Outplace
Yourself

Outplace Yourself

Secrets of an Executive Outplacement Counselor

Charles H. Logue, Ph.D.

ADAMS PUBLISHING
Holbrook, Massachusetts

Published by Adams Media Corporation
260 Center Street
Holbrook, Massachusetts 02343

ISBN: 1-55850-505-9
Printed in the United States of America

J I H G F E D C B A

Library of Congress Cataloging-in-Publication Data
Logue, Charles H.
Outplace yourself : secrets of an exectuvie outplacement counselor / Charles H. Logue.
    p.   cm.
Includes bibliographical references and index.
ISBN 1-55850-505-9
1. Job hunting. 2. Executives—Recruiting. 3. Employees—Dismissal of. I. Title.
[HF5382.7.L64   1995]
650.14—dc20   94-46696
                                                       CIP

This publication is designed to provide accurate and authoritative information with regard to the subject matter covered. It is sold with the understanding that the publisher is not engaged in rendering legal, accounting, or other professional advice. If legal advice or other expert assistance is required, the services of a competent professional person should be sought.
— From a *Declaration of Principles* jointly adopted by a Committee of the American Bar Association and a Committee of Publishers and Associations

COVER DESIGN: Marshall Henrichs

This book is available at quantity discounts for bulk purchases.
for more information, call 1-800-872-5627.

Foreword

There has been an endless discussion throughout human history concerning the relative importance of social destiny. The truth, of course, must surely lie in the multifaceted variety and unlimited possibilities of the interrelationships between and among humankind and its social structures.

In this period of dramatic social and economic change, indeed upheaval, when so much of what was established in the post-World War II period, which seemed to promise a future of continuous improvement, has fallen apart around us, some of us look to the social and economic circumstances for both explanations and solutions. We look to statistics today—unemployment, underemployment, trade imbalances, plant shutdowns, business collapses, health care needs, and on and on. We look for policies and programs that will address these needs and enlist each individual, who wishes in his or her own opportunity, to grow and to contribute.

Dr. Logue, in this remarkable book, comes at the challenges of our time from exactly the opposite direction. He provides us with a fascinatingly precise "how to" manual for those who are the victims—for Dr. Logue, only temporarily—of this period of such pervasive change, disruption, and loss of employment.

There was a time when layoffs were essentially a blue-collar phenomenon and were cushioned as well, in good union situations, by supplementary unemployment benefits and other such arrangements. Layoffs and terminations were rarities in offices, at least at the higher levels, and in such "secure" employment pursuits as government and the financial institutions. In any event, for most of the postwar period there also seemed to be reason for considerable confidence in the invisible hand of the business cycle. What went down not only came up but seemed to rise to higher levels.

It is now a very different world. Restructuring, lean and mean, reducing the layers of management, retraining, and multi-job careers are the order of the day. In this dramatically different circumstance, whatever the social and economic theorists may say, whatever societies' leaders may do or fail to do, individual human beings must somehow cope.

It is to the individual's needs that Dr. Logue directs his book in impressive, often surprising, detail. It's all here, from understanding the psychological mechanisms of depression, through motivational stories and poems, through the fine points of the job search and interviewing processes to diets and exercises so that health and fitness may prevail.

Dr. Logue has accomplished a monumental task in assembling such a mass of useful material. There is something here for everyone. The writing is clear, crisp and direct; the material is so varied that it's always interesting.

He has provided us with a one-volume support network for chaotic and challenging times.

LYNN R. WILLIAMS
President, United Steelworkers of America

This book has four cornerstones of dedication: to God for spiritual and motivational leadership; to my terrific family, Cheryl, Jon, Michael, Bob, and especially my wife Dr. Ina, for continued love, support, and many cherished times; to my parents, Ethel and Charlie, for believing in me; and to the countless clients and friends that I have had the pleasure of working with or knowing who have helped me to continue to grow and to be a better person.

Acknowledgements

The friendship of those we serve is the foundation of our progress.

— ANONYMOUS

My co-workers at R. Davenport Associates have helped me to understand, refine, and excel in the job-hunting field—Bob Davenport, Joan Trombetta, Mac Matter, Jim Barry, Dorothy Bannow, Pam Barney, Rick Joyce, and Linda Buick-Campbell—all "pros" in their areas.

Hundreds of clients helped me build this book, and their assistance, encouragement, and friendship have meant a great deal, especially the following: Gerry Vozel; Andrea Yaksick; Mark Schwartz; John Murray; Gordon Phillips; Bill Henkel, Esq.; John Stokes; Dave Boyer; Paul Hindes; Art Victor; Michael Steur; Jim Bird; Clyde Vandall; John Runco; Elmo Cecchetti; Joe Burnich; Marvin Zalevsky; Ed Sheets; Glen Schillo; Glenn Swaim; Phil Koechline; Karl Van Gurp; Darryl Mills; Melanie Swan; Dennis Snedden; Ralph Burris; Tom Cunningham; Ed Pribonic; Gary Bash; Olga Torriero; Duane Hope; Bob Flodstrom; Maryjo Klimas; Michael Havlin; Dan Campbell; Bill Cline; Bill Gernert; Steve Cohen; Art Victor; Charlie Gilmore; Dennis Kanuck; Arden Biggar; Bill Jersey; Jim Kimbrough; Bill Loftus; Mark Miller; John Perfetti; Bill McLaughlin; Phil and Rita Marcinek; Jack Buser; Duane Ready; Ed Curran; Ken Banks; Marty Dekker; Rob Hilles; Bob and Marion Riley; Dick Sinewe; Finn Overlie; Bill Strait; Brian Dingle; Marc Albert; Dick Bombardieri; Ken Fenush; Rob Murray; Lou Goodman; Dale Meisel; Elaine Beck; Kerry Burgan; Bob Andrassy; Jack Welch; Jerry Wanichko; Tom Szuba; Meg Whaling; Jim Shanahan; Bob Roy; Gary Shiwarski; Bob Reeves; Scott Robinson; Terrance Roman; Bill Kriebel; Larry Miorelli; Bruce Emmett; Harry Meyers; Chuck Johnston; Mark Daniels; Les Boord; Alf Butler; Greg Moore; Jon Emley; David Haines; Gordon Conn; Paul Lee; Norm Goodlin; Paul Formichella; Ron Anthony; John Anstead; Rich Schneider; Ken Scharding; Connie Schott; Joe Ewing; and Joe Stiger, as well as others who allowed me to serve them.

I have had the pleasure of working with many professionals, friends and family whose collegial good will and/or friendship provided inspiration: the Logue clan (Jimmy, Barry, Richard and their families; Rita, Leo and family; Elizabeth, Henrietta and Theresa; Cheryl, Chip Grabowski and family; Ellen, Richard Klein and family; Evelyn and Mac Smith; Ran and Sue Yardeny; Henry, Margaret Wischusen and family); Pat and Dave Gallaway; Carole and Jeff Creamer; Dale, Chris and Craig Wilson; John and Lois Yates; Helen and Ed Palasak; Dave Fleming; Bob Ryan; John Yeager; Bill Neff; Ralph and Connie Gilbert; Brian Lindsay; Pat and Mary Ann O'Hara; Mary Ann Raymer; Dennis Pad; Bill and Aylene Kovensky; Shirley and Max Money; Chuck and Becky Gough; Montie and Harriet Rea; Ted Polk; Charlie Timmins; Ann Maers; Joe Rotondi; Vera Green; Gene Egan; Jim Tricco; Tom Samuels; Dick Connors; Jack Winemiller; Don Plagman; Ben Del Prince; Myrtice Edwards; Barbara Swan; Bob and Joan Engebretson; Thelma Harris; Tom Powers; Ron and Sally Beaumariage; Joanne and Robbie Robinson; Fred Jones; Lynne Berkowitz; Vince Donnelly; Tom Yun; Rob Monte; Shirley Spring; Larry Noddin; John Laverty; Bob Berkebile; Fred Kocher; Pat Olliffe; Joe and Gayle Breman; John Lymburner; Leo and Marge Kane; Jim Stalder; Gary Spina; Bill Lauer; Tom Hanson; Bill Fueller; Janet Harberth; Tracy Smith McCarthy; Bill Few; Dave Donohue; Dr. Wally Chang; the brothers at Sigma Chi; Jim Sanders and "The Bicycle Club"; former Oil Company School students and faculty; and last but not least friends at Highland.

In memory of four very special friends—Jim Sehn, Jim Ferriman, Joe Newell, and John Portella—I acknowledge their help.

I would also like to acknowledge my typist, Valerie Kearney, whose dedication, hard work, and patience with my "hen scratching" were greatly appreciated.

Finally, I want to acknowledge those who will be conducting future job campaigns and will endure stress, hard work, and the unpleasantness of a job search. May you all be determined to succeed! Good luck!

Special thanks to Brian Dingle and Ross Feltz for their editing; Dan Campbell for his collating; Marc Schwartz, who worked on many of the charts; my son Michael, who drew the sketches; Mary Bonach, Laurie Cohen, and Rhonda Kopchak, who assisted in the research on books and other publications; my editor Brandon Toropov, of Adams Publishing; and my publisher Bob Adams, of Adams Publishing.

Contents

Introduction

It's not what you are but what you got left with and what you do with it.

— F.D. ROOSEVELT

My experience at two *FORTUNE* "Top Ten" companies as well as in other organizations has enabled me to establish instant rapport with most of my clients. The fact that I have found myself looking for employment several times during my career also has given me "real world" feelings that allow me to empathize and sympathize with my clients effectively. Serving as an educator, counselor, and business manager has given me valuable insight into client problems and situations.

The following are some of the categories of people that I have worked with: fired or laid-off employees, afraid of the unknown and with outdated skills; people unhappy with current jobs, who have feelings of being burned out; overextended, taken-for-granted employees who are looking for a way "out of their misery"; people going through midlife crisis or "career menopause," not knowing where to turn and maybe for the first time "trying to find themselves"; concerned parents wanting to help a son or daughter find a job that will make everyone happy; people over fifty who question whether they will ever be able to do productive work again; career counselors and outplacement specialists in need of better counseling skills; students graduating from high school, college, or graduate school scared to death about venturing out into "the real world of business"; a career military person who is trying to return to the civilian work world; and a concerned organization or union officer who wants to have a "top-notch" outplacement manual and process for assisting employees who are going to be discharged or terminated due to cutbacks, an untimely acquisition or the need for a cost-effective operation.

What have been the feelings of some of my former and current clients before turning themselves around and starting this process? These are some I would like to share with you:

I was scared and frightened about what was going to happen to me.

I was afraid of the unknown, not knowing where I was going to be working or how disruptive it would be to my family.

I experienced daily mood swings like being on an emotional yo-yo or roller coaster.

I felt helpless due to anger and disbelief with my former boss and organization, as they repaid loyalty by putting me in an unbearable, hurting situation.

I was angry, frustrated, and bored with myself; I felt there was nowhere to turn.

I had feelings of deep hurt, rejection, loss of status, loneliness, hopelessness, worthlessness, and unhappiness with life, and thought that my spouse had given up on me; therefore I wanted to quit or give up on myself.

I felt degraded and I lacked pride, especially when I found myself standing in line for unemployment checks where others could see me.

I didn't want to talk to family or friends about my feelings or situation, I wanted instead to crawl further inside myself. I hurt so much that I didn't think I could go on.

I walked around aimlessly due to a lack of self-esteem, not believing in myself or feeling that I could do anything anymore, trying ways to survive that were not working.

I gave myself messages that I can't succeed or won't succeed, as with a pre-mental-breakdown state.

I was willing to take whatever morsels might be thrown my way just so I could start my way back or try to survive financially.

Many of these feelings are no different from those exhibited in other stressful situations such as the three "ds"—death, divorce, and dying. Unfortunately, one has to initially go through a grieving period! In my case, it was three months, for others longer. Then you never really get over it because of some of the psychological scars that remain, even though they have been repressed as well as possible into the subconscious. Somehow and in some way most people, though, survive these humbling trials and tribulations. I have seen individuals make speedy recoveries when given the right support group, professional counselor, and marketing package. As one client said to me, "When you need to see a physician, you see one; when you need a career marketing counselor, you find one you can work with": a job doctor.

I am reminded of the words of John Dewey: "Education isn't a preparation for life. Education is life itself." So it is with individuals in a career counseling program. Their task is living a commitment on a day-to-day basis, striving to be at their very best, as tough as that challenge may be, and realizing that they are responsible for their own behavior and attitude toward the job campaign.

The success formula in today's highly competitive, uncertain job market combines the need for the correct marketing techniques with the right attitude to get you where you want to be. This book can serve as a companion piece to an institutional inplacement program, as a complement to an outplacement program, or as a guide for those in situations described at the beginning of this section.

Outplace Yourself shows you how and describes successful techniques with models, and whether you have just started your career or have been at it for a while, you will want to use this book as a resource time and time again.

Who Should Use This Book?

This book is written for and dedicated to the individual who may or may not be working with a professional career counselor. It is meant to be a ready tool to help you through a process equivalent to a top-level executive outplacement counseling program. Nothing can take the place of a teacher/coach/counselor and the interaction (give and take) that you get from being in a one-to-one situation. ("Every teacher a leader, every leader a teacher, every student a success.") The same is true with a dedicated, qualified, and committed counselor. If you have one, consider yourself fortunate. If you don't, you honestly should find a reputable career management/outplacement firm and work with it. I am prejudiced when it comes to effective one-to-one counseling. I have seen it work its magic time and time again.

This book also can be used by human resource managers as a companion to their internal "outplacement" program. If they have not yet designed a program or selected an outside outplacement counseling consultant, it will at least give them some ideas to consider.

Loved ones can buy this book for someone who wants to get ahead, even for a very special friend whom they care about who either has lost his or her job or is going to lose it. Such buyers can even read it themselves to understand what is and will be taking place. It was written with both users in mind. Granted, a book isn't everything, but it's the thought that counts, and rest assured there are many valuable thoughts contained within that represent over fifteen years of experience in the business and well over a thousand clients served.

Executives and union leaders alike will find this book useful when they are faced with cutbacks of personnel, as a valuable "how-to" source of key ideas that will not only help their employees feel whole again but assist them in getting to where they want to be by outplace-counseling themselves.

— CHARLES H. LOGUE, PH.D.

It's a recession when your neighbor loses his job; it's a depression when you lose yours.
— HARRY S TRUMAN

PART I

Where You've Been,
Where You Are Now, and
Where You're Going

1.

Being Fired/Terminated, Laid Off, or Making a Career Change

A life that is not examined is not worth living.
— Socrates

What's Happening

The label may be different, but the result is always the same. You've been called into the boss's office, or the Personnel Office, most likely late on a Friday afternoon (a Monday would be better so you wouldn't have a weekend to fret) or to the Personnel Office for no more than a 30-minute meeting. You may be told any of the following: "We have to let you go; your services are no longer needed." "You are being terminated, outplaced, dismissed, laid off, axed, or furloughed." Whatever—a "rose by any other name" is still a rose. Very rarely, according to my clients' experiences, is the f-word—*fired*—used in these discussions. I know it wasn't in my case. You've been asked to clean out your desk and leave in a matter of minutes. There are generally no goodbyes to anyone.

Over the last ten years in our country, millions of employees have lost their jobs (business divorces), and countless others are forecast to lose them in the nineties as companies go through buyouts, competitive mergers, acquisitions, business spinoffs, reorganizations, divestitures, reductions in force, hostile takeovers, downsizing (rightsizing), or streamlining (restructuring) of their operations. Most people have been fired or terminated at least once in their career. No one today is immune or safe anymore, as companies attempt to "trim the fat" and make themselves more "lean and mean" to survive. Certainly with more and more foreign investments taking place, more streamlining will occur through the nineties. With more and more of this happening, being fired, like being divorced, doesn't have the stigma it once did. If we haven't been fired yet, at least we know of some neighbor or friend who has been.

Feelings

The outcome of these "pink-slip" meetings is quite predictable. Sometimes it is an emotional shock with complete disbelief and dismay and a hurting experience with a sure loss of the fired person's self-esteem, "soul," dignity, and self-confidence. You can feel totally expendable and all by yourself and have a strong tendency to give yourself an inner verbal tongue-lashing. You will experience an emotional roller coaster ride. The ostrich syndrome may even prevail: you may want to bury your head in the sand. Stress becomes the order of the day. It's like being hit by a truck. You also can feel tense, worried, embarrassed, ashamed, isolated, depressed, alone, frustrated, angry, lost, nervous, frightened, and very insecure (helpless). It can be paralyzing. It is important to try to accept the way you feel, to realize that it is normal, and tell yourself you are going to feel better. Dealing honestly with your emotions, especially during the first week of unemployment, will be one of the toughest challenges you have ever had to face. It's almost like dealing with culture shock. Don't phone other companies as soon as you've been fired or laid off. The tendency will be to try and get a job right away. You're too emotionally upset to really help your case. You need to heal! If you do call before you have healed, you may lose an opportunity forever. Put all big decisions aside for the time being.

For many, their thoughts will not be what they appear to be. I had a client tell me that shortly after he lost his job, a neighbor made the following comment: "I see you're playing hooky from work today. How do you do it?" When he replied seriously that he had just been laid off, she walked away, not knowing what to say. He initially reacted defensively by asking himself, "What's the matter with me?" rather than, as he decided later, his neighbor was lost for words, and her reaction didn't have anything to do with his personality. Unemployed people think and generally react immediately and now rather than in the future. Talk things over with family and friends to "clear the air." Know that being out of work is very common today. Others have survived it, and you will too. Get the negative thoughts out of your system and move on emotionally with your life! You are in control! Don't take it personally. Tell yourself this will only be a short period of time for you. Soon your survival instincts will kick in and you will be emotionally fit. Try and find out early from the company their level of commitment to helping you find new employment. Know what your rights are and whether the company has a termination procedure. If you feel you've been wrongly laid off, consult an attorney.

People Lose Jobs for a Variety of Reasons

Why do people get fired or lose their jobs? Why did you? Is there a pattern if it's happened before? Some of the reasons could be these: Things aren't or haven't worked out, especially during the three- or six-month probationary period. Maybe the working image you initially created wasn't one that jelled with how things were done at this company. "Sales are down;" therefore support services such as public relations, advertising and/or human relations (training and development) are cut, many times "to the bone"; the firm will rehire when times get better. Your dress or hairstyle caused friction with the company's unwritten codes, office power plays, and politics. Some people are not politicians and never will be able to "play the game," and thus are doomed to fail within an organization; employees have to remember that "the walls have ears," and if you say anything against the company or don't "let the boss be the boss," ways will be found to move you out. Maybe the Peter Principle (you were promoted to your level of incompetence) has prevailed and you are in over your head; you either lack the technical expertise, the people skills, or both.

Usually the company documents these supposed shortcomings over a period of time, so that when you lose your job, the facts will speak for themselves. The firm may cite poor "chemistry and fit," or say that "you don't fit in with the climate, culture, or environment of the organization." You perhaps have been labeled as "not one of them," and if you don't get along with your boss, it's double jeopardy. You may be told that your attitude is strictly one way, or that "you were very rigid in your thinking and not about to try things the way the company wants you to."

After you have been fired, you need to consider several strategies:

> *We can throw stones, complain about them, stumble*
> *on them, climb over them, or build with them.*
> — WILLIAM ARTHUR WARD

1. Keep your cool—don't get angry with your former boss or company. The die is already cast. Leave the premises quietly, without lashing back at your boss, although that would be the natural thing to do. Suppress the desire to lash out. Don't "bad mouth" anyone. You need time to cool down when your thinking won't be as emotional or clouded. You don't want to do anything that will "burn your bridges" with the company. You will need references. Try to arrange a follow-up get-together for a time when you have your wits about you, you've cooled down, and you are less emotional, if you haven't done this before you leave (Figure 1.1). Items on your list should include severance pay (usually one week's to a month's pay for each

✦ ✦ ✦

FIGURE 1.1
Sample letter for terminated person

Personal Letterhead

Name
Address
City, State, Zip

PERSONAL AND CONFIDENTIAL

Dear _____ :

I wish I were writing under better circumstances, but because I see you as both a friend and someone who was very instrumental in hiring me for (Position), I am writing this letter to you in hope that you can help me. As you can appreciate, since I left the company, the "grieving process" has been extremely hard on both me and my family.

I know that when employees serve an organization well and then leave, the company tries to help them land successfully back on their feet. This I believed to be true at (Company Name), which is not a "Job Shop," but a place where employees are generally not laid off between assignments. As you know, in my case, I was laid off virtually without any advance notice. Be that as it may, I wanted to call you and Mr. (Person's Name) to see if the company can assist me and my family in the following ways:

1. Severance pay.
2. Extending my major medical group coverage for at least several additional months beyond the cutoff date of (Month). As you know, my wife has multiple sclerosis, and for me to pick up treatment for her would be impossible outside the group policy. This, I feel, would be a most humane act for the company during this transition.
3. Sending me a "To Whom It May Concern" reference letter that I may use in my job search. I am attaching a draft of one for your possible use.
4. Allowing me to use the services of an outplacement firm that would assist me in my job campaign, with the billing sent to the company.

I have already registered for unemployment compensation, which amounts to only $274 per week and lasts only six months.

Your attention to these concerns would be greatly appreciated. As you will note, I am also sending copies of this letter to (Person's Name) and (Person's Name). I will plan to call you within a week for your guidance and help. Thank you.

Sincerely,

(Your Name)

Enclosure

cc:

◆ ◆ ◆

---

year of service, with a minimum of four weeks of pay) and bridge money (to help you until you find a new job). Large organizations tend to pay one week's salary for every $2,000 of annual executive compensation. (*Note:* Many companies today are starting to cut back on severance pay.) This is based on the assumption that lower-level workers have an easier time finding jobs than do highly paid executives (not necessarily true in today's market). You should also cover the following: unemployment compensation (do you qualify?); grievance procedures (if applicable); and continuation of insurance—firms with over 20 employees must let you stay with their group medical plan, paying for it yourself for up to 18 months, if you desire. (It is recommended that you sign up unless you can switch to your spouse's plan; ask for feedback.) See if you can reach some sort of mutually agreeable settlement as to how the company is going to treat your release, i.e., "We had some disagreements about the organization's direction. We also talked about ways to satisfy both our feelings, but in the end we felt it was in both our interests for me to look elsewhere," or "my boss and I had some philosophical differences and we had an amicable parting of the ways." Most know what that expression means. Also, you will want to know what the firm will say in a reference letter (Figure 1.2).

2. Tell your spouse and children. Some individuals hesitate, at least initially, to tell family members. This is a true test of your relationship. All family members need to know. Their emotional support and understanding are vital to you during this traumatic time. Ask for it. Express your feelings, but pay attention to their feelings also. They really feel helpless, and the tendency is to snap back. Spouses need to acknowledge that the situation is bad, that they, too, are grieving, but that things will be better. They need not criticize or nag but show that they care and are concerned,

✦ ✦ ✦

FIGURE 1.2
Sample reference letter

Company Letterhead

To Whom It May Concern:

Re: (Your Name)
I have known (Your Name) for over three years and would give him my highest recommendation as a person of integrity, with a warm and outgoing social style, deep caring for others, with a high sense of responsibility. His character, in all aspects, is flawless. For three years I have been in a position to watch him work. He has a work ethic that is superior and an attitude to go with it that he must achieve success. (Your first name) loves a challenge.

(Your first name) has always followed through and completed his assignments with the utmost of professionalism. He has enormous potential and would be a fine asset to any company he chooses to work with. As you can appreciate, with the cutback of our projects, we have had to eliminate a lot of positions under a new realignment. This, of course, had nothing to do with previous working assignments.

Should you wish to discuss (Your name) in greater detail, please do not hesitate to give me a call.

Sincerely,

Former Boss (signature)

✦ ✦ ✦

that they love the spouse and stand behind him or her 100 percent. Share upbeat, positive events with them. Be reassuring to your family. Tell them you have everything under control, and all will be okay. Remember we are conditioned by our attitudes. You are starting with a "clean slate." You have many options. They need to know you're moving ahead with options. Being out of work is an interim thing, and with the proper mind set it can be a time of opportunity.

3. Put together a list of your fixed expenses and plan your job hunting budget. Talk to all your creditors, especially if you have a mortgage with a bank, about your situation. You may be able to arrange smaller payments by just paying the interest or even having a grace period until you find a job. Determine how much you need to live on. Possibly borrow from IRAs if need be. Remember, you can take money out of an IRA once annually as long as you replace it within 60 days. Don't cash in your IRAs, because you will have to pay penalties as well as taxes. Once your employment compensation runs out, or even before it does, consider taking an interim, temporary, or part-time job to pay your bills while searching. (See also chapter 5, on budgets.)

4. *If your company is paying for an outplacement service or if you need to se-lect one, refer to your local Yellow Pages, firms that do career counseling or the Di-rectory of Outplacement Firms published by Kennedy Publications, (603) 585-2200.*

Another source is the National Association of Career Counseling Consultants. These outplacement firms usually are offered only through companies that want to save possible legal expenses or severance pay, avoid job discrimination charges, or want to make a bad situation at least a little more palatable. These outplacement firms provide office space, sec-retaries, phones (office number/answering service), research material, copi-ers, fax machine (sometimes), and computers, but most of all a tried and true support system to work from. In short, as Bob Davenport says, "they provide hope." These services don't find new jobs for fired or terminated employees, but they can allow clients to tap into the outplacement com-pany/counselor's network of former clients and the companies they work for. If the organization has been in business for some time, naturally there is a bigger network to tap. These firms will help you to assess your skills, write resumes, package yourself, prepare for interviews, and plan an effec-tive marketing campaign. As you go through the mental gymnastics of self-assessment, you soon realize, through some behavioral modification, that you are a valuable person. You begin to hold your head high, telling your-self that you still have a lot to offer. Also, if a company doesn't hire you, "their loss is someone else's gain!" That's the way you must think!

Most of your investment in a career managing firm can be deducted under the current tax laws. You have to realize that it can cost you between $3,000 and $8,000 (depending on your level) but that it is an excellent in-vestment in yourself/career/family to work with a reputable firm. Interview several companies, and select one that will best fit you and that offers the best support. Some evaluative criteria to use when selecting one of these firms can be: how long have they been in business; what professional or-ganizations are they registered with; do they have testimonial letters on file that tell not only of satisfied customers, but of people whom you can call; profiles of staff members, showing which counselors have advanced de-grees, especially in guidance/counseling or psychology; talking to friends who may have had positive experiences with the firm; the business back-ground of customers. Ask to see their manager's and staff's resumes and to interview them. Caution: There are bad firms out there wanting only to take your money and giving little in return. Beware!!

5. *Check to see, if applicable, whether there is a Forty Plus Club or job club in your town.* These self-help groups are for unemployed professionals over 40 years of age.

6. *Realize that your job hunt will take time, that it is a full-time, 40-hour-a-week challenge if you are unemployed, and that you are going to work harder than you have ever worked on a job!* Keep your days structured. Set goals for yourself! Take control of what you can. Don't get discouraged. Remind yourself that others before you have been "in this boat" and survived, and you will, too. Don't feel sorry for yourself; you are not a quitter or a loser! You are tough and you will "suck it in and spit it out!" This is only a temporary setback. You haven't lost your skills and abilities. Don't get discouraged with the present and appear desperate. Be determined not to accept pity or feel ashamed. Hold onto your pride and confidence as hard as you can.

7. *Realize that today's work force, because of the economic climate, moves often.* As many union workers would verify, since they have been furloughed frequently, one of the keys to survival is being flexible by keeping your options open. Maybe, just maybe, you have to consider going back to school, being retrained, or even moving to another state.

8. *Use this situation as an opportunity for self-evaluation and direction by clarifying what did go wrong and what might have been past signs of job trouble and what your new career goals are.* Did you receive no salary increase or very little? Did you have trouble getting in to see your boss, a poor office location, or very few support services? Did you notice others not talking to you, or many of your duties being taken away from you? Focus on the future, and not on self-pity and anger toward your former boss or situation. That's behind you now. Learn from the past.

9. *See if there is an interfaith church or fraternal support group locally that you can join.* Remember, failure is never final! Don't go this road alone.

10. *Realize that between 60 to 86 percent of people in similar situations get jobs by networking.* Perfect your networking skills, even if you are an introvert. Think can, will, and do!

11. *If you are thinking about starting a business of your own, talk to others who have made similar investments.* Talk to representatives at the Small Business Administration's office. Adopt a never-say-die attitude! Don't be afraid to fail! (See Part III.)

12. *Also talk with your spouse, financial advisor—and yourself.* Will you be able to spend long hours and endure times of uncertainty? Are you able to do the dirty work if need be? Realize that for a management position, a job search can take one month or more for each $10,000 of one's former salary. That has been a reliable guideline in the past. Today it is more like two or more months for laid-off managerial types. (As an aside, most laid-off

people come from larger companies and then go to smaller ones.)

Although there is no true, proven way to avoid or prevent job loss from happening another time (most people never want to experience the pain and those negative feelings again), ideas to prevent mismatches or problems may include doing better "homework" on the company you're thinking about joining. Observe or better yet try to meet and talk with people who work at this firm, vendors and suppliers who service this company, and some customers to gain insight into the way it does business, how it operates, and its products, pricing policies, and growth rates. How successful (financial history) is it? What is its competition (kinds), management style and company culture? Develop a profile of its work force. Many of these things may be hard to do. Answers to these questions can tell you (or at least give you clues as to) whether this is the company that you want to work for.

During your probationary period (usually the first three to six months of your new job) you will be watched closely to see how well you fit in. Exhibit a positive attitude and work hard on all assignments, keeping a daily log of all work completed. Note chapter 25 in this book about taking a new assignment, and follow it.

If you think you are beaten, you are.
If you think that you dare not, you don't.
If you would like to win, but think you can't,
It's almost certain you won't.

If you think you'll lose, you've lost.
For out in the world you'll find,
Success begins with a person's will,
It's all in the state of mind.

If you think you are outclassed, you are,
You have got to think high to rise.
You have got to be sure of yourself before
You can ever win a prize.

Life's battles don't always go
To the stronger or faster man,
But sooner or later the man who wins
Is the man who thinks he can.

— EDGAR GUEST

2.

Changing from the Service to Civilian Career: "Follow Me!"

*There are risks and costs to a program of action.
But they are far less than the long-range risks and
costs of comfortable inaction.*

— JOHN F. KENNEDY

Counselors and Transferable Skills

Most professionals, when confronted with the need to change, feel they can handle the situation themselves with or without a plan. Some can, but most need an expert to interpret tests. Any counseling professional worth his or her salt can correctly administer and successfully interpret a battery of tests to help a person focus on the best second-career direction. Find yourself a career management firm, if you can, that has had successful experiences with ex-servicemen, and then work with them. If for whatever reason you can't, use *Outplace Yourself.*

Professional Organizations That Can Help

As a former infantry/airborne officer, I feel it makes a lot of sense to consider joining the Retired Officers Association. You can do that by writing to 201 North Washington Street, Alexandria, VA 22314 and asking for membership information together with any free booklets they have. You might even check to see if there is a chapter in your community where you can do some networking. There may also be an American Legion or VFW chapter locally that can be of assistance.

Check to see if a nearby Veteran's Administration office offers career counseling and testing services. If you are not satisfied, look into contacting reliable career-counseling firms for the kind of services they offer and go with the one that you feel will do you the most good.

Over and above the battery of tests you'll take, you will want to assess your service skills and see how they can transfer to civilian life. Some will be more obvious than others, i.e., military police into safety and security, transportation into a similar service, and ordnance into a warehouse and distribution operation. You will want to look at your skill areas and see which ones would be transferable, i.e., leadership skills used in the general management arena or communication skills being used in the public relations/advertising/radio/ TV fields.

You should look for organizations where there are perceived needs and fill them. Certainly the health care industry and high-tech firms are two areas in the private sector where one can market one's talents. It's important to take note of what the employment trends and occupational outlook are for specific areas of the country. [Refer to *Occupational Outlook Handbook* (Annual), U.S. Government Printing Office, Washington, DC 20402, (202) 783-3238.]

A Wish For Leaders
May you have enough happiness to keep you sweet;
Enough trials to keep you strong;
Enough failure to keep you humble;
Enough success to keep you eager;
Enough friends to give you comfort;
Enough faith and courage in yourself, your work,
and your country to banish depression;
Enough determination to make each day a better
day than yesterday.
— ANONYMOUS

3.

Self-Esteem and Attitude
Are Where It's At

To me, self-esteem and attitude go hand-in-glove; you are what you think you are! If you think of yourself as a winner, you become a winner. It's the Pygmalion effect or the self-fulfilling prophecy. Henry Ford was quoted as saying, "Whether you think you're right or whether you think you're wrong, you're right." Reflect and concentrate on positive thoughts, and positive results will develop for you. You are what you think! In the six and a half years that I worked full-time and as a consultant in the hospital-health care field, I found that patients who felt positively about their sicknesses, recovered more quickly than those who didn't. Some feel that negativism undermines the body's immune system. I tend to agree.

If your attitude is positive, self-confidence is a powerful force that you will convey to others when you meet and talk to them.

> *As a person thinketh in their heart, so will they be.*
> — ANONYMOUS

And we know that the more positive and confident people are, the better their results are with others. They become more creative, productive, confident and successful. Success leads to other successes!

It's hard to be upbeat and positive initially, especially if you have just been laid off or if you have been looking for employment to no avail for some time. It's as if you're going through the motions and not getting anywhere. You may be feeling shock, anger, self-pity, disbelief, numbness, guilt, bitterness, discouragement, shame and fearful of the unknown, the future. You can even be down on yourself and confused about how to go about conducting an effective job campaign feeling as badly as you do. You might even be more confused if it has been a long time since you last conducted a campaign—twenty or more years. These feelings are all quite predictable and a natural reaction to a job loss.

Self-Improvement Ideas

To improve both your attitude and self-esteem, you will need to realize several things:

1. *You are not alone, even though it's easy to feel you are.* You have family, friends, loved ones, church/neighbor support groups and career management organizations that can provide a strong support base for you as you go through this unpleasant time dealing with stress, as hard as it may individually be for you. Keep your cool, practice relaxing, and realize that you are not the first person nor will you be the last person to be in this situation. Others have traveled down this rocky road and survived; you will, too. Most people today experience as many as five different jobs during a career. Some researchers say it may go higher in the future. So be determined to succeed no matter what the obstacles.

2. *Remember you still have your skills, abilities, talents, and personality going for you.* Once you recognize that you are special and have many things going for you, you're well on your way to success again. Erma Bombeck once wrote about a women who realized this when she returned to the work force after being a housewife for 15 years. During her interview she told the personnel manager that she had been a wife and mother for all those years and needed extra sheets over and above those on the application form to list her background and skills. Needless to say, she got the job.

Make a list of all of your good points and accomplishments. You do make a difference! Self-confidence and self-respect are the key! Focus on the things you like about yourself, especially when you are feeling a little down. You are still an important person even when you are between jobs. Believe in yourself even when others don't. Remember, if you don't, others won't either. Do daily conditioning for a positive mental attitude and mindset.

> *Today begin a new life. Each day of your new life begin by reading these few short paragraphs. The wisdom and principles you read will become a part of your inner self and guide you to success and happiness.*

> *You are nature's greatest miracle. All men are your brothers, yet you are different from each. Do not imitate others. Put your uniqueness on display, you are rare, and there is value in all rarity.*

Greet each day with love in your heart, for this is the most important secret of happiness. Love all mankind even though their good qualities may be hidden. Learn to recognize the mystery of moods in men; do not judge another on one meeting.

Be master of your emotions. Try to sing when you feel depressed and laugh when you feel sad. Try each day to bring joy, enthusiasm and laughter into the lives of others and automatically joy, enthusiasm, and laughter will become a part of yours. Refrain from using profanity and strive to improve your manners and grace for they are the spices to which all are attracted. Remove from your vocabulary negative words such as quit, cannot, impossible, and hopeless, for they are words of the nondoers. Exercise your body and mind daily, and avoid habits of excess which can cause physical or mental degeneration.

Waste not a moment of your new life mourning yesterday's mistakes, defeats, or heartaches, for that would be throwing good after bad. Life is a measure of time; do not waste time, or you will waste life. Destroy procrastination with action, destroy doubt with faith, and destroy fear with confidence. Act now: the procrastination which has held you back is no longer a part of your life, for tomorrow is when the failure acts and the weak become strong.

Though you may stumble and fall, realize that few march straight to success and happiness. Persist until you succeed, knowing this is one of the greatest principles of success. Learn to turn adversity into something of value with the belief that each adversity has within it the seed of an equal or greater benefit and adversity is actually a tonic to strengthen you.

Be careful not to become so dignified that you cannot laugh at yourself, for although you may accomplish greatness, are you not still an insignificant part of the universe?

Pray for compassion and love for others, for patience and guidance to reach your goals, and for gratefulness and humility when you reach them. In your prayers, give credit and thanks to the real source of all you will accomplish or acquire in your life, your Creator.

— ANONYMOUS

3. Realize that you may have to work harder at getting a job than you may have had to on any other previous job. There are no shortcuts or "cookbook solutions" to a successful campaign. It requires a full commitment of your time, patience, energy, perseverance, control of emotions, and intenseness, as well as a nonquitting attitude ("snapping turtle behavior"—once they get hold of something, they don't let go). Tell yourself that you will succeed no matter what because if you don't nobody else will do it for you. Adopt a "can do—will do" attitude and show it nonverbally as well as verbally. In scientific research multiple failures often lead to success. You control your own life—you can be down and negative after failure—or you can choose to go on to higher things. Take note of an example of this determination of past experience not being a solid indicator of future success in Figure 3.1.

✦ ✦ ✦

FIGURE 3.1
You control your own life!

- lost job, 1832
- defeated for legislature, 1832
- failed in business, 1833
- elected to legislature, 1834
- sweetheart died, 1835
- had nervous breakdown, 1836
- defeated for speaker, 1839
- defeated for nomination for Congress, 1843
- elected to Congress, 1846
- lost renomination, 1848
- rejected for land officer, 1849
- defeated for Senate, 1854
- defeated for nomination for Vice-President, 1856
- again defeated for Senate, 1858
- elected President of U.S., 1860

(Abraham Lincoln)

✦ ✦ ✦

4. Don't put yourself down, and don't broadcast your shortcomings to others. Take time (twice or more) each day to use positive affirmations ("Our life is what our thoughts are"—Marcus Aurelius) as an aid in programming your mental computer to get you to where you want to be. They become your own the more you say them, and they really work. Remember your attitude projects your self-esteem. We almost always measure up to our image of ourselves. Keep everything positive; i.e., "I deserve to be rich and prosperous." If you do feel negative at times, realize that it is perfectly natural to feel the way you do and try and eliminate the feeling by focusing only on positive things. If you can't do this, tell yourself you are going to think about the past only one day a week, for only two to three hours at the most. Period. The end.

5. *Have faith that all will work out for the better.* Look at your job situation or problem as a challenge that you will overcome. Be enthusiastic as you look to the future and forge a new beginning for yourself. Realize, too, that you may be better off than you were when you started! You've grown into a stronger fighter. Hone your existing skills and learn some new ones—"Behold the turtle, who makes progress only when he sticks his neck out."

6. *Keep things in perspective.* Things could be worse. Take charge! "Don't make a mountain out of a molehill" or overdramatize the situation you are in. Make each hour and day a busy and productive one. The starting point of all achievement is desire.

> *I've been beaten, choked, kicked, swindled, taken*
> *advantage of, and laughed at. The only reason I*
> *hang around is to see what happens next.*
> — ANONYMOUS

7. *Keep a good sense of humor.* Realize that if you have your health, you have everything. Set-up a daily exercise program for yourself, even if only a brisk walk that rewards you for positive thinking.

8. *Resist the temptation to call everyone right away about your situation and ask them if they know of jobs you might apply for.* That really puts them on the spot and can be embarrassing to both parties when none surfaces. Let the healing process start to take shape before you start contacting anyone. Don't waste time on might-have-beens ("couldas, shouldas, wouldas") and dwelling on the past!

> *If we like what we thought, we'll get what we got.*
> — JIM HUGE

9. *You make the decision to smile or frown, to give or take, to love or hate, to*

build or destroy, and to win or lose. "When life gives you lemons—make lemonade."

10. Don't procrastinate. Remember, "results expected equals results achieved." Set-up daily activities and plans for yourself to follow. Do something every day that you do well, whatever it may be. Make a daily "to do" list consisting of tasks that are part of the overall campaign goals and plan of action. Keep your mind active. Determine to learn new things each day. Note your results.

11. Start acting and looking like a winner. Look people in the eye ("eyeball to eyeball") when you talk with them. Shake hands firmly, smile, have a pleasant manner, and dress well. Cultivate friendships with people who make you feel like a winner. Stay away from people who make you feel lousy. Tell yourself you have marketable gifts and skills! Visualize yourself as a success (act confident) and as too good a person to be out of a job for too long. Remember, no company will offer you a job while you feel and look "like a truck just hit you." Companies don't like problems; they hire people to solve them.

> *A man is what he thinks of all day.*
> — RALPH WALDO EMERSON

12. Focus on success stories of others. Choose people who accomplished things that they never thought possible because of the "fire that burned within them," even when others said they couldn't do it. Make a success list of your best and refer to this "plus list" when you've having a bad day or face a big challenge.

13. Get some audio-visual aids. Write to Success Motivation Institute, P.O. Box 2508, Waco, TX 76702-2508, (817) 776-1230; Nightingale-Conant Corporation, 7300 N. Lehigh Avenue, Niles, IL 60714, (708) 647-0300; or The Pacific Institute, Inc., Seattle, WA 98164, (204) 628-4800 for lists of self-help tapes. Select and order the best for you.

14. Make your own inspirational posters. Put them up in your bedroom and bathroom. For example:

> *The fullness of life does not come from things*
> *outside us; we ourselves must create the beauty in*
> *which we live.*

♦

To lengthen your life, shorten your meals.

✦

Love with the realization that what you love might be lost.

✦

Few have all they need, none all they wish.

✦

Observation is more than seeing; it is knowing what you see and comprehending its significance.

✦

The biggest room in the world is the room for improvement.

✦

The greatest source of human happiness is in personal achievement.

✦

Do not criticize the faults of others, but seek to correct your own faults.

✦

When you reach the end of your rope, tie a knot in it and hang on!

✦

Success is not a destination; it's a journey.

— Anonymous

15. *Listen to relaxing, soothing music while you are doing positive things for yourself.*

16. *Consider, in addition to a career management specialist, working with a*

relaxation therapist and psychologist while you are going through these times. Have a professional team working for you. These expenses may be covered under your medical benefits.

17. *Don't settle for a pretty good job search campaign; strive for the best.* Remember, you are a winner! Have the vision and determination to set and reach your career goals. Have the attitude of never giving less than your best to this endeavor.

18. *Contact Soundview Executive Book Summaries.* They're at 5 Main Street, Bristol, VT 05443. Learn about their book summary program and speed reviews. Call (800) 521-1227, in Vermont; elsewhere (802) 453-4062.

Emotional Journeys

As you work your job campaign over a period of weeks and months, you will experience an emotional roller-coaster ride. I call it "the yo-yo syndrome." A person has to realize that he or she is going to go though a grieving process and should allow enough time to work through the emotions. Many of my clients have talked about "hitting the wall" in their campaign, with respect to their attitude and self-esteem. This generally can occur when a person has gone through his or her contact list to no avail, a personal crisis arises within the family, telephone calls are not returned, and letters go unanswered. When this happens the natural tendency is to abandon networking or early campaign objectives and retreat to writing broadcast letters and answering ads, a strategy proven to be only 20 percent effective. Handling rejection and coping with "no's" is mentally tough. Naturally your attitude and self-esteem can take a nose dive as you doubt yourself.

Believe In Yourself

Most people who have been in this situation will tell you that they "bite the bullet," "suck it in," and continue on, determined to succeed. As difficult as it sometimes is and as lousy as they sometimes feel, they are determined to succeed and because of this determination and commitment, they will succeed. You have to believe in yourself to get to where you want to go. The rebuilding of self starts there.

Mental Attitudes

Sports psychologists have identified the eleven mental attitudes directly related to success in competitive sports:

Drive. Drive that provides the athletic desire for success. Committed athletes have a strong desire to do better, to compete, and to win. No one gets to be best without a burning desire to be the best.

Aggressiveness. Winners make things happen instead of waiting for them to happen. They take charge, force action, and produce results. They assert themselves strongly, make their presence felt. They thrive on competition.

Determination. Determination makes winners: the refusal to quit or accept defeat; the persistence to try and try and try again; the willingness to practice long and hard. Determined athletes are relentless in their efforts to improve and to win.

Responsibility. Winners accept total responsibility for their actions. They recognize their own mistakes and the need for change and improvement. They admit errors and will not blame others or make excuses.

Leadership. Winners tend to enjoy the role of leader. When leadership is needed, they step forward and take charge. They are dynamic people who like to influence others and take control of situations.

Self-Confidence. Self-confidence builds winners. Winners have confidence in their abilities and can act decisively. They believe they can successfully meet challenges and handle unexpected situations. They never doubt their own ability.

Emotional Control. Successful athletes can handle the pressures of competitive sports. They keep their cool, adjust quickly, and are not upset by bad breaks or bad calls. They deliver top performance regardless of the circumstances.

Mental Toughness. Mental toughness is a big factor in athletic success. Winners can accept strong criticism and rigorous training from a demanding coach. They recover quickly from setbacks. They don't fall apart when the going gets rough.

Coachability. Winners respect the coach and the coaching process. They know that coaching is important to their development and progress as an athlete. They are receptive to the coach's advice and follow it.

Conscientiousness. Winners have high standards of character. They have a deep sense of obligation, and know a team must have discipline to be successful. They put the welfare of the team first. They don't bend rules or regulations to suit themselves.

Trust. Winners are believers. They accept people at face value, and know that mutual trust is a major factor in building team morale and unity. Trusting athletes communicate and cooperate better with their teammates and coach.

— ANONYMOUS

4.

Coping With Stress:
Get Rid of Hang Ups

After a while you learn
the subtle difference
between holding a hand
and chaining a soul.
And you learn
that love doesn't mean leaning
and company doesn't mean security.
And you begin to learn
that kisses aren't contracts
and presents aren't promises.
And you begin to accept your defeats
with your head up and your eyes ahead
with the grace of a woman or a man,
not the grief of a child,
and learn to build all your roads on today
because tomorrow's ground is
too uncertain for plans,
and futures have a way of falling down
in mid-flight.
After a while you learn
That even sunshine burns if you ask too much.
So plant your own garden
and decorate your own soul
instead of waiting for someone to bring you flowers.
And you learn
that you really can endure
that you really are strong
and you really do have worth.
And you learn

and you learn
with every goodbye
you learn . . . .

— ANONYMOUS

What Stress Feels Like

You are out of work for the first time in your life. You are asking yourself, "where do I go from here with my life?" How am I going to survive? Will I have to move? For most people, fear of the unknown can be debilitating. You are experiencing stress. Stress is a perceived threat (imagined or real) that causes us to tense our bodies. Note the successful ways you have dealt with stress. Try them again.

When I was out of work for the first time, friends would say, "take it one day at a time." I was saying "no way," and "how about one hour at a time?" My self-esteem was at an all-time low, and I was probably the best self-flagellator of all times. It was devastating. All the messages I was giving myself were negative, like, "you dumb jerk, how could you let this happen? If you're so good, why haven't you got another job?" I'll never forget taking those warm, soothing showers as I let the water beat down on me, hoping to ease the pain I was experiencing. The mental pain and anguish really hurt, and I didn't know how I was going to make it over those hurdles of pain. Also, while taking a shower, I took long, deep breaths. I would hold my breath for a period of time and then let the air out slowly. This seemed to help. I somehow, with the emotional help of loved ones, had a support system of friends who really cared about me and told me so, resulting in a determination on my part that I would triumph and survive the grieving process which took me all of three months to go through. When I read Dr. Elizabeth Kubler-Ross's best seller *On Death and Dying* in the mid-seventies, little did I realize that her book would have implications for me in dealing with unemployment.

Termination Responses

Usually, a person terminated for whatever reason responds in one of the following ways:

1. *"I saw the handwriting on the wall and knew it was just a question of time before the axe would fall."* It still can be a blow for one's ego, though, when it does occur.

2. *"I can't believe this has happened to me."* After all, you were indispensable, a hard worker, an excellent performer, and, above all, loyal. Some-

times one experiences numbness. I read that 90 percent of jobs are lost not because of job performance but because of personality differences, politics, or simply the arrival of a new manager who is bringing his or her own team. Sad as this may seem, it has nothing to do with performance.

3. *"I feel like taking a vacation to just get away from it all."* It's the "fight or flight" syndrome. Somehow you feel that the farther away you are from this unpleasant situation, the more soothing it will be. It doesn't work this way and delays facing up to the situation. You can't confront the problem when you are on a trip!

4. *"I feel relieved that I am away from that situation."* A great burden has been lifted from you. Had it not been for "your security blanket" (benefits and seniority), you might have left some time ago.

5. *"I am extremely angry and feel like arguing with whoever represents the establishment."* You occasionally read about some cases where a fired employee has returned later with a gun and killed several people. Fortunately, situations like this are few and far between.

Try preparing an "angry list" and tape it to the bottom of one of your old pairs of shoes that you can stomp around in. This is a great way to vent one's anger (suggested by a former client).

Other possible responses to unemployment are wanting to sleep most of the day and not doing anything (I call this returning to the womb); working on hobbies or using other delay tactics rather than getting on with your job search; panicking—sending out hundreds of resumes in hopes that something will click; practicing the ostrich syndrome—not wanting to talk to anyone, especially your spouse or friends. You feel too embarrassed and feel locked-in to a specific field rather than examining your options.

Five-Stage Grieving Process

Having experienced some of these feelings initially, you most likely enter, as in Kubler-Ross, into a fluctuating five-stage grieving process that becomes the "yo-yo syndrome," which has no set time frame. With me, it lasted three months. The stages (denial, bargaining, anger, depression, and eventual self-acceptance, Figure 4.1) can overlap and many times, just when you seem to move ahead, you find yourself moving backward. "Getting on with it" can be facilitated by realizing that it is perfectly normal to feel this way. Countless numbers of people did before you and countless numbers after you will also react this way. This acceptance by you of the fact that this is normal will help in your mental recovery. Our response to job loss can be shaped, though, by our personal history, as well as how we have behaved under stress in the past. Talking to your doctor if you have chronic headaches or sleeping problems, seeking assistance from the clergy, buying and reading self-help books on coping, seeing a psychiatrist, and going to a public health clinic may also be suitable strategies that will help one to cope.

❖ ❖ ❖

FIGURE 4.1
The unemployment cycle index

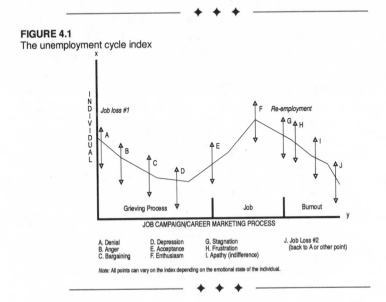

A. Denial D. Depression G. Stagnation J. Job Loss #2
B. Anger E. Acceptance H. Frustration (back to A or other point)
C. Bargaining F. Enthusiasm I. Apathy (indifference)

Note: All points can vary on the index depending on the emotional state of the individual.

❖ ❖ ❖

Let us examine this five-stage emotional process and how it can affect us:

1. Denial

"They must have made a mistake. I am expecting them to call me back because I'm indispensable. They need me. This can't be happening to me. I was their best performer." When one is in this stage the bottom falls out not only for you but also for your spouse and other family members. I had a former client's wife say, "what am I going to say to the neighbors? They will see your car in the driveway and they will know. How can I deal with the embarrassment?" Honesty always is the best policy. This stage can be and should be a time for family and friends to rally around the "unfairness" of the situation. The emotional nurturing from all concerned is one of the ingredients to help an individual rebuild self-esteem. Couples need to communicate even more as a team and talk about their feelings about what this unemployment situation has done to their relationship and what they can do for one another to help them through the grieving process. The person directly affected by the job loss has to realize that the spouse, more often than not, also goes through extreme trauma. Timely, soothing words like "everything will be all right" and "this is just another challenge for us to continue growing" may help. It must be realized that healthy denial can serve the purpose of temporary stress reduction and thus help one rehabilitate oneself faster.

> *To have a crisis and act upon it is one thing. To*
> *dwell in perpetual crisis is another.*
> — BARBARA GRIZZUTI HARRISON

2. Bargaining

"Maybe they will take me back if I recontact them." This stage is an action stage where you feel *you have to do something* to survive. Most individuals feel they need to send resumes out by the truckload and start taking interviews right away. This is the worst thing they can do. A person going through grieving "stinks," as a former boss said. Not literally, but the interviewer quickly senses that there are problems. Maybe it's the person's handshake, walk (droop), lack of eye contact, or closed body language. A job seeker has to collect his or her thoughts and realize the need to heal before rebuilding a career. This healing may take several weeks or even several months. You've heard the expression, "different strokes for different folks." Well, people react to stress differently. Most of my clients, when I get them, want their resume developed yesterday and a sixty-hour process reduced to the shortest passage of time. It just doesn't work that way; never has, never will! The client going through this stage soon realizes that the former employer is not now about to bargain (the bargaining was only in the client's mind), that there is no other job to go back to, and that perception leads them to the next stage.

> *The sun is already there.*
> *It is I*
> *who must come*
> *from behind the clouds.*
> — PATRICIA THUNER JONES

3. Anger

"Why me, Lord? It always happens to me!" A person with a strong faith may get mad at God. There are usually feelings of sadness, together with feelings of persecution. It's often hard to know where to direct the anger; e.g., steel workers, especially in Pittsburgh, caught in the web of a fluctuating economy and the importing or dumping of steel. Most direct it toward the former employer. "I never really liked working there anyway." The anger can also be displaced toward loved ones or friends. If the marital relationship was rocky to begin with and not built on commitment, caring, and open communication, both would not possibly have the right foundation "to weather the storm." As people usually get worse before they get better, loved ones usually react neutrally to any outbursts, holding their feelings within. It's important for the listening person, spouse, friend, or counselor to help draw out feelings while being both supportive and nonjudgmental. It's also important for feelings to be ventilated so that they can be healthily dealt with. A person could say that he or she is angry and know what has made him or her angry. It is interesting to note that some seemingly irrational displays of anger can be attempts to avoid feelings of remorse.

Eventually, though, depression and remorse come, that is, unless the person still remains in an earlier stage and doesn't deal with the loss. Note how a confederate soldier dealt with his losses (Fig. 4.2).

✦ ✦ ✦

FIGURE 4.2

A Confederate Soldier's Prayer

I asked God for strength, that I
might achieve;
I was made weak, that I might
learn humbly to obey.
I asked for health, that I might
do greater things;
I was given infirmity, that I
might do better things.
I asked for riches, that I might
be happy;
I was given poverty, that I
might be wise.
I asked for power, that I might
have the praise of men;
I was given weakness, that I
might feel the need of God.
I asked for all things, that I
might enjoy life;
I was given life, that I might
enjoy all things.

I got nothing that I asked for,
    but everything I had hoped for;
Almost despite myself, my
    unspoken prayers were answered.
I am, among all men, most
    richly blessed.

— ANONYMOUS

✦ ✦ ✦

4. Depression

This is probably the toughest stage. I know it was for me. I withdrew. I didn't want to talk to anyone. Some experience jitteriness, feelings of being worthless, sleep problems, self-blame, inability to concentrate, feelings of "doom or gloom," and a loss of control—even recurrent thoughts of death or suicide, or attempted suicide. One of my former clients said, "thanks for being there; had you not, I would have committed suicide."

My self-worth was at an all-time low when I was out of work. Friends saw me as being on edge, irritable, impatient, and suffering occasionally from aches and pains. If it had not been for the persistence of some of my supporting friends to "drag me out" to lunch or social events from time to time, I would have had a tougher time making the adjustment. You have the feeling that you are on a downward roller-coaster ride that will never make it to the upswing. You feel you don't have any control of yourself or your future. The fear of the unknown is awesome. It can cause your internal support system to be at an all-time low if you let your mind get away from you. "As a man thinketh, so is he." We need to get rid of "the garbage," throw it out and think about how we want things to be. We need to take responsibility for this.

"Turn your scars into stars."
                        — THE REV. ROBERT SCHULLER

The strengthening part of this stage can be to withdraw to plan and rethink one's life as you grapple to put the pieces back together again, like putting together a giant jigsaw puzzle. Some individuals do volunteer work or yoga, use biofeedback, seek psychological help, increase their religious activity, get more rest, work on hobbies, change their diets, adjust work activities to their biorhythms, learn to meditate, listen to motivating audio tapes, read books on how to get out of depression and concentrate on relaxing techniques.

Daily exercise can also be a great stress reducer, whether it involves taking brisk walks (also, walking the stairs instead of taking the elevator), bicycling, swimming, jogging, or working out at a local health club, which I strongly recommend, especially if you have a sedentary job. Other proven suggestions for reducing stress that came from a friend are as follows:

Breathing deeply, as I suggested earlier, can be an effective way of coping with stress. Imagine that all the tension in your body is leaving as you exhale (fresh air provides extra oxygen when combined with deeper breathing brought on by exercise); *roll your shoulders* forward and back several times each way; *use humor*. Ask yourself what your favorite comic would do in a similar situation. For example, meditate on Rodney Dangerfield's line "Look out for number 1 and don't step in number 2." Keeping a sense of humor, if possible, will help you through the tough times. Laugh your way through it; *visualize*, with your eyes closed, the most tranquil, peaceful place you have ever been to, such as the ocean with the sound of the waves moving in and out, the sea breeze, the seagulls, the smells you sense—or a cool mountain stream. Put yourself into that scene for a minute or two and enjoy it. I have even suggested to clients that when they start this exercise they should focus on a corner of a room. They soon associate the corner of the room with a pleasant, relaxing scene that they can "switch to" during a stressful interview or situation. They look at a corner of a room at a convenient time and associate it with a naturally relaxing scene; if you do this, turn your head from left to right and back again slowly as you look over your shoulders. Take at least several seconds to make the turns to release tension; and, last but certainly not least, backrubs, neckrubs, and shoulder rubs from a friend can be a wonderful way to help you through this depression stage.

The Twenty-third Psalm

The Lord is my shepherd; I shall not want. He maketh me to lie down in green pastures: He leadeth me beside the still waters. He restoreth my soul: He leadeth me in the paths of righteousness for his name's sake. Yea, though I walk through the valley of the shadow of death, I will fear no evil: For though art with me; Thy rod and Thy staff they comfort me. Thou preparest a table before me in the presence of mine enemies: Thou anointest my head

*with oil; my cup runneth over. Surely goodness and
mercy shall follow me all the days of my life: and I
will dwell in the house of the Lord for ever.*

This is the time for reflection about how you again want to live. A
close friend or family member should be supportive by listening (as you
ventilate) and being supportive as the job seeker comes to grips with his or
her situation, realizing that depression will not last forever. Try and relax
your mind and body.

5. Acceptance

We need to realize that as we experience a variety of emotions and
feelings, they can tell us many things about ourselves. We might see anger as
a source of energy and creativity, hurt as a source of compassion for others that
may also be going through the hurt that we are; depression as a time of withdrawal to reflect on who we are and where we are going. Then we allow ourselves also to move toward some kind of acceptance of ourselves.

We need to focus on the good of what we are and not on what we are
allowing ourselves to presently feel. Our mind-set should be focused on
the positive, and we should be feeding ourselves positive mind tapes such
as, "I am a good and capable person who is now feeling depressed, alone,
and worthless." We need to realize that it is all right to feel the way we are
feeling and that most of the negative feelings will soon pass. "Time heals
all wounds."

*Two Rules of Dealing With Stress
Rule One — Don't sweat the small stuff!
Rule Two — Everything is small stuff!*
— ANONYMOUS

As we examine ourselves in this stage, we might reflect on what Socrates was quoted as saying, "A life that is not examined is not worth living." This situation provides an opportunity to examine our past work
situations and learn from them; i.e., were there problems with management, peers? was there a lack of commitment? did you "let the boss be
boss"? were you involved in your work? We should also look at past behavioral patterns to see how we handled previous crises and what worked for
us to cope with the situation. Many of those coping mechanisms might be
applicable now. We need to realize that this adverse situation presents a
time for us to grow within ourselves, to learn new skills, and even to possi-

bly make new friends. Many of our clients make friends with others who are also going through "hard times." They not only become a peer support group for one another as they work to get on with their lives, but they sometimes provide network contacts. Most realize that acceptance doesn't mean forgetting about the loss, but profiting from it. They move through the pain and the heartaches to their new selves. As another, anonymous philosopher said, "Pain makes a person think, thought makes a person wise, and wisdom makes life endurable."

As we move through life and our careers, we realize that there are only three things we can really count on: taxes, death, and change. Nothing remains constant. We all will experience losses, and many will come quite unexpected.

If we can develop character-building inner mechanisms that help us to cope with those kinds of situations, help to reduce stress and fear and give us more self-control as we cope with them, our self-esteem will improve as we accept our own reality and what we have been dealt. We need to keep our minds "positively active." People are never hired out of pity. We need to see our situations as positive opportunities and take action! If we had heart disease and needed bypass surgery, we would accept the necessary surgery. So it is when we lose a job or do not have meaningful employment, we need to be of the positive mind-set that this is an opportunity to rebuild ourselves, to expand or further develop our career horizons.

Peace

> *One night I dreamed I was walking along the beach with the Lord. Many scenes from my life flashed across the sky. In each scene I noticed footprints in the sand. Sometimes there was only one.*
>
> *This bothered me because I noticed that during the low periods of my life, when I was suffering from anguish, sorrow or defeat, I could see only one set of footprints. So I said to the Lord, you promised me Lord, that if I followed you, you would walk with me always. But I noticed that during the most trying periods of my life there has been only one set of footprints in the sand. Why, when I have needed you most, have you not been there for me? The Lord replied: "Sometimes you have seen only one set of footprints, my child, because that's when I have carried you!"*

> — ANONYMOUS

5.

Your Budget: Determining Your Financial State with the Right Moves

When a man
Does not know
What harbor
He is making for,
No wind
Is the right wind.

— ANONYMOUS

Budget Survival with Checklists

When a person loses a job for whatever reason, the question naturally surfaces as to how to survive economically. The first thing you will want to do is to file for unemployment. Second, you will need to ask yourself the question, "How do we pay our bills and, simply, live?" It is important, therefore, to assess what your cash-on-hand and expenses are and generate extra income ideas that you may be able to tap to keep yourself afloat. By using the following checklists, together with your accountant's help if you have one, you will be able to at least come up with a figure on what it will take to keep your head above water. You will want to involve the whole family and get their input as you figure out your financial status. (Note: See Fig. 5.1.) Use a pencil as you fill in the figures. Put yourself on a budget.

Having completed your cash-on-hand checklist, you next need to tackle your expense checklist (Fig. 5.2) and your job campaign expense checklist (Fig. 5.3). Project for six months and even have a back-up plan in case your campaign takes longer—e.g., temporary or part-time work.

You should also keep a campaign expense travel report (Figure 5.4) as you incur the expenses. At the end of your campaign, it will be easier for you to total these deductible campaign expenses. Most job search expenses are still tax deductible. Keep your receipts!

─────────────── ◆ ◆ ◆ ───────────────

FIGURE 5.1
Cash-on-hand checklist

Calculate possible sources of money

Primary sources
Check if applicable:

Amount

☐ Checking/savings account _____
☐ Credit union _____
☐ Leases (sale value) _____
☐ Money owed _____
☐ Negotiable securities _____
☐ Refinancing mortgage(s) _____
☐ Relative loan(s)
☐ Sale of other assets, i.e.,
jewelry, silver _____
☐ Severance pay _____
☐ Tax refund _____
☐ Unused vacation days _____
☐ Whole life insurance (cash in) _____
☐ Other _____
TOTAL _____

Other sources

Amount

☐ Alimony/child support _____
☐ Consulting fee(s) _____
☐ Dividends (stocks) _____
☐ Income from spouse _____
☐ Interest (bonds) _____
☐ Rental income (if applicable) _____
☐ Retirement funds—401K,
profit-sharing and pension funds* _____
☐ Unemployment compensation _____
☐ Other income _____
TOTAL _____
GRAND TOTAL _____

*Check to see what your penalties would be if you withdraw these and
don't roll them over within 60 days.

─────────────── ◆ ◆ ◆ ───────────────

✦ ✦ ✦

FIGURE 5.2
Expenses checklist

Calculate average monthly expenditures:

Average monthly payments
Check if applicable:

		Amount
☐	Alimony/child support payments	_____
☐	Automobile insurance	_____
☐	Babysitting/child care	_____
☐	Barber shop/beauty salon	_____
☐	Bus/car pooling/parking/taxi	_____
☐	Car payment(s)	_____
☐	Car repairs/maintenance	_____
☐	Cigarettes, tobacco, beverages	_____
☐	Clothing	_____
☐	Clubs	_____
☐	Dues/subscriptions, (newspapers, books)	_____
☐	Entertainment/hobbies/recreation	_____
☐	Gasoline/oil	_____
☐	Gifts/birthdays/holidays	_____
☐	Groceries (food)	_____
☐	Health (medical/dental) drugs/ prescriptions	_____
☐	Home maintenance	_____
☐	Hospitalization	_____
☐	Job campaigning costs (see Fig. 5.3)	_____
☐	Laundry/cleaners	_____
☐	License/registration/tax	_____
☐	Life/disability insurance	_____
☐	Lunches/food away from home	_____
☐	License/registration/tax	_____
☐	Life/disability insurance	_____
☐	Other loans/installments/bills	_____
☐	Property insurance	_____
☐	Property (local) taxes, state taxes	_____
☐	Religious and other contributions	_____
☐	Rent or mortgage	_____
☐	Tuition/education/payments	_____
☐	Utilities:	
☐	Oil/heat	_____

- ☐ Natural/bottled gas   _____
- ☐ Electricity   _____
- ☐ Water/sewer/trash collection   _____
- ☐ Telephone   _____
- ☐ Other:
- ☐ Lessons   _____
- ☐ Personal items (cosmetics, etc.)   _____
- ☐ Travel   _____

TOTAL   _____

_____   ✦ ✦ ✦   _____

_____   ✦ ✦ ✦   _____

FIGURE 5.3
Job campaign expense checklist

List expenses associated with your job campaign

Check if applicable:

                                  Expenses
                                  anticipated

☐ **Career counseling**   _____

☐ **Directories/newspapers for search**   _____
Recruiter directory
Industry directories (i.e., Chamber of Commerce)
Local directories
Out-of-town newspapers
National help-wanted newspapers (i.e., National Ad Search)

☐ **Equipment**   _____
Telephone answering machine
Typewriter (rented or bought)
Tape recorder
Fax use

☐ **Long distance phone calls to
friends or firms**   _____

☐ **Postage**   _____
Introductory/thank you letters

Resumes to recruiters/agencies
Resumes to friends
Broadcast letters
Letters answering ads

☐ **Printing** _____

Resumes (one, two or three pages)
Cover letters to agency/recruiting firms
Broadcast letter (if not on word processor)
Stationery (Regular and Monarch with envelopes)
Business cards

☐ **Secretarial assistance** _____

Needs/wants ad response
Thank you letters after interviews (advice/job)
Broadcast letter (if on word processor)
Envelopes addressed (to agencies/recruiters, companies)

☐ **Travel and entertainment** _____

Drinks, meals for individuals seen personally
Hotel/transportation to cities where you are "on your own"
Car expense to library, interviews, to network
Note: see Fig. 5.4

☐ **Other** _____

TOTAL _____

✦ ✦ ✦

Saving and Cutting Expenses

As you worked on your expenses checklist (Fig. 5.2), it was probably a good idea to brainstorm for family ideas as to how you might save or cut expenses. Check bills for computer mistakes. They do occur. Barter with neighbors: Tell your CPA, if you have one, you'll trade his doing your income taxes for painting or gardening services if that is your specialty. Make long-distance calls, if you have to make them, after 5 p.m. or wait for weekends. Buy generic foods. Buy things on sale. Charge nothing. Rent videos, if you have a VCR, (there's a place near me that rents them 3 for 3 days for $1.50) for entertainment. You may want to temporarily eliminate all entertainment expenses, gifts, extra telephones (if applicable), lessons for the children, contributions, etc. You may consider consolidating all of your bills

FIGURE 5.4
Campaign expense travel report
Keep accurate record in the space provided

Date	Person Visited	Company	Miles	Amount	Parking	Meals	Other

Name _____
Period Start/Ended _____

(possibly with a home equity loan) so that you can make easy payments. Call Select Quote at (800) 343-1985 for low-cost term insurance. You could also call all of your creditors and tell them about your situation and what you can pay. Maybe they will settle for token payments until you get back on your feet again. Try and pay at least a little on each of your bills. Use the creditors checklist (Fig. 5.5) to log your results. Note: After you get back on your feet you can let your creditors know and then pay off your remaining balances as soon as possible.

✦ ✦ ✦

FIGURE 5.5
Creditors checklist

Check if applicable:

Item	Monthly Payment	Creditor's Name
☐ Appliances		
☐ Bank that holds your mortgage (pay principle only)		
☐ Car payments		
☐ Credit cards		
☐ Furniture		
☐ Home-equity loan		
☐ Rental agent		
☐ Sewer		
☐ Utilities		
☐ Water		
☐ Other bills		
TOTAL OWED		

✦ ✦ ✦

Generating Income

To generate additional income for yourself during this time, you might borrow against your life insurance or retirement policy if you have one. Usually the interest rate is lower than prevailing ones. Also, you may qualify for some government assistance programs, e.g., food stamps, although it has been my experience that you would have had to be making a rather low salary from your last position to qualify.

Another idea for the generation of income would be to consider a part-time job. Look into registering with a temporary agency. Also consider taking out an ad for specialty work that you might be able to do, i.e., wallpapering, painting, fixing VCRs. Be creative! Think of two quotes to guide you: "Necessity is the mother of invention" and "act, not react."

As a last resort you may consider items from off the extra income checklist: (Fig. 5.6)

✦ ✦ ✦

FIGURE 5.6
Extra income checklist

Check if applicable:

Source of supplemental income	Value
☐ Automobile (second car)	_____
☐ Automobile (first car)	_____
☐ Sporting equipment (boats, planes, snowmobiles, campers)	_____
☐ Expensive cameras (or other hobby equipment)	_____
☐ Jewelry	_____
☐ Musical instruments	_____
☐ Stamp/coin collection	_____
☐ Works of art	_____
☐ Unused furniture	_____
☐ Old clothing	_____
☐ Other equipment (unused lawn and farm equipment, appliances, etc.)	_____
☐ Secondary properties	_____
☐ Your home (see realtor for appraisal)	_____
☐ Loans from relatives	_____
TOTAL	_____

✦ ✦ ✦

6.

Appearance: Business Attire, Exercising and Diet Can Help Create Your Image. Time is on Your Side

By a man's finger-nails, by his coat-sleeve, by his boots, by his trouser-knees, by the callosities of his forefinger and thumb, by his expression, by his shirt-cuffs—by each of these things a man's calling is plainly revealed. That all united should fail to enlighten the competent inquirer in any case is almost inconceivable.

— SHERLOCK HOLMES

Business Attire

Clothes not only help to make the person but certainly project a statement about yourself to others. With first impressions being lasting ones, especially at an initial interview, it's important that you dress properly. You may be meeting a person for the first time and a first impression will definitely be based on how well you are dressed. If you are dressed well and you know it, you will most likely come across as being confident, ambitious, and successful. If a person looks polished, others will feel he or she is polished. Generally speaking, if you look and feel good, your performance will be good as well.

Assess Your Wardrobe

Before you assess your wardrobe and buy additions to it, do some research to find out what others that you might be working with are wearing. Take your "winning" wardrobe cues from them. If you have been invited to an informal interview, always dress up. It's easier to dress down than to dress up. If all is informal, you can always ask if it's all right to get informal too. Also note pictures in annual reports, business/fashion magazines, and clothing books for traditional and conservative ideas that will enable you to blend into an organization. You could even visit some clothing specialty stores to seek some professional advice.

Stick to professional clothing that won't attract attention and to tasteful attire that you feel you look good in, yet clothing in which you could even step into a board meeting if you had to. Your winning image will also project a positive attitude and label you with having used excellent judgment in your wardrobe selection. Let's now examine some noteworthy wardrobe suggestions for your consideration:

Men

Suit. Select an expensive, conservative, two-piece, two-button gray, navy, or dark blue flannel (wool blend) pinstripe or solid suit during store sales at upwards of 50 percent off. (Note: The darker the suit, usually the more trust and credibility it transmits.) Good suits cost more but last longer, and you'll find that professionals will identify with a "quality, trustworthy look." If you want to project a winning look, you have to invest in it! Find a good tailor so that your suit will fit you well. The cut of your suit should be single-breasted with natural shoulders. Suit trousers should have cuffs of $1\frac{3}{4}$" if you are under 6'0", 2" if you are over 6'0", and should be long enough to break as they touch the shoes. A double-breasted suit or any with an extreme pattern or cut should not be worn.

Don't clutter the pockets of your suits, that makes them baggy. Also, carry a slim leather wallet in the inside pocket of your jacket (less bulky!). Stay away from pocket handkerchiefs (too flashy). Use leather belts for your suit that complement or match the color of your shoes (stay away from flashy, ornate belt buckles). Note: If you are invited back for additional interviews, make sure you don't wear the suit that you wore to the first one.

Shirt. Use only nonpatterned white oxford (100 percent cotton) shirts that have been professionally laundered, lightly starched and ironed with long sleeves (even in hot weather) $\frac{1}{2}$" to 1" below coat sleeve, and with straight collars. Avoid button-down collars and initials on sleeves as they are too sporty. Wear a plain, pointed collar. Never wear a new shirt to an interview, as it will look like you just put it on for the first time.

Ties. Should be 3" to $3\frac{1}{4}$" wide. Use conservative silk-styled challis (lightweight worsted fabric in solids or printed designs), dots, stripes or traditional foulards in classic checks (lightweight silk tie with small intricate figures). Don't wear solid ties with solid suits, but bold-pattern ties are best with solid-color suits; stay away from the clasps, and use darker ties to complement lighter suits. Consider small patterns, bias stripes, club ties, or dots; no bright prints or bow ties. Use the four-in-hand knot rather than the windsor.

Shoes. Select lightweight, thin-soled, and leather (not patent) shoes with three or four eyelets in well-polished black (go with blue and grey suits)—or cordovans which go with everything. Note what people in charge wear! A classic laced wing-tip or cap-tip shoe in black, brown, or cordovan is best. Avoid saddle shoes, bucks, patent leather or loafers, which convey an informal attitude. Check your shoes for worn soles and heels. If they need to be repaired, take them to a cobbler and keep them polished.

Socks. Wear solid over-the-calf or knee-high socks that match the suit you are wearing. Never wear white socks unless you want to attract negative attention. If the elastics are gone in your socks, replace them.

Overcoat. Burberry trench coat with zip-in lining in beige or khaki. Never black in the U.S., although it's acceptable in England.

Jewelry. Keep simple and tasteful, although the less you wear, the better. No flashy cufflinks. If you wear cufflinks, gold is preferred to silver. A conservative, businesslike watch with a black or brown leather band is acceptable.

Hair. Your hair should be cut short, neat, and combed. All facial hair and sideburns must go. If you have a question about your hairstyle, go to a reliable barber and ask for a business cut.

With respect to facial hair, I realize that those with moustaches are going to take offense; check out any number of annual reports at random. If you see any facial hair, it usually will only be with the owners or individuals from the advertising or research/development departments. My suggestion is to stay away from any facial hair. Remember, the bad guys in the movies always wore black and had moustaches! You might laugh today but I honestly believe that this negative image still carries over even into peoples' subconscious minds.

Accessories. Use a high-quality leather attaché with a dial lock. Stay away from the key types. Too basic. Buy yourself a gold pen and pencil set.

Topcoats/Overcoats. Use classic style of solid or herringbone. Camel hair coats are too tough to keep clean. Stay away from them.

Asides. Don't use toothpicks, chew gum, or bite your nails; keep nails trim and clean; keep hands out of the way when you are seated; make sure if you wear glasses that they are clean and in good repair; use quality cologne. Above all, don't take magazines with you to an interview unless they are related to the subject you are being interviewed for. Note: consult John Malloy's *Dress For Success*, Alan Flusser's *Clothes and the Man*, and James Bradford's *Investment Dressing*.

Women

Suit. Wear a two-piece, conservatively stylish, button, lapel, wool or wool-blend, navy, black, burgundy, or grey suit. Buy an expensive suit on sale. Consider it as an investment in yourself. Skirt length is best at the knee or slightly below it. No high slits or side openings.

Blouse. Buy a white silk, cotton, or polyester blouse with side closure, it's the safest; ruffled neck or band collar with or without pleats. Avoid bold stripes or loud prints or V-necks. Accent with multicolor scarves. Long sleeves and shoulder pads help to achieve a powerful image. Avoid short-sleeved blouses and sheer fabrics, even if worn with a slip or camisole.

Dresses. Business dresses should have simple, classic lines; silk prints and wool are best.

Shoes. Wear plain black, brown, or navy 2" pumps. Flats and high-heeled shoes are out. Avoid heels that are too high (2" to $2\frac{1}{2}$" heels are best).

Coat. Solid color wool and a Burberry-type trench coat for rain wear; in cold weather wear a tan, navy or blue woolen coat.

Stockings. Hosiery should be sheer, light, and untextured; pantyhose in a neutral color. Note: Always carry an extra pair in case of an unexpected run. Avoid opaque, colored, or patterned stockings. When in doubt, always dress conservatively.

Jewelry. Be discreet. Don't wear too much. Avoid gaudy pieces. One ring per hand.

Belts. Replace the belts that come with your skirts or dresses and add a good-looking leather belt.

Hair. Neatly styled and shoulder length. If you have long hair and don't want to cut it, keep it pulled back. Keep hair away from your face. Strive for balance in hair and makeup.

Purse/Handbags. Don't use them. Invest in a brown or cordovan leather briefcase or attaché case.

Asides. Use cosmetics and perfume sparingly, e.g., light fragrance; use skin moisturizers, especially during the winter months; keep nails short (long fingernails are out); carry a gold pen with you. Note: Read Emily Cho's *Looking, Working, Living Terrific 24 Hours a Day* and John Malloy's *Dress For Success* (women's version).

Reminders for both sexes:

1. Check to see that all of the wardrobe you are wearing is clean and pressed, properly fitted, shirt or blouse tucked in, colors are coordinated, shoes are shined, nails clean and properly cut, and hair neat.

2. Refer to *Esquire* and *Working Woman* magazines for a guide to conservative dress. *GQ* and *Vogue* would be more high fashion. See how TV evening newscasters dress.

3. See a color consultant to find out what your best colors are.

4. Rule: Better too plain than too fancy!

To The Man In The Arena

"It is not the critic who counts, not the man who points out how the strong man stumbled or where the doer of deeds could have done them better. The credit belongs to the man who is actually in the arena; whose face is marred by dust and sweat and blood; who strives valiantly; who errs and comes short again and again; who knows the great enthusiasms, the great devotions, and spends himself in a worthy cause; who, at the best, knows the triumph of high achievement; and who, at the worst, if he fails, at least fails while daring greatly, so that his place shall never be with those cold and timid souls who know neither victory nor defeat.

— THEODORE ROOSEVELT

Exercise

Why the Interest

Exercise, conditioning, physical fitness and athletics have always been a part of my life. My brothers Jim, Barry, and Richard and I were involved in a variety of sports and conditioning programs as we grew up. Out of all of us, Jim excelled the most, receiving All-American honors in ice hockey at Boston College, as well as being on the U.S. team for several years, culminating in being a goalie for the 1968 Olympic team. He was honored by his alma mater in 1985 when he was inducted into the Boston College Hall of Fame.

My dad played baseball. My uncle Leo centered for Frank Lahey's Boston College Sugar Bowl champions before the coach left for Notre Dame. My uncle Bud was a scratch golfer and club champion and my son-in-law Chip was a high-school All-American hockey player who became captain of his college team at Plattsburg State College and was drafted by the New Jersey Devils.

Because of this sensitivity to the importance of the development of "the complete person" (the three-legged stool of mind, spirit and body), I involved all of my four kids in sports and exercise programs from an early age. Cheryl was our figure skater, Jon and Michael played hockey, and Bob became football co-captain of his high-school team and went on to become a starting linebacker and special team player at Cornell.

I personally think the discipline of being active in sports, an awareness of what conditioning does for your body, and the sensitivity to the importance of team play, provides us with a mental toughness essential for surviving.

Champion Creed

I am not judged by the number of times I fail, but by the number of times I succeed . . . and the number of times I succeed is in direct proportion to the number of times I can fail and keep trying.

— ANONYMOUS

Reasons for Exercise

Most athletes who test and condition their bodies with exercise will tell you that they are able to handle stress a lot better when they are mentally and physically tough than when they are not.

Companies such as Bonnie Bell, Phillips Petroleum, PepsiCo, Xerox, and Boeing have long been committed to providing subsidized in-house exercise programs for their employees, believing there is indeed a positive correlation between physical fitness and mental alertness (productivity). A longitudinal study of almost 40 years was conducted at Harvard University with the results proving that correlation. (It was published in the December, 1979 issue of the *New England Journal of Medicine.*)

We know people exercise for a variety of reasons, but mostly, to control their weight. The *Wall Street Journal* (December 30, 1986) reported that men who are at least 20 percent heavier than the standard weight for their size lose an average of $4,000 a year in pay. Other reasons include stress reduction, making one feel better from a health standpoint, and enabling one to be active in their lives.

It is important to exercise when you are not emotionally in the best of states. You can run, walk, swim or bike. It's an excellent way to get the "poisons of stress" out of your system, and you will feel better for your efforts. Be physically active. You will need to have a physical from a physician, especially if you haven't been very active physically, and then, assuming that you pass your physical, begin to do some exercises that will put you in touch with your body.

Daily exercise should go hand-in-hand with a proper diet schedule for yourself. As you start to feel better about yourself, you will find yourself being able to control stress a lot better.

Kinds of Exercise

See if there are some local health clubs, YMCAs or YWCAs, or company or school facilities in your community where you can start your exercising. You might decide what exercise or exercises that you want to participate in by referring to the following overall activity chart (Fig. 6.1) compiled by the President's Council on Physical Fitness and Sports. Each of the fourteen activities was rated by seven medical experts according to their overall fitness value. You may want to experiment with different kinds of exercise, utilizing the ones you enjoy and can work into your schedule. Several friends of mine have a Nordic Trac in their homes that they use daily. They love them!

✦ ✦ ✦

FIGURE 6.1
Activity chart—
overall fitness value

	Stamina (Cardio-respiratory)	Muscular Endurance	Muscular Strength	Flexibility
Jogging	21	20	17	9
Bicycling	19	18	16	9
Swimming	21	20	14	15
Skating (Ice or Roller)	18	17	15	13
Handball/Squash	19	18	15	16
Cross-Country Skiing	19	19	15	14
Basketball	19	17	15	13
Alpine Skiing (downhill)	16	18	15	14
Tennis	16	16	14	14
Calisthenics	10	13	16	19
Walking	13	14	11	7
Golf	8	8	9	8
Softball	6	8	7	9
Bowling	5	5	5	7

REFERENCE: The President's Council on Physical Fitness and Sports. Each activity was judged on its overall fitness value by seven leading medical experts. A score of 3 was the highest possible rating each expert could give each factor of an activity.

✦ ✦ ✦

You should leave enough time for both a warm-up and a cool-down period. You will need a slow, gradual warm-up period to increase your circulation and stretch the muscles of your body, getting them ready for exercise. I have been a victim here in the past by either not stretching long enough or doing the wrong stretches. The result can be shin splints or, worse than that, a pulled Achilles tendon. A proper warm-up period of fifteen to twenty minutes will avoid muscle pulls.

Group exercise appears to be a motivating way to go. In many exercise activities today it is not uncommon to have many half-hour to one-hour aerobics classes with the masses "doing their thing" to lively music. Exercise, though, should be moderate, regular (20 to 30 minutes per day, three days per week) and not exhausting. They say if you can't talk while you are exercising, you are pushing too hard.

A sample YMCA industrial fitness program that was shared with me by Norman Joyner (a YMCA executive) is as follows: (Fig. 6.2)

If you record this YMCA program on any audiotape with background music, it could then become your home Jane Fonda tape.

Note: As you cool down from your exercising, do so by walking or by doing mild stretching exercises from the warm-up sheet.

♦ ♦ ♦

FIGURE 6.2
Industrial fitness program

1. Jog laps to warm up.
2. Standing position with legs apart, touch hands on floor then extend arms over head 1-2 count - 15 times.
3. Standing position with legs apart and arms extended over head. Count 1-2-3 to left; 1-2-3 to right - 15 times.
4. Standing position with legs apart and hands on chest, swing arms back and up 1-2-3 count (box) - 20 times.
5. Jumping jacks 1-2-3 count - 25 times.
6. Standing position, legs apart, hands over head, touch both hands on left foot; touch the floor beneath your feet; touch right foot, return to starting position 1-2-3 count -15 times.
7. Deep knee bends, half way down 1-2-3 count - 10 times.
8. Hops, 1-2 count - 15 times.
9. Lying on stomach, arms extended forward, raise left arm and right leg; then raise right arm and left leg 1-2-3 count - 15 times.
10. Lying on stomach with hands behind neck, arch the trunk upward and down up/down - 15 times.
11. Lying on stomach with hands behind at sides and legs raised, open and close count 1-2-3 count - 15 times.

12. Lying on stomach, arms extended to side, cross left leg to right hand; cross right leg to left hand 1-2-3 count - 15 times.
13. Lying on stomach, raise legs, move arms in breast stroke motion 1-2-3 count - 20-25 times.
14. Push-ups - 12-15 times.
15. Standing position, raise both arms overhead, while arms are going up inhale; when going down exhale, inhale/exhale count - 10 times.
16. Standing position with legs apart and hands behind head, turn left; turn right 1-2-3 count - 15 times.
17. Arm circles, arms out to side, forward; backward 1-2 count - 20 times.
18. Standing position, raise left knee to chest; raise right knee to chest 1-2 count - 20 times.
19. Windmill 1-2-3 count (alternating toe touching) - 20 times.
20. Sitting position, legs straight and hands on chest, swing arms from left to right 1-2-3 count - 20 times.
21. Sitting position, legs straight, touch both hands to both feet 1-2-3 count - 15-20 times.
22. Sitting position, legs apart, arms at sides, touch left hand to right foot; touch right hand to left foot 1-2-3 count - 15-20 times.
23. Lying on left side, raise right leg and lower it to starting position, repeat on right side up/down count - 15 times.
24. Lying on back, bring both hands up to a 45 degree angle. Raise both legs up until they touch finger tips; return to starting position up/down count - 10 times.
25. Lying on back, raise up, circles, 6 right then 6 left.
26. Lying on back, arms at sides; raise neck up and down 10 times.
27. Lying on back, arms extended over head; tighten up muscles, relax.
28. Lying on back with legs and knees on stomach, rotate trunk right to left - 15 times.
29. Lying on back, raise legs 12 inches off floor - kick up/down - 15 times.

✦ ✦ ✦

The California Department of Health Study

The California Department of Health has been conducting longitudinal studies on individuals since 1962 and found that people who practice the following habits had a greater longevity and better health than those who didn't. (The study found that if six out of seven rules were followed, men could add 11 years to their lives and women could add 7 years.)

1. Get adequate sleep (7 to 8 hours).
2. Eat a nutritious breakfast (not just coffee and a danish).
3. Eat regular meals and don't eat between them. (Avoid foods with refined sugars and fat. They can increase your cholesterol. Studies have shown that cholesterol readings of 250 mg or above increase the potential coronary risk to twice the normal rate).
4. Control your weight. (The tendency when you are under stress is to eat, eat, eat. Exercising will reduce the desire to eat.) Remember, people are not overweight but overfat.
5. Don't smoke cigarettes. (Give them up "cold turkey." If you smoke, take the American Cancer Society's test to see where you stand.)
6. Drink moderately or not at all.
7. Exercise regularly.

Immediately following exercise, take your pulse to determine your exercise heart rate and how that compares with the ideal rate for your age. There are several ways for you to determine your pulse. You can count the carotid pulse at the carotid artery in front of the large vertical muscle next to your Adam's apple. Count for only ten seconds, since the pulse rate returns to a slower resting state quite fast. Then multiply your ten-second count by six to get your 60-second exercise heart rate. The heart rate should fall somewhere between 70 and 85 percent of the maximum for your age.

Now that you know how to take your pulse, you may want to take your pulse before exercise, several times during exercise and immediately after when you are ready to cool down. You should ideally be back to normal within ten minutes after you exercise.

Exercise not only can help you survive through periods of stress but, as was mentioned, can also help you toward longevity. It helps not only your physical well-being, but such qualities as strength, agility, endurance, breathing, flexibility, and how you feel about yourself. "If you feel and act like a winner, you will be a winner." Therefore, as the Nike ad says, "Just Do It!" Get your spouse or friend involved also.

Exercise Programs

Physical exercise provides relief from stress. You don't have to exercise until you are fatigued in order for the activity to be beneficial. Do not attempt strenuous exertion without first checking with your family physician. Exercise provides physical as well as psychological benefits.

A Physical Fitness Test

These tests will give you some indication of your overall state of fitness. If you're under a doctor's care, don't attempt them without your doctor's consent. Stop if you feel overstressed. Do these exercises and then answer the questions with a "yes" or "no":

_____ When you pinch your waist, while standing, is the skin fold an inch or less?

_____ Can you hold a deep breath for 45 seconds?

_____ Is the difference between your chest full of air and your chest not full of air at least $3\frac{1}{2}$ inches, if you're a man and $2\frac{1}{2}$ inches if you're a woman?

_____ Can you do 10 situps?

_____ Can you do 5 pushups without undue strain?

_____ Can you step onto and off of a strong chair with a seat about 15 inches from the floor 20 times?

_____ While sitting on the floor with legs apart and hands clasped behind your head, can you lean forward and touch each elbow to the opposite knee without undue effort?

_____ Can you do 10 deep knee bends? (Omit this one if you have cartilage problems.)

_____ After running in place for three minutes, lifting your feet up at least four inches off the floor, is your pulse under 120 beats a minute?

A "no" answer to any of these questions suggests that you are not as physically fit as you should be. If you struggled to complete some of the items, you may not be in overall good shape, either.

Diet—You Are What You Eat

Monitoring

Research supports the belief that nutritional mistakes (eating the wrong foods) and a variety of emotional ills—i.e., depression and suicides—go hand in glove. It's important, therefore, that we monitor what we eat. If we are overweight, our productive output can be sluggish at best. As you need to exercise to reduce stress, so do you need to balance exercise with eating the right foods, especially if you are under a lot of stress or tension. Keep track of your calories using this chart (Fig. 6.3) and with an inexpensive calorie counter that you can buy.

◆ ◆ ◆

FIGURE 6.3
Food and calories

(Obtain a more complete list from your physician or from books on dieting)

Food	Calories
Bread and Cereals	
White bread (1 slice)	64
Whole wheat bread (1 slice)	55
Doughnut (1)	136
Rice (1 cup)	201
Beverages	
Coffee or tea (plain)	0
Milk, whole (1 cup)	166
Dairy Foods	
Butter (1 T.)	100
Cheese, cheddar (1 oz.)	113
Egg (1 medium)	77
Cream, light (1 T.)	30
Dessert	
Pie, apple (4″ section)	331
Pie, lemon meringue (4″ section)	302
Ice cream, vanilla (½ cup)	200
Fruit	
Apple, raw (medium)	76
Banana, raw (medium)	88
Grapefruit (½ small)	48
Orange (medium)	70
Pear, raw (medium)	95
Fruit Juices	
Grapefruit, fresh (1 cup)	87
Orange, fresh (1 cup)	108
Tomato, canned (1 cup)	50

Liquors

Brandy (1 oz.)	75
Scotch whiskey (1½ oz.)	125
Beer (12 oz.)	170
Wine (3 oz. glass)	75-100

Meat, Fish and Poultry

Beef, sirloin steak (9 oz.)	750
Pork chop (3 oz.)	284
Veal chop (3 oz.)	193
Chicken, broiled (2 pieces)	100
Tuna (3 oz.)	169
Salmon, canned (3 oz.)	173
Frankfurters (2)	250
Leg of lamb, 1 slice (4"x 4"x ¼")	250
Codfish steak (4"x 3"x ¼")	100

Vegetables

Carrots (1 cup)	44
Corn (1 cup)	140
Peas, fresh (1 cup)	111
Potatoes, mashed (1 cup)	159
Tomato, raw (medium)	30
Potatoes, french fried (10)	165

✦ ✦ ✦

To lose weight, try eating fewer fried and sugary foods. Cook vegetables and meats without fat or sauces. If you have to use oil, use olive oil. Broil or bake stews or roast meats. Try eating only one serving per setting, avoid gravy and eating after 6:00 p.m. Use the Kovensky diet (named after a lawyer friend of mine):

Eat None	*Eat Less*	*Eat More*
Caffeine	Meat	Vegetables
Alcohol	Sweets	Fruit, salads
Fermented liquids	Sugar, salt	Fish, seafood
Ripe cheese	Other dairy products	Grains
Cured products	Nuts	Rice
Ice cream	Salad dressing	Pasta
Anything containing fat	High calorie food	Poultry
MSG	All foods	All carbohydrates
		(Use chopsticks—you
		have to eat more slowly)

Nutritional Planning

You will want to plan your meals. Try and include the three major nutrients: protein, fat, and carbohydrates every day. Remember that good nutrition is a way of eating; choose lean meats and trim off the fat. Broil, bake, or steam when you cook. Buy ice milk or frozen yogurt rather than ice cream. Use low-fat or skim milk rather than whole milk. Eat more chicken and fish. Choose crisp, "grainy" breads or popcorn rather than high-fat crackers. Use oil and vinegar rather than high-calorie dressings. When you have to snack, do so on raw vegetables, fruits, or juices.

If you've been invited out for a luncheon interview, be on time and let the host or hostess select the place. Never order an alcoholic drink. Tell the host it's your doctor's orders. Select food that is easy to eat and not necessarily the one that your host has selected. Never criticize anything about the food, service, or place, as that is a direct insult to your host. Take your time eating the meal and thank your host for it. He or she should get your thank-you note within the next two or three days. Some luncheon pointers: never season food that you haven't tasted; the butter on your butter plate is for bread and not vegetables; and don't offer to pick up or divide the tab when it was someone else's invitation.

> *The doctor of the future will give no medicine but will interest his patients in the care of the human frame, in diet, and in the cause and prevention of disease.*
>
> — THOMAS A. EDISON

PART II

The Complete Career Marketing Process
(Boot Camp): "Take One Day at a Time"
Strategies for Tomorrow

7.

Self-Assessment:
It's the Key to Your Future

When you stop to think, don't forget to start again.
Eat less, breathe more; talk less, think more; ride
less, walk more; clothe less, bathe more; worry less,
work more; waste less, give more; preach less,
practice more.

— ANONYMOUS

Career Direction

Many people at various times in their careers, want to assess where they've been, where they are, and where they are going. Times change and people with them. Goals, values, vocations, and interests (identity issues) have a way of changing as people gain experience (good or bad). Some people want to confirm their direction, some know they want to change careers but are uncertain where their strengths lie and what they should aim for; some need help through a midlife crisis—they feel trapped while others are looking for options. In short, they want to find out what they would like to do at this time.

Self-assessment takes many shapes. It first, I believe, starts with your education and experience. Then you need to take a battery of tests. The best adult vocational interest indicator, I feel, mainly because it's been around since 1933 (with seven updates), is the Strong Campbell. This can at least give the person an occupational direction with some suggested vocational choices.

Other considerations are the *current needs* of the person, the person's present job values, what the person feels would be the perfect job (take a fantasy trip), what interests the person, what the person is good at, and whether the person has the education and experience to make it work. Not only does the person need to truly know himself or herself, but he or she needs a positive self-image and the ability to honestly visualize themselves as a success, if he or she is to complete the self-assessment process. As you go through this process, take note of what makes you unusual or different as well as what you enjoy doing. What do you like? What turns you on? What do you want out of life? Don't be limited to just what you have done in the past. Also note what you didn't like in your previous jobs.

When Socrates said, "Know thyself," he wasn't that far off the mark when it comes to looking for a job. Coming to know oneself, if done right, can be multifaceted, as you are about to see.

First, you need to develop a list of ideas about yourself from the following variety of sources (see Fig. 7.1).

Jobs

Review any jobs (part-time or full-time) that you have had and the duties, responsibilities, and/or projects that you were responsible for and what authority you had in carrying them out. How many people did you supervise? Did you fill in for a supervisor? How many committees did you serve on? What equipment or material did you use? How large was your budget? Did you receive any recognition (awards or certificates), save money or time, point out or create something, improve customer service, or reduce turnover? Job descriptions, if available, can be a helpful tool.

Personal

Think about any personal, recreational, or community projects that you worked on that made you feel good or proud, that you enjoyed, that provided the greatest satisfaction, or that at least in your mind was a success. What challenged you? What "turned you on?" Did this occur with things, numbers, people, ideas, or words? Put your conclusion on your idea list.

Skills Inventory

Review the alphabetized inventory list of skills, abilities, and talents in Fig. 7.2. Circle those that you feel you honestly have and have successfully demonstrated in an educational, vocational, community, or recreational environment. After doing that, review those that you have circled and double check your top twenty. Now check over your top twenty and circle and check your top ten skills. These are your primary skills; the second ten are your secondary skills or strengths. Add these ideas to your list.

✦ ✦ ✦

FIGURE 7.1
Idea assessment list

1. Job(s), Duties, Responsibilities, Projects

   _____

   _____

   _____

2. Personal, Recreational, Hobbies, Community Activities

   _____

   _____

   _____

3. Skills Inventory

   _____

   _____

   _____

4. Action Verb List

   _____

   _____

   _____

5. Dictionary of Occupational Titles (DOT)

   _____

   _____

   _____

6. Resumes (Dossier, Vitae)

   _____

   _____

   _____

7. Umbrella Ideas (Projects)

   _____

   _____

   _____

8. Work Values

   _____

   _____

   _____

9. Journalistic Questions

   _____

   _____

   _____

10. Challenges Solved

   _____

   _____

   _____

11. Needs Solved

   _____

   _____

   _____

12. Friend(s) Ideas

   _____

   _____

   _____

13. Organization/Location/Salary Preferences

   _____

   _____

   _____

14. Other Factors

   _____

   _____

   _____

✦ ✦ ✦

✦ ✦ ✦

FIGURE 7.2
Skills inventory (abilities learned)

A
Abstracting ideas
Accounting
Achieving goals or objectives
Acting
Administration
Advertising
Advising
Analyzing data and problems
  quantitatively
Anticipating events or moods
Appraising programs, services, or
  property
Approving layouts, equipment, or
  orders
Arbitration
Arranging events, meetings
Artistic qualities
Assembling apparatus, equipment,
  or data
Assigning responsibilities for work
  schedules
Assuring contractual compliances
Auditing
Other(s)

B
Budgeting
Building teams, tools, dies, etc.
Buying
Other(s)

C
Calculating
Carpentry
Checking for accuracy
Checking receiving records against
  invoices
Classifying information
Collecting money, information
Committee work
Communicating

Comparing people, things
Compiling and maintaining
  statistical data
Composing things
Computing quantitative data or
  information
Conceiving relationships
Conceptualizing numbers or ideas
Conducting safety meetings, research
Conferring with boss to plan
  activities
Confronting other people
Constructing buildings or other
  things
Controlling situation (financial,
  behavioral)
Convincing
Cooking
Coordinating, controlling
  events/activities/tasks/labor—
  management teams
Coping with pressure
Copying
Correspondence
Cost analysis
Counseling, coaching, tutoring
Crafts
Creation, invention
Credit analysis
Customer relations
Other(s)

D
Dancing
Data processing
Dealing with pressure
Dealing with unknowns
Dealing with volunteers
Debating
Deciding uses of money, setups,
  production rates
Decision making

Decorating
Delegating
Designing art, processes, products,
  programs, systems, buildings
Detail-oriented
Determining and planning product
  testing, objectives, changes
Developing budgets
Developing mathematical models,
  systems, standards, programs
Diplomacy
Directing and coordinating sales,
  products, services
Directing preparation of
  administrative directories/people
Discipline
Dispensing information/goods
Displaying ideas/materials
Distribution
Dramatizing ideas/problems
Drawing diagrams, charts, drafts
Driving, operating machinery
Other(s)

E
Economical
Editing
Enduring long hours (physical
  hardships)
Energy, drive
Engineering
Entertaining
Enthusiasm
Equipment operating
Estimating space or cost
  requirements
Evaluation
Examining, assessing situations
Exhibiting
Expediting (speeding up)
Explaining
Expressing feelings individually or
  those of a group
Other(s)

F
Fast worker
Figures
Financial analysis
Financial management
Finding information from
  sources/people
Fixing machines
Follow-through on instructions
Foresight
Fund raiser
Other(s)

G
Generating cost-saving ideas
Getting along with others
Goal setting
Government relations
Group dynamics
Group facilitating
Group work
Other(s)

H
Handling business correspondence
Handling complaints
Handling detail work
Handling financial transactions
Handling objects
Helping others (physically)
Human relations
Other(s)

I
Idea generating
Identifying surplus space or
  equipment
Imagining new solutions, ideas
Implementation
Improving situations, materials
Individualism
Initiating contacts/new ideas
Interpreting languages/contracts/
  laws/regulatory requirements
Interviewing
Inspecting

Installing
Instruction in quality/production
    standards
Insuring optimum efficiency,
    economy, compliance
Investigation
Invention of new ideas
Inventory control
Investigation of problems,
    complaints
Other(s)

J
Joining things together
Judging
Jumping
Other(s)

K
Keeping records
Kindling objects
Other(s)

L
Labor relations
Laboratory work
    (equipment/experiments)
Landscaping
Language use
Leadership
Learns quickly
Legal expertise
Liaison
Library research
Listening to others
Loading goods (transportation)
Other(s)

M
Maintaining inventory of
    materials/coordinations
Making deals
Making layouts, tooling changes
Making financial decisions
Managing information, projects,
    resources, programs

Managing money
Managing people
Manpower planning
Manual dexterity
Manufacturing products
Mapping events
Marketing goods
Material handling
Measuring boundaries
Measuring objects
Mechanical work
Media relations
Mediating conflicts
Meeting deadlines
Meeting the public
Memory
Mentor to others
Merchandising
Methods and controls
MIS
Monitoring the progress of
    others/quality
Motivating others
    (groups)/individuals
Moving with dexterity (athletically)
Multilingual
Other(s)

N
Negotiating contracts, etc.
New business development
Number-oriented
Other(s)

O
Observing
    people/animals/things/detail
Obtaining information (detective
    work)
Office work
Operating equipment, machines,
    devices
Operating as a liaison person
Operations management
Orders equipment/material
Orderly recordkeeping

Organizes people, tasks, materials, information, leisure time, data
Outdoor work, travel
Ownership
Other(s)

P
Painting objects
People
Perceptiveness
Performing analysis, audits
Persevering
Personal warmth
Personnel administration
Personnel development
Persuading others
Physical work/skills (body, hands, fingers)
Planning agendas/organizational needs, goals, programs, layouts, budgets
Policy making
Politics with others
Practicality
Precision work (data)
Predicting the futures
Preparing materials, written documents, schedules, statements, orders
Printing
Problem solving
Processing human interactions, data, orders
Product development, control
Project development
Program development
Programming computers, events
Promoting events
Proposal writing
Protection of property, people
Providing personal service
Providing technical support
Purchasing
Public relations
Public speaking
Other(s)

Q
Quality control
Questioning others
Other(s)

R
Raising funds
Reading technical manuals/numbers/symbols
Recommending employee hiring/dismissals
Recordkeeping of data/records/files
Recruiting
Reducing costs
Rehabilitation
Releasing material
Remember (recall) information/detail
Repairing mechanical devices, equipment
Repeating same procedures
Reporting results
Representing an organization, association, other
Research
Results-oriented
Reviewing (reassessing) programs, reports, records, costs, testing
Rewriting articles/language
Running meetings
Other(s)

S
Safety operations
Sales/marketing
Scheduling
Scientific investigation
Secretarial duties
Self-starting
Selling products, ideas, service
Service
Setting deadlines
Setting up demonstrations (shows, exhibits, displays)
Sewing
Showmanship
Sketching

Solving problems
Speaking in public
Sports skills
Staffing (hiring, delegating)
Studying proposals (bids), etc.
Supervising installations, workers,
  programs, buildings
Supporting others
Surveying work areas
Synthesizing numerical data
Systems procedures, analysis
Other(s)

T
Taking instruction
Talking for long periods
Taxation
Technical applications
Technical writing
Territory development
Time organization
Toleration of interruptions, lack of
  support, misunderstandings
Training, teaching, developing others
Translation
Treating people, illnesses, animals
Troubleshooting (people, machines)
Typing data
Other(s)

U
Updating files, information
Using intuition
Using instruments (scientific,
  medical)
Using numbers
Using words

V
Values clarification
Visualizing new formats, patterns,
  shapes, sounds
Other(s)

W
Working with committees
Working with hand tools
Working with large machines, i.e.,
  earth movers
Working with precision
Working with scientific equipment
Working with small machines (i.e.,
  duplicating)
Working with visual media
Writing reports, publications,
  materials, proposals, instructions
Writing talks, presentations
Other(s)

X
X-raying
Other(s)

Y
Yelling words
Yodeling songs
Other(s)

Z
Zooming lenses (motion pictures,
  TV)
Other(s)

✦ ✦ ✦

Action Verbs

Review and circle the action verbs in Fig. 7.3 that trigger in your mind things that you have done and can write about. Put these on your list. Also, some of these verbs may be used in writing about your accomplishments later. Let the words you select reveal your initiative and enthusiasm and strong intent. You will want to choose active, exciting, and action-oriented verbs that best describe you and your background.

✦ ✦ ✦

FIGURE 7.3
Action verbs

Circle the words that best describe actions you have taken.

Accelerated	Arranged	Changed
Accepted	Ascertained	Charted
Accommodated	Assembled	Checked
Accomplished	Assessed	Circulated
Accounted	Assigned	Clarified
Achieved	Assimilated	Classified
Acquired	Assisted	Cleaned
Acknowledged	Attained	Closed-up
Acted	Attended	Coached
Activated	Attracted	Collaborated
Adapted	Audited	Combined
Added	Augmented	Communicated
Addressed	Authorized	Compared
Adjusted	Automated	Compiled
Administered	Averted	Completed
Admired	Avoided	Complied
Adopted	Awarded	Composed
Advanced (to)		Compounded
Advertised	Balanced	Computed
Advised	Benefitted	Computerized
Advocated	Boosted	Conceived
Affected	Bound	Conceptualized
Agreed	Bought	Conciliated
Aided	Broadened	Concluded
Allocated	Budgeted	Condensed
Altered	Built	Conducted
Amplified		Conferred
Analyzed	Calculated	Confined
Answered	Called	Conserved
Anticipated	Capitalized	Considered
Applied	Carried (out)	Consolidated
Appointed	Carved	Constructed
Appraised	Catalogued	Contemplated
Apprised	Celebrated	Consulted
Approached	Centralized	Consummated
Appropriated	Chaired	Contracted
Approved	Challenged	Contributed
Arbitrated	Championed	Controlled

Converted
Convinced
Cooperated
Coordinated
Copied
Corrected
Corresponded
Counseled
Created
Credited
Criticized
Cultivated
Cut

Danced
Debated
Decentralized
Decided
Decorated
Decreased
Defined
Delegated
Delivered
Demonstrated
Designated
Designed
Detailed
Detected
Determined
Developed
Devised
Diagnosed
Diagrammed
Dictated
Differentiated
Dimensioned
Directed
Disapproved
Disbursed
Discharged
Disciplined
Discovered
Discussed
Dismantled
Dispatched
Dispensed

Displaced
Displayed
Disposed
Disproved
Dissected
Disseminated
Distinguished
Distributed
Diversified
Diverted
Documented
Doubled
Drafted
Dramatized
Drew (up)
Drove
Dug

Earned
Edited
Educated
Effected
Elaborated
Eliminated
Emphasized
Employed
Enacted
Encouraged
Enforced
Engaged
Engineered
Enhanced
Enjoined
Enlarged
Enlisted
Ensured
Entertained
Enumerated
Equipped
Established
Estimated
Evaluated
Examined
Exceeded
Exchanged
Executed

Exercised
Expanded
Expedited
Expended
Experimented
Explained
Expressed
Extended
Extracted

Fabricated
Facilitated
Familiarized
Favored
Figured
Filed
Financed
Fired
Finished
Fixed
Focused
Followed
Forecasted
Formed
Formulated
Found
Founded
Framed
Free-lanced
Fulfilled
Fund-raised

Gardened
Gathered
Gave
Generated
Got
Governed
Graduated
Grouped
Guided

Had (responsibility
for)
Halved
Handled

Harmonized
Headed
Helped
Hired
Hosted
Hypothesized

Identified
Illuminated
Illustrated
Imagined
Implemented
Improved
Improvised
Inaugurated
Incorporated
Increased
Indexed
Induced
Influenced
Informed
Initiated
Innovated
Inspected
Inspired
Installed
Instigated
Instituted
Instructed
Insured
Integrated
Interested
Interpreted
Intervened
Interviewed
Introduced
Invented
Inventoried
Invested
Investigated

Joined
Judged
Justified

Kept

Keynoted

Landscaped
Launched
Laid (out)
Learned
Lectured
Led
Licensed
Lifted
Lightened
Liquidated
Listened
Located
Logged

Made
Maintained
Managed
Manipulated
Manned
Manufactured
Marketed
Mastered
Maximized
Measured
Mechanized
Mediated
Memorized
Mentored
Merchandised
Merged
Met
Minimized
Mixed
Mobilized
Modeled
Moderated
Modernized
Modified
Molded
Monitored
Motivated
Moved

Navigated
Negotiated

Nominated
Notified

Observed
Obtained
Occupied
Offered
Opened
Operated
Optimized
Orchestrated
Ordered
Organized
Oriented
Originated
Overcame
Overhauled
Oversaw

Packed
Painted
Packaged
Participated (in)
Penetrated
Perceived
Performed
Personalized
Persuaded
Photographed
Piloted
Pinpointed
Pioneered
Planned
Played
Positioned
Postulated
Predicted
Prepared
Prescribed
Presented
Presided
Prevented
Printed
Probed
Problem-solved
Processed

Procured
Produced
Profited
Programmed
Projected
Promoted
Proofread
Proposed
Protected
Proved
Provided
Published
Purchased
Put (together)

Questioned

Raised
Reached
Read
Realized
Reasoned
Rebuilt
Received
Recognized
Recommended
Reconciled
Recorded
Recruited
Rectified
Redirected
Redesigned
Reduced (losses)
Re-established
Referred
Refined
Regulated
Rehabilitated
Reinforced
Rejected
Rejuvenated
Related
Remembered
Rendered
Renegotiated
Renewed

Reorganized
Repaired
Replaced
Reported
Represented
Requested
Required
Researched
Reshaped
Resolved
Respected
Responded
Restored
Restricted
Restructured
Retailed
Retrieved
Returned
Revamped
Reversed
Reviewed
Revised
Revitalized
Revived
Rewarded
Risked
Routed

Safeguarded
Sang
Satisfied
Saved
Scanned
Scheduled
Screened
Secured
Selected
Sensed
Separated
Served
Serviced
Set
Settled
Set (up)
Sewed
Shaped

Shared
Shipped
Showed
Shut (down)
Signed
Simplified
Simulated
Sketched
Slashed
Sold
Solicited
Solved
Sorted
Sparked
Spearheaded
Specified
Spoke
Sponsored
Staffed
Staged
Standardized
Started
Stimulated
Stipulated
Straightened
Streamlined
Strengthened
Stressed
Stretched
Structured
Studied
Submitted
Subordinated
Succeeded
Suggested
Summarized
Superseded
Supervised
Supplied
Supported
Surpassed
Surveyed
Sustained
Symbolized
Synergized
Synthesized

Systematized

Tabulated
Tailored
Talked
Taught
Team-built
Tended
Terminated
Tested
Theorized
Tightened
Told
Took (charge,
   instructions, over)
Traced
Tracked
Traded
Trained
Transacted
Transcribed
Transferred

Transformed
Translated
Transmitted
Traveled
Treated
Triggered
Trimmed
Tripled
Troubleshot
Turned (around)
Tutored
Typed
Typeset

Umpired
Uncovered
Understood
Understudied
Undertook
Unified
Unraveled
Updated

Upgraded
Uplifted
Used
Utilized

Vacated
Validated
Verbalized
Verified
Vitalized

Washed
Weighed
Wholesaled
Widened
Withdrew
Won
Worked
Wrote
Wrought

✦ ✦ ✦

DOT

Refer to the *Dictionary of Occupational Titles* (1991). This government publication has over 20,000 abbreviated mini-descriptions of jobs and can give you some additional insight into positions similar to those you have had in the past. Add any ideas to your list.

Other People's Resumes

Look at other people's resumes as idea sources of what to write about, especially if the people are close to your age group and area of expertise. Jot down ideas from the resumes and add them to your list.

Umbrella Ideas

Review your ideas. Maybe the larger ones ("the umbrella") can be broken or reduced down into several smaller ones, especially if you are having trouble adding to your idea list.

Work Values Inventory

Check the work values that are important to you, using Fig. 7.4. Double check your top ten. Circle and check your top five. Maybe this will give you ideas to add to your list.

——————————— ✦ ✦ ✦ ———————————

FIGURE 7.4
Work values inventory checklist

Check if applicable:

☐ Precise work routine, use of printed words or numbers
☐ Work under pressure, lots of deadlines, under close supervision
☐ Physical work (use hands)
☐ Variety of work assignments, different things to do
☐ Authority and control over others (boss/decision maker), organize activities
☐ Work with people
☐ Help others
☐ Work outdoors
☐ Work requires little or no travel, same town or geographic area
☐ Work fast-paced, competitive, i.e., selling
☐ Boss you get along with, who appreciates you, without close supervision
☐ Job security (stable environment)
☐ Work is intellectually stimulating, involves solving problems, learning new ideas; is challenging
☐ Good fringe benefits (pension)
☐ Annual pay increases, performance reviews
☐ Profit sharing
☐ Need for creative, artistic, idea-oriented work (aesthetics)
☐ Recognized in your field as an expert (influence others)
☐ Freedom and independence at work
☐ Location, community, work setting favorable
☐ Form and develop friendships at work; one of the team; friendly people
☐ Public contact
☐ Reasonable work hours
☐ Opportunities for advancement, self-development
☐ Educational benefits
☐ Telephone work
☐ Research—using information or numbers, detail, precise work
☐ Working with machinery, tools, equipment (things)
☐ Inventing or designing things
☐ Giving advice and counsel

☐ Working for reputable company, steady work, agree with firm's direction

☐ Excellent salary

☐ Work with plants, animals

◆ ◆ ◆

Journalistic Questions/People Values Inventory

Think about the journalistic questions of who, what, where, when, why and how much, how many, and how long. Answers to these questions as they relate to things you've done may provide further knowledge and understanding. Add any additional thoughts they promote to your list, i.e., in what ways do I want to work with people? Some examples can be found in Fig. 7.5.

◆ ◆ ◆

FIGURE 7.5
People values inventory checklist

Check if applicable:

☐ *Enlighten others.* Inform or enlighten others with specific knowledge, ideas.

☐ *Understand others.* Study the behavior of people to understand them.

☐ *Public contact.* Have a lot of contact with people.

☐ *Instruct others.* Instruct or train others in various tasks or skills.

☐ *Peacemaker, mediator.* Help people solve conflict differences.

☐ *Investigate others.* Obtain information about people.

☐ *Help people.* Help people with personal problems.

☐ *Improve health.* Relieve the physical distress or sickness of others.

☐ *Dominance.* Use leadership, skills, have power, give directions or influence others.

☐ *Information gathering.* Collecting information by directly contacting others.

☐ *People come to me.* People needing services or advice will come to me.

☐ *Going to others.* Want to seek others opinions.

☐ *One-time contact.* Frequent contact with the same people.

☐ *Regulate people's contact with me.* Decide when people can see me.

☐ *Independence.* Little or no supervision.

☐ *Want supervision.* Need a lot of supervisory direction.

☐ *Work closely with others.* Work as a team or in a group, i.e., committee, task force.

☐ *Work alone.* Work by myself, without help from others.

☐ *Supervise others.* Supervise, lead or direct others in their work.

✦ ✦ ✦

Challenges Solved

Think about any exciting challenges (problems, opportunities) that you have either solved or resolved. Put them down on your idea list.

Needs Filled

Think about any needs (plans, products, services or programs) that you might have identified and then filled. Add your ideas to the list.

Input from Friends

Ask loved ones, relatives, former and present associates and teachers, sales representatives and customers what fields they think you are best in—what your greatest talents are. Add these ideas to your list. Note: Make a list of jobs that use these kinds of skills and abilities.

Focus Checklist

Make choices about what institutions (companies), locations, salary and role you visualize yourself in as you start your campaign (Fig. 7.6). You can even envision your ideal or dream job. Do these selections relate in any way to the career direction you want to be going toward? If so, list the ideas that relate to previous successes and that match favorably with them.

✦ ✦ ✦

FIGURE 7.6
Focus checklist

Check if applicable:

Institutions (Companies)

☐ Public	☐ Indoor	☐ Profit	☐ Urban
☐ Private	☐ Outdoor	☐ Nonprofit	☐ Rural

- ☐ Small
- ☐ Medium
- ☐ Large
- ☐ Travel
- ☐ Relocate
- ☐ Retail
- ☐ Wholesale
- ☐ Consumer
- ☐ Processing
- ☐ Distribution

- ☐ Blue Collar
- ☐ White Collar
- ☐ Manager
- ☐ Worker

- ☐ Local
- ☐ State
- ☐ National
- ☐ International

- ☐ Service
- ☐ Industrial
- ☐ Manufacturing
- ☐ High-Tech

Government
Service:
- ☐ Local
- ☐ State
- ☐ Federal

Education:
- ☐ Elementary
- ☐ Secondary
- ☐ Higher

- ☐ Consulting
- ☐ Ownership
- ☐ Church

Salary Desired (excluding fringe benefits)
- ☐ $20s
- ☐ $30s
- ☐ $40s

- ☐ $50s
- ☐ $60s
- ☐ $70s

- ☐ $80s and above

Relocation Preferences
- ☐ Housing
- ☐ Cost of Living
- ☐ Economy
- ☐ Weather
- ☐ Crime

- ☐ Unemploy-ment
- ☐ Entertainment
- ☐ Taxes
- ☐ Recreation
- ☐ Transportation

- ☐ Shopping Facilities
- ☐ Friends/ relatives in area

Note: Contact moving companies, realtors, or Homequity Destination Services (800) 243-1033 for relocation information. Contact the Commerce Department's Bureau of Economic Analysis (202) 523-0977 for local income/statistical information (note growth rates) and the National Reference Center of the Library of Congress (202) 707-5522 for list of local sources. Check or subscribe to local newspapers.

✦ ✦ ✦

Miscellaneous Factors With Idea Assessment List

Other factors that can be part of your idea assessment sheet can be your educational background, test results, the use of standard industrial classification (SIC) codes, hobbies, community and school activities, and military service if applicable; think what you would do if you won the state lottery for ten million dollars; draft the obituary you would like to see written about yourself; describe the ideal job you would like to have before retiring or if you had six months to live.

Now complete your assessment list of your success ideas (Fig. 7.1). This list should tell you about ingredients in your life experiences which make you the person that you are. You should interpret your composite idea list or have a career counselor do it. Determine what your focus will be. This will show you what your job objective should be.

Now select your top ten or eleven accomplishments (most resumes have only that many) that you want to write about as they relate to your career direction and that best represents you either as a "total work professional" or as a "total person." You decide! A.S. O'Neil says in his book *Summerhill* that "there are two ways to measure a person, from the eyes up and from the feet up." Some individuals like to be measured only in one way; that is their choice.

Writing About Your Ideas

You will now need to spend time writing about each of your selected ideas describing what the *challenge* (problem, actively defined) was and the SAR: the situation (environment, culture) that it took place in, what actions (steps, obstacles overcome, how you did it) you took to either correct, alleviate, or minimize the problem, and what were your results (outcome). The results should be in specific, quantitative, and measurable terms using, where appropriate, numbers, people, money, percentages, savings, improvements, quantities, dimensions, amounts, income, service, etc. There is no limit to the number of pages to be used as you write out your accomplishments. My clients are told that these are "mental gymnastic" exercises where nothing is set in concrete. If one can't give me an exact specific, I tell him or her I want at least a ballpark figure or the best guesstimate—after all, he or she lived it and did it. I certainly didn't. An example of a completed accomplishment description that reflects the above is provided in Fig. 7.7):

--------------------- ✦ ✦ ✦ ---------------------

FIGURE 7.7
Accomplishment description

Challenge (problem, activity defined): To design several credit union courses which would appeal to local members of the CUNA (Credit Union National Association).

Situation (environment, culture): A four-course curriculum was developed by CUNA to improve the overall knowledge of the credit union employee or volunteer at the local level.

Action (steps, obstacles overcome, how you did it):

1. Approached Continuing Education Division at the Community College of Beaver County (CCBC) about the possibility of the courses being offered.
2. Convinced six CCBC officials of value of courses, despite relatively small market (44 CUs in Beaver County) and accepted challenge of being the instructor.
3. Publicized eight courses through three mailings to 15 credit unions and by 60 personal calls and 60 visits.
4. Developed a second four-course curriculum (Marketing, Credit and Collections, Management, and PCs in CUs) of specialized courses, choosing the 34 texts to be used; developed 125 lesson plans.
5. Because of the specialized nature of the PCs in CUs course, worked with eight CCBC faculty members to develop course content to ensure that credit union personnel received desired information.

Results (outcome):

1. First course attracted 44 people and four-course core curriculum (Introduction, Accounting, Operations, and Financial Management) was attended by 161 people.
2. Second four-course program was attended by 108 people.
3. Nowhere else in Pennsylvania has the first four-course program been so well attended and nowhere else in the state has the second four-course program ever been attempted.
4. Emphasized the need for education well enough that attendance at PA Credit Union League educational sessions by Beaver County Credit Unions was 37 percent higher than in the rest of the state.

Note: If it is truly impossible to have any quantitative data, a qualitative statement can be used.

———————————— ✦ ✦ ✦ ————————————

Impact Statements

After preparing statements about all of your accomplishments (believe me, you need to spend time doing this thoughtfully; I have had clients spend an entire weekend just on this exercise), you will need to prepare impact statements (sometimes referred to as bullets). Figure 7.8 gives examples of boiled down SARs. These statements should be fairly concise (no more than 1 to 2 sentences) and consist of the following three parts: *action* verb or verbs (no more than three), a *specific* situation, and *specific* results. The key to these statements is having the necessary specifics which bring life to them and thus give them impact. The reader should be able to actually visualize the situation coming to life from your description (a "technicolor statement" if you will). These impact statements, although the foundation for an outstanding resume, more importantly help an interviewee communicate abilities or skills during an interview very effectively. When the interviewer says, tell me about yourself, the person can then speak with an air of confidence. This confidence continues to improve as you go through a variety of mental gymnastic exercises. That confidence and self-assuredness does help to give you the competitive edge. I really believe that!

✦ ✦ ✦

FIGURE 7.8
Impact statements

Researched and developed the first Performance Appraisal System, designed and directed 120 training sessions for 300 managers, and directed a 12-month process evaluation. 95 percent of surveyed managers reported that they had conducted more objective performance reviews and provided a more equitable distribution of salary increases.

Instituted a program to train internal staff as supervisor development faculty rather than using external consultants training (saving $35,000) doubled the number and frequency of course offerings from once biweekly to four courses per week, increased by 30 percent the attendance and number of departments that received training.

Designed, organized, and implemented the organization's first Employee Assistance Program for chemically dependent and troubled employees. During the first operating year, it was projected that 5 percent of the work force would use the service (the national average for EAPs), and the organization would save an estimated $250,000 annually in absenteeism, tardiness, sick leave, and lost productivity.

Designed, developed and implemented a six-month-long agency-based teacher-training program for teachers of the visually handicapped to help relieve a teacher shortage at the agency. Staff was increased from two to 11 in three years, making it the second largest in the nation. The program also earned $12,000 annually in tuition from other agencies which requested the service.

Researched and published one article in a national professional journal and two curriculum guides for teachers of the visually handicapped. As a result, was invited as guest speaker to five national and regional conferences and served as consultant to two universities in establishing their teacher education programs.

Managed improvement project across five departments in ammunition manufacturing plant of 1,200 employees resulting in productivity increases in three key areas of 47, 60, and 67 percent. Maintenance costs dropped $1.8 million and inventory fell $1.5 million (out of $16 million). Achieved $2 million profit to business after previous-year operating loss of $8 million.

Increased production in heavy union environment from 9,000,000 units/year to 36,000,000 units/year. Overtime fell 30 percent and product yield increased from 40 to 85 percent.

Designed and implemented a parts shortage system in an aerospace manufacturing company that saved $26,000,000 in three years.

Coordinated an approach to standardize units of measure and nomenclature for seven manufacturing plants in six countries for over 110,000 employees simultaneously.

Organized, produced, and managed a marketing plan to address an unproductive vendor program. Created a database, initiated six monthly mailings, an incentive plan and three corporate presentations to impact a 300 percent increase in lease volume over six months.

Calculated and presented 50 "Lease versus Buy" analyses as part of a strategy to open 22 new accounts; financed 32 CPUs in nine months which generated $5.6 million over lease contract term and led to *Million Dollar Club* status.

Planned and supervised six equipment exhibitions as a key role in a photo typesetting system sales strategy in a remote region; sold $1.3 million in equipment over 12 months and achieved *Blue Chip Club* honors.

Researched, developed, and implemented a sales strategy to introduce 600 insurance agents to specialty insurance programs, leading to $5 million in volume after the first 12 months and *Sales Rep of the Year* recognition.

✦ ✦ ✦

As was suggested to me by a client, you may want to circle all of the action verbs in both your SARs and impact statements. Then note whether you have recurring skills and/or skills that match. Those are the labels that you can use on your resume. Target companies can then be selected, with the assistance of SIC codes; these should be companies that can use the kinds of skills, expertise, and interests you have.

As an aside, when you take a new job, keep adding to your list of achievements. Make note of them for further reference, especially if you worked as a member of a team, committee or task force. *Team players are the order of the day.* Determine what areas you need to improve on and what conditions/duties you need in your work to stay or be happy!

There has never been a statue erected to the memory of someone who let well enough alone.

— JULES ELLINGER

8.

Using Tests to Put the Pieces Together

*If a man does not keep pace with his companions,
perhaps it is because he hears a different drummer.
Let him step to the music which he hears however
measured or far away.*

— HENRY DAVID THOREAU

A Part of the Puzzle

People of all ages turn to the alleged magic of tests to help give them clues
as to who they are and where they should be heading vocationally. These
people can be young adults entering "the real world" of work for the first
time unsure as to what they really should be doing; women who may be returning to the work force having raised a family; individuals who have lost
their jobs through downsizing, mergers, or cutbacks; or people who are just
unhappy with life and their jobs and looking for a change. All of these people need answers, whether to help with a first career, a second or alternative career, part-time employment, or leisure-time activities—and whether
they should be working for others or themselves.

A test or tests by themselves are not necessarily the answer. They are
just part of the puzzle: a guide, if you will. The other parts would be working hand-in-glove with a skillful counselor who can not only interpret the
test results correctly but also incorporate them with the clients autobiogra-
phy, educational background, work history, and goals. For clients who really need direction, I put together a chart. I got this idea when I was
Director of Education for a women's hospital and noticed that when the
doctor visited his patients, he always referred to their charts. Thus, an idea
was born, and I now use charts with clients who are experiencing career
difficulties. A sample chart of mine is in Fig. 8.1.

✦ ✦ ✦

FIGURE 8.1
John Doe chart

1. STRONG CAMPBELL
   (Basic Interest)
   a) Store Management
   b) Restaurant Management
   c) Realtor
   d) Elected Public Official
   e) Marketing Executive

2. TEMPERAMENT AND
   VALUES INVENTORY
   (Personal Characteristics)
   a) Flexible
   b) Active
   c) Attentive
   d) Sociable
   e) Persuasive

3. MYERS-BRIGGS
   a) Dominant-Extraversion
   b) Auxiliary-Sensing
   c) Third-Thinking
   d) Least-Judgment

4. JOB MUSTS
   a) Influence Others
   b) Speak
   c) Manage Others

5. FACTORED CAPABILITIES
   a) Leader/Sales
   b) Initiative/Persuasive
   c) People/Personnel
   d) Perceptive/Analysis

6. LONG-RANGE GOALS
   a) Career: Business/Education
   b) Role: Manager/Professional
   c) Function: Owner/Employee
      with Policy Influence
   d) Size: Medium

7. SIC INDICATORS
   a) Investor
   b) Advertising Agency
   c) Real Estate Agent, Broker,
      Manager
   d) Short-term Business
   e) Direct Selling
   f) Coaching

8. IDEAL JOBS
   a) Quick Decision Making
   b) Planning
   c) Influence People
   d) Allow Flexibility
   e) Visible

9. EDUCATION
   B.S. in Industrial Engineering

10. SKILLS
    a) Selling
    b) Planning
    c) Coaching
    d) Motivating
    e) Managing

11. VALUES
    a) Economic Return
    b) Management
    c) Way of Life
    d) Independence
    e) Prestige/Intellectual
       Stimulation

12. INTERESTS
    a) Business
    b) Social
    c) Craft
    d) Arts
    e) Scientific

13. SELF-DIRECTED
    a) Head Coach/Athletic Director
    b) Business Manager
    c) Real Estate Agent
    d) Sales Rep Advertising
    e) Operations Manager

14. JVIS
    a) Finance
    b) Dominant Leadership
    c) Teaching
    d) Business
    e) Sales

15. POSITIONS
    a) Salesman
    b) Manager
    c) Staff Consultant
    d) Senior Staff Consultant
    e) Project Manager
    f) Assistant Chief of Operations

◆ ◆ ◆

Once a chart has been completed, I ask the client whether he or she wants to interpret it or whether they want me to. Inevitably, I end up doing the interpretation. Funny that it always turns out that way.

Vocational Tests

Vocational tests can generally be broken down into three large categories:

Interests

The Strong Campbell Interest Inventory (SCII) is the most widely used adult interest inventory. This test measures interests in a wide range of career areas including professional, technical, nonprofessional and vocational-technical. Your results are compared and contrasted to those of other adults who represent six major occupational themes and 106 occupations. The Strong Campbell has been around since 1933, updated seven times (most recently 1985) and has, in my opinion, excellent validity and correlation with other tests. It takes about 25 to 35 minutes, and it's a test that all Davenport clients take and have interpreted. Write to Consulting Psychologists Press, Inc., 3803 E. Bayshore Road, Palo Alto, CA 94303 for information, or call (415) 969-8901.

Other vocational interest tests include the Jackson Vocational Interest Survey (Sigma Assessment Systems, Inc., 1110 Military Street, P.O. Box 610984, Port Huron, MI 48061-0984, (800) 265-1285) and The Self-Directed Search (Psychological Assessment Resources, Inc., P.O. Box 998, Odessa, Florida 33556, (813) 968-3003).

No trumpets sound when the important decisions of our life are made. Destiny is known silently.

— AGNES DeMILLE

Personality

We use the *Myers-Briggs Type Indicator* (MBTI) (1962) to determine our client's and spouse's (if any) personality type. There are four bipolar scales to this test: Extraversion–introversion, sensing–intuition, thinking–feeling, and judgment–perception, with 16 described personality types. On the basis of the scale results, it is possible to determine frequent career choices made by each of the 16 types. This test takes 20 to 30 minutes. This test is nonthreatening, as there are no right or wrong answers. Write to Consulting Psychologists Press, Inc., 3803 E. Bayshore Road, Palo Alto, CA 94303 for information.

Another profile system that has been tested and proven to be effective is the Personal Profile System published by Performax Systems International, Inc., Minneapolis, MN. Others that can be used are the Adjective Checklist, The Career Orientation Placement and Evaluation Survey, the California Psychological Inventory, and the Executive Profile Survey by the Institute of Personality and Ability Testing, Champaign, IL.

Aptitude

These tests measure your performance ability for specific jobs. Some of the most popular are the Wide Range Achievement Test, Nelson-Denny Reading Test, the Watson-Glaser Thinking Appraisal, and the Otis-Lennon Mental Abilities Test.

Other aptitude tests are the California Aptitude Survey, the General Aptitude Test Battery, and the Differential Aptitude Test Battery. The Johnson O'Connor Research Foundation, Inc., which gives a battery of tests, is headquartered at 201 Maryland Avenue, N.E., Washington, DC 20002, (202) 547-3922. This organization has other offices around the United States.

Sources

If you need to do some research about tests, I suggest two sources:

Mental Measurements Yearbooks, Ed. Conoley and Kramer
University of Nebraska Press
Buros Institute of Mental Measurement
901 North 17th Street, 327 Nebraska Hall
Lincoln, NE 68588-0520
(402) 472-3581 or 2023

Check with your reference librarian on this source. Also write the address below for *Tests in Print*.

ProEd
8700 Shoal Creek Boulevard
Austin, TX 78757-6897
(512) 451-3246

If you need to be vocationally tested, I would first check with the schools, colleges, and community colleges in your area. You may find one that will administer a battery of tests for a very reasonable price, i.e., self-guided computer programs called "Discover."

Another idea would be to check the Yellow Pages under "Vocational, Career, Job, or Employment Counselors" to see if they offer such a service. Caution: If I was going to be tested and have the results interpreted, I would want to check out the educational background and qualifications of the person doing the interpreting. That is a must!!

Testing Materials

Other testing material of possible use are as follows:

Descriptive Check List
Personnel Predictions and Research, Inc.
200 Fillmore Street
Denver, CO 80206
(303) 388-5451

Idak Career Match
Idak Group, Inc.
Banfield Plaza Building, 7931 NE Halsey, Suite 309
Portland, OR 97213-6755
(503) 252-3495

MBS Profile Report (Management by Strengths)
11810 Quivera Road
Overland Park, KS 66210
(913) 469-6700

Career Decision-Making System
American Guidance Service
P.O. Box 99
Circle Pines, MN 55014-1796
(800) 328-2560

Executive Profile Survey
Institute for Personality and Ability Testing
P.O. Box 1188, 1602 Coronado Drive
Champagne, IL 61820
(217) 352-4739

Personalysis, James R. Noland
Manatech, Management Technologies, Inc.
1200 Post Oak Boulevard, Suite 520
Houston, TX 77056
(713) 961-4421

Teleometrics International (Jay Hall)
1755 Woodstead Court
The Woodlands, TX 77380
(713) 367-0060
Variety of tests—send for catalog.

The FIRO-B test (Fundamental Interpersonal Relations
    Orientation-Behavior)
Consulting Psychologist Press Inc.
3803 E. Bayshore Road
Palo Alto, CA 94303

Life Styles Summary Profile, J. Clayton Lafferty
Human Synargistics
39819 Plymouth Road
Plymouth, MI 48170
(313) 459-1030

Note: Most companies no longer send you to be psychologically tested. That is almost a screening tool of the past. Maybe they want you drug tested, but having a psychological test is a different story. If a company is still operating in the "dark ages," using psychological tests for screening purposes, my suggestion is to respectfully decline to take the test, saying that at this stage in your life and career you would just as soon stand on past work accomplishments and education. Also say that you would be willing to provide any personal or business references that the firm may need. It's been my experience that if someone in truth really feels that "the chemistry and fit" regarding your candidacy are right, refusing to take some tests is not going to stand in the way of employment. They may respect you more! If not, their loss is someone's gain! That is how you have to look at it.

If you feel you have to take the test, reflect on what kind of employees this organization hires. Then react accordingly. You may even consider contacting a college psychology department to help prepare you for taking the tests before you actually take them and/or read *The Art of Taking Tests* by D. Huff, which tells how to beat those tests.

If a man does not know to what port he is steering,
no wind is favorable to him.

— SENECA

9.

Goals Help You Get Where You Are Going

Keep Climbing

Life is a struggle, a continual climb,
If we're ever to reach our goal;
Requiring real effort from dawn to dusk,
Ere we slip and mar our soul.
For the road of life is rough and rugged,
With many a stone in the way;
And only with courage and a will to win,
Can we reach the summit one day.
God never intended that the going be easy,
That our pathway be strewn with flowers;
But by overcoming hardships day by day,
We grow stronger in our various powers.
Then up with your chin and out with a smile,
Start pushing your way to the top;
The higher you climb, the better the view;
Keep right on going, never say stop.
There will be many on the road of life,
To caution you of the dangers you face.
Suggesting you turn back, give up the goal,
And with them your footsteps retrace.
Right then is the time to show your courage,
And decide for once and for all;
That your life's task lies directly ahead,
And on this decision, rise or fall.
Then in faith push on to heights sublime,
Not back to the land of ease;
You'll always find light, facing the sun,
And shadows in the rear, if you please.
The higher you climb, the greater the zeal,
More courage will be given if you ask;

*Only be sure you're guided by truth, and
He'll supply strength for the task.*

— ANONYMOUS

Organizations Do It—Why Not You

Most successful people, if you interviewed them, would tell you that they are goal-oriented. They take the initiative and participate in an ongoing process: a form of self-management and a statement of what you are after. For years companies have offered management-by-objectives and goal-oriented supervision workshops for their managers. This allowed them to periodically measure their performance and results against mutually agreed upon goals as they relate to the mission of the organization. Appraisal of performance against these goals has provided organizations with a basis for their salary administration program together with promotions, lateral moves, and releases.

*If one advances confidently in the direction of his
dreams, and endeavors to live the life which he had
imagined, he will meet with a success unexpected in
common hours.*

— HENRY DAVID THOREAU

Workable Road Map

Now that you know more about your strengths and who you are because of the tests you have taken, accomplishments you have written about, and skills that you have determined you have as well as the work values and needs that are important to you, you are ready because of a pattern that has emerged to plan a "road map" for yourself. This will help you to get where you want to go based on your strengths and an improved self-image. This road map will come to life with realistic, useful, challenging, measurable, timed goals to help you get to where you want to go within a set time span, and observable goals that you set for yourself. These specific goals should be in eight different categories (family, financial, personal, professional, spiritual, social, community, and health) for both the short range (less than one year, Fig. 9.1) and long range (more than one year, Fig. 9.2). Specific time frames are important. Keep yourself busy! All of these ambitious goals should be interrelated, since "the whole is made up of the sum of the parts," and so it is with you.

After you write out at least two specific goals (don't be afraid to let

FIGURE 9.1
Short range goals

FIGURE 9.2
Long range goals

your creative juices flow) in each of the eight categories, you should then state definite actions for you to do each week that are going to help you achieve those goals. Ask others to review them and give you their feedback. Potential barriers should be minimized or eliminated. Note: the more specific you make your goals as you write them, the more tangible they become. Written words tend to become more fixed in our minds. That is why it is good to write them out. Your goals can then be constantly assessed with respect to your performance to see how well you are doing in reaching them.

There are two kinds of people in the world—those who are always getting ready to do something and those who go ahead and do it.
— ELBERT HUBBARD

Daily "To Do" Lists

Procrastination is definitely not "the order of the day" in the carrying out of your plan. Prepare a daily "to do" list (do it one day at a time if need be) and classify the things you need to do as "A" (significant) and those that would be nice to do as "C." Note: Since C tasks are low priority, leave them to last even if they are rather easy to accomplish. Any leftovers would fall in between as a "B" item. An old saying states, "plan your work and work your plan." A word to the wise should suffice.

Time is the most valuable thing a man can spend.
— THEOPHRASTUS, 278 B.C.

At the end of your work day you can assess your list and carry over items that were not completed. Above all, even if you are having trouble with your list, don't give up. Don't take rejections personally. Avoid feelings of failure. Be more determined to succeed. Don't be afraid to select, if need be, three or four different job target areas. Stay with your plan. Take charge. Make things happen with constructive actions. Don't procrastinate! Plan to do something each day if possible toward the successful completion of your goals.

Note: Goals to be achieved must be constantly reinforced by self-affirmations, together with a positive self-image. You need to visualize yourself reaching your goals and naturally believing that you will achieve them.

Don't expect that others are going to do it for you. Face up to your new responsibilities! Measure and monitor your progress constantly. You are the creator of your own destiny. "What you do today determines where you will be tomorrow." Be persistent! You are the dreamer, the planner, and the doer! You alone! Set your goals, establish an order of priority and a time limit to reach them. If you don't reach some of your goals, learn from what happened and get on with your life! Some goals will take longer than others. Don't become discouraged! Be determined to succeed. If you need to "research" some areas before writing out some of your goals, do part-time work, volunteer, talk to others in those positions of interest, join organizations in an active way and talk to others.

> *Lose this day loitering; t'will be the same old story*
> *tomorrow, and the next more dilatory. . . .*
> *Each indecision brings its own delays and days are*
> *lost lamenting o'er lost days. . . .*
> *What you can do or think you can, begin it boldness*
> *has genius, power, and magic in it.*
>
> — GOETHE

Goal Questions

Have some questions that can help you sort through concerns as you write your goals:

Where have you been?

What is your track record of success? Someone who has been a success in the past most likely will be a success in the future. What have you done that has made you feel good? What skills did you use, and what can be improved or newly learned? Are there any recurring themes that keep running through your life? Are there any things that you would change from your past?

> *It's not only what we do, but also what we do not*
> *do, for which we are accountable.*
>
> — MOLIÉRE

Where are you now?

What seems to be important to you? Where are your strengths and values? What's preventing you from getting to where you want to be? What are you doing about it?

Time stays long enough for anyone who will use it.
— LEONARDO DA VINCI

What do you want to be?

Where would you like to be five to ten years from now? Do you have
the necessary skills to do it? What obstacles will you need to overcome?
What are your alternative plans? What kinds of organizations (profit/non-
profit, private/public, manufacturing/service, size, consumer/industrial, do-
mestic/foreign, travel/no travel), positions, working climates, geographical
areas and amounts of money are you after? What kind of a budget will you
need?

Dare to Dream

*How can you be true to your future if you don't
know what it holds? Good question! Although the
future is unpredictable, everyone can have a direct
influence on how things turn out. The most
successful individuals understand the importance of
having a plan which will help them accomplish
their dreams. Unfortunately, a majority of
individuals seem to exist on a day to day basis. To
these people, life consists of "marking time."*

*Although planning for the future is always
tentative, without a plan, there is less chance of a
dream coming true. Thus it is important when
planning your future to include some high
expectations, even though they may appear slightly
out of reach. If you do not set your goals high, you
may miss out on some great life experiences.*

— ANONYMOUS

Get Them Down On Paper

As any good reporter will tell you, think of the who, where, what, when,
how and why of your situation. *Who* are you and *who* are your contacts;
where is your career going and where is the labor market demand not only
locally but nationwide; *what* will your new duties, responsibilities, authority, and accountability be in the job you are seeking; *what* are the strategies
necessary for you to obtain the job you are looking for, and what will your
rewards be for reaching them; *what* are the obstacles that you have to over-

come and your solutions to overcome those obstacles; *what* help do you need from others, and *what* are your alternatives; *when* will this take place; *how* will you deal with potential negatives; *why* are you interested in going in this direction, and *how* does it interface with your other goals; *how* excited and determined are you to achieve your goals? Now write them out. Get them down on paper.

> *In whatever arena of life one may meet the*
> *challenge of courage, whatever may be the sacrifices*
> *he faces if he follows his conscience—the loss of his*
> *friends, his fortune, his contentment, even the esteem*
> *of his fellow men—each man must decide for*
> *himself the course he will follow. The stories of past*
> *courage can define that ingredient—they can teach,*
> *they can offer hope, they can provide inspiration.*
> *But they cannot supply courage itself. For this each*
> *man must look into his own soul.*
> — JOHN F. KENNEDY

> *People whose lives are affected by a decision, must*
> *be part of the process of arriving at that decision.*
> — JOHN NAISBITT, *Megatrends*

Try setting up a "T" account for each of your written goals (Fig. 9.3).

State your goal and then list the pluses for achieving that goal on one side of the "T" and the negatives on the other side. You could also list ways to minimize or eliminate those negatives.

Then list the strategies that you will be using to achieve that goal. Have sheet(s) of paper for your strategies. Consider writing customized short (daily/weekly) and/or long range (monthly) campaign goals (note samples) if applicable, i.e., number of phone calls and advice meetings (Figs. 9.4, 9.5, 9.6).

Goal Tips

1. Plan your work and work your plan! Set both short- and long-range goals with time frames (starting/finishing dates) that are manageable for you, but don't be afraid to "stretch" yourself.

✦ ✦ ✦

FIGURE 9.3
Setting up a "T" account for each goal

Goal defined: _____

_____

_____

Goal Pluses (+)   Goal Negatives(−)

Strategies planned to achieve the above goal

_____

_____

_____

✦ ✦ ✦

FIGURE 9.4
Short- and long-range campaign goals (sample)

Activity	Target Date
Preparation & Review	
1. Review videotapes and presentation materials	Complete by 2/27
2. Develop A-B-C List	Complete by 3/1
3. Rewrite, rehearse advice presentation	Complete by 3/1
Personal Contacts	
1. Phone calls for advice interviews	Begin 3/1
2. Advice Interviews	1 per week minimum
Advertisements	
1. Response as suitable	Immediately
Employment Agencies	
1. 3-4 selected agencies	Complete by 3/5
2. Follow-up calls	Every 3 weeks
Direct Mail	
1. Develop target list	Complete by 3/5
2. Review alumni directories	Complete by 3/5
3. Send broadcast letters	Complete by 3/12
Other	
1. Follow-up Florida opportunity	Call 2/23

FIGURE 9.5
Short-range campaign goals (sample)

Goal	Target Date
1. Networking	
a) Follow-up previous contacts with letter.	3/2
b) Obtain appointments for advice interviews.	ongoing
c) Attend advice interviews, plan one per day.	ongoing

2. Advertisements

    a) Review Help Wanted advertisements: ongoing

        Wall Street Journal

        Pittsburgh Press

        National Business Employment Weekly

        National Ad Search

    b) Answer all adverts with possible fit.   ongoing

    c) If possible, follow up on answered

       advertisements.   ongoing

3. Executive recruiters

    a) Previously registered with:

    _____

    _____

    _____

    _____

    _____

    _____

    b) Register with: 3/2

    _____

    _____

    _____

    _____

    _____

    _____

4. Revised list of target companies

    Revised list: 3/2

    _____

    _____

    _____

    _____

    _____

    _____

5. Consulting assignments

    a) Follow-up meeting with:

       Richard Roe   2/24

       Harry Lane   3/2

    b) Letter to D. Smith

       for reference   3/2

    c) Follow-up with J. Jones   3/2

    d) Arrange appointment with M. Martin.   3/9

✦ ✦ ✦

✦ ✦ ✦

FIGURE 9.6
Short- and long-range campaign goals (sample)

I. Local Campaign
1. Personal contacts
   Phone calls for advice interviews
   Advice interviews — 1/week minimum
   Letters to former clients for contacts

2. Employment agencies
   Letters and resumes to 3 or 4 agencies
   Follow up-phone calls

3. Ad letters
   2 to 3 letters if suitable and available

4. Local companies
   Broadcast letter followed by phone calls

II. Long Distance Campaign (Raleigh-Durham, NC)
1. Write Chamber of Commerce for information
   Subscribe to newspapers
   Purchase manufacturing directory

2. Write broadcast letters with phone call/follow-up

3. Ads — 2 or 3 letters per week

4. Letter and resume to 3 or 4 agencies in Raleigh area

5. Locate Alumni directory — letters and phone contacts

Overall goal is to work campaign through April 199__.

✦ ✦ ✦

2. Plan to revamp and revise your goals at least weekly but certainly no less often than each month. Be flexible and not hard on yourself.

3. Try and list easy tasks first to insure successes. They don't all have to be hard and/or nearly impossible.

4. Don't get hung up on experiences as a limiting factor. New skills can be learned. Assess your present skills (note earlier chapter).

Learn from others who have the kinds of skills you desire and read magazines and books that give you new ideas. See yourself as succeeding. Work at it! Realize that most goal barriers are self-imposed. Try and minimize and/or eliminate these barriers.

5. Be determined to get what you set out for. Plan to invest in your career and work with a career counselor whom you have respect for. If you can't, follow the many ideas in *Outplace Yourself.*

6. As you write your goals, try to be as specific as possible. List a step-by-step process of how you plan to achieve your goals: your subgoals.

7. Avoid procrastinating on your goals. Eliminate the excuses by disciplining yourself. Plan to do something every day toward their completion. Work out solutions to potential barriers. If you have fears, i.e., fear of rejection or failure, try and understand, or get a "pro" to help you understand why you think that way.

8. Try rating your goals by their importance to you and what kinds of feelings their successful completion would give you.

9. Try and analyze yourself as to where you've been, where you are now, and how all this impacts on your future. Ask yourself what jobs have given you the greatest happiness and what things you have done that weren't so terrific? What did you learn from these events and how do they help with setting present goals? If you had only a short time to live, what would you be doing? Where would you like to make your mark? Who can help you obtain your goals and what will they need to do to help get you there? How will you measure the achievement of your goal? Are you really committed toward that end?

10. Most psychologists will tell you to set your goals and keep the positive image of successful completion of them in your mind with daily, positive self-talk. Don't concentrate on the negative or negatives, as you are then programming yourself to fail at your goals. Turn negative thoughts into positive ones by telling yourself that you will succeed.

10.

References and Exit Statements
and Their Importance

Recipe for Friendship

1 package concern	*2 tsp. sympathy*
¼ cup warm feelings	*1 tbsp. helpfulness*
2 cups understanding	*5 cups loyalty*
2 tbsp. thoughtfulness	*1 tsp. love*

Soften concern in warm feelings. Combine understanding, thoughtfulness, sympathy and helpfulness. Stir in five cups of loyalty to make a strong dough. Turn out on floured surface and knead until smooth and harmonious. Shape into loaf and let rise in a warm heart for many years. Sprinkle top of loaf with teaspoon of love. Bake in a sturdy pan and serve for a lifetime.

— ANONYMOUS

Check Them

Because any job campaign or search centers around references, you need to check the past and present professional contacts that you will be using. You should have business references familiar with your job skills for each company you've worked for over the last ten years. Rest assured, if you don't check them, your prospective organization will. Organizations will most likely verify employment dates, titles, salary, and duties as well as other information they may be able to obtain. You may say that you don't need to because you trust what everyone on your list would say about you. You honestly feel there would be no surprises. Believe me, in the years that I have counseled and worked with clients from all backgrounds and of all ages, your references need to be checked. You need to find out whether you can count on them to confirm information about your performance and background. If you leave it to chance, all you might get is the unexpected, which may be embarrassing (note Fig. 10.1).

———————————— ✦ ✦ ✦ ————————————

FIGURE 10.1
A bad reference letter

——————————————
——————————————
——————————————

February 2, 199__

Mr. Charles H. Logue Jr., Ph.D.
R. Davenport & Associates
1910 Cochran Road
Pittsburgh, PA 15220

Dear Mr. Logue:
I really appreciate being given an opportunity to provide a reference for one of your clients, Brian D. I have known Brian socially for a period of just over four years. During this time, I have grown to appreciate his personality characteristics and traits. I can honestly say that I have not met too many people in my life like Brian. His eagerness to pick up a challenge and his ability to maintain a high level of intensity when working on different kinds of problems and projects is truly impressive. I am only sorry that these two characteristics are almost totally offset by his "bitchy"-like behavior and the incredible difficulty people have in communicating with him.

When I first got to know him, a lot of these deep-seated characteristics were fairly well hidden, and only in recent years have they come forward. What I expect is an important feature for you to understand about Brian is his ability to totally undermine an individual's expressive capabilities through badgering. This is truly a talent that most people do not have: Brian seems to have it and, unfortunately, uses it for his own well-being, even to the disadvantage of people trying to befriend him.

A recent experience which will exemplify his behavior occurred when we played golf together last summer. Brian, as you probably know, is the world's worst golfer, but he refuses to admit his own limitations. Myself, of course, am a scratch golfer, and this drives Brian absolutely crazy. One afternoon while we were playing together, I hit a drive about 360 yards on a 540 yard par five hole. Brian then followed with a shot that went all of 40 feet. He immediately claimed he had been distracted by a low flying duck and was going to hit another shot. He asked if I could pick up his first shot while he went to get another ball from his bag. I should have been less trusting because, when I reached his ball, he had already teed up his second shot and was swinging with a vengeance. Fortunately for me, his second shot was not quite as good as his first and landed about five feet in front of me but dead on line with me. At this point, Brian yelled and screamed that it was just unfortunate that he heard that duck again because his second shot was right on target except for its distance. It is this kind of attitude of getting even and making it difficult to deal with him that I think you will find to be most prevalent in all of his behaviors. It is perhaps these characteristics that make him most suited for the positions that he has had in the past and those that he attempts to get in the future. I presume that someone who can achieve the results that Brian has, totally through the expense of others, might be considered somewhat of an asset by some senior executives.

While I cannot judge Brian on his performance in a business setting, I must resort to examining his performance at home and use this as a surrogate for his behavior at the office. I especially admire Brian's ability to deal with his wife. Rosemary is a bright, active woman who Brian keeps on a very close reign. She does all the housekeeping, cooking and shopping. She makes time to shine his shoes and takes extra-special care of Brian's needs. She also takes care of their house, cuts the grass and recently did a very good job of painting the exterior of their house. I think she will be getting out of the hospital within the next few weeks—she is recovering from a bad fall. It seems that she slid off the roof the other day trying to fix the fireplace chimney which was blocked. Brian asked her to fix it and was careful to warn her to take off her heels before climbing onto the roof. But apparently, Rosemary would not listen. Brian said it was totally her fault because he specifically told her to take off her heels and she refused to listen.

Brian's ability to control and motivate his children is also outstanding, and I take notice of his abilities and try to apply them to my situation. His son, Robert, is an outstanding student who responds well to his father's wishes. He studies a great deal and gets very good grades. Brian has not had to reprimand him in months—since the last time when he was forbidden to go to the bathroom until he fully understood Chinese literature. His daughter, Lisa, is doing very well in her first year in college. Again, due to Brian's ability to motivate her. It is fortunate that she can write with both hands since it will be another few weeks before the cast from her right hand will be removed. The cast was a result of a motivating session between Brian and Lisa concerning grades.

As you can tell, I have really been impressed with Brian. I recommend him highly. He is a delight to be with and, in a sadistic sense, represents the ultimate manager which most companies would do well to have on board.

Sincerely,

I. O. Yew

✦ ✦ ✦

I responded accordingly (Fig. 10.2):

——————————— ✦ ✦ ✦ ———————————

FIGURE 10.2
Response to bad reference letter

R. DAVENPORT & ASSOCIATES

February 11, 199__

———————————————
———————————————
———————————————

Re: Brian D.

Dear Mr. Yew:

I am in receipt of your letter dated February 2, 199__. Your reply to my inquiry and the honesty of your reference is appreciated! It is indeed a rare person who is as honest and candid as you. You know they say "first impressions are the lasting ones." Indeed this character more than proves the point, doesn't he?

Your remarks more than confirm my early impressions about "Mr. D." and he has on a number of earlier occasions pompously strutted about the office reprimanding our secretaries! He never has had a good word to say and as a matter of fact, the secretaries now go out of their way to avoid him. We even had one the other day call in sick when she knew he was going to be here. Has he always had this uncanny way of bringing out the best in people? The office undercurrent now is "don't mingle with D." Sad, but true!

On first blush you would swear when you meet him that he had "bad breath," "loose dandruff," (actually he does have both) or "a limp handshake," but it unfortunately goes beyond that. He persists in wearing the same suit day after day. It is a rather nice tweed but clearly outdated. It has some tears in the material. He claims you can't see them because they've been "superstitched" but whoever did it, did a poor job. Also, the aroma of his suit is something remarkable. What has always caught my eye, though, have been the soup stains that somehow have made their way to his collection of ties. I think I have seen tomato, onion and even mushroom. "All collector's items!"

Brian claims he should be paid a salary commensurate with that of a senior executive in the $150 to $200,000 range. I told the bloke as his counselor that he should be paid what he's worth but unfortunately there's a minimum wage hour law. Maybe you have some ideas on this— I'm currently doing a Pittsburgh wage/salary survey.

As an aside, most clients treat for muffins or danish from time-to-time. In the almost two months he has been here, never has he offered! He truly does have "short arms and long pockets." Why the other day, someone saw a moth fly out of his wallet. We are currently waiting to see how his credit ratings are going to fare. Rumor has it that his wife is still wearing the same clothes she got married in.

I was particularly interested in your comments about golf. I, too, am a scratch golfer playing out of the XYZ Golf Club. I think we should plan an outing, make the stakes high and "nail him" to his score card for starters. His arrogance regarding his game will be his undoing, wouldn't you agree?

Sent a get-well card to Rosemary. Let's hope she's home soon and again carrying on with her chores. Does he pay her an allowance? Probably not—knowing "Mr. D."

Regards. Please keep my comments confidential! Thanks.

Sincerely,

Charles H. Logue, Jr., Ph.D.

CHL/dtb

✦ ✦ ✦

Make Sure You Have Them

Naturally none of the above inserts were real, but hopefully the point is well made that one should never gamble on what references might say. It is better to get at least a "to whom it may concern" letter or better yet, prepare a draft of a letter for your former boss. Make an appointment to see him or her to review the draft. Tell him or her that they are free to change anything about the letter that they want to and that you are submitting it for their consideration and review. I would, if it is true, stress that you are moving along with your life and career, that you have a family to support, and that this letter of reference is an important link in a successful campaign. Hopefully you both can reach a consensus that it will be in the best interest for each of you. Figure 10.3 shows a reference solicited from a client's former boss, who had fired him. Naturally, with the negatives as a part of this letter, I had to recontact the person by phone, stress the importance of having *only* a positive letter, and request a rewrite. Figure 10.4 was the result and the one we use.

Obtaining this letter not only helped in changing the client's attitude to a more positive one, but enabled him to move ahead with his campaign.

✦ ✦ ✦

FIGURE 10.3
Reference letter before rewrite

You had requested that I write to you about the occupational capabilities of my former partner.

_____ has very high intelligence, associated with excellent powers of analytical and conceptual thinking. In short, his cognitive abilities place him among the highest I have known.

Additionally, he is industrious and willing to work hard. He places a high value on obtaining and keeping the respect and esteem of his peers through personal achievement. Indeed, he was respected by his colleagues, and popular with them as well.

On the negative side are the problems which _____ has coping with stress. The problems are manifested by episodic displays of temper, resentment of authority (perceived as a source of stress) and resistance to accepting organization positions.

Although highly committed to middle-class values and the work ethic, surprisingly _____ is relatively unimpressed by the conventional signs of that commitment, namely, the accumulation and display of wealth.

About _____, there is the touch of the poet-philosopher. Unless driven by more stress than he can handle, _____ is always highly moral and ethical and has a real compassion for those less gifted.

If properly insulated from excessive stress, _____ could perform very capably in a _____ related position. Teaching—especially courses like logic, rhetoric, ethics or philosophy—would be something at which he would excel. He would grow quickly bored, frustrated and resentful in a job which did not exercise and stimulate his intellect.

I hope I have successfully answered your questions.

Very truly yours,

✦ ✦ ✦

✦ ✦ ✦

FIGURE 10.4
Reference letter after rewrite

To Whom It May Concern:

I am writing to you about the professional capabilities of my former partner.

_____ has very high intelligence, associated with excellent powers of analytical and conceptual thinking. In short, his cognitive abilities place him among the highest I have known.

Additionally, he is industrious and willing to work hard. He places a high value on obtaining and keeping the respect and esteem of his peers through personal achievement. Indeed, he was respected by his colleagues, and popular with them as well.

_____ rhetorical and forensic skills and accomplishments are outstanding. Because of his powers of legal reasoning and grasp of medical evidence, he was able to compile an outstanding record of "wins" in cases brought under the Federal Black Lung and the Pennsylvania Workmen's Compensation Acts. His successes were in every instance achieved without sacrifice or compromise of the highest ethical and moral standards.

_____'s departure from our firm has left a gap which is yet to be filled by a satisfactory replacement.

Very truly yours,

✦ ✦ ✦

It should be noted that most bosses and former supervisors are not vindictive people who hold grudges! They will usually give you a reference or at least tell you what they will do. "Time tends to heal all wounds." It's important to make peace and reach an amicable consensus. If you can't, find a co-worker you had excellent rapport with.

Although companies seldom hire back individuals they've let go, one never knows. It doesn't hurt to be in the firm's good graces. Don't leave behind any enemies if possible. "Mend your fences, don't burn your bridges."

Unless my client had had this meeting and received this letter, his campaign would have remained stagnant due both to his lack of self-esteem and his wondering how he would ever explain his most recent job departure. It was certainly one of the keys to his rehabilitation!

Organizations Usually Check Them

Some companies don't check references, but in this day and age of "resume inflation" most do, primarily because some applicants have been known to falsify degrees and work experience, like one who put on his resume that he was a sanitation engineer when in fact he was no more than a garbage collector. You may laugh, but it's a true story.

Little friends may prove great friends.

- Aesop

When companies check references, they mainly check by telephone or use a firm like Equifax (out of Atlanta, Georgia) to call the Human Resource Director or where they can, the person that the applicant reported to. Some of these calls sometimes elicit, I am sure, negative feedback at an unthinking moment, especially the question "Would you rehire this person?" Sometimes the way the speaker responds or the tone of voice says, definitely no. A sample checklist used in such telephone calls is below (Fig. 10.5).

✦ ✦ ✦

FIGURE 10.5
Reference checklist

Reference Checklist
- What was his/her title, duties, and length of time with the company?
- Good work habits? Showed initiative?
- Personality?
- Describe their limitations?
- Outstanding skills and strengths?
- He/she indicated their salary was _____ a year. Verify compensation.
- Bonuses?
- Communication skills?
- Any personal or financial problems?
- Why did they leave?
- Would you rehire?

✦ ✦ ✦

We check references for our clients in advance of their job search (Fig. 10.6).

✦ ✦ ✦

FIGURE 10.6
Sample reference check

REFERENCE: _____

The individual referred to above has retained our firm to provide an objective evaluation of his capabilities and to assist him in obtaining a new career position. As part of the evaluation process, we are contacting his business and personal associates who are in a position to comment on his character, work habits, and potential for greater or different responsibilities.

XYZ Associates provides professional counsel to executives seeking to advance their careers. We are also consultants to major corporations, non-profit institutions and government agencies. Since 1968 our firm has been known as a successful marketing and career management group and has made significant contributions in the area of human resource development.

Our client has specifically given us permission (as documented below) to solicit your comments with the understanding that you may wish to respond in complete confidence. If you do, please indicate. We, of course, will then guarantee to respect that confidence.

We would greatly appreciate your candid comments in a short note, and we thank you in advance for your cooperation.

Sincerely,

I authorize XYZ Associates to solicit business references on my behalf.

Name	Date

✦ ✦ ✦

I have found that many clients would give me what they felt were reliable references only to find out after we requested a reference letter that they would not respond or if they did, they would do so only over the phone. Early in my counseling career I fell into the trap of accepting verbal testimonials only to be accused sometime later of taking the remarks out of context. After that incident, I would accept only written references. If they wouldn't put it in writing, I didn't want it.

If you want to check what a former organization is saying about you, have a friend or counselor call the organization under the guise of considering you for employment. Let them then conduct their inquiry and give you the feedback.

If you are approaching friends, a current boss, ex-boss, colleagues (former/present), customers/clients you have served, professors, teachers, deans, department heads, neighbors, a high-ranking politician and/or company official who are familiar with your recent work, personality or both, get quality references from them, not a quantity of references. Select them carefully and keep them informed about how you are doing. No more professional references are necessary. Don't include religious references or references from personal friends. If you want to add extra ones for a reserve in case some prove to be negative, or to see what others will say, go for it! Keep a written record of the current addresses and phone numbers of your references. They, too, change from time to time.

Issues To Be Addressed

Reference letters should be clear, concise, and no more than one page, preferably typed on good quality bond paper. These letters can address some of the following issues:

1. What is the relationship of the individual to you?
2. Examples or highlights of how he/she knows or is familiar with your work/personality.
3. How you relate and work with others (interpersonal skills)?
4. Areas that need to be or could be strengthened regarding your job/community performance.
5. How you came to leave the organization—"downsizing or right-sizing," "restructuring," "philosophical differences and an amicable parting of the ways," "merger/acquisition with new management team," etc.
6. What this person sees as your strongest strengths/capabilities/traits.
7. Whether this person can be contacted for further information.

Some Sample Reference Letters:

Sample Reference Letter A

Dear _____:

I have known and worked closely with _____ since 198__. In that time period I found him/her to be a very valuable asset on all projects he/she was involved in. In my opinion, _____ is a very intelligent, detail-oriented, and has an analytical ability to find the answer or problem in very complex situations.

I feel _____ would be an asset and able to meet the challenge in any number of corporate positions.

If I can be of any further help, I would be more than happy to speak on his/her behalf.

Sincerely,

Sample Reference Letter B

Dear _____:

Despite the outcome of his employment at _____, _____ possesses not only solid management skills but also outstanding personal traits. Without sounding too much like a testimonial, let me list some of those skills _____ demonstrated during our business relationship:

- Leadership—He knew how to build a team, he acted decisively.
- Analytical Ability—He seemed to be able to grasp the core of problems and break it into manageable segments.
- Action Oriented—Bordered on impatient but certainly had a bias for action.

In my opinion, _____ also handled well the constant and often unreasonable pressure and demands of his superiors. At times he was asked to do too much with too little.

His departure from _____ dealt them a major blow. Someone else will benefit, regardless of the industry or the job.

Sincerely,

Sample Reference Letter C

Dear _____:

Thank you very much for your note concerning _____. I am pleased for the opportunity to share my thoughts about this individual.

First, I must tell you that _____ is a great person. His character, in all aspects, is flawless. For two years I was in a position to watch _____ work. He has a work ethic that is superior, and an attitude to go with it. I have no doubt that he will achieve success. _____ loves a challenge.

I will share with you what I think happened to _____ and his position. First, his entire career was spent in sales, and as you know, he was extremely successful. He was taken from that arena and put in the position of C.E.O. I do not believe that _____ was given enough time or assistance to make that transition. He certainly is capable and is C.E.O. material, but, again in my opinion, should work as an assistant for a period of time and be brought up to that level.

_____ has enormous potential and will be a fine asset to any company he chooses to work with.

Should you wish to discuss this individual in greater detail, please do not hesitate to give me a call.

Cordially,

Keep Them Fresh

Once you have your references, you should send them an updated resume with a handwritten note (Fig. 10.7) saying how much you appreciate each being your reference. Remember never to put the following statement on your resume: *References furnished upon request.* That is a given! Besides, people usually do not furnish bad references. At least I haven't known many clients who did. It would be suicidal or the "kiss of death" for your campaign.

✦ ✦ ✦

FIGURE 10.7
Sample handwritten note

Dear _____:

Thank you very much for agreeing to be one of my references. Your support is greatly appreciated!
I will keep you advised regarding my job campaign, and will call you if anyone asks for my references. If anyone calls, please let me know so I will know what companies are seriously considering me.
I have enclosed my updated resume for your information and use.

Sincerely,

John Doe

Enclosure - Resume

✦ ✦ ✦

Have a typed list of your references available on one sheet during interviews, so they can be provided if needed (Fig. 10.8).

✦ ✦ ✦

FIGURE 10.8
Reference list

JOHN DOE

REFERENCES

Business

Charles H. Logue, Jr., Ph.D.
Faculty Member - Evening School
Graduate School of Business
University of Pittsburgh
Pittsburgh, PA 15260   Phone Number

Joe McBayer, Vice President, Technology
XYZ Co.
P.O. Box 151
Anycity, PA 01234   Phone Number

Ray Sawyer, Vice President
National Bank
P.O. Box BK
Anytown, PA 43210   Phone Number

Michael D. Lebo, Vice President
Painters, Inc.
9th Avenue
Anycity, PA 01234   Phone Number

Personal

Tom M. Jones
Z Street
Anytown, PA 01234   Phone Number

Betty C. Stebbins
Lee Place
Anycity, PA 54321   Phone Number

Lou Cunningham
P.O. Box 123
Anytown, PA 01234   Phone Number

✦ ✦ ✦

Negative Information

Many companies today have a policy of not giving out negative information for fear of being sued for slander or libel. With your current company, you should protect your future company references by making sure that if there is any negative information in your file, it be removed within a year or two. Many companies make it a policy to remove negative materials within a reasonable length of time if the person improves his/her behavior or changes his/her ways. If the company doesn't remove the negative documentation, try to get your supervisor to write a letter stating that the problem no longer exists.

Note: Make a list of good people (if possible with impressive titles) who know your job skills, i.e., politicians, chief executives, etc. Call and ask them if they will be references for you and whether it's all right to use their names. Provide references only when asked or as part of your portfolio. Have your references call you when they've been checked.

Reference Tips

1. Always inform all of your references when you accept a new job. Keep them updated.

2. Note the reference/telephone question lists. References should address the appropriate issues in their one-page letters.

3. Remember: poor references can keep you from getting the job you really want. Check out all of your references.

4. Don't be afraid to draft letters of reference for former bosses' consideration if you don't have one. Send them a cover letter, together with a drafted reference letter for their consideration, changes and signature on company letterhead. If they can't put it on company letterhead due to company policy, ask them if they can put it on their own personal stationery.

5. Ask references to enthusiastically endorse your candidacy. If a company detects the slightest hesitancy or "reads" the wrong tone of voice in a response to a telephone check, that position may be lost.

6. References can be checked by phone (most common), mail (second choice, although least effective), and in person.

So much to say. And so much not to say! Some things are better left unsaid. But so many unsaid things can become a burden.

— VIRGINIA MAE AXLINE

11.

Phone Techniques:
Telemarketing Yourself

Behold the turtle: He only makes progress when he sticks his neck out.

— James Bryant Conant

Using The Telephone

The telephone can and should be one of your most important job campaign tools, especially after you've done your homework (prospecting) and have put together a market list of companies together with the names of the decision-makers. Call the switchboard operator and ask her for the correct spelling of the name of the person in charge and verify the mailing address. A call can be effective in following up a broadcast (direct mail) or introductory letter (see letters). In addition to setting up an advice meeting, it can also be used to give, clarify, or get information, to contact agencies/recruiters, to provide contacts and telephone updates from time to time, or to follow up a job interview.

The only way to get comfortable when using the telephone is to write out your script so that you leave nothing to chance and to practice, practice, practice with a friend, spouse or tape recorder until you feel confident ("Confidence is success remembered." — Anonymous), comfortable and relaxed. This is the best way to do away with phone fright. Never read your script over the phone. Memorize it so that it becomes a part of you. Be persistent! You will then feel in control of yourself rather than just trying to "wing it," which I feel is next to impossible. Also it helps to eliminate the fear of using a telephone if you've never used one for business purposes to any great extent in the past. If you are somewhat fearful of using the phone, you may want to remind yourself that the phone is the most used communicative device for doing business in the world today and it has been for some time. If organizations didn't want to be "bothered" by phone calls, they wouldn't have telephones. It certainly is necessary as a followup to an introductory letter and later on for a telephone update to an advice interview.

I would recommend that the script you write be short, less than two minutes, and have an upbeat, enthusiastic tone! Keep the tone of your voice friendly and pleasant to all you talk to.

As you develop leads and work your campaign, you will be using the telephone a lot due to the following sources: referrals, Yellow Pages, direct classified ads, key hiring persons who have been identified from directories, and telephone updates that need to be made. Identify and make lists of organizations that use skills like yours. Write introductory letters before you make your calls, indicating the day you will be calling.

In order to succeed, double your failure rate.
— TOM WATSON, *founder of IBM*

Telephone Sample Script—Setting Up the Advice Interview

A sample "sales pitch" script for setting up advice interviews follows:

Mr. Beck (Note: make sure you have checked the correct pronunciation of the name before you say it), or if I may call you "Cap," this is Gerry Herron. We have not had the pleasure of meeting yet, but we do have a mutual friend in Ken James whom I saw *last week*. While we were talking, he suggested that I give you a call. Did you get my letter? Do you have a minute? (Show consideration.)

I am at an important time in my career right now where I need some sound advice and counsel. Ken said that you would be a good person for me to visit with. (Notice that I didn't say to talk with if I wanted a local visit.)

I want you to know that I'm not coming to see you for a job but more importantly, I want to run some ideas and strategies by you to see what you think. As a matter of fact, I have some things I want to show you. All I need is approximately 30 to 40 minutes of your time. How does your calendar look for later this week or early next week? (*Note:* I wouldn't ask this question late in the week.)

Thank you. I look forward to our meeting.

He is not only idle who does nothing, but he is idle
who might be better employed.
— SOCRATES

Alternative Scripts

My name is Jane Doe. I have 20 years of experience in the training and development field with one of your competitors. I am currently considering a change. I would like to arrange a meeting at your office to discuss working for your organization. How does your calendar look for later this week or early next?

My name is John Doe, and I am doing a hi-tech survey to learn all I can about computer careers with your firm. What are their major duties of and qualifications for this position? What are the best and worst parts of this work? You have been most helpful to me. Would it be possible for me to visit your office to see these people in action? From what you have shared with me, I am interested in researching this some more. Can we set a mutually convenient time for this visit?

If you know there is an advertised position: My name is Mark Doe and I am calling you at the suggestion of Joan Doe. Do you have a minute?

I have a strong background in _____, with a proven record of accomplishments as a sales engineer. My reason for calling is to set up a meeting to discuss a project I'm working on. Is there a convenient time we could meet?

Mr. _____ or if I might call you _____, this is Ed Doe. Do you have a minute? I have been with the XYZ Company (can use present or former company name for credibility) since the early 1980s and my most recent position has been _____ (can also use title). I now find that I am ready to make a move. I know your company has been growing and I would like to contribute to it.

While with XYZ, I have accomplished some interesting things (mention one or two select impact statements). I would appreciate the opportunity of meeting with you and learning more about your company. Could we set-up a mutually convenient time, say this coming Thursday afternoon or next Tuesday morning? Which would be better for you?

I have not failed, I have (successfully) discovered 1200 methods that won't work.

— THOMAS EDISON

Send Letter before Telephone Call

When you send a broadcast or introductory letter before your telephone call, you might, after identifying yourself, ask whether the person you called received your letter and if so, if he or she has any questions about it. If not, proceed with a modification of the above scripts, setting up your advice interview. If you are unable to do so, try and turn it into a brief phone advice/information interview. I had a successful client who conducted his local campaign primarily using the phone. A sample of the introductory letter that he used before his telephone call is as follows:

Dear Mr. _____ :
I am writing to you to introduce myself and my interest in _____.
While I have had little direct experience in _____, I do have skills which would allow for a transition to that sector.

I am a conscientious, thorough, and dependable individual, as evidenced by my daily work. I have very good analytical skills and give careful attention to detail.

Regarding my attributes of persistence and dedication, I overcame a language barrier to take thirty oral examinations in school en route to my degree.

I researched, organized and effectively presented eleven assigned topics during _____ training.

Having seven years of training, I have completed specialties in _____ and _____. I also have training in the areas of _____ and _____. I feel the above training would aid me in any administrative position that I would undertake.

As for interpersonal relationships, throughout my career I have maintained good relationships with peers.

Enclosed is an updated copy of my resume.

I would like to call you in approximately one week to discuss the above.

Thank you.

Sincerely,

(Answering service phone number)
(Residence phone number)

Enclosure: Resume

This kind of letter and a modified telephone script could be used for long distance campaign calls. When making these calls, have several items ready for possible use: calendar for setting appointments, list of references, your two or three best SARs, written responses for handling rebuttals, research on the organization including known problems they are "wrestling with," and the correct name (including pronunciation) and telephone number of the person you will be talking to. Program yourself positively by looking forward to using the telephone and making new business acquaintances.

If you are unable to arrange an advice interview or even obtain referrals, ask if the person would mind if you could call back in three to four weeks. If that doesn't work out, maybe the person will give you some information that you can use.

If you are fortunate enough to have arranged an advice interview and to have obtained a list of contacts and companies, you will need to conduct a telephone update presentation two to three weeks later. A simple sample script for that followup telephone presentation is as follows:

Telephone Sample Script—Update Presentation

Do you have a minute? (Remember their time is valuable.)
I called for three reasons:

First, did you get my thank you letter? If you did, you know I appreciated our get-together. I ask only because letters sometimes get lost in the mail. (Aside: If he or she says your letter hasn't arrived yet, say it's in the mail.)

Second, I promised you an update, and here it is. I met with _____, and he was very generous with his time. [*add personal note*].

And finally, the third reason for my call, and a most important one—might there be some additional people or companies that you have thought about since we last met that you feel I should be contacting? [*this should be an excellent chance for additional contacts*].

> *It matters not how straight the gate,*
> *how charged with punishments the scroll.*
> *I am the master of my fate.*
> *I am the captain of my soul.*
>
> — W.E. HENLEY

Telephone Tips

1. Start with low-key companies (companies that you are lukewarm about) from your market list of companies to practice on and modify or refine your approach. Make these low-key calls also to friends, where it's okay for you to make and correct your mistakes. Get some easy wins first! Ask for their assessment and ideas for improvement. Remember that information and feedback from telephone contacts is second best to a face-to-face interview because it too is a multidimensional process.

2. Avoid calling people on Mondays and Fridays, for obvious reasons. Tuesday and Wednesday mornings and late afternoons, are reported to be the best by our clients.

3. Telephone calls require privacy. If you're employed and can't get to the phone because "the walls have ears," have a friend or spouse serve as "your secretary" to make appointments for you.

4. If you've been asked to send a resume and are planning to, mention your telephone conversation in the cover letter that accompanies the resume.

5. Schedule phone calls over a two- to three-hour period. You start to warm up after a while and get on a roll.

> *Acceptance is not submission, it is acknowledgement of the facts of a situation, then deciding what you're going to do about it.*
> — KATHLEEN CASEY THEISEN

6. Never conduct a local interview over the phone if you can help it. Face-to-face meetings where you have the chemistry of the situation working for you are the best! Strive to get them.

7. Use 800 numbers (1-800-555-1212) or WATS lines for all long-distance calls. If that is not possible, call person to person or by title only. Tell the operator that you would like the time and charges after the call has been made. If the person isn't there you can leave your number at no expense to you in the hopes the person will call you on their nickel. This works some of the time, especially around or during lunchtime, but not all of the time.

8. Never make a call when you're feeling lousy. The tone of your voice should be confident, friendly, appreciative, and polite.

Smile as you talk into the receiver as if you were speaking to the most important person you've ever talked to and you are really enjoying yourself. Act enthusiastic and you will be.

9. Have a list of questions to ask, written responses to possible rebuttals, and an outline of the script in front of you. Note: If you don't want a "no" for an answer, don't ask those kinds of questions. Try open-ended questions, i.e., "How is the business climate there?"

10. When you get your appointment for a meeting, get off the telephone! If you can't get an appointment, express disappointment and ask the person if he or she knows any people in the field who they think can offer you some advice?

11. After leaving a job interview and sending your thank-you letter, make a telephone call to see if you are still a viable candidate and reiterate your continued interest in the position (tell them they are still your "number one choice"), your availability to make it in for another interview, and your readiness to supply additional information and references if need be. Then follow up this telephone call with a brief thank-you note referring to the telephone conversation and reassert that you honestly feel that you can make a contribution to the organization.

Life is either a daring adventure or nothing.
— HELEN KELLER

12. Keep accurate records as to how well you are doing with your calls by keeping a daily Job Campaign Phone Log (Fig. 11.1). Record information while it is still fresh in your mind. Don't rely on your memory. Keep records together with pen or pencil and calculator (you never know when you need one).

13. Determine whether the person you are talking to is people, detail, or results oriented. Try to "mirror" that person by tone of voice, rate of speech, and word choice.

- *People-oriented:* emphasize feelings and relationships
- *Detail-oriented:* emphasize facts and specifics (stress who, what, where, when, why and how).
- *Results-oriented:* emphasize what you have accomplished as specifically as you can.

FIGURE 11.1
Job campaign phone call log

Note: Keep an accurate log of all calls; this information should be transferred to your alphabetized 3" x 5" index cards so you can find company information quickly.

Number	Date	Out	In	Person Called	Secretary's Name	Area Code & Phone No./ & Ext.	Results

14. Do research on the people and companies they work for before your conversation. Verify titles and name pronunciation. Use your title, if you have one, when calling. Practice; be determined and persistent with all the calls you make.

15. Don't take or make telephone calls when you have someone in your office.

16. Prepare a well-written "introductory telephone commercial" on yourself should you need it, i.e., my name is _____. I am (job title) qualified to do (special, specific skills). I also have completed (additional skills/accomplishments). I have (education). May we set a mutually agreeable time for me to tell you how I can make money for your organization?

17. If your introductory letter was not yet received by the person you were calling, offer to call back in a few days; or, if the person has time, briefly summarize what your letter was about.

18. Take a public speaking and/or Dale Carnegie course. Plan to join the nearest community toastmaster club. Write to the following for free information: Toastmasters International, P.O. Box 10400, 2200 N. Grand Avenue, Santa Anna, CA 92711, (714) 542-6793; National Speakers Association, 5201 N. Seventh Street, Suite 200, Phoenix, Arizona 85014, (602) 265-1001; and the International Platform Association, 2564 Berkshire Road, Cleveland Heights, Ohio 44106, (216) 932-0505.

19. If you have a bad experience over the phone, take a breather and start again at a later time. From time to time you may come in contact with rude people. Try and keep your cool when you do. Don't take it personally.

20. Know that if you haven't used the telephone in the past very much for business purposes, it can be a stressful experience. Realize that it is a normal reaction and that your approach will get better as you spend more time using the phone. Learn from your mistakes, and modify your approach. Work with a "pro," if you can't conquer your fear.

21. Set and meet your daily phone call goals. If you can't get to a phone, have your spouse or a friend make them for you. If you have trouble meeting your goals, work on your efficiency.

22. Don't waste time with poor contacts. Move on to your next one. As I say all the time, "their loss is someone else's gain."

23. Identify potential employers from the classified ads, regional

magazines, Yellow Pages, business news stories, product literature, newspapers, city directories, lobby directories, and network contacts that you can add to your market list of organizations.

24. If you are conducting a long distance campaign and making a cold call to a decision maker (never talked to this person before), ask how working conditions are in that town and what organization or companies they would suggest you contact. The local chamber of commerce would be a good place to start and chambers usually sell local directories of organizations for a reasonable amount.

> *Even if you are on the right track, you'll get run over if you just sit there.*
> — WILL ROGERS

Telephone Techniques for Negative Responses

You should review this list of suggestions for overcoming barriers at the switchboard, with the secretary, and by the hiring person in your area of interest:

Negative Responses at the Switchboard

If you receive a negative response, ask the following: Could you give me the correct spelling and how do you pronounce the name (if the name is difficult to pronounce) of the person in charge of _____ and the official title (you can also verify the address)? Thank you. (Obtaining the correct name will help you in answering direct ads and in sending broadcast/introductory letters to this firm.)

Is that person in? What is his/her secretary's name and the correct spelling of his/her name? Does he/she have a direct line? Could I please be connected to him/her? Can he/she be paged? Thank you.

Could you please give me directions to your office?

> *Success is more than knowing how. It's knowing when.*
> — ANONYMOUS

Negative Responses from the Secretary

Establish rapport with the secretary. Ask for his or her name (make note of it) and for his or her help. If you have to call back, you can use the secretary's first name. When asked:

What is this in reference to?

Answer: We've been in correspondence with one another (if you sent an introductory letter and you mentioned you'd be calling), and he/she's expecting my call, or "tell him/her that _____, is holding on the line, please. Is he/she in a meeting?" Or, "Good morning, my name is _____. I would like to speak to Bob (using the person's first name only can sometimes get you through the secretarial barrier) please. I am calling at the suggestion of our mutual friend, _____. It's about a marketing project I am working on" or "_____, a mutual friend, suggested that I contact Mr./Ms. _____ to assist me in my job search."

What company do you represent?

Answer: If you are still on severance pay, you can use your former company or your own name, i.e., The Logue Company or that you are "self-employed" (if you are working for yourself).

Have you spoken with him/her before?

Answer: We have had recent correspondence, dated _____. Mr./Mrs. _____, President of XYZ Corporation suggested that I contact him/her to discuss the information in my letter.

He/she is not in.

Answer: To whom am I speaking? When is he/she expected back? _____ (name of secretary), I need your help! What time of day is he/she usually available to take a call? If she asks for your telephone number, tell her you are at a number you won't be at much longer (you're on the road or you are planning to be out of the office), and maybe she could give you a better time for you to call back. This enables you to keep the initiative and control!

When did he/she hear from you last?

Answer: I sent him/her a letter dated _____. He/she is expecting my call.

He/she is on another line.

Answer: I'll be happy to wait if you'll let him/her know that I'm on hold.

He/she is in a meeting.

Answer: When will he/she be free? At what time would it be convenient for me to call back?

He/she is out-of-town (on vacation).
Answer: When does he/she return? I'll contact him/her then.

He/she has left the company.
Answer: When did he/she leave? Where has he/she gone? Who is the new _____? What do his/her friends call him/her (if name provided)? May I be connected to him/her?

He/she passed away.
Answer: I'm sorry to hear that. Who has taken his/her place as the new _____?

> *As soon as you trust yourself, you will know how to live.*
>
> — GOETHE

Notes:

1. Obtain the secretary's name from the switchboard before you call the office. Use his/her first name to establish a friendly relationship. Be polite, firm, positive, and courteous. Make a friend.

2. When you ask for the boss, make sure there is a sound of familiarity in your voice. Ask for the boss (hiring person) by the first name, i.e., "Is John in? Would you please put me through?"

3. If the secretary says that the boss referred your letter to another department, thank her and ask to be transferred to that department. If that department happens to be Human Resources, you can tell her that the boss must have misunderstood your letter as you weren't asking him/her for a job or looking for a job with their company. Could you talk to him/her so that you might clear up this matter?

4. If you are connected to Human Resources anyway, you can tell them you were referred by the boss's office and that you would like to set up a date for an interview. If you are not given one, it is suggested that you recontact the boss' secretary and ask her to recommend someone else. If you know the name of the hiring person, mention that individual to the secretary and ask her if he/she would be a good person for you to contact.

5. Never tell a secretary that the reason for your call is a personal matter. Believe me, that turns them off completely and sends up a red flag that they will defend against.

6. If you are having problems getting past the secretary, try calling between 7 and 8 a.m. or 5 and 6 p.m. or during lunch time. If this doesn't work, write a letter to this contact saying that you've tried to reach them a number of times and have had trouble getting through. Maybe he or she could leave some suggested dates or times with the secretary for you to select from. If that fails, as a last resort, try getting back to your original referral source, if you have one, to see if he or she might intercede in your behalf.

7. Don't put or have anything in your mouth while you are talking to someone. It gets amplified. Talk slightly above the center of the mouthpiece.

Negative Responses from the Hiring Person

What is the purpose of this call?
Answer: As I mentioned in my letter dated _____, Mr./Ms. _____ said that we should get together. I'd like to make an appointment to speak briefly with you about _____. I need more information and your expertise makes you an excellent choice.

We have no openings.
Answer: Tell him/her you are sorry to hear that and then ask, "Who do you know that you might recommend that I be talking to? Would it be possible to use your name as a referral?" Or, "As you'll note from my letter, I wasn't planning to ask you for a job but only for your advice. I'm sure you will be able to give me the help that I need. Is later this week or early next week better for you?"

I am too busy for a meeting.
Answer: I realize your time is valuable and I would therefore be very brief. I would be happy to meet you before or after work if that would be more convenient. Would Tuesday or Thursday be better (have your appointment book handy)? Or, "I knew you would be. Could we get together one afternoon after work . . . say tomorrow, or would Tuesday morning be better?" Note: In this day and age though, five minutes over the phone may be better than trying to arrange a twenty minute meeting in person, especially if it's with an executive.

I get a lot of letters like this.
Answer: Then you're exactly the person with whom to speak if I am to obtain information on _____.

I'm scheduled all this week and most of next.
Answer: Very well. How would next Tuesday be? I'll only take twenty to thirty minutes of your time. I know how busy you are.

It is company policy that we not schedule appointments not related to company business.
Answer: I'd be happy to meet you for breakfast or come in before or after work. Would morning or evening be more suitable?

I don't really see how I can help you.
Answer: Your experience and expertise in the field of _____ are very valuable to me at this time. If you could see your way clear to giving me 20 minutes, I would be most appreciative. Or, doesn't your company have a problem with _____? Would additional expertise in this area help you?

I'm new to the area.
Answer: But well-respected and knowledgeable in the field.

I think you need to speak with Mr./Ms. _____ our Director of Operations.
Answer: I'll certainly contact Mr./Ms. _____. Hopefully, he/she will be able to add another dimension to the insights I will gain from you.

I think you need to speak with Mr./Ms. _____, our Director of Human Resources.
Answer: I have no interest in the personnel field. My interests lie in the field of _____, and you are by far the best qualified to supply information in that area. Or, "I am perfectly willing to go through Personnel but I had hoped that we could first meet and discuss possibilities in your department. All I need is twenty minutes of your time."

Send me a letter describing your background or a resume.
Answer: I'm not necessarily seeking a position. The reason I want to see you is to run some strategies and some ideas by you to see what you think. Or, "I would be glad to send you my resume. However, I will be in your area in the next two days and would rather stop by and give it to you in person if that's possible. What time would be more convenient, 10 a.m. or 2 p.m.?" Or, "Before I send you my letter describing my background, I would like to ask you a few questions." (See questions to ask about a company or department). Again try to arrange a mutually convenient time for a meeting. Be persistent yet calm and cool. Or, "I've been with your compe-

tition and I'd like to keep this meeting confidential. Might I bring it with me when we meet this afternoon, or would tomorrow morning be better?"

We hired someone else.

Answer: "I really am interested in working for your company. Just in case things don't work out with that individual, I would like to drop off my resume so that it can be kept on file. I'll be in your neighborhood tomorrow. Would it be all right that I drop it off in person in the morning?" Or, "Yes I know you have a good team. In fact, that's why I felt you could help me at this crucial time in my career. Could we get together later this week or early next?"

A Client's Long Distance Phone Campaign

Since relocation plans were open, and the expense of visiting different geographical locations was prohibitive, I was forced into generating a long distance telephone campaign. During my campaign, I made over four hundred telephone calls and was rebuffed by approximately five people. People will talk with you and are willing to help, by providing names for further networking, by providing suggestions as to the course of action you should pursue, or a combination of both.

The candidate should perform all the same actions as if he were searching for a job in the local area, except that letters of introduction need not be sent. Time is of the essence to the candidate, and the sooner he can talk with people, the happier he will be. Get right to the phone call!

It is very important before a candidate begins his long distance telephone campaign, that he is very strong in his presentation, and that he expresses a degree of self-confidence. This can be best accomplished by conducting a series of advice interviews with companies and personnel in his discipline within the local area.

You always need two names when you are networking, the name of the person to whom you wish to speak and the "introduction" name (the name of the person who suggested you make the call). Contact the person to whom you wish to speak, use the "introduction" name, and make the presentation. When you are provided names for additional networking, ask the person if you can use his/her name as an introduction name. Make it very clear to that person that you are not asking for a reference, since you already have your own.

When you do not have an "introduction" name, contact the person to whom you wish to speak and make your presentation. Remember, the vast majority of people are willing to help.

When you have only the name of the company, just call the company and ask the operator who is the responsible person for the department that you are interested in. You may have to use your imagination in obtaining the name, i.e., you are Mr. Jones with the Best Advertising Agency and you are compiling a manual with all the names of the business executives in your field. Be prepared to handle this!

Remember, you always have to have a name! Follow-up on whatever course of action develops from the conversation.

I found that calling on Tuesday, Wednesday, Thursday, and Friday morning was successful. The best time to call varied. Sometimes it was before 8 a.m., sometimes at lunch time, and sometimes after 5 p.m. local time at the number being called.

If the person is not there, ask the secretary what is the best time to contact the person and then call back at that time. Don't lose control of the situation by having the secretary return the call. After two direct calls, I would then inform the secretary that I would call person-to-person next time.

It is easy after a few calls—practice makes perfect!

— Courtesy of BOB FLODSTROM

What kind of man would live where there is no daring? I don't believe in taking foolish chances, but nothing can be accomplished without taking any chances at all.
> — CHARLES AUGUSTUS LINDBERGH

To know and not do is not yet to know.
> — ZEN SAYING

12.

Marketing Yourself with Letters

The Lord's Prayer has 56 words; Lincoln's
Gettysburg Address, 226; and the Ten
Commandments (which set a whole moral code for
mankind), 297. In contrast, the words used in a
Federal Order dealing with the price of cabbage
contained a total of 26,911 words.

— ANONYMOUS

Effective Writing

Letters will play an important part in your campaign as you communicate with a variety of friends and strangers. Letters that are well written will set you apart from other candidates and ensure that you are marketing yourself correctly. Communication is an art, though; and to effectively do it with writing, you will need to use many of these ideas and models:

- Order good rag bond stationery (25 percent rag or better), classic laid. Note: If you are employed, don't use the firm's stationery or business cards. Quality stationery usually has a watermark that is visible when held up to the light. You will want to have your name, address and telephone numbers on it (office or answering service and residence). Put your address on the envelope flap. If you have retained a career counselor, use his number as your business phone or get yourself an answering service. Stationery stores, printing services, and commercial firms like Daytimer, Allentown, Pennsylvania 18001 sell luxury-line stationery. They also will show you different styles of printing to choose from.

- Order both Monarch size stationery ($7\frac{1}{4}$" x $10\frac{1}{2}$") with envelopes ($3\frac{7}{8}$"x $7\frac{1}{2}$") and standard size ($8\frac{1}{2}$"x 11") with number 10 size ($4\frac{1}{8}$" x $9\frac{1}{4}$") envelopes for them.

- Since most offices have "white correspondence" coming across the desk, select matching off-white (e.g., antique, beige, ivory, or light gray) for envelopes and stationery. Stay away from dark colors.

- Keep the content concise, positive, and neat. Write short sentences and paragraphs. Think and plan what you're going to say before you do it. Divide long sentences into two if need be. Show a lot of white space in your letter, use wide margins (1"–1½") and adequate spacing between paragraphs, and have your letters one page (maximum) with no more than 3 or 4 paragraphs. Letters can be arranged in one of the following styles:

Style

1. *The Blocked Style.* The date, the complimentary close and the writer's identification (name and signature) all begin at the center line of the page. All other lines begin at the left margin.

2. *The Semi-blocked Style.* This is exactly like the blocked style, except that the first line of each paragraph is indented five spaces.

3. *The Full-Blocked Style.* All lines begin at the left margin. Nothing is indented (except for displayed quotations, tables and similar material).

Short words are always best.
— WINSTON CHURCHILL

- Always address your clean letters to a correctly-spelled name and not just to a title. Never "Dear Sir" but "Dear Ms./Mr. _____." Check with research sources or the switchboard operator about the name, title, and address. I prefer the latter because people can change jobs overnight. Put *Personal and Confidential* on both the letter and the envelope. The letter ideally should be sent to the person who can hire you (the decision maker—if he/she doesn't have a job open, maybe one can be created). Never send the letter to the person who has the job you are after or to the personnel or human relations department. Remember: that department, with all due respect, is a staff department and is there to disqualify candidates, not qualify them. The only exception would be if you are sending a letter in answer to a blind ad. I have, though, worked with clients who used a "double-edge" approach by sending a letter to personnel as well as to the hiring person. Use "To Whom It May Concern" as your salutation. Stay away from Dear Sir/Madame, Dear Sir, and Gentlemen as you may well offend someone.

- Write the letter as if you were talking to someone. Keep it natural, and use your own language. Remember: letters reflect you and your style. All letters should be typed, single-spaced, with double spacing between paragraphs.

The meaning of a communication is the response that it elicits.

— R. BANDLER and J. GRINDER
authors of *Frogs into Princes*

- If you plan to write to many organizations, you may want to consider photo-offset printing. Prepare the master copy of the letter you will be using on the same typewriter that will be used to address the envelope and provide the letter heading and salutation. Take the master without your signature on it to a printer and have it reproduced. You can then sign each individually, as you use them, with your full name, and using a blue or black pen. Use only ink for your signature.

- Select the companies and specific people that you will be writing to who can use your skills. This also would include organizations that are vendors or suppliers serving companies horizontally and vertically (one step removed). Use a variety of "homework" sources as well as: Yellow Pages, local Chamber of Commerce directories, alumni/alumnae directories and the companies represented by Board of Trustee members (mutual interest in school) and community leaders. Don't mass mail, primarily because you have to follow letters up at the same time. Feed them out five to ten letters per week.

It takes less time to do a thing right than to explain why you did it wrong.

— LONGFELLOW

- Choose your words to fit the reader's personality and background. *Customize it!* Avoid words like *believe, hope, feel*; use *should* and *know*. Be positive in word and deed! Don't give the reader a chance to disagree with you (be more positive). Remember: your writing and the words you use say something about how you think and organize your thoughts. Use a dictionary and a thesaurus if need be.

- If you need help with your writing, see an English teacher or use business writing books (see bibliography), friends, or Strunk and White's *Elements of Style.*

- Sleep on your writing and proofread (edit) your letters before sending them out. Don't use letters with any erasures or white-out. Your letters need to be error free. Have friends proofread for you.

- Save copies of all correspondence for followup purposes, e.g., telephone. Send only originals, never a copy. Use your calendar for followup dates.

- Consider writing to recently promoted people whose names you learn from "the people on the move" section of the newspaper or trade or business magazine who may well be bringing in their own teams. Try and personalize your letters with things you might have in common and/or research items. Refer to published articles or quotes.

- Realize that although campaigns can be seasonal, anytime is a good time to launch your mail campaign. If, for example, it is around the holidays, you might very well connect with someone who is otherwise hard to reach, because business might be slow.

- Some people use a variety of creative writing supplements to gain attention: video presentations about themselves; drawing their foot and attempting to get their "foot in the door" along with their letter (sounds rather corny); certified or registered mail or mailgrams; issuing a "BEWARE—if you don't take action on this letter, you will be stricken by a seven-year itch"; a poem about your qualifications; a statement of your credentials on a T-shirt, etc. The bottom line is, though, if it works, why not! Most organizations are conservative. Realize that creative and cute things may get a reaction—a negative one.

- Be sure of the gender and the correct spelling of the name and title of the person you are contacting. The name and/or initials may fool you. Better to check beforehand. Remember Johnny Cash's song, "The Boy Named Sue."

- Never attach your resume to any broadcast letter unless it was previously requested or you are conducting a long distance campaign.

- Timely and well-written letters are an essential part of your campaign. Don't be discouraged if you don't hear from a majority of the recipients of your letters. Response rates can be as low as five percent. Hang in there! Be determined to succeed. You want to put the majority of your campaign time into conducting advice interviews, since 65–85 percent of people get jobs this way.

- Consider using a short cover letter with a resume for long distance campaigns. Indicate your willingness to make a trip for a personal interview. Followup by phone could be optional. If the resume you are attaching is more than one page, staple the pages together and attach them to your cover letter with a gold-colored paperclip that adds a stylish touch.

- If you are unsure what jobs may be available, include several questions in your letter.

- Don't mention present, last, or desired salary.

- Remember: write the way that is the most comfortable for you. Again, try to "individually customize" letters where possible.

- Confidential campaign letters—use a friend's address on stationery; this enables the friend to receive calls and letters for you. This can be effective if you are conducting a long distance campaign to a city where you have a friend who is willing to help you.

Broadcast Letters

Your broadcast letters, for the most part, can be broken down into three parts: the introduction (one paragraph), body (one to three paragraphs), and the closing (one paragraph).

There are several types of ways to introduce yourself ("attention grabbers") by letter: *accomplishment* ("I made a $300 million business, with a long and nearly perfect record for losing money, profitable the first year"), *reference* ("our mutual acquaintance, Fred Jones, suggested that I contact you"), *homework* ("I recently came across an article that you wrote for the *Pittsburgh Magazine* that was of interest to me"), and *creative ideas* ("Foreign competition getting to you? Tired of sales approaches that don't seem to work anymore? If these questions hit a nerve, please read on!").

The body (your value) contains the meat of the letter. No more than four to five specific impact statements as they relate to the specifics (needs and wants) of the job you are seeking and how you can help that organization! All statements should be quantified to the best of your ability whether they be number of customers worked with, courses taken or coordinated, savings, dollars, sizes, and/or amounts. Quantifying your results will definitely help your interviewing skills to be more exact and visual. Also, try and include a new or interesting idea that will cause the person to want to meet you.

Try and retain control in your closing. That is, tell the addressee that you will be contacting him or her within the week (allow yourself ample time for a followup) to set up a mutually convenient time, or if you are conducting a long distance campaign, you may ask the recipient to contact you if interested. It would be rather costly to follow up long distance letters by phone unless you had access to a WATS line or the organization you were contacting had an (800) number. You can quickly determine (800) numbers by dialing directory assistance at 555-1212 or by using the 800 directory at a library.

Creativity Counts

Opening paragraphs can be the key to your letters. I worked with a client who creatively wrote to key company executives stating initially, "Reducing costs while increasing profits is the bottom line that executives like yourself are concerned about. If I could show you ways to do both of these things, would you be interested in meeting me?" This statement very well might attract someone's attention, but a lot depends on how the rest of the letter is packaged. Consider having your state senator or a top executive that you, a friend, or parents know write a broadcast letter on your behalf.

Sample Cover Letters

As "a picture speaks a thousand words," so do the following 32 sample cover letters give you ideas to use or refer to in your campaign. You may want to rewrite these and change them to your own writing style.

Sample Reference Letter

DRAFT

COMPANY LETTERHEAD

Date

To Whom It May Concern:

Re: (Your Name)

I have known (your name) for over three years and would give him my highest recommendation concerning being a person of integrity, a warm and outgoing social style, deeply caring for others and a high sense of responsibility, His character, in all aspects, is flawless. For three years I have been in a position to watch his work. He has a work ethic that is superior and an attitude to go with it that he must achieve success. (Your first name) loves a challenge.

(Your first name) has always followed-through and completed his assignments with the utmost of professionalism. He has enormous potential and would be a fine asset to any company he chooses to work with. As you can appreciate, with the cutback of (description) projects, we have had to eliminate a lot of positions under a new realignment. This, of course, had nothing to do with previous working assignments.

Should you wish to discuss (your first name) in greater detail, please do not hesitate to give me a call.

Sincerely,

(Name)
(Title)

Broadcast Letter
(Also known as Confetti, Popcorn, PAR (Problem-Action-Result), Guidance, Overview, Motivating Letters; the greater the distance, the smaller the effect of this kind of letter. Try and get a high-powered person to write on your behalf.)

Letterhead

Name   Date
Company
Address
City, State, Zip

Dear _____: PERSONAL AND CONFIDENTIAL

I am in the process of relocating from a position of Manager of Sales and Marketing for (company name). Because of the complex nature of your company, I would appreciate some guidance from you as to the person in your organization to contact regarding my qualifications.

With twenty years management experience, I am seeking a Senior Position in Sales/Marketing or Management. Skills have been demonstrated in the areas of organizing sales and marketing teams, penetrating new markets, developing new products, and profit and loss responsibility. I have functioned as National Sales Manager, Product Manager, and Technical Service Manager.

Some of the highlights of my career are:

- Responsible for sales and marketing activities of "XYZ" and private-label antifreeze with annual sales of $40 million.
- Customer groups included oil and rubber companies, mass merchandisers, chemical companies, steel and mining industries, O. E. M., brokers and reps, and chemical and warehouse distributors.
- Responsible for profitability of ethylene products which included antifreeze, industrial glycols, ethylene oxide, glycol ethers, and ethanolamines.
- Managed advertising and promotional programs.
- Developed short and long-term sales and marketing plans.
- Directed research, development, and technical activities in automotive, aircraft, and industrial specialty chemical formulations.

I will call you for your advice, within the week, on who to contact.

Very truly yours,

(Your Name)

Note: These letters serve as organizational introductions.

Sample Broadcast Letter (Local)

Date

Address

PERSONAL AND CONFIDENTIAL

Dear _____:

As a respected and successful member of the Pittsburgh business community, I would like your help. I am involved in a program to assist me in changing careers. I am presently interested in building and spreading a personal communication network in Pittsburgh to identify mutually appropriate needs in the manufacturing field.

For the last nine years, I have consulted both domestically and internationally in all types and areas of manufacturing. Some of my experiences and projects are as follows:

- Managed improvement project across 5 departments in ammunition manufacturing plant of 1,200 employees resulting in productivity increases in 3 key areas of 47%, 60% and 67%. Maintenance costs dropped $1.8 million and inventory fell $1.5 million (out of $16 million). Achieved $2 million profit to business after previous year operating loss of $8 million.
- Increased production in heavy union environment from 9,000,000 units/year to 36,000,000 units/year. Overtime fell 30% and product yield increased from 40 to 85%.
- Designed and implemented a parts shortage system in an aerospace manufacturing company that saved $26,000,000 in 3 years.
- Coordinated an approach to standardize units of measure and nomenclature for 7 manufacturing plants in 6 countries for over 110,000 employees simultaneously.

My education includes a Bachelor of Science Degree in Economics from (university name). Company-sponsored training includes structured group problem solving, finance (from Kellogg, Northwestern University), Total Quality and Total Manufacturing concepts and applications.

I will appreciate your guidance and suggestions in helping me build and spread my communication network. I will phone your office within the week for your suggestions. Thank you.

Sincerely,

(Your Name)
(Residence Telephone Number)

Sample Direct Ad Resume Letter
(Call and get name, spelling, and address of person in charge of Marketing)

Dear Mr. _____ :   PERSONAL AND CONFIDENTIAL

Since you are looking for a manager of Industrial Marketing, you will be interested in my qualifications.

I am currently the Operations/Marketing Director of a large utility company. In this position my primary marketing concern is with the industrial customer. I also function as an internal marketing, planning and engineering consultant on matters relating to promotional rates, area development, competitor's activities and design and construction of service facilities.

My experience, education and abilities meet and exceed all of your requirements and includes senior management experience with a large consulting engineering practice. Some examples of my completed experiences are as follows:

- As a member of a four-man planning team, I developed a twenty year business plan for a $1 billion dollar utility company, analyzed the options for future supply, markets and allocation of resources.
- I authored an energy-audit program that saved $125,000 and is being used nationally by a respected research organization.
- Initiated a heating sales program that sold $3,500,000 the first year.
- Exceeded ambitious sales goals by $4,600,000.
- Created and gained approval of new rate that has profit potential of $74,000,000.

In all of my personal activities, I have exhibited creativity, common sense and a natural feel for the marketplace. Most of my assignments over the past 18 years have required superior analytical, persuasive and communication skills as well as foresight.

We should meet to discuss this opportunity and my qualifications. I will call your office within the week to arrange a mutually agreeable time.

Thank you,

John Doe

JD/ef

Notes: If salary history is "demanded," state that you are sure that salary can be worked out. Never attach a resume to this letter. This letter for all intents and purposes is a "resume letter."

Blind Ad: Indirect Box Letter Response

Name/Address   September 29, 199___

P-3023
CHEMICAL WEEK
Class. Adv. Dept.
P.O. Box 900
New York, NY 10020

Dear Sir:

Your specifications in CHEMICAL WEEK for a General Manager of a chemical processing plant closely match my background and qualifications.

With a large chemical industries company I have gained wide functional experience. Skills for initiating, planning and getting things done complement this strength.

You seek a "candidate with early background in chemical engineering." My qualifications fit, as I:

- Earned a Bachelor of Science Degree in Chemical Engineering from Purdue University.
- Designed and operated major equipment and pilot plants that led to a $30,000,000 chemical plant investment.

Your preferred candidate would then have had "general management responsibility." This fits because:

- As General Manager, I led a manufacturing subsidiary in a major expansion. In two years we increased sales by 60 percent to $11,500,000 and raised earnings by 30 percent.
- While managing a marketing unit, I strengthened a sales staff and agent network. We increased chemical product sales by 40 percent to $15,500,000 annually.
- In another assignment I organized two, profitable joint venture manufacturing companies that represent sales of $51,000,000.

We should meet to review the full scope of the General Manager position and further details of my qualifications. Please contact me at the address above or at (412)_____ so we can arrange a convenient visit.

Very truly yours,

Jane Doe

JD/ef

Note: Stress that your qualifications "fit" the majority of their needs.

Sample Long Distance Ad Response Letter

Name
Company
Address
City, State, Zip

Dear _____: PERSONAL AND CONFIDENTIAL

INTRODUCTION   In view of your need for a Warehouse-Fleet Manager as described in the June 7, 199__ issue of the Courier Journal, I know that my qualifications will be of interest to you.

Your request of five years' experience is more than adequately met by my seven years' experience as supervisor for the nation's largest common carrier. As supervisor, I was responsible for improving dock production and city drivers' performance, while at the same time having our first perfect audit in inventory control.

Totally responsible for maintaining and licensing all of the equipment for three terminals; one each in Pittsburgh, PA, Morgantown, WV, and Wheeling, WV. After reading the text of your advertisement, I am confident that I can furnish the managerial talents you seek. Some of my other demonstrated accomplishments include:

BODY

- Organized and taught a one-day course to management personnel on how to drive a tractor trailer and what the DOT safety requirements are for tractors.
- Reduced annual maintenance expense from $146,000 to just over $45,000 per year.
- Trained others on proper methods of reporting overages, shortages, and damages by computer so as to minimize cargo claims and cluttered warehouse space.

Money is important to me and you but is not everything. I am interested in the opportunity, responsibilities, personal relationships, and value to the company. If these items are a fit, I would expect to be able to arrive at an acceptable compensation plan to our mutual satisfaction. I have enclosed a copy of my 199__ compensation report as it represents the halfway point in my career.

CONCLUSION   Since my experience matches your requirements so well and I am willing to relocate, I know we should meet to discuss any further questions. Please phone me at 412/ _____ (business) or 412/ _____ (residence) so that we may make mutually convenient arrangements. I look forward to hearing from you.

Sincerely,

John Doe

Enclosures

Sample Box Follow-Up Letter
(Made three to four weeks after original letter was sent, when you don't have a response and when "fit" was good.)

Address/Date

Box VY, Suite 816
City, State, Zip

To Whom It May Concern:

Regarding your search for a Director of Sales and Marketing position, I fit your specifications exactly.

As I have not heard from you in response to my letter of August 12, 199__ (copy attached), I am concerned that it may have been mislaid or lost in the mail.

At present, I have some other situations developing rapidly, so it becomes important that we have a prompt exchange of information if we are to give fair consideration to what could be a mutually beneficial relationship.

Please contact me, in confidence, at my office: 412/_____ or at home: 412/_____. Thank you.

Sincerely,

Ralph Jones

Enclosure - Resume

Sample Agency/Recruiter Cover Letter

Address/Date

Name
Agency
Address
City, State, Zip

Dear Mr. _____: PERSONAL AND CONFIDENTIAL

I am seeking a challenging opportunity at a senior management level in general management with profit and loss responsibility or in sales/marketing management. Your firm has been highly recommended as a respected and extremely successful executive recruiting firm.

The enclosed resume highlights my 30-year career in the metals industry with emphasis on my executive management skills in sales/marketing, and as president and chief executive officer. Proven skills in leadership, policy making, strategic planning, cost management, communications and human resources are commensurate with my career objective.

My current compensation is in excess of $100,000. However, the base salary is negotiable dependent on the challenge, future opportunities, incentive fringes, etc. It should however be in excess of $80,000 and I am flexible on relocation.

If a client's position responsibility requirements are compatible with my background and objectives, I would welcome the opportunity to discuss the situation. I can be reached at 412/ _____ (business) or 412/ _____ (residence). Thank you.

Sincerely,

Jane Doe

JD/ef
Enclosure - Resume

Note optional closing: "I will call your office within the week to see if you received this letter and resume and determine whether you have any questions." Recruiters will want to know salary history/range if it is not on the cover letter, when you are available or can be available for interviews (make yourself available for interviews on comparatively short notice) and why you are looking for a job.

Sample Agency/Recruiter Cover Letter (Longer Version)

Address/Date

Name
Company
Address
City, State, Zip

PERSONAL AND CONFIDENTIAL

Dear Mr. _____:

For the past ten years I was employed in the corporate Controller Department of _____ Corporation. While at _____ I was promoted from staff accountant to progressively more responsible positions. My last position was Director-Corporate Controller.

As you are aware, _____ has been acquired by _____ Corporation. I have decided not to accept a new position with _____ and am now seeking employment with another organization.

I am interested in a Financial Management position including responsibility for a full range of financial and accounting functions. I am flexible on salary if the right position is available. My salary when I left _____ was $60,000.

As the enclosed resume indicates, my background includes public accounting and college-level teaching experience. I am a CPA and have an MBA from the University of Pittsburgh. I would prefer to work someplace along the East coast, but would consider relocating to any part of the country.

I would be pleased to detail my qualifications more thoroughly and how I could be of value to your clients. I will call your office, therefore, within the week. May I have the opportunity to talk with you?

Sincerely,

John Doe

Enclosure - Resume

Sample Agency/Recruiter Cover Letter (Shorter Version)

Address/Date

Name
Company
Address
City, State, Zip

PERSONAL AND CONFIDENTIAL

Gentlemen:

Your clients frequently are in the market for qualified people with my background. I would welcome the opportunity to be interviewed by any interested parties.

You will understand the need to treat both this letter and the accompanying resume as confidential.

Yours truly,

Jane Doe

JD/ef

Enclosure - Resume

Sample Agency/Recruiter Letter

This is a request to remove your name from the active file.

Address

Date

Name
Company
Address
City, State, Zip

PERSONAL AND CONFIDENTIAL

Dear _____:

This is to advise you that I am no longer available for a position and therefore request that you remove my application from your active files.

Although I did not get a position through your firm, your courtesy and personal interest are very much appreciated.

I plan to recommend your firm to anyone who may be looking for a position in _____. Thanks again.

Sincerely yours,

John Doe

Sample Thank-You Letter After Job Interview

Date

Name
Title
Company
Address
City, State, Zip

Dear _____:

It certainly was a pleasure meeting you and (name).

I would like to thank you for the opportunity to visit your plant. I had a most interesting tour through the operation and I can really appreciate the need for good control and firm direction in the leadership required for this type of business.

(Name), I am certainly more than just interested in the position as Director of Manufacturing. I don't feel I would have any problem at all in changing from steel to brass or bronze and I would seriously like to be considered for the position and for the opportunity to become part of your organization.

I am attaching an explanation of the expenses incurred by me during my visit to your plant.

Thanks again for the professional manner and courtesy in which I was treated by you and (name) during my visit. I am looking forward to hearing from you soon.

Incidentally, I made it home from the airport in 1 hour 40 minutes (with coat in hand); the flight only took 45 minutes.

Sincerely,

Jane Doe

JD
Attachment - Expenses

Note: After an interview, send thank-you letters to reinforce your positive qualifications for the position, the contributions you feel you can make and your continued interest in and enthusiasm about joining this organization. All the people that you interviewed with should get one (or at least the person who coordinated the interview). Obviously, you want to change each letter.

Sample Follow-Up To An Interview (Basic Business Etiquette)

Letterhead

Date

Name
Title
Company
Address
City, State, Zip

Dear _____:

Thank you for inviting me to _____ last Saturday. I am very interested and enthused about the sales position that we talked about and know I can do an outstanding job for you. I liked the "all for one and one for all" attitude that you talked about.

My goal is to channel the energy it takes to manage a dozen people, six outside drafting services and 50 contracts into a sales position.

I feel very comfortable talking to architects and contractors. For example, last Monday, I needed some information on a project but my customer's office was closed for the holiday. I found the name of the architect and his phone number on the design drawings. I called Mr. _____ that day and got the information I needed.

As you know, the personal "chemistry and fit" between me and any organization I would join is important. I sensed an excellent fit as we talked and am confident we can arrive at a mutually agreeable compensation package.

I look forward to our next discussion.

Sincerely,

John Doe

412/ _____ (Business)
412/ _____ (Residence)

Sample Acceptance Letter

Address/Date

Name
Title
Company Name
Address
City, State, Zip

Dear Mr. _____:

I was very pleased and excited to receive your letter of March 25, in which you extended me an offer to join your organization following graduation. I am enthusiastically accepting your offer of employment at a monthly salary of $2,000.

The description of the duties which will be assigned to me as a Production Management Trainee fit in well with my career goals. I am certain that my educational background and previous internship experience will be of value to me and will permit me to be a contributing member of the ABC Corporation.

You indicated that as a full-time employee I will be eligible for the complete medical program and employee tuitional educational reimbursement programs as of my starting date. Also, as agreed, I will be granted one additional week of vacation during my first year of employment for my wedding and honeymoon.

I look forward to a lengthy and mutually profitable relationship with ABC Corporation. I will report to your office at 8:00 A.M. on September 1, 199__.

Sincerely,

Jane Lewis

P.S. Enclosed is the voucher you gave me for reimbursement of out-of-pocket expenses.

Sample Announcement/Thank-You Letter

Address

Date

Name
Address
City, State, Zip

Dear _____:

    It is with great pleasure that I announce my new position of Sales Engineer with _____ Industries, Inc. in _____. _____ Industries distributes and installs insulation for residential, commercial and industrial buildings.

    This is an exciting and challenging position for me. _____ Industries is a small, but well-respected, contractor that has exhibited steady growth. I will be responsible for creating additional growth by developing new business in _____ and _____, then expanding markets in _____.

    (Name), I want to thank you for your help during my job search campaign. It was your suggestion to talk to _____ that eventually led me to _____ Industries.

    I am enclosing a business card for your reference. _____ and I will be moving to _____ as soon as we sell our home in _____. I look forward to getting together with you soon. Please, let's keep in touch!

    Once again, thanks very much for your help.

Sincerely,

John Doe

JD/dtb

Enclosure - Business Card

Sample Follow-Up Letter After Rejection

Date

Name
Title
Company
Street Address
City, State Zip Code

Dear _____:

Thank you for your letter of (date) in which you advised me of your decision regarding the Marketing Management position. As you can imagine, I was disappointed that I was not selected for the opening. I felt that it offered so many opportunities in which I could have productively applied my considerable knowledge and experience in the _____ industry. However, I do realize that evaluations more objective than mine were involved in your final choice. I understand and respect the basis for your decision.

Because of the rapport that I felt we had established, and because of my conviction that I could really do an outstanding job as your assistant, I want you to know that, should your selection not work out, I would still be interested in being considered for the position or any others that might open up.

In the meantime, the thought occurred to me that you might wish to help me in a rather special way. Since you have an understanding in depth of my capabilities and objectives, you can probably think of the names of one or two of your acquaintances in other companies whom you feel I should make aware of my availability. I would very much appreciate any suggestions you might have.

Thanks again for all your courtesies and consideration. I sincerely hope that we meet again and perhaps sometime in the future a way can be found to continue our association.

Sincerely,

John Doe

Sample Thank-You Letter After Advice Interview

Letterhead

Date

Name
Title
Company
Street Address
City, State, Zip

Dear _____:

Thanks again for meeting with me last _____. Your input and suggestions on my career objectives and presentation were of great value to me.

The information you gave me regarding _____ was most informative. I appreciate your suggestion that I contact _____ for further suggestions. I will also be following up with the other individuals you suggested that I contact.

Thanks again. I know now why _____ holds you in such high esteem. Please keep my objectives in mind in case you hear of other opportunities. And as we discussed, I will be back in touch with you in two to three weeks to see if you have any further suggestions and to keep you informed of my progress.

Sincerely,

John Doe

Sample Publication Response Letter

Date

Contact's Name
Title
Company
Street Address
City, State, Zip Code

Dear _____: PERSONAL AND CONFIDENTIAL

I recently read with interest in (Publication, Date/Name) of your organization's growth over the past several years. As an experienced manager, I am interested in joining an organization like yours and working on your staff.

My work experience with _____ has given me the chance to gain significant experience in the areas of quality control, management/union relationships and, of course, interpersonal management skills.

My resume is enclosed and highlights some of my career achievements and skills. As you read it, you will quickly note why I am interested in your organization.

I would welcome the opportunity to personally meet with you to discuss how my qualifications might match some of your current or planned management needs. I will, therefore, call your office next week to arrange an appointment. (Local)

OR

If it seems appropriate for us to meet, I would be available to fly to _____ for a meeting. (Long Distance).

Sincerely,

Jane Doe

Enclosure

Note: Use format also for contacting people you learned of from convention and trade show speeches, chance meetings, annual report names, radio/TV speeches, and promotion announcements.

Sample Long Distance Letter

Letterhead

Name   Date
Title
Company
Street Address
City, State, Zip Code

Dear _____:

I am relocating from Detroit to Pittsburgh and am interested in making a connection as a manager of management services and computer systems, either in real-time process control or in a business system applications.

OR

I am considering relocating to Pittsburgh. With your knowledge of the area, you might be able to provide me with some answers to questions that I have.

Since 1985, I have served in the Management Information Department of _____ with responsibilities ranging from Manager or _____ to my most current position as Manager of _____.

I clearly understand that it is unlikely that there is a connection within your company, however, since we are peers at our management level, I would like to visit with you to get some professional advice and direction to what activity there is in Pittsburgh.

I will ask my office to call and arrange a mutually convenient appointment so we can exchange some information. I will be in Pittsburgh from October 1 through 10. Hopefully we will be able to meet at that time.

Sincerely,

John Doe

JD/ac

Note: Letter can be sent to: Executive Director of Chamber of Commerce, key hiring company personnel, civic leaders, directors of organizations like YMCA/YWCA, Lions and Rotary clubs, religious leaders, school and government leaders. Plan a trip to your target area of two to four weeks if possible. Send thank-you letter to responders.

Sample Long Distance Letter

Name & Address

Name   Date
Title
Company
Address
City, State, Zip

Dear _____: PERSONAL AND CONFIDENTIAL

It was very enjoyable talking with you last week. Thank you for taking time out from your busy schedule to allow me to tell you more about my background, present work situation, and future career goals. As I mentioned to you, I am seeking a position in Technical or General Management. I can envision myself as managing a technical group that includes R&D, engineering, tech services, etc. or running a small manufacturing operation involving a number of functions and responsibilities.

I have enclosed a draft of my resume. It is, as you will notice, not finished at this date and I am still contemplating some minor changes. I would like your thoughts on the overall effect of the resume and whether you think it is properly focused for the goals that I have stated.

Knowing that "networking" is my most important job-seeking strategy, I would also appreciate it if you could recommend any individuals that I should talk to for the purpose of increasing my exposure. These individuals do not have to be involved in the _____ industry or related businesses.

I have also enclosed an initial list of target companies in the _____ area that I am currently considering. I have just begun to assemble the list and it is still in the refining stages. You will notice that there are some "non-_____" related companies listed. Perhaps you know of some individuals in these companies that you could also recommend for furthering my "networking" campaign. I am also interested in any additional companies that you might suggest.

I will give you a call within the week to get your comments. Thank you again for the interest you have shown in helping me with my career plans.

Sincerely,

John Doe

JD/ab

412/ _____ (Business)
412/ _____ (Residence)
Enclosures (2)

Sample Sales/Market/Contact/Letter Resume/Bullet Letter (Long Distance)

USE CURIOSITY;
ATTENTION GETTER

I made a $300 million business, with a long and nearly perfect record for losing money, profitable the first year. Over the next four years, profits were increased at a rate over 100% per year.

Your company may need someone with the experience and results orientation I have gained as a Corporate V.P. and Division COO of a top performing $3 billion consumer food company. I have, for example:

ACCOMPLISHMENTS
IN QUANTITATIVE
TERMS (BASED ON
NUMBERS)

• Managed capital and inventory programs to maintain gross assets at a constant level over the last four years. R.O.I. improved over 20%.

• Initiated marketing strategies which resulted in sales and share increases for two $80 million brands dominated by competitors with over 70% shares. Marketing spending rates were maintained.

CREATING
INTEREST—
RELATING TO
THEIR NEEDS

• Set priorities and directed R&D, engineering and purchasing plans. Improved product quality while reducing variable costs over 5.0% on sales.

• Reduced employment from 2500 to 2000 people. Reduced fixed overhead by over 2% on sales.

• Constructed a new plant to vertically integrate one operation. Consolidated two operations into one plant. Result produced a lower investment base and $10 million additional profit.

• Added one new size to an existing line which is now the company's largest profit maker and the industry's largest volume item.

EDUCATION—
CREDIBILITY

I have an MBA from the Graduate School of Business, Indiana University. My Bachelor of Arts Degree, with honors, is from University of Maine.

MEETING
ACTION
STATEMENT

I would be glad to discuss the details of my experience with you in a personal interview. You can contact me at the above address or by calling 412/ _____ or 412/ _____.

Very truly yours,

John Doe

JD/ab

Sample Introductory Letter Using Mutual Friend

Personal Address

Title   Date
Company
City, State, Zip

Dear _____ :   PERSONAL AND CONFIDENTIAL

ATTENTION GRABBER   I have been referred to you by Cas Welch. He felt that the knowledge and insight gained through your career and experiences would be very helpful to me. As I am at a critical point in my professional career, he also thought that you might be willing to talk with me to share your advice and suggestions in regard to my career goals and assistance in gaining market exposure.

BRIDGE   To avoid any possible awkwardness, the purpose of this discussion is not to ask for a job. However, Cas felt you could be of great help to me in gaining market exposure and perhaps offering an idea or two for new directions in which I might target my career program. (Note below) My professional background, experiences and areas of activities include:

INTEREST BUILDER

• Eighteen years of experience in technology management with proven demonstrated skills for leadership, management and coordination of multi-discipline projects, problem identification and solution, facility and strategic planning, and written and oral communication.

• Coordinated corporate facility planning activity and developed a $1.2 billion 5-year capital and major maintenance plan.

• Implemented an on-line computer process control system that resulted in an $8 million annual operating savings through improved product uniformity and productivity.

• Directed corporate-wide quality study that resulted in successful requalification of products in three critical markets and impacted $350 million in annual sales.

INITIATIVE/ CONTROL   I will appreciate your suggestions for broadening my exposure and will call your office within the week to arrange an appointment at your convenience. Thank you.

Sincerely,

John Doe
412/ _____ (Business)
412/ _____ (Residence)

As an aside, you would be getting reactions to: your overall campaign objective, your campaign plan, your presentation, and the target areas that you are concentrating on.

Sample Letter Requesting Advice By Phone

Letterhead

Date

Name
Title
Company
Address
City, State, Zip

Dear _____: PERSONAL AND CONFIDENTIAL
    I was referred to you by _____ of _____ in _____.
    I am a licensed physician, currently practicing _____. No longer interested in the _____ section of Medicine, I would welcome other opportunities where I could utilize my Medical degree, such as work in evaluation and/or review.
    My educational background includes a Bachelor of Arts Degree from Tufts University, post graduate course work in Biology and a Doctor of Medicine degree.
    Having completed residency training in _____ and _____, I also have training in _____ and _____.
    Since completing residency training, I have practiced _____ in three hospitals and two out-patient settings.
    I have enclosed my resume for your review.
    I will appreciate your suggestions and will call you in approximately one week. Thank you.

Sincerely,

Jane Doe

412/ _____ (Business)
412/ _____ (Residence

Enclosure - Resume

Sample Third-Party Referral Letter—On Disk with Variety of Responses

Name   Date
Title
Address
City, State, zip

Dear _____

In a conversation with _____, you were recommended as a person who is knowledgeable and could be of assistance to me. I am planning a career move and need assistance both in the areas of what is happening within the industry and help with certain strategies.

To avoid any misunderstanding, Mr. _____, this letter is not a request for a position with your company. Without key information which you have available, my opportunities will be limited. I am in need of 5-10 minutes of your assistance by telephone.

In an effort to provide you with information about myself, some of my accomplishments have been:

TILE INDUSTRY

- Directed the expansion and negotiated with Italian suppliers for state-of-the-art equipment.
- Developed operating budget, with goals, for performance measurement.
- Managed multiple plant operations.

ADVANCED CERAMIC INDUSTRY

- Experience in beryllia, high alumina, zirconia, yittria/thoria in all methods of forming and machining.
- Directed standard cost and engineered standards systems in both union and non-union environments.
- Strong belief in quality as a means of cost control and cementing customer relationships.

Attached is a resume, also for your review. I will telephone your office on _____, 199__ to arrange for 5-10 minutes of your time. I will appreciate the help of someone of your stature and look forward to talking with you at that time.

Thank you.

Sincerely,

John Doe

412/ _____ (Business)
412/ _____ (Residence)
Enclosure - Resume

Sample Reference—Thank You

Letterhead

Date

Name
Title
Company
Address
City, State, Zip

Dear _____,

Confirming our telephone conversation of yesterday, I am enclosing a copy of my resume. Your assistance in my job campaign is appreciated.

My goal is a steady job where I can utilize my experiences in warehousing. I am familiar with all types of fork lifts including propane, electric, and gasoline engines. If possible, I would like to remain here in Pittsburgh.

Although you had no immediate suggestions, please review my resume and keep my availability in mind. I will contact you in about two weeks to advise you of my progress and check on any ideas you might have. Thanks again.

Sincerely,

John Doe

Enclosure

Sample Contact Letter Through a Referral Source (friend referral letter)

Letterhead

Date

Name
Address
City, State, Zip

Dear _____:

Dave Gallaway is a personal friend of mine and one for whom I have the highest regard. He is currently involved in a job campaign. To avoid any awkwardness, I am not introducing him as a job candidate for you but rather I would like to ask you to spend some time with him and offer whatever advice and direction that you feel is warranted.

I have suggested that Dave contact you to set-up a meeting. Thanks for your help.

Sincerely,

John Doe

Sample Friend Referral Letter

Letterhead

Date

Name
Title
Company
Address
City, State, Zip

Dear _____ :

I met recently with Ron Martin, who is shortly departing _____ Bank in the wake of the reorganization taking place there. I have known and worked with Ron for a number of years while he has been at _____ Bank and before that at _____ Bank. I have the highest regard for his analytic and personal skills. Ron's talents lend themselves to a position in investment banking, lending or corporate finance.

I have taken the liberty of enclosing some background material about Ron. In view of our work together, I had mentioned to Ron that he might benefit from meeting with you and gaining your guidance in his search for a new position.

Very truly yours,

John Doe

JD/an

Enclosure

Sample New Graduate Letter

Letterhead

Date

Name
Title
Company
Address
City, State, Zip

Dear _____:

    I have just graduated from the University of Maine with a Bachelor of Science Degree in mathematics, and I am seeking a position as an actuarial trainee.

    Although I have no working experience except for miscellaneous summer employment while in school, I can offer hard work, enthusiasm and a desire to succeed in return for an opportunity with your firm.

    I am enclosing a resume for your consideration, and would appreciate the opportunity of an interview.

Yours very truly,

Mary Ann Doe

Enclosure - Resume

Sample Graduating Student Letter

Letterhead

Date

Name
Address
City, State, Zip

Dear _____:

As a candidate for the degree of Master of Business Administration with a strong interest in (concentration), I have become aware of the career potential offered MBA graduates by (name of company). For this reason, I would like to meet with you to discuss management opportunities in the field of (career field). This August 199__, I will receive my MBA from the Graduate School of Business, University of _____, and will be available for employment immediately thereafter.

(Company name) is recognized as (descriptive adjective) in (descriptive adjective) and, I believe, provides the potential for that manner of professional development I desire. My background in (career area) coupled with a predisposition for (career interest), I believe, foretells a mutually beneficent fit between your firm's philosophy and my personal goals and objectives. Enclosed please find my resume which will more fully apprise you of my professional qualifications.

I plan to be in the (location) area within the next (time frame) and desire to meet with you during this visit to discuss such opportunities further. As my plans firm up, I shall be in touch with you to propose a mutually agreeable date. In the interim, I may be reached at (phone and area code) and messages may be left at (phone and area code). Thank you very much for your kind attention to this matter.

Sincerely,

John Doe

Enclosure

Sample Letter to Friend Requesting Advice Interview

Letterhead

Date

Name
Title
Company
Address
City, State, Zip

Dear _____:

We have been friends over the past several years. During this time I have always respected your business judgment and technical financial knowledge. It is with this in mind that I could use some advice regarding my current job situation.

Currently, I am investigating the job market in the areas of accounting and finance. My experience and achievements relate to these areas and they are areas in which I am very much interested. Enclosed you will find my resume which describes my background.

Please understand, (person's name), that although I am currently conducting a job search, I do not anticipate you would have or know of any openings. Your suggestions and advice concerning my objectives and presentation would be greatly appreciated.

Realizing you are very busy, I still would like to meet with you. Therefore, I will be calling within the next week to arrange a mutually convenient time.

I am looking forward to our discussion. Thank you.
Cordially,

Mary Doe

Enclosure - Resume

Sample Ex-Serviceman Transferring to Civilian Life

Letterhead

Name   Date
Title
Company
Address
City, State, Zip

Dear _____:

Recently I successfully completed 13 years with the United States Navy as an officer and I am now reentering the civilian sector. Your organization has many stateside operations and you may need a person with my transferable skills.

The following are examples of my effectiveness:

- Organized, trained and led a 12 man Emerging Reclamation Team that earned the squadron favorable comments during Mid- and Post-Cruise Inspections; saved the Navy 120 manhours and aircraft downtime when they were called on during shipboard accident, and significantly added to squadron combat readiness.
- Developed and instructed a series of five one-hour simulator trainers for the squadron's 16 Naval Flight Officers that accomplished more comprehensive training than 30 actual flights, saving the Navy 160,000 hours and maintained 100% combat readiness of the aircrew during a nine-month turnaround period.
- Rescheduled and coordinated a 700 man, 35,000 ton carrier on-load during adverse weather conditions that permitted the carrier to meet its scheduled sailing date and saved the Navy a day's use of 5,000 men and $10 billion in assets.
- Rescheduled and supervised the modification of 16 DC-9 flights to accommodate a change in a ship's docking that enabled 500 men and 30,000 pounds of cargo to get home a day early after a six-month development.
- Supervised and was responsible for 150 men squadron customs program that ended with it being the first of twenty shipboard groups in submitting correct and accurate customs forms and no squadron member having to pay duty or fines.

We should meet to talk about possible opportunities within your firm and for me to expand on my experiences. I will therefore call your office within the week to arrange a mutually convenient time. Thank you.

Sincerely,

Name

Sample Exit Statement

JOHN DOE

John Doe joined XYZ Corp. in August 198__ as a _____. He successfully initiated a _____ and coordinated _____.

Recently, however, XYZ has moved from a decentralized organization to a centralized operation. This involved many changes throughout our company. Because of the downsizing, John recognized that his future career advancements and responsibilities were significantly reduced. Therefore, he has chosen to seek another position with the full agreement and support of this company.

John's talents, loyalty and honesty would be assets to any company hiring him.

March 27, 199__

Note: The above is not to be given to anyone but will serve as a "mental cover letter" for you, if applicable, in your interviews.

✦ ✦ ✦

On the fields of friendly strife are sown the seeds which in other years on other fields will bear the fruits of victory.
— GENERAL DOUGLAS MACARTHUR

13.

Tools of the Trade:
Tune-up Your Campaign

The only way to discover the limits of the possible is to attempt the impossible; the difficult we do right away, the impossible takes a little longer.
— ANONYMOUS

One of the keys to conducting an effective campaign is to have all the necessary tools of the trade together, ideally, with a well-qualified career counselor at your disposal. You'll need to be well-organized, and the following tools will help you to be.

A. Get yourself a *six-ring pocket binder* (for women a "purse binder") with optional alphabetized tabs and lined paper to list all contacts, i.e., National 80-141 (virgin vinyl)—your prospect file. There should be a separate page for each contact with the contact's name, where that contact came from (research, friend, publication, article, trade journal), method of contact, company, address, zip code, title, business (home phone optional) and secretary's name in pencil on one side of the lined paper. I suggest putting the secretary's name in pencil because secretaries sometimes change positions and all you have to do is erase the existing name, and write in the new one.

On the reverse side of the lined contact page, you can put the dates you talked to this person and in a capsule way, what you talked about. At least put enough key ideas to jog your memory. Some clients have even noted spouse's and children's names, whether they have any other information about the contact (annual report, 10K, etc.), and what the status of their contact is.

Franklin International Institute, Inc., has forms they sell which will be of interest: Prospect File (#4056) and (#4021); Meeting Planner (#4022).

B. Keep a daily *to do list (A–Must Do, C–Nice To Do and B–In Between) pad* to list daily priorities, appointments, together with a *monthly activity calendar* to schedule on (Fig. 13.1). Review at the end of each day what you've accomplished and revise for the next day. Set up a "battle slogan" for yourself like Abraham Lincoln's, "It is better to try and fail than fail to try." Items such as phone calls, appointments, correspondence and personal activities can be included.

✦ ✦ ✦

FIGURE 13.1
ABC to do list

Date: _____		ABC	Done
1			
2			
3			
4			
5			
6			
7			
8			
9			
10			

KEY: A = top priority tasks   B = all in between   C = nice to do tasks if I have the time

✦ ✦ ✦

C. *Three-ring binder* ($8\frac{1}{2}$" x 11") with 3" rings to organize and keep most of your campaign materials such as copies of letters sent, ads answered, companies contacted, expense sheets, campaign summary sheets, and research materials.

D. *Telephone answering machine* at home or answering service to handle campaign messages when you are away. Include these costs with campaign expenses. Consider having your message written and recorded professionally, as well as having a cellular car phone to make calls while traveling.

E. *Portfolio or addendum sheets*—additional in-depth personal and professional information to support your resume but only as an optional campaign choice.

F. *3" x 5" or 4" x 6" index file* as an alternative source for keeping information in six-ring binder; use an $8\frac{1}{2}$ "x 11 "plastic business card notebook holder (usually 6 or 8 card slots per page). Always get business cards from everyone you meet.

G. *Typing service or borrowed typewriter.* If you are working with a reputable and reasonable secretarial service, all correspondence should be handled in a professional and proofed way. That takes a lot of pressure away from you and/or spouse (friend).

H. *Copy machine* or access to one, as well as access to a fax machine (use for long distance campaign).

I. *Three-hole* and *two-hole punch* together with a *stapler.*

J. *Research materials* or access to them. Work with a competent reference librarian, i.e., literature, job search books, annual reports, 10K reports, trade journals, magazines, and newspapers. Write down names of organizations that appeal to you. Also, get information about the job market relevant to your job and job objective(s). Note trends from professional trade journals. Order yourself an expandable ("accordion"), 21-pocket letter file (10 "x 12 "), No. 35280 from the Mead Corporation, Dayton, Ohio 45463 or from your nearest office supply store. This file is not only alphabetized but it also has the months of the year. This can be used as a "tickler file" in conjunction with your weekly/monthly calendar as you plan and follow through on your campaign activities. A second file or folder could be used for "inactive" materials.

K. *Market list* of key organizations and some *target lists* of organizations of strong interest from your research. Develop a list of at least 100 organizations you could realistically see yourself working for/fitting in with and then develop a second list of 100.

L. *ABC contact list.* (See chapter 15.) Remember to follow up and follow through with your contacts. Keep an organizational contact sheet (Fig. 13.2).

A friend is one before whom I may think aloud.
— RALPH WALDO EMERSON

✦ ✦ ✦

FIGURE 13.2
Organizational contact sheet

KEY:

Type
N - Network
A - Ad
R/A - Recruiter/Agency

Means
P - Phone
L - Letter
R - Referral

Results
D - Dead
P - Pending
L - Lead
F - Follow-up

Date	Organization	Phone/Fax	Type	Means	Results	Comments

✦ ✦ ✦

*Love is patient, love is kind. It does not envy, it
does not boast, it is not proud. It is not rude, it is
not self-seeking, it is not easily angered, it keeps no
record of wrongs. Love does not delight in evil but
rejoices with the truth. It always protects, always
trusts, always hopes, always perseveres.*

— I CORINTHIANS 13

M. *A daily calendar/day planner system* is a must (Figs. 13.3 and 13.4).
Contact the following for their catalogues:

Daytimers, Inc.
One Day-Timer Plaza
Allentown, Pennsylvania 18195-1551
(215) 395-5884

Franklin International Institute, Inc.
2640 Decker Lake Boulevard
Salt Lake City, Utah 84119
Order: 1-800-654-1776
Customer Service: 1-800-654-1775

Executive Scan Card System
814 W. 3rd Avenue
Department 697A
Columbus, Ohio 43212
1-800-848-2618

✦ ✦ ✦

FIGURE 13.3
Daily calendar/daily planner

✦ ✦ ✦

✦ ✦ ✦

FIGURE 13.4
Daily calendar/daily planner

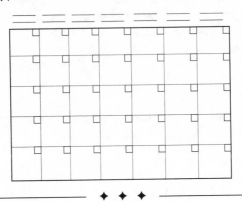

✦ ✦ ✦

N. *An office to work from* if unemployed. Might even be in a church or social service agency.

O. *A portable hand dictaphone or tape recorder* is useful to talk to right after advice interviews, or to record thoughts, etc. while dressing. Later on, when relaxed, you can review key ideas.

P. Use a *gold Cross pen/pencil set* when filling out applications and/or have in your shirt pocket for interview notes if need be. Write to A.T. Cross Company, One Albion Road, Lincoln, Rhode Island 02865-3700, (401) 333-1200. Note: As a companion piece to this set, consider having a *quality attaché case or leather folder* to carry all necessary items including a leather folder (8½ "x 11 "with brass corners) into which you can insert a pad of paper. I call it a presentation kit.

Q. A *portable video camera* that you can at least borrow to videotape any mock presentations that you care to make; consider making a video or computer disk resume on yourself.

R. Purchase a *tape recorder* for you to practice and critique your presentations (telephone presentations, advice interview presentations and mock interviews). The more you practice, the smoother and more confident you'll come across. "Practice does make perfect."

The tape recorder can also be used to play back purchased or borrowed relaxation, stress/coping management and self-confidence/self-imaging tapes. One excellent source for these audio tapes is Effective Learning Systems, Inc., 5221 Edina Industrial Boulevard, Edina, Minnesota 55435, (612) 893-1680.

You can get an excellent "two for one" when you're driving your car and listening to these audio tapes at the same time.

S. Keep a *pad of paper and a pencil beside your bed* for any brainstorms that occur to you while you're lying in bed. It's important to jot them down right away rather than wait until the morning when you've forgotten what they were all about.

T. A *positive mind set*, just taking each day as it comes.

Just For Today

1. Just for today I will be happy. This assumes that what Abraham Lincoln said is true, that "most folks are about as happy as they make up their minds to be." Happiness is from within; it is not a matter of externals.

2. Just for today I will try to adjust myself to what is, and not try to adjust everything to my own desires. I will take my family, my business, and my luck as they come and fit myself to them.

3. Just for today I will take care of my body. I will exercise it, care for it, nourish it, not abuse it nor neglect it, so that it will be a perfect machine for my bidding.

4. Just for today I will try to strengthen my mind. I will learn something useful. I will not be a mental loafer. I will read something that requires effort, thought and concentration.

5. Just for today I will exercise my soul in three ways; I will do somebody a good turn and not get found out. I will do at least two things I don't want to do, as William James suggests, just for exercise.

6. Just for today I will be agreeable. I will look as well as I can, dress as becomingly as possible, talk low, act courteously, be liberal with praise, criticize not at all, nor find fault with anything and not try to regulate nor improve anyone.

7. Just for today I will try to live through this day only, not to tackle my whole life problem at once. I can do things for twelve hours that would appall me if I had to keep them up for a lifetime.

8. Just for today I will have a program. I will write down what I expect to do every hour. I may not follow it exactly, but I will have it. It will eliminate two pests, hurry and indecision.

9. Just for today I will have a quiet half hour all by myself and relax. In this half-hour sometimes I will think of God, so as to get a little more perspective into my life.

10. Just for today I will be unafraid, especially I will not be afraid to be happy, to enjoy what is beautiful, to love, and to believe that those I love, love me.

— ANONYMOUS

14.

Portfolios:
Knock On The Right Doors

*The difference between possible and impossible is
hard work and commitment.*

— Bob Dole

A Companion Piece

A portfolio, according to Webster Dictionary, means "a flat, portable case for loose papers." A portfolio is not for everyone. Some people use colored art work, graphs or charts, and photos to make it visually appealing and professionally packaged.

A portfolio can and frequently does become a "companion piece" to a resume. It's like the one-two combination of a boxer. I advise any client who has taken the time to prepare a portfolio to use it discreetly. You don't leave or show this brochure to everyone. If a client has had an especially good interview and is invited back, it may, if the timing seems right, provide the opportunity to say, "I've taken the time to prepare a portfolio on myself that I believe will give you additional insights into me not only as a person but as a professional as well. I would like to leave this with you, if that's all right with you, to review at your leisure, and I will pick it up when we next meet." Not much of the competition will have taken the time to prepare such a document and people who have them seldom leave them behind. If your portfolio has been well-packaged with a soft, rich-looking cover stock slightly larger than the contents, the pages ($8\frac{1}{2}$ "x 11 ") encased in transparent acetate jackets with a table of contents with tabs for easy access, it will be like sharing a treasured book with a friend. In this case, that book is a treasure of successful things about yourself.

Portfolio Tips

1. The portfolio, like your resume, should not contain everything you have ever done, but should give the viewer a taste of your work, an overview, if you will. Make sure what you include is clear and concise. Keep your portfolio simple and neat. Remember it reflects you, your personality and style.

2. Make sure the look of your portfolio is professional. Spend time putting it together. Use quality white stock and have as much of the contents printed by laser as possible.

3. Try to slant the portfolio to the organization's needs and wants in a creative and innovative way. Show that you have an understanding of its problems.

4. Consider including examples and a variety of successful past projects in greater detail than on your resume.

5. Highlight key words or phrases in your portfolio that you want your reader to focus on and that show that your experience (assets) "fits" their problems.

6. Use a table of contents to ensure the even flow of information.

7. Graphics in black and white or color can be used effectively to illustrate or clarify other things in the portfolio. Pie charts, bar graphs, and project summaries can be nicely displayed. "A picture speaks a 1000 words."

8. A good proposal can contain a cover sheet, table of contents, overviews (one page biographical sketch of self and career), project summaries, addenda, education, graphics, patents, miscellaneous information, organizations, published articles, performance appraisal results, pictures (illustrations), list of references and copies of reference letters.

9. Consider also doing a job campaign portfolio consisting of planning calendars, organization contacts, progress reports, campaign reports and tally sheets as well as negotiation results. It's important to keep your campaign on track and well organized and all information up to date. This kind of portfolio helps you do that.

10. A graduating student, in addition to number 8, can list ideas on why he desires employment with a particular firm based on research, an overview of summer or part-time employment and what was learned from it, what courses, awards and activities he was involved in, letters of recommendation from teachers and department heads.

11. The length of your portfolio can fluctuate depending on the message(s) you want to convey.

12. Portfolios should contain only typed or printed material. Leave handwritten materials out of it.

13. A portfolio is *not* meant to be your scrapbook. If you treat it as such, it will in fact be treated as scrap. Remember, it is a well thought out and carefully orchestrated sales instrument to help you get to where you are going.

Portfolio Page Samples

1. Cover Sheets — Figs. 14.1 and 14.2

2. Table of Contents — Figs. 14.3 and 14.4

3. Self/Personal Summary — Figs. 14.5 and 14.6

4. Career Overview (one-page biographical sketch) — Fig. 14.7

5. Project Summaries — Figs. 14.8–14.12

6. Visual Presentation — Figs. 14.13 and 14.14

7. Charts and Graphs — Figs. 14.15–14.18

8. Miscellaneous Information — Figs. 14.19 and 14.20

9. Education — Fig. 14.21

10. Organizations/Affiliations — Fig. 14.22

11. Diplomas/Certificates — Fig. 14.23

12. References (one sheet) — Fig. 14.24

Note: Actual letters of reference may also be included.

You Shall Be Judged By Love

Do not be influenced by that which men count as valuable, or successful, or as achievement. A person is successful who causes happiness, and a reflection of the Divine in the lives of those he touches. If there is never the building of a talent or the accumulation of money or a recognizable accomplishment of any kind in life, yet that soul provides happiness and fosters growth spiritually in others, bringing pleasure into the life of others and ease in communications, then that one has succeeded at the level of the soul.

There are those on your plane who will make a great mark in history and become known. There are those who will develop talents and abilities recognizable to others and yet not a shred of evidence of that accomplishment will be found in these records of karma and soul growth. For it is not what men recognize as accomplishment that is recorded here or set down as achievement of a soul. But that one who causes the son or daughter, the husband, the wife, the neighbor to have a little more light, a little more pleasure, love, energy, happiness with which to accomplish his day to day living - he has lifted himself and the race a little closer to God.

— ANONYMOUS

FIGURE 14.1
Cover sheet

FOR YOUR CONVENIENCE

DOSSIER

MICHAEL S. ROMAN

123 Main Street	508 / 555-1212
Middleton, Massachusetts 01949	508/554-1212

✦ ✦ ✦

FIGURE 14.2
Cover sheet (alternate approach)

Portfolio

of

ROGER J. MOORE

✦ ✦ ✦

✦ ✦ ✦

FIGURE 14.3
Table of contents

TABLE OF CONTENTS

SECTION ONE . . . . RED TAB
- Self Assessment, Capabilities and Traits
- Resume

SECTION TWO . . . . BLUE TAB
- Computer-Related Experience
- Visual Presentation Major Projects and Products
- Visual Presentation Working Patents and Trademarks

SECTION THREE . . . . YELLOW TAB
- References

SECTION FOUR . . . . GREEN TAB
- Letters of Reference and Acknowledgements

SECTION FIVE . . . . ORANGE TAB
- Miscellaneous Information

✦ ✦ ✦

✦ ✦ ✦

FIGURE 14.4
Table of contents (alternate approach)

TABLE OF CONTENTS

✦ ✦ ✦

✦ ✦ ✦

FIGURE 14.5
Self/personal summary

RE: SELF-ASSESSMENT, CAPABILITIES AND TRAITS

To Whom It May Concern:

As an individual, I strive to be the best at whatever I do. As an experienced executive, I am an honest, creative, hard working, persuasive leader with success-oriented work ethics and attitudes; including a sense of humor. I have deep respect and a high sense of responsibility toward my employees-associates-peers-family and friends.

My manufacturing and management experience covers 26 years, of which 17 years are in executive management as Partner, Vice President, President and Chief Executive Officer. My background encompasses all facets of business operations for a manufacturing company, including demonstrated "entrepreneurial expertise," full responsibility for "profit and loss," financing, marketing, plant design and development.

I have successfully developed two divisions and a new corporation, including the organization and implementation of their sales, marketing, engineering and purchasing functions. In addition, I developed numerous products, patents and trademarks, wrote promotional literature and designed brochures.

Included in my personal qualifications is my ability to analyze and solve problems relating to human resources or material resources with leadership "finesse" and negotiation; the ability to plan and effectively execute those plans with a deep personal "commitment to excellence."

Sincerely,

_____

Name

✦ ✦ ✦

✦ ✦ ✦

FIGURE 14.6
Self/personal summary

PERSONAL SUMMARY

- A businessman with twenty-three years of experience of steadily increasing responsibility, a high degree of computer literacy, a proven track record of sales accomplishments and ten years of senior-level positions in sales and operations, including eight years of full P&L responsibility.

- Comfortably at ease with computers, software and the use of computers to solve business problems. Fifteen years of increasingly responsible experience in programming, systems analysis, field sales, customer support and management for computer manufacturers and computer service companies.

- A demonstrated propensity to "coach" and be a mentor to people associated with him. Committed to training and development of co-workers. A suitable replacement has been groomed and moved into place for each responsible position vacated.

- Described by others as: "[He] has a business-like sense of responsibility"; ". . . impressed with his performance and, in particular, his problem solving expertise"; "[Jack has] the ability to recognize a problem and the need to resolve it"; "Skeptical, critical, independent, determined, often stubborn."; ". . . a fine power to organize a job and carry it through with or without help."

- Has a track record of success in turning around difficult and slow-moving situations. A leader who is able to reconcile differences between groups of people and get them working together on the common problem.

- Driven by a sense of urgency to get started, to get problems solved, to move toward a worth-while purpose.

- Highly adaptable, with ". . . a willingness to be involved in risky or adventuresome undertakings." Has a ". . . readiness to make changes." Capable of adjusting quickly to new or shifting situations.

- Paid 100% of his own expenses for college—both undergraduate and graduate.

✦ ✦ ✦

✦ ✦ ✦

FIGURE 14.7
Career overview

CAREER OVERVIEW

Upon graduation from VPI in 1967, accepted a position as Systems Engineer with Western Technologies in Pittsburgh, PA. Responsibilities were applications programming, systems analysis, and computer training for engineers. While at Wesern Technologies, attended University of Pittsburgh Graduate School of Business, evenings and weekends. Master of Business Administration Degree in 1970.

In 1973, joined General Technologies Information Services Company as Technical Representative. This firm sold timesharing and consulting services. Programming, training, trouble-shooting and customer service responsibilities. Secured promotion to Senior Sales Representative with direct field sales responsibility. Achieved top G.T. award for field sales people. Promoted to Technical Manager with responsibility for three technical support offices.

Left corporate world to join consulting service as V.P. of Sales. Sales, client training, equipment selection, installation and programming of PCs. Landed account with large international retailer in less than three months.

Returned to the corporate world in 1981 with Information General Corporation as Manager, Systems Engineering. IG is a manufacturer of minicomputers and PCs for commercial and industrial markets. Customer service, training, trouble-shooting and sales presentations for three offices in four states, based in Pittsburgh.

From Data General, was recruited to develop marketing and sales for Footwear Central in Chicago, as Vice President of Sales and Marketing. Responsible for sales and operations for 7 athletic shoe stores. Annual volume growth of over 20%. Asked to run operation as President after one year, with complete P&L responsibility. In less than three years, chain grew from 7 stores to 10 stores, sales were up 58% and margins had improved 10%.

Chicago stores were sold in 1985. Moved back to Pittsburgh to Yankee Supply Company, as President. Challenge was to shake up company but not affect profits. As products sold were commodities, business and marketing plan was to compete on service, not price. Instituted regular deliveries, formalized customer financing, developed computerized inventory stocking programs. Introduced new lines with better margins.

In less than five years: sales grew 250% (with industry norms at 5-10% per year), margins increased 21%, credit policies were developed reducing uncollectibles and receivables (a chronic problem for distributors) and our employees say Yankee is a much more "fun" place to work.

✦ ✦ ✦

✦ ✦ ✦

FIGURE 14.8
Project summary

GREEN HILLS AUTO PARTS — ABC AUTO PARTS

PROJECT SUMMARIES

Marketing Analysis

Organized, planned and implemented a marketing study of North suburban Pittsburgh to determine feasibility of a new auto parts jobbing store. Analyzed competition, assessed market size, interviewed prospective customers, investigated possible store locations. Convinced LOBA of desirability of store placement in this market and opened new store, growing business to $435,000 annually in four years.

Sales/Customer Service

Reviewed market conditions and competitive business practices. Developed major account acquisition program based on providing superior customer service and delivery. Within a three year period, doubled sales gaining consistent high volume business from mass merchandiser accounts such as Goodway Muffler, A-1 Tire, Rockway, J.R. Dollar's, Warden Montclair's, and J-Shop.

Store Layout and Design

After selecting new store location for Green Hills Auto Parts, created, designed and implemented an action plan for layout of retail lobby display, efficient placement of warehouse inventory stocking, offices and machine shop area.

Computer Conversion

Outlined, reviewed and assessed current inventory control and accounts receivable systems being performed manually. Researched and reviewed available computer systems designed specifically for the automotive aftermarket. After deciding upon a _____ System, planned and implemented installation bringing system to full automation within four months resulting in more effective accounts receivable and credit control, increased inventory turns from 1.7 to 2.9. With far less time spent controlling this area manually, more effective use of time to sales activities was realized.

Market Demand Analysis

Monitored and analyzed automotive aftermarket trends recognizing increased market demand for import parts. Expanded inventory coverage for import automobiles which was instrumental in acquiring the $60,000 per year Goodway account, and provided incremental sales volume and market share before the competition could react.

✦ ✦ ✦

✦ ✦ ✦

FIGURE 14.9
Project summary

ENTERTAINMENT PROJECTS

YEARS	PROJECT/ LOCATION	ACTION	OBJECTIVE RELATED RESULT
1986–1987	Played guitar part-time in blues/rock band (location)	Practiced with 4 piece band a minimum of 10 hours weekly; played at house parties; played with other local musicians. Transported and set-up equipment for 15 performances.	Experienced the work of a musical performer and stage technician.
1985–1986	Music Chairman of Sigma Chi (location)	Responsible for maintenance and operation of the fraternity's audio system. Produced over 50 hours of recorded music to be played at over 100 fraternity social functions.	Cultivated a sensitivity for what people would like to hear at the various types of social functions (parties, formals, mixers, etc.)
1983–1984		Sponsored, via the fraternity, live entertainment at social functions; participated in acquiring local bands to perform.	Experienced small scale production of shows. Experienced the risks and benefits of sponsoring different types of acts.
1978–1982	Studied guitar at Oliver Music Studios (location)	Attended $\frac{1}{2}$ hour lessons and practiced a minimum of 7 hours weekly.	Acquired considerable knowledge of different types of music.

✦ ✦ ✦

✦ ✦ ✦

FIGURE 14.10
Project summary

PARTIAL LIST OF PROJECTS

PROJECT	CUSTOMER	SCOPE OF WORK
Midtown Power & Light Co. Port City Nuclear Generating Station Port City, TX	Smith & Adams	Fabricate and erect containment and fuel pool liners.
General Tech Manuf. Plant Expansion College City, PA	Edward Powers Corp.	Fabricate and erect structural steel and metal deck.
NYC Transit Authority Subway Rehabilitation Brooklyn, NY	Abbey Structural Enterprises, Inc.	Fabricate replacement columns and brackets.
NYSDOT, Coney Island Viaduct Rehabilitation New York, NY	Abbey Structural Enterprises, Inc.	Fabricate steel for $\frac{1}{2}$ mile repair and widening.
Ithaca Metal Blasting Co. Plant Expansion Ithaca, NY	Ithaca Metal Blasting Co.	Fabricate and erect steel, roofing, and siding.
Battery Park City Commercial Center New York, NY	F.M. Powell, Inc.	Fabricate heavy beams and columns.
527 Madison Ave. Hi-Rise Office Building New York, NY	JBJ Construction, Inc.	Fabricate metal roof and floor deck.
Mt. Sinai Hospital Expansion New York, NY	Colfax Construction Co.	Fabricate metal roof and floor deck.

✦ ✦ ✦

✦ ✦ ✦

FIGURE 14.11
Dealer projects

1985–1987
Set up procedure for dealer financial statement analysis and 5 year planning
Originally 7 Northeastern states, then national
Implemented system for monthly dealer statement analysis and 5 year plans.
Dealer financial knowledge, profits and sales increased. Dealer statement submission increased from 15% to 90%. 70% of dealers started 1, 3 or 5 year plans.

1987–1989
Provide operational audits of dealers
New England and Middle Atlantic states
Designed and initiated program for dealer departmental operation audits and reviews.
Improved dealer performance in all departments. Dealers able to cope with down turns more effectively.

1989–1990
Refranchise and recontract dealers
New England and Middle Atlantic states
Insure compliance with company policies, objectives and programs. Negotiated contract renewals.
Refranchised - dealer body. Reduced dealers from 124 to 87. Stronger more profitable operations.

1990–1992
Set up Regional Dealer Development Dept. Sign dealers of major open points
17 Northeastern states
Successfully closed Boston, Pittsburgh and New Jersey - New York Metro Market open points. Established department for dealer development with special emphasis on financially troubled and low performing dealers.
Combined sales increased $24 million. Market share increased 1.5%. Increased sales, profits and market share of regional dealers. Assisted other regions in U.S.

✦ ✦ ✦

FIGURE 14.12
Project summary

MAJOR PROJECTS

Year	Project	Total Cost ($ Million)	Engineering Firm	Major Contractor	Subcontract
1977	Oilway Exim (Belgium)	4.2	Oilway Group (U.K.)	C.S. Smith	P.D. West Co.
1986 1987	Regional Water (U.K.)	1.3	Regional Water Engineering	Janeway & Porter	Oilway Services (U.K.)
1988	Irish Oil	5.6	Western Brake	Western Brake	Patrick Simmons
1989	JD Malaysia (Port Kelang)	2.3	Western Brake	Western Automation	Van Dyke Electrical/ Swag Eng.
1989	Fairweather Oil (U.K.)	30	Western Brake	Fairweather Engineering	G.G.I. (West Germany)
1990	Fields (Sweden)	1.8	Steven Corp.	Galloway Technical	Technomeas. (U.K.)
1990	Real Technogique (France)	1.4	Steven Corp.	Seals Engineering	Western Power Systems
1991	Arpatco (USA)	3.8	Steven Corp.	Stephen Automation	Technomeas. (U.K.)
1992	Desasidena (Spain)	12	Western Automation	Western Site Services	

FIGURE 14.13
Visual presentation

SALES ENGINEER
125 J.D. CUSTOM AIR COMPRESSORS
MARKET: INDUSTRIAL
CUSTOMER: KLD BARGE
1991

[[USE APPROPRIATE PHOTOGRAPHS
OR DRAWINGS FROM SALES LITERATURE]]

- Initiated routine sales call.

- Supervised 2 technicians in making field modifications.

- Discovered application for standard product.

- Specified required modifications to plant I.E. for outdoor service.

- Provided field start-up service and aftermarket follow-up.

- Generated proposal and established selling price.

- Sourced-out special accessories for low temp. service.

- Sold 2 units for $39,618

✦ ✦ ✦

FIGURE 14.14
Visual presentation

MAJOR PROJECTS AND PRODUCTS
Industrial control panels and systems
Dedicated micro-processor control systems
SCR proportional power controllers
Power/temperature regulating systems
Signal conditioners
Toroid assemblies and winding
Infrared pyrometer

[[*USE APPROPRIATE PHOTOGRAPHS
OR DRAWINGS FROM SALES LITERATURE*]]

✦ ✦ ✦

FIGURE 14.15
Charts and graphs

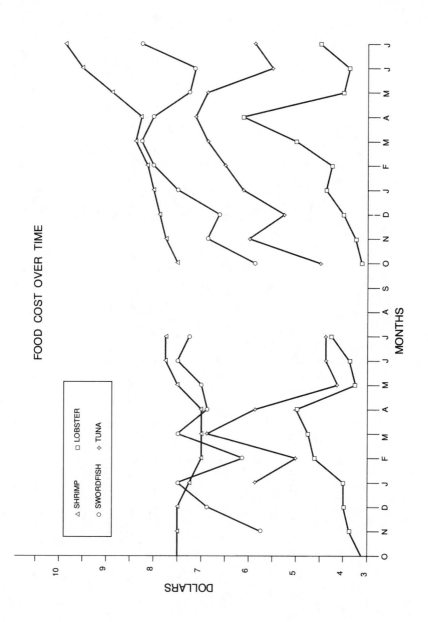

✦ ✦ ✦

FIGURE 14.16
Charts and graphs

	JAN	FEB	MAR	APR	MAY	JUN	JUL	AUG	SEP	OCT	NOV	DEC	YEAR
CumAvg%	7.5	14.2	21.8	29.5	40.1	48.7	56.4	66.9	74.2	84.5	92.3	100	
Predct													40000
#Above	30000	56800	87200	118000	160400	194800	225600	267600	296800	338000	369200	400000	
CumNum	30000	26800	30400	30800	42400	34400	30800	42000	29200	41200	31200	30800	40000
Actual	29850	27448	31112	30587	43841	35492	29524	42400	29659	42031	28774	30911	401629
CumNum	29850	57298	88410	118997	162838	198330	227854	270254	299913	341944	370718	401629	
R		56516	86764	117410	159598	193826	224472	266262	295316	336310	367354	398000	JAN
E			87965	119034	161806	196508	227578	269946	299402	340963	372437	403507	FEB
E				119637	161775	196446	228730	271314	300918	342690	374323	400550	MAR
F					16262	19705	227506	269861	299308	343238	374812	403380	APR
O						197761	229029	271668	301311	340856	372220	406080	MAY
R							229688	272449	302178	344125	375890	407248	JUN
C								270273	299765	341377	372888	403996	JUL
E									299744	341352	372862	403967	AUG
A										341545	373072	404195	SEP
S											373507	404667	OCT
T												401645	NOV
												401629	DEC

✦ ✦ ✦

✦ ✦ ✦

FIGURE 14.17
Charts and graphs

RESTAURANT OPERATING REPORT

	Sat	Sun	Mon	Tue	Wed	Thu	Fri	Total
LUNCH								
Plan covers	100	150	123	124	145	160	148	950
Actual covers	108	134	139	159	158	167	139	1004
Variance	8	-16	16	35	13	7	-9	54
Plan kitchen hours	50	60	55	55	58	63	60	401
Actual kitchen hours	51	59	47	49	64	62	60	392
Variance	1	-1	-8	-6	6	-1	0	-9
Plan dining hours	57	69	60	61	68	75	68	458
Actual dining hours	60	54	55	51	60	80	67	427
Variance	3	-15	-5	-10	-8	5	-1	-31
Total lunch hours plan	107	129	115	116	126	138	128	859
Total lunch hours actual	111	113	102	100	124	142	127	819
Total variance	4	-16	-13	-16	-2	4	-1	-40
DINNER								
Plan covers	450	300	225	300	340	375	500	2490
Actual covers	490	338	246	289	337	357	520	2577
Variance	40	38	21	-11	-3	-18	20	87
Plan kitchen hours	107	75	65	70	82	88	115	610
Actual kitchen hours	105	70	90	87	84	90	120	654
Variance	-2	3	25	9	2	2	5	44
Plan dining hours	210	140	109	140	158	170	225	1152
Actual dining hours	197	159	110	136	176	181	213	1172
Variance	-13	19	1	-4	18	11	-12	20
Total dinner hours plan	317	215	174	218	240	258	340	1762
Total dinner hrs actual	302	237	200	223	260	271	333	1826

✦ ✦ ✦

FIGURE 14.18
Charts and graphs

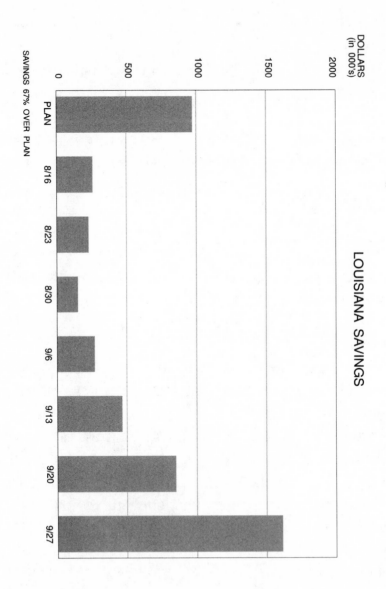

+ + +

FIGURE 14.19
Miscellaneous information

MISCELLANEOUS INFORMATION

Samples of continuing education, seminars, and training:

CDP certification, 1971 (a national program for certification of professionals in the data processing industry; covers hardware/software, systems analysis, programming and general business).

Seminars and continuing education

General Technologies Company Management Seminars:
  Supervisory Skills
  "Coaching" Management
  Sales Management

Time Management

Docupro Corporation Selling Skills.

Honeywell 6000 Mainframes and Operating Systems

IBM 360 and 370, JCL Operating Systems, Executive

Data General Minicomputers, PC's, Operating Systems

Allegheny Community College
  COBOL
  Musicology

The Language Center - German language refresher

University of Pittsburgh Seminars:
  Finance for Non-Financial Managers
  Management Techniques
  Effective Warehousing

Member

National Electrical Sign Association (national trade group)
  Tri-State Sign Association (Founding Member, local trade group)
  Southern States Sign Association (regional trade group)

Head Coach, Shady Side Academy Soccer Team (Junior School). Our team was undefeated for the past three years of play (Fox Chapel League "83s").

+ + +

✦ ✦ ✦

FIGURE 14.20
Miscellaneous information

COMPUTER-RELATED EXPERIENCE

* OPERATING SYSTEMS: CP/M, MSDOS

* MICROCOMPUTERS: Z80, 8080, 8086

* PC'S and PLC'S: IBM AT, IBM XT, KAPRO PC,
OSBORNE PC; General Electric
Series 3 and 6, Allen-Bradley, Texas
Instrument.

* LANGUAGES: CBASIC, Microsoft BASIC,
Assembly-Language.

* SOFTWARE: WordStar, Word Plus, SuperCalc,
Mailmerge, Business Master Plus-
Accounting and Payroll, PeachTree-
Accounting-Payroll-Inventory.

* OTHER: Also have experience of software
for Assembly-Language process
control applications, (CAD)
Computer Aided Design and other
Graphics.

✦ ✦ ✦

◆ ◆ ◆

FIGURE 14.21
Education

EDUCATION

Business Administration/Engineering Program (2 years)
University of Pittsburgh, Pittsburgh, Pennsylvania

Electrical Engineering Program (1,600 hours)
Air Force Training Command
Lowry Air Force Base
Denver, Colorado

Chemistry/Math Program (2 years)
St. Vincent College, Latrobe, Pennsylvania

Extensive on-the-job training during 29 year period.

Corporate Seminars in Production Engineering,
Manufacturing, Management Safety and Glass to Metal Seals Technologies

PMA Seminars in Hazardous Materials in Work Place
Storing and Transporting Hazardous Waste
Reporting and Maintaining Records for Hazardous Waste

Smith & Tragert Seminars in Finance and Accounting

TransContinent Seminars in Corporate Bonding and Securing Lines of Credit

IAS Seminars in Patent Law

IAS Seminars in Corporate Law

IAS Seminars in Process Control

Western Technologies Seminars in Magnetic Amplifiers

Western Technologies Seminars in High Voltage Discharge

General Technologies Seminars in Silicon Controlled Rectifiers

General Technologies Seminars in Engineering with High Voltage Rectifiers

General Technologies Seminars in I^2t Fusing of Semiconductors

John Hopkins Seminars in High Frequency Pulsed Radiation

◆ ◆ ◆

✦ ✦ ✦

FIGURE 14.22
Organizations and affiliations

ORGANIZATIONS AND AFFILIATIONS

Instrument Society of America

Junior Chamber of Commerce

Thornhill RIDC Association

Boy Scouts of America

Save the Whales Association

Pennsylvania Manufacturing Association

Benevolent and Protective Order of Elks

✦ ✦ ✦

✦ ✦ ✦

FIGURE 14.23
Diplomas and certificates

WESTERN TECHNOLOGIES ELECTRIC
CORPORATION CERTIFICATE

Western Technologies Corporation

This certifies that **ROBERT MOORE**
has attended

ADVANCED SUPERVISOR'S TRAINING PROGRAM

provided for Western Technologies personnel

This certificate is awarded and attested
this day May 4, 1976

[signature]

Industrial Relations Manager

[signature]

Division Regional Headquarters Executive

✦ ✦ ✦

✦ ✦ ✦

FIGURE 14.27
References

REFERENCES

Mr. Sanford Addington, Esq.
Addington, Frank and Steiner
2320 Grant Building
San Francisco, CA 01234
(415) 555-1212

Mr. Robert N. Powers
Diamond Way Supply Company
3524 Bell Street
Pittsburgh, PA 43210
(412) 555-1212

Mr. Mark Houghton, Esq.
Bennett and Grigsby
2900 DDY Tower
625 Masonic Avenue
Pittsburgh, PA 01234
(412) 555-1212

Mr. Alan Clemson, President
Clemson Group
200 Wellington Road
Belle Vernon, PA 54321
(412) 555-1212

Mr. John White, President
The Patriot's Inn
Old South Road
South Egremont, MA 12345
(413) 555-1212

✦ ✦ ✦

15.

Contacts: Networking
Constructive Involvement Today
(An Ongoing Process)

You will meet Me often as you work—
In your companions who share your risks . . .
In your friends who believe in you enough to lend their own dreams
   their own hands
   their own hearts
   to your building . . .
In the people who will find your doorway,
Stay a while,
And walk away knowing they, too, can find a dream.
                                          — CHARLES PEGUY

Networking:
Always Has Been and Always Will Be The Main Way to Campaign

Job search studies for almost the last twenty years indicate that as many as 60 to 86 percent of people get their jobs by networking (prospecting) or through personal contacts. Mostly the low-paying jobs are advertised, whereas the better jobs are neither advertised nor ever listed. Because of these studies, we know that to have your best chance at a successful job campaign in this day and age, you are going to have to learn how to network, as it doesn't come naturally. It's a necessary part of any career change or campaign. The name of the employment game today, as it has been for a long time, is contacts, contacts, and more contacts. It's never ending and should be for giving as well as getting. It's not what you know but whom you know, "Networking," according to the March 8, 1991 issue of *The Kiplinger Washington Letter*, "is the way most managers latch on to new jobs." It used to be called the "old-boy network."

Today it is still functioning but has given way to the social process of networking, which lets people know you are available for work, enables you to practice your interviewing skills, and opens doors to possible job leads. It helps you learn skills that you are able to use in the workplace. Every person conducting a job search needs to spin a web of personal contacts of his or her own called a *network*. It can be very supportive (no person is a failure who has friends). If Will Rogers was alive today he would be saying, "I never met a person yet I didn't think was a good contact." People enlarge their webs by using personal contacts and their own initiative and persistence to tap into other people's ready-made webs. This process, if successful, is what is called penetrating the hidden or unpublished job market (Fig. 15.1). These positions are hidden in the sense that they have not been released to formal recruiting sources (i.e., search firms) nor have they been advertised in trade journals or the newspaper. In short, they have not been made public. They include jobs created by unreleased new plans, emerging new problems, impending retirements, and company expansions, as well as the jobs that could be advertised in the near future. Other areas to note are changes in government regulations, emerging markets (acquisitions), reorganizations or restructuring, and reported personnel or labor problems that could forecast job openings. And yes, even taking note of the obituaries!

◆ ◆ ◆

FIGURE 15.1
How new jobs are found

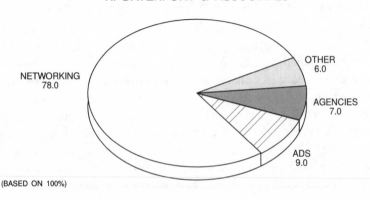

HOW CLIENTS GOT JOBS FROM 1986-1992
R. DAVENPORT & ASSOCIATES

OTHER
6.0

NETWORKING
78.0

AGENCIES
7.0

ADS
9.0

(BASED ON 100%)

◆ ◆ ◆

Reverse Pyramiding

The technique of reverse pyramiding puts a person in touch with as many people as possible who can provide job leads, contacts, ideas, and names of companies who may be hiring; some may have the power to hire. This process may be thought of as reversing the links in a chain or of a business organization chart (Figs. 15.2 and 15.3).

✦ ✦ ✦

FIGURE 15.2
Business organization chart

Research and development
Experimental development
Product development

Raw materials
Machinery
Warehousing
Disposal

Consumer surveys
Sales forecasting
Plant location
Trend analysis

Training
Compensation
Benefits
Employment

Stockholder relations
News releases
Speech writing
House publications

Systems and procedures
Auditing
Budget
Taxes
General accounting
Plant accounting
Cost accounting
Data processing
Capital investment

Methods
Design
Plant layout
Standards

Scheduling
Quality control
Supervision

Routing
Rates
Claims
Transportation

Regional
District
National
Production management

Brochures
Media
Space buying
Time buying
Agency liaison

Contracts
Patents
Copyrights

Grievances
Negotiations (labor)
Contract administration

Environmental affairs
Lobbying
Regulations

Controller

Treasurer

Engineering

Research

Production

Purchasing

Traffic

Sales

Market Research

Advertising

Legal

Human Resources

Labor Relations

Government Relations

Public Relations

Vice President Finance

Vice President Manufacturing

Vice President Marketing

Vice President Administration

Board of Directors

President

✦ ✦ ✦

FIGURE 15.3
Networking (reverse pyramiding)

Assumption: Averaging three leads per contact, you will have 121 leads at the fifth stage.

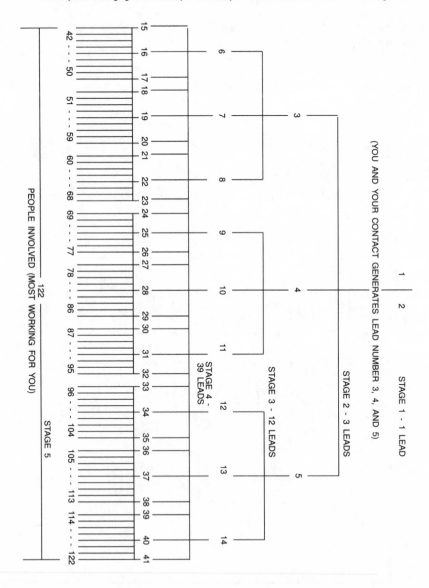

ABC Lists

To "spin your own web," you must develop a subjective A (primary) list, generally about 20 people you know well enough to call on the phone; B (secondary) list, about another 20 people you have met or not met who can refer you to decision makers (the power brokers); and a C (miscellaneous) list, which can consist of referrals or others, i.e., clergy (see Figs. 15.4 and 15.5) of your own contacts using a network circle (Fig. 15.6) of people you know (take out all the business cards you've saved, or use your Rolodex) and people that you don't know within their communities (as large as you make them) that they should know or can make the acquaintance of. Start slowly, with low key meetings only of people you know quite well and branch out from there with your list. The list may be developed by brainstorming with your spouse and/or friends. Salespeople call this prospecting. The contacts are subjectively evaluated by you as those who you think can help you with ideas, advice, support, suggestions and contacts (whether they do or do not remains to be seen) or those who might refer you to key decision makers or community leaders (Fig. 15.7). You never eliminate or prejudge any contacts because you never know whom they know, whom they might refer you to, and who can create a job for you. The more you see, the better your chances. Be persistent, and follow through! Take action! If need be, give yourself daily positive pep talks before making your contacts. Most people who come in contact with others are what I call "power contacts"; that is, they get their power from others they know. They may also be able to put you in touch with target companies, companies that you've identified by SIC code research and that you feel you would like to work for (Fig. 15.8). Most people who land a job at a company of interest through networking usually have used people two, three or four times removed from the original contact. That is why it's important to keep your network going. Another source of desirable organizations might be mailing lists purchased from direct-response marketing firms.

> *You need circles of community to sustain your*
> *continual growth . . . and they must be of your*
> *choosing and your building.*
> — PAULA P. BROWNLEE

> *The best way to get on in the world is to make*
> *people believe it's to their advantage to help you.*
> — JEAN DE LABRUYÉRE

✦ ✦ ✦

FIGURE 15.4
Network circle of acquaintances

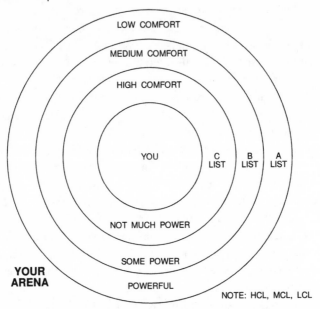

Note: This Network Circle of Acquaintances is generally aimed at low to middle level arenas (situations) for the most part; it would not be applicable to high level position arenas as key decision makers can and do know other key decision-makers. Thus, their lists usually are high comfort.

Key

Note: As you move from the center of your network circle toward the outer circles, the greater the importance of contacts.

High comfort level: People who generally do not have the authority to hire you but do know of companies and/or people that you should be talking to. These are people in your arena that you either know or do business with. Possible "key" (power) contacts limited—*C list.*

Medium comfort level: People who, if they knew you were available, could introduce you to others who can hire you. These are people in your arena that possibly could know of people that you don't know, that maybe you should know. Possible key contacts within the *B circle* that can refer you to the A circle list.

Low comfort level: People who are in a position to hire you. High-level powerful people who generally are the decision makers, position makers, shakers, doers and have powerful contacts—*A list.*

✦ ✦ ✦

FIGURE 15.5
Networking sheet

Date	Name/Address	Company	Position	Telephone Number	Contact	Result

✦ ✦ ✦

FIGURE 15.6
Sample contact sheet format

WEEK ENDING DATE: POSITION:

#	NAME	PHONE/TITLE	DATE	CONTACT	AFFILIATION	COMMENTS

Key: #—ABC contact rating; O—outstanding; P—pending; 1—reg. opportunity; 2—schedule; E—executive recruiter;
T—telephone interview; W—special; X—met; Y—thanks, Z—telephone follow-up; L—letter; N—newspaper;
LM—left message; SR—sent resume

✦ ✦ ✦

FIGURE 15.7
Developing your ABC list

Use 6 ring notebook or 3 "x 5" index cards (one card for each contact). Keep it in your pocket or briefcase. Jot down all names, title, address, phone number, secretary name (on one side of the card). On the reverse side, date(s) and what you talked about. List a few persons in each category.

DEVELOPING YOUR ABC LIST
Everyone Can Provide Leads

COMMUNITY
Toastmasters; country club listings

Retirees; unemployed/outplacement friends

Restaurants—fast food owners; bartenders

Funeral Parlor—(obituaries)

Clubs—membership listings, i.e., Rotary, Lions, Kiwanis

Entrepreneurs; Industrial Development Boards

Newspapers/Magazines—people on the move;

Publishers, editors, stock reports

Community organization officers; city manager

Politicians, lobbyists, congressmen, public officials, senators; driver training; political organizations

Conventions/Trade shows (companies attended)—use business cards

Travel agencies; hotels; florist

Government agencies; TV/radio stations

Car agencies; landscapers; TV repairman

Police/fire chiefs; plumber; electrician

VFW—American Legion; truck drivers

Public Relations/Advertising Personnel

YMCA/YWCA; movers; taxi service; photographers

Event sponsors, i.e., performing arts

Librarians (reference)

40 Plus Club; express companies

PTA; builders; caterers; cooling/heating

Service organizations (officers); school board

Chamber of Commerce/Directories; contractors

Community Fund; decorators; bus drivers

Fund Raisers; dry cleaners

Realtors, lumber, printers, sports stores, scouts

PROFESSIONAL
Past/present Employers; successful people; new hires

Placement office/Registrar/Advisor

Workshops/Seminar participants

Alumnae (directory), alumnae associations

Part-Time Instructors

Teachers/Deans/Profs—Letters of Recommendation; Classmates, Counselors

TROA Chapters; manufacturers

Board of Trustees, Board of Directors

Personnel Officers; receptionists

Development Office—Company Donors

Co-Workers (present/former)

Company recruiters; secretaries;
   interviewers
Workers who worked for you
Purchasing—Company dealt with
Consultants; customer (past/present)
Trade, Business
   Associations—Officers Union
   members/Lenders; trade journal
   editors/writers
Competitors/Sales
   Reps/Vendors/Suppliers
College Presidents
Annual Reports; prospectus; 1OK
   reports
Professional/Trade Association
   Officers
Temporary Agencies; part-time
   contacts
Manufacturer representatives; credit
   bureaus

SPIRITUAL
Interfaith support groups
Priest (pastor)
Rabbi
Minister
Religious organizations
   (officers/members)
Sunday School Teachers, ushers
Choral groups

FINANCIAL
Financial/investment advisor
   (brokers)—stock
   brokers/holders/underwriters
Bank presidents/lawyer/
   managers/leasing agents
CPAs (accountants); stockholders;
   patent attorneys
Insurance representatives/agents/
   brokers/underwriters
Leasing/rental agents
Wealthy people; creditors

FAMILY
Met while Traveling

Friends; acquaintances (social)
Neighbors (past/present)
Mailcarrier
Armed Forces (present/former)
Card groups
Sports groups; exercise clubs
In-laws, brother(s), sister(s)
Relatives (yours/spouse)
Mother (other children contacts)

PERSONAL
Creditors; others looking for jobs
Classmates (past/present) - night
   school
Barber; beautician
Merchants (small business owners:
   funeral parlor, hardware, clothing,
   grocery, lounge, jewelry, furniture,
   shoe)
Yearbooks (past/present);
   checkbooks (who you've written
   checks to)
Holiday/gift lists; telephone book
Volunteer Associations (part-time)
Coaches—Athletic Director (schools
   played)
Local golf pro/country club directory
Appliance repairman; dry cleaner

HEALTH
Doctor; druggist
Dentist; veterinarian
Health club; hospital trustees
Psychologist
Psychiatrist

SOCIAL
Associations—memberships lists;
   officers
Club memberships—Jaycees,
   (monthly meetings); athletic,
   campus, off-campus
Fraternities/Sororities (National
   Directory)
Bowling leagues; social services;
   team mates

OTHER

College/Career fairs; workshop/
seminar meetings

Newspapers/magazine articles about
companies

Various industrial register/directories
(S&P, D&B, Trade, Moodys,)

Individuals who recently changed
positions (People on the Move
Register)

Newspaper Ads—*National Ad
Search/National Business
Employment Weekly*

Consultants; quoted people

Yellow Pages/telephone books

Mailing Lists

Target companies

Outplacement Class Associates

Note: Use alumnae, club, association, country club directories; check with your school placement office to see how they work (if there is a fee, newsletter, job postings—bulletin boards, resource center, etc.).

✦ ✦ ✦

✦ ✦ ✦

FIGURE 15.8
Target companies list

	COMPANY	LOCATION	COMPANY PRODUCTS
1.			
2.			
3.			
4.			
5.			
6.			
7.			
8.			
9.			
10.			
11.			
12.			
13.			

✦ ✦ ✦

How to Set Up and Conduct Advice Interview Meetings

Introductory Letter Setting Up Advice Interviews

These *meetings* (not interviews) have also been referred to by many other names such as guidance, personal, exploratory, focus, reaction, contact, indirect, informational (research), marketing, and referral meetings. They are easily arranged after you have verified the name and address of the person to contact, which you initially do by a friendly, personal, typed, introductory letter, except in the case of a close friend, when you can call, or someone to whom you are referred to by another person (Fig. 15.9).

◆ ◆ ◆

FIGURE 15.9
Introductory letter for setting up advice interviews

Name
Address
Telephone

Date

Name
Company Name
Address
City, State, Zip

Dear Ms. (Last Name),

Mr. (Name), a mutual acquaintance (or use "friend") of ours, suggested that I write to you in regard to my interest in finance. He thought you would be a good person to give me some advice.

I am interested in pursuing a career as a financial analyst. My knowledge of finance is a result of a number of project-oriented courses taken as part of the MBA Program at the University of Pittsburgh. I will be graduating in July of 1993 and would like to begin to explore the possibilities that are available in the area of finance.

I would appreciate the opportunity to meet with you in person. I am certain that your advice and counsel would be most helpful as I begin to gather information and advice for my job search. I will call your office next week to see when you would be available to meet with me.

Sincerely yours,

Jane Doe

◆ ◆ ◆

Note: The meeting should be primarily for advice. Anything else connotates false pretenses on your part. If your contact changes the agenda to a job interview, so be it!

Do not include a resume! After the letter has been sent and several business days have gone by, you can follow up the letter by making a telephone presentation (preferably call, early Tuesday through Thursday) to arrange a timely meeting. If you have difficulty getting by the secretary, tell her politely and in a courteous way that you have been in correspondence with the boss and that he or she is expecting your call. Identify the secretary by name. Make a note of it. Mention not only your name, but your title if you have one. The tone of your voice should be upbeat! If you still can't get through, try calling between 7 and 8 a.m., at noontime, or between 5 and 6 p.m. when the secretary most likely will not be there, especially if you have the number to a direct line. If that also doesn't work, write a second letter and ask the boss if he or she would be kind enough to leave some meeting dates/times for you to select from. As a last resort, if none of these ideas work, you will have to go back and ask your original source to intervene on your behalf.

Telephone Presentation

Assuming that you have no difficulty in reaching the boss, you then make your telephone presentation that you have rehearsed by using a tape recorder, spouse, or friends (Fig. 15.10):

✦ ✦ ✦

FIGURE 15.10
Telephone presentation

(Usually as a followup to an introductory or broadcast letter)

Hello, Mr. _____, or if I might call you _____, my name is _____ and I've been referred to you by a mutual friend, who said that you would be able to give me your help. Do you have a minute? (Yes) Fine. Did you receive my letter (if sent)? Good. Then you know I'm at a pivotal point in my life right now regarding my career in sales and sales management. I'm developing a few strategies and would like your advice and comments. (Note: If the person says that they haven't received it yet, tell them that a letter is in the mail and they should be receiving it shortly.)

_____ said that you were a good person for me to visit. *I'm not going to ask you for a job but would like to get your advice on some of my strategies and your reaction to some of the things that I have prepared.* When would be a good time for us to get together, say for about 30 minutes? How does your calendar look for later this week or early next? Thank you. I really look forward to our get-together!

$\blacklozenge \ \blacklozenge \ \blacklozenge$

Alternative Opening Paragraph Remarks

I am in the process of making a career change and would like twenty to thirty minutes of your time to ask some questions and get some advice.

Due to a recent restructuring (or downsizing) at my past employment, I'm in a career transition. I am exploring some alternatives and would like to meet with you for no more than a half an hour to share some strategies, show you some things and get your reaction to them.

Note: People don't like to be pressured or feel uncomfortable regarding job positions. If there is one within that firm or the person knows of one it will surface during the discussion.

Advice Meeting Presentation (The 10 Steps)

When setting an appointment, set it on the half-hour if possible. It communicates that you are interested in a block of time and most likely have an agenda. You arrive for your advice meeting (interview) no later than ten minutes *before* your scheduled time. A suggested format for this meeting is shown in Fig. 15.11 (don't memorize it). Keep it light, relax and enjoy! Rehearse what you will say!

$\blacklozenge \ \blacklozenge \ \blacklozenge$

FIGURE 15.11
Suggested format for advice meeting presentation

RELAX AND TAKE A FEW MINUTES TO GET TO KNOW ONE ANOTHER. ACT ENTHUSIASTIC (IT'S CONTAGIOUS) AND SMILE!

1. *Establish Rapport (Breaking bread, ice-breaker)*
   "Your office is very nice and your secretary couldn't be nicer. I really appreciate you taking time from your busy schedule to talk to me today; it really means a lot to me!"

RE-EXPLAIN THE PURPOSE OF THE INVERVIEW.

2. *Diffuse Situation - You want no hidden agendas.*
   "I'm not here to ask you for or to see if you know where there is a job, as you may recall, but I do need your advice and counsel." You most definitely want the interviewee to think that the sole object of this exercise is not to ask for a job but more importantly to obtain that person's advice. If the person knows of a job, it will surface during the interview.

3. Mission

I'm determined to become a senior member of a corporate management team with a dynamic organization. I'm an experienced Marketing/Engineering Manager currently functioning as Director of Customer Accounts for XYZ Company. During the past five years I have had full responsibility for reorganizing and operating the engineering, marketing and customer service functions for 250,000 customers representing $400,000,000 in sales. It now appears that opportunities at XYZ Company are limited due to recent changes in the organizational structure. Therefore, I have decided to evaluate other opportunities that would enable me to better realize my goals.

4. Strategies

I'm currently using three strategies that I'd like to share with you:

STATE YOUR COMMITMENT

— I've registered with a few select recruiters.
— I'm answering ads from select trade journals, Sunday papers, and the Tuesday *Wall Street Journal.*
— And the most important method that I'm using is called networking, which is critical in tough job markets. I am meeting good people like you and hoping something will surface along the way. Here is an article from the *Wall Street Journal* that someone shared with me, and as you can see 70% land jobs through personal contacts. This is what I'm focusing on. Are there any other campaign methods/strategies over and above these that you think I should be using?

5. Resume Draft — *"testing the waters with your resume"*

GET THEM INVOLVED

Notes - "I brought a rough draft of my resume with me today and I'd like you to look at it and make comments. Would you mind if I took notes?" Your resume should be a copy, have DRAFT penciled in at the top with a few penciled notes on each page. If the person wants a resume, tell them this is your only copy and that when you finalize it, you will send a copy. Note: Never leave a stack of resumes and let others distribute them for you. You want control.

AFTER RESUME REVIEW

(Roadblocks and obstacles) — "Now that you know me a little better, do you see any roadblocks or obstacles that might prevent me from getting to where I want to be and if so, how can they be minimized or eliminated?" Find solution(s) together.

(If you get a rosy answer or what I call a "glad hand," counter with) "I feel that I don't have the in-depth experience that I may need (or some problem you are willing to share, or what would you do next?). How would you handle this if you were in my shoes?"

6. *People*

TRY AND OBTAIN AT LEAST THREE REFERRALS. IT'S THE QUALITY OF THE CONTACTS THAT COUNT, NOT NECESSARILY THE QUANTITY. DECISION MAKERS ARE THE KEY!

"Knowing that networking is the most important part of my campaign, who do you know that I should be talking to? I need a few people who can help me continue the process of building a contact network and who can add to the information that I already have gained. Who do you feel I should show my resume to?" Or, "who would know the kind of person I need to meet?"

(If put off, use "hard sell" but use only once; show discomfort: move, clear throat)

"I was really counting on you for some names today; time is important! They can be friends, neighbors or maybe even customers of yours. (Make sure that the person is not just trying to think of people who are presently hiring or who are in need of someone with your skills. Do you have a minister, doctor or stockbroker? What about sales reps, vendor distributors and/or suppliers that call on you?" Note: Follow-up all referrals within the week, while they are still hot!)

7. *Companies/Target List*

KEEP YOUR EYE ON THE TIME. DON'T OVEREXTEND YOUR WELCOME.

"Are there any companies/industries that you know about or recently read about that you think I should be contacting?"

(If no suggestions, show target list—you may have more than one list) — our retired senior project manager used to call this "a pump-primer" (a memory jogger).

"This is a partial list of companies that I feel that my background would mesh with. Do you recognize any of these companies or better yet, know any of these people?" (Hopefully you'll develop leads and/or contacts into your targeted organizations!)

8. *Verbal Thank-You*

"I want to thank you for your time, interest and suggestions. You've been a great help and I appreciate it."

9. *Telephone Update*

"Because of all your help I'd like to get back to you with a telephone update in two or three weeks—is that OK? Fine. I'll be talking with you!"

After the meeting, write down as much as you can remember as to what occurred. Some people put this information on file with index cards whereas we have all of our clients complete a report sheet on all meetings.

10. *Written Thank-You Letter*
(Send right away, but certainly no later than three days after the meeting, thanking the person for their time and suggestions.)
Example: See letter section of this book.

———————————— ✦ ✦ ✦ ————————————

Tips to Make Your Advice Interviews Successful

As for these meetings, it is most important to:

- *Be well-groomed and dressed conservatively.*

- *Be well-organized and use a presentation kit.* This kit should be a leather folder, containing a paper tablet, a network article, your resume "draft," a target list of companies, a copy of your list of personal references, business cards, certificates and (if appropriate) your portfolio and/or proposal.

- *Make sure your handshakes are firm and eye contact solid.* Create both a favorable impression and an upbeat (enthusiastic) attitude.

- *Maintain an open posture with your body language when conducting the meeting.*

- *Realize that the Pareto Principle ("the vital few and the trivial many") comes into play while networking.* That is, approximately eighty percent of your quality leads will come from approximately twenty percent of your contacts. Therefore, you will want to concentrate on the 20% that you feel can do you the most good, especially if you have a lot of people to contact and only so many hours to do it.

> *From the standpoint of everyday life . . . there is one thing we do know; that man is here for the sake of other men—above all, for those upon whose smile and well-being our own happiness depends, and also for the countless unknown souls with whose fate we are connected by a bond of sympathy.*
>
> *Many times a day I realize how much my own outer and inner life is built upon the labors of my fellow men, both living and dead, and how earnestly I must exert myself in order to give in return as much as I have received.*
>
> — ALBERT EINSTEIN

- *Don't overstay your visit timewise unless the other person invites you to.* Have this person introduce you to his secretary. Now you have a friend on the inside.

- *Use a good pen for your meeting.*

- *Try and have your meeting in an office setting* rather than at a restaurant, cocktail lounge, or some other informal place where distractions are the order of the day. It should be noted, though, that these settings are ideal places to meet people socially who might work for some of your target companies.

- *Realize that networking can be fun and that the secret of success is to stay active* in continuously developing new contacts and renewing old ones. Enjoy it! The more you devote to building, nurturing, and maintaining relationships, the more will be returned to you. Believe it! Most people can think of reasons not to meet with others, especially if they are shy, introverted types (i.e., "its too tough, won't work for me, makes me feel uncomfortable, can't reach certain people, takes too much time"). True they must work extra hard at practicing their script, but they surely can do it successfully, like many introverted clients I have worked with through the years. It primarily is either assertively networking, or not working. That is the bottom line! Remember: most people want to help and give advice. They like to be treated as experts and give their opinions. Don't feel you are exploiting them. You have to ask to receive! Make a mental note of that.

Believe in the Impossible

If you think you are beaten, you are.
If you think you dare not, you don't.
If you like to win, but you think you can't,
It is almost certain you won't.

If you think you'll lose, you're lost,
For out of the world we find,
Success begins with a fellow's will—
It's all in the state of mind.

If you think you are outclassed, you are,
You've got to think high to rise,
You've got to be sure of yourself before
You can ever win a prize.

Life's battles don't always go
To the stronger or faster man,
But soon or late the man who wins
Is the man WHO THINKS HE CAN!
— E. GUEST

- *Realize that you could be rejected for (someone refuses to see you) or at (not receive any leads) a meeting.* Don't be thin-skinned. Say to yourself that "their loss is someone else's gain" and continue on with your campaign.

Much can be done—"if people care."
— ANONYMOUS

- *Join a local association if you are not already an active member* (Note: use the *Encyclopedia of Associations*). Then plan to attend regular meetings and volunteer for association work, i.e., membership committee, so you can make contacts for possible future meetings. Become active and involved! Get yourself known.
- *Realize that because of your work schedule, you may not be able to conduct advice meetings during the work day.* One might say to a person that "it would be unfair to your employer to interview on their time and you know their time is valuable. That if you made the effort, you could be at his or her office by 6 p.m.; would he or she be able to briefly meet with you at this time?" Or, "I have a problem leaving work early, but I also know you are very busy. If I hurry, I would be there by 5:30 p.m.; I'll only take a few minutes of your time. Is that okay?"

Tell me I'll forget, show me, I may remember, but
involve me and I'll understand.
— CHINESE PROVERB

- *Realize that you now will soon develop a new circle of professional friends and contacts.* Record them all in your six-ring binder. Find out if they know of anyone getting promoted, moving out of town, or being transferred or of someone who will soon be retiring. Use the *first* names of telephone book listings to jog your memory as to whether you know someone who has the same first name.

> *Your wealth is where your friends are.*
> — PLAUTUS (254-184 B.C)

- *As a student, start your junior year developing your network*, i.e., deans, administrators, professors, teachers, fraternity/sorority friends.
- *Know that networking can be a dirty word with a lot of executives* because a lot of job seekers don't approach it correctly. If you are well-prepared and focused and make your contacts through friends or friends of friends, you will most likely be granted an advice interview.

Fig. 15.12 is an example from one of my former clients of how advice meetings can work.

———————— ✦ ✦ ✦ ————————

FIGURE 15.12
A client's successful network plan

- "I contacted the Columbus, Ohio, Purchasing Management Association Secretary and requested a membership directory.

- Broadcast letters were sent to companies of interest. One letter was sent to the Purchasing Manager of Columbus and Southern Ohio Electric Company.

- I followed up each broadcast letter with a telephone call. During my discussion it was suggested that I contact the Vice President of Purchasing at American Electric Power (AEP owns Columbus and Southern Ohio Electric).

- I sent a letter with a resume to him mentioning in the letter that the Purchasing Manager suggested I contact him.

- I telephoned to make sure he received my letter. During our conversation it was suggested a position may be opening up in the spring. I closed our conversation by asking him if I could keep in touch, and he said "okay."

- Two months passed and one Saturday evening I got a call from AEP to arrange the interview.

- As you suggested, before interviewing, I met with the Purchasing Manager, whose office is across the street from AEP.

- During my first interview I was asked if I knew the Purchasing Manager, and I said yes and that I had just talked with him at his office.

- AEP had me back for a second interview. Between the first and second interview, I spoke with the Purchasing Manager by telephone to keep him abreast of my progress. I was interviewed a second time by three other Purchasing Department managers; all three asked if I knew the original Purchasing Manager, and I said yes.

- A job offer was made.

- I accepted the job and telephoned the Purchasing Manager to let him know; he was happy to hear the good news.

- He now wants me to have lunch with him once I am settled.

Courtesy of BILL KRIEBEL

✦ ✦ ✦

Other Network Ideas

1. *Start with low-key (low-stress) contacts and practice advice interviews initially with friends and neighbors first.* Set weekly goals for yourself. Make sure you get out and do it! It will be as good as you make it. Job hunting is not for the weak at heart. Push yourself if you have to. Talk to as many people as you can. Take the initiative!

   A friend is a present you give yourself.
   — ROBERT LOUIS STEVENSON

2. *Never pass up an opportunity to network.* It's a compliment to ask another person for assistance. Talk to everyone. Don't underestimate their value to you. "To one who waits, a moment seems a year." Know that networking does require hard work and practice (use role playing and/or a tape recorder) until your presentation is natural and comfortable. This holds true for everybody.

3. *Follow up every contact* as quickly as you can. Strike while the iron is hot! If a person gives you a name, it's for a reason. Be sure to make the contact and get back to your original source with an update within two to three weeks.

> *To know one's self is wisdom, but to know one's neighbor is genius.*
>
> — MINNA ANTRIM

4. *When you have accepted a new position, send out an announcement/ thank you letter and your new business card* to all who impacted on your job campaign (Fig. 15.13). Still keep your network active and aware! Follow up at least once a year. Keep your contacts fresh! You never know when you'll need them. Use creative ways to keep in touch, i.e., holiday cards, timely articles with notes, pictures, etc. Invite contacts out to lunch or coffee with no strings attached. Make it low key.

-------------------- ✦ ✦ ✦ --------------------

FIGURE 15.13
Sample thank-you letter

1910 Cochran Road
Pittsburgh, PA 15220
May 8, 199__

Mr. Larry Martin
Vice President
XYZ Company
1 Overview Drive
Pittsburgh, PA 15228

Dear Mr. Martin:

Mr. John M. was right when he said you would be helpful in giving me advice and counsel regarding my career.

I appreciated you taking time from your busy schedule to meet with me. Your advice was most helpful and I have incorporated your suggestions in my resume. I will send you a copy when I finalize it.

Again, thanks so much for your assistance. As we agreed, I will give you a telephone update within the next two to three weeks as to how I made out with the following suggestions you gave to me:

(Listings of suggestions, companies, people, etc.)

As an aside, you are to be complimented on your choice of secretaries. Mrs. Jones was most cordial and friendly. She made me feel most welcome when I arrived the other day and that was appreciated.

Thanks again.

Sincerely,

Note: You really now have a friend in Mrs. Jones.

✦ ✦ ✦

5. *You may not get in touch with all people on your list. Use the list as a starting point.* Work with and through others! Get them working for you. Separate the weak contacts from the strong! Rate/evaluate them.

6. *Keep your ears open at all times and be an active listener.* Remember: the Lord gave us two ears and only one mouth so we should listen more than we talk. (Every person is the architect of his own fortune — Chinese proverb.)

7. *Keep a record of all contacts* by using 3" x 5" index cards or a six-ring pocket binder. List the name, position, company address, phone, extension number, individual secretary contacted, how you came by the name, date, referrals/organizations/ideas obtained, followup dates, and action planned.

> *A real friend is one who walks in when the rest of the world walks out.*
> — WALTER WINCHELL

8. *Remember that networking allows a person to be evaluated by the contact even when no job exists.* Sometimes the individual can create a job for himself. Your expectations, talents, personality, and attitude will hopefully shine through. Because you are so well-focused, they may want you for their team.

*The image of myself which I try to create in my own
mind that I may love myself is very different from
the image which I try to create in the minds of
others in order that they may love me.*

— W. H. AUDEN

9. *If an advice interview turns into a job interview, ask what the organization's needs and wants are.* Indicate your fit by mentioning some
past achievement of yours that shows that you can handle the position. Say you are excited about what you've heard so far.

10. *Don't get discouraged or take it personally if a contact doesn't give you
any leads.* Most people will. Remember Proverbs 15:22 and 16:9;
Winston Churchill said, "Never, never, never give up." Keep
pushing! Perseverance is the order of the day!

Don't Be Afraid To Fail

*You've failed many times, although you may not
    remember
You fell down the first time you tried to walk.
You almost drowned the first time you tried to swim,
    didn't you?
Heavy hitters, the ones who hit the most home runs, also
    strike out a lot.
English novelist John Creasey got 753 rejection slips
    before he published 564 books.
Babe Ruth struck out 1,330 times, but he also hit 714
    home runs.
Don't worry about failure.
Worry about the chances you miss when you don't even try.*

— ANONYMOUS

11. Because of seeing different people with different personalities,
all advice interviews are different. If you have difficulty meeting
and talking to people, take a Dale Carnegie course or one similar
to it. If you don't, take one anyway to hone your presentation
skills. Either way, you win!

*The way to gain a good reputation is to endeavor
to be what you desire to appear.*

— SOCRATES

12. *Look for evidence of memberships* displayed in offices that you visit as well as other memorabilia (don't touch). Ask the person you are visiting if there is a member of that organization that they know that you should be talking to. Also observe the following: display areas with company literature (usually in reception area), kinds of people calling on that firm, impressions given by all you meet, type and kinds of equipment, age of staff, cafeteria, geographical location, etc.

13. *Don't be too impatient* or look too hungry when you meet contacts. Ask people for *advice* not *favors*.

> *Make the most of yourself, for that is all there is of you.*
>
> — RALPH WALDO EMERSON

14. *Lead-ins or purpose for a contact can be varied creatively:* desiring information on field, industry or geographical area, presenting a proposal, or doing a class project or research project; networking can be used for long distance campaigns by targeting a geographical area, its industries and people by letter and phone, then arranging visits to those areas.

15. *Have business cards printed up* with your answering service number listed. Don't use your present organization's business cards or stationery; it's too tacky (Fig. 15.14).

16. *Note that networking isn't necessarily being at the right place at the right time* when a job opportunity surfaces. It is more a strategic positioning of yourself so that when something does surface, your name is there. Consider getting personal contacts for introductions to key organization decision makers who are in positions to hire people (people at least two or three levels from the position you are interested in). If you've done your homework, show how you fit that firm. Try and find areas of their needs where you have both knowledge and experience, i.e., operational changes, international expansion, future opportunities, market/product improvements, etc. Gear the conversation to them rather than to you.

17. *People generally will see you* because you stroke their ego by asking for their advice, it can expand their network with fresh ideas, you possibly mentioned a mutual friend and they feel obligated to that friend and this friend may help them one day. I suggest that

✦ ✦ ✦

FIGURE 15.14
Sample business card

JOHN A. DOE

— ✦ —

1 Smith Drive   Res 412/123-4567
McMurray, PA 15317   Bus 412/561-4003

✦ ✦ ✦

you wait until after you have launched your campaign to start and use your contacts, so that you can get your campaign shaped up. And once you have made an appointment, call the day before to confirm it. It might save you from making a needless trip.

> *Don't walk in front of me*
> *I may not follow*
> *Don't walk behind me*
> *I may not lead*
> *Walk beside me*
> *And just be my friend.*
> — ALBERT CARNUS

18. *If you have very few contacts initially,* try writing introductory letters to influential people as a starter; take a part-time job; attend seminars, trade association or supplier meetings; take an active role in community affairs, politics, service organizations; volunteer your services for community activities; attend trade shows and conventions to develop contacts, and use program brochures for organization leads; search for organizations' needs by researching business articles and preparing a proposal that can be

presented to management; brainstorm with friends as to what creative methods they are using to generate both target companies and contacts. Remember organizations are interested in people that bring more value to them than they cost.

19. *Set daily and weekly goals for yourself* in terms of calls and advice meetings that you will make and hold. Results expected equals results achieved. Have faith, and take it step by step.

> *Others judge us by what we have already done.*
> — LONGFELLOW

20. *Once you've landed back on your feet, plan to help other people who are networking.* Paybacks begin once you are employed; pay your dues willingly! Also, maintain an active network even when you are happily employed because you never know when the axman cometh. As one client told me, "I found myself in the past turning down possible job opportunities while I was happily employed and later regretting that I had not at least looked into them" Remember: the only job security today is yourself and your transferable skills. Finding job security within companies, I believe, is a thing of the past!

21. If you've identified a mutual need, prepare a proposal to be hired as a new employee or as a "temporary" consultant. I have had a former client hired as a consultant for three months and then get put on the permanent payroll.

22. *Remember the key rules of networking: never ask for a job, always ask for suggestions.* Don't ask for favors, always ask for advice.

23. *You should always strive to network in person.* You may, if you are conducting a long distance campaign, conduct one over the phone with some minor changes, i.e., send your resume draft by fax ahead of the call.

24. *If you have an important decision to make, ask key people from your network for their opinion.*

25. *When networking, group people that you have to see by geographical location.* It will cause you less stress and strain.

26. *It's a fact that the average adult person knows at least 400–700 people,* the best being those they come in contact with daily. Realize that everyone knows someone who in turn knows someone else!

27. *When unemployed, don't be afraid to contact your creditors about your situation.* Maybe easier financial arrangements can be made and who knows, maybe you can turn it into an advice meeting.

28. *Keep your eyes and ears open for leads.* Stickers on vans and cars, especially school stickers, or travel stickers, give you clues that the people who have them most likely have contacts there.

29. *Know and believe that networking gets people jobs!* The statistics don't lie. Don't be misled by people who say it's outdated because they've been upset by people approaching them who weren't prepared and credible in their total presentation (letter, telephone, actual presentation, and followup).

30. *Remember that networking works and that you are determined to make it work in your campaign.* Keep a positive attitude! Realize that you will meet people who will be indifferent to what you are doing and there will be many no's to referrals (don't take it personally) and tell yourself that these are the hurdles *for you* leading to job campaign success!

Student Networking
A Student Learns What They Experience

If a student experiences warmth,
    they learn that they are welcome.
If they experience friendliness,
    they learn to smile.
If they experience kindness,
    they learn to be kind.
If they experience unhurriedness,
    they learn that they are important.
If they experience thoroughness,
    they learn confidence.
If they experience competence,
    they learn respect.
If they experience frankness,
    they learn trust.
If they experience concern,
    they learn appreciation.
And if they experience all of this,
    they learn that positive attitude is what sells.
— ANONYMOUS

Career Research

If you are a student, you are in a choice position where you can contact people in the name of career research and yet at the same time interview for information. Your introductory letter should use your school's, dean's, or professor's name as a bridge to your meeting. The key to a successful meeting is to be well prepared with a written list of questions that you seek answers to from the following (select those most applicable and incorporate these into your modified advice interview approach): short or long term trends affecting the field; procedures, products, and programs used or being developed; what professional publications in this field you should be reading; names of other people to contact; additional sources for research; what salaries are paid for your skills and degree; what does the interviewee feel is the hardest/easiest part of his or her job; why did you choose this field; what types of people do you deal with; what personal qualities are necessary to succeed at this type of work; how would a person get an entry-level position in this field; what are the fields and positions that have the most opportunities for advancement; are there any spinoffs or developing areas I need to know about; what skills and degrees are most important to have today; are there magazines, trade journals, and books that I could begin reading; is there a local professional group that meets regularly that offers student memberships; what about my competition (do others seeking similar positions possess similar backgrounds); what are the biggest obstacles I could possibly face in this field; what kind of position could a college graduate or a person with my educational background or training anticipate when entering this field; in what ways is this field changing (trends); can I keep in touch with you regularly; who are the recognized leaders in this field; if you were in my shoes, how would you prepare for an interview or job search in this field; what should I stress from my resume; what kinds of problems and challenges do you face; hints on how to break into the organization or field; if you could give only one piece of advice to a young person seeking a career such as yours, what advice would that be; if you did not know me and had just seen my resume, would you endorse me for an interview; does your company invest in the training and development of its employees; can I present myself better, etc.

Note: Read published information for possible business contacts, as exemplified in Fig. 15.15.

✦ ✦ ✦

FIGURE 15.15
Seeking possible business contacts

_____ Rittelmann Associates recently named seven employees in the firm to the position of associate. New associates employed in the _____ office are: _____, a certified public accountant and director of finance for the firm; _____, AIA; and _____, AIA, both project managers/ architects. Other new associates are _____ and _____ in the _____ office, and _____ in the _____ office.

_____ Architects announced the appointment of three new professional staff members. Joining the firm are _____, _____, and _____. _____ assumes the responsibilities of project manager for health care commissions; _____ serves as a project manager and equipment planner; and _____ joins the firm with seven years experience in the architectural field. _____ also joined the firm as a construction coordinator.

The _____ Group Inc. has added three certified financial planners to its consulting and planning staff: _____, CFP; _____, CFP; and _____, CFP. In addition, _____ has joined the company as database coordinator.

_____ & Co. promoted _____ and _____ to partners in the firm. _____ concentrates in individual, partnership and corporate taxes, with a special focus on the construction industry and manufacturing companies. _____ concentrates in individual, corporate and partnership taxation, with a special focus in the construction industry and post-secondary educational institutions.

_____ Associates added _____ as manager of accounting and auditing services. _____ will assume overall responsibilities of the public accounting firm's accounting and auditing practice. He has worked with emerging and growth-oriented companies, including start-up and high-technology companies throughout the area. _____ formerly was employed as a manager in the emerging business services group of _____.

✦ ✦ ✦

It is love that asks,
that seeks,
that knocks,
that finds,
and that is faithful
to what it finds.

— St. Augustine

Working with Friends

Ask yourself the question, would your friend(s) come to you if they were in a similar situation to yours? Would you be disappointed after a period of time to learn that a friend in need hadn't turned to you for help? If your answers to these questions are clearly yes, don't hesitate in contacting your friend(s).

Your initial contact to all friends (in-town and out-of-town) should be a personal one by phone which conveys a sense of urgency. Your followup to this call could be a letter similar to Fig. 15.16:

✦ ✦ ✦

FIGURE 15.16
Long distance letter to a friend

Dear _____:

It was great talking to you yesterday. I enjoyed catching up on what's been happening in your career.

As I mentioned to you, I am conducting an active job search seeking a position within the industry. As we discussed, I am enclosing my resume to update you on how my career has been doing. I'm also enclosing a list of several companies I could easily see myself working for.

Obviously, it would be terrific if there were something appropriate within your own organization. I realize, however, that this may not be the right time to inquire about opportunities in your company.

As such, I hope you will also do me the favor of thinking about your friends in other organizations with whom you have regular contact. Perhaps some of them are in the list of companies I have enclosed, or might have business connections with those companies or similar concerns. I will plan to give you a call to discuss any person and/or company that you feel I should be contacting. An introduction from you would mean a lot to me.

Thanks for all your support and for any names you may come up with. I look forward to talking to you within the next week.

Sincerely,
(Your Name)

Enclosure

✦ ✦ ✦

When working with friends or friends of friends, note the following:

1. *Don't ask friends to conduct a job search for you.* Ask them for contacts that you can contact. Tell them you will do the contacting. That enables you to maintain control (Fig. 15.17).

✦ ✦ ✦

FIGURE 15.17
Ask your friends for contacts

Dear Joe:

It was great to talk to you yesterday after all this time. Glad to hear things are going so well for you.

To confirm our conversation, I'm doing a full-fledged job search right now, and I've been advised that the best way to get a job in today's market is by networking through my friends and associates.

In this regard, I'm enclosing my resume to bring you up to date on my career, plus a list of the 150 companies I'd most like to join. I hope you'll look it over to see if you know anyone in any of these companies, or someone who might know anyone in these companies.

As a matter of fact, even if you don't know anyone associated with these companies, if you do know someone in a similar company, I'd sure like to get his or her name . . . and an introduction . . . from you!

Joe, per our conversation, I'm looking forward to talking with you again at 6:00 p.m. on Thursday evening, the 8th. I promise I won't take up more than a few minutes of your time, but hope that we can think up some names for me to contact by then. It would sure speed my job search along.

Thanks in advance for thinking about my request. I sure do appreciate it!

Sincerely,

✦ ✦ ✦

Note: Send your resume only to close friends, as it will appear to others that you are too anxious to get a job.

> *And in the sweetness of friendship let*
> *there be laughter, and sharing of pleasure.*
> *For in the dew of little things the heart*
> *finds its morning and is refreshed.*
> — KAHLIL GIBRAN

2. *Remember you are asking friends only for names—not a job.* No one lives as a hermit and everyone has neighbors, customers, friends, business associates, sales representatives, vendors or merchants they do business with. Try and obtain a wide sampling of ideas from a variety of people. Cover the bases.

> *A friend is one to whom one may pour out all the contents of one's heart, chaff and grain together knowing what the gentlest of hands will take and sift it, keep what is worth keeping and with a breath of kindness blow the rest away.*
>
> — ARABIAN PROVERB

Questions to Ask Recent Alumni (for graduating seniors)

1. What is your current functional area of responsibility?

2. What has your career path been up until now and where do you anticipate it going in the future? Are there spin-offs or developing areas that I should know about? Trends? What's new? What is needed or wanted in your field?

3. How is your degree helping you in your current position? What other careers are similar to yours?

4. Did you have previous work experience in another industry? Has it helped you on your present assignment?

5. What are the basic prerequisites for careers in this industry? What kinds of prior experience are most essential?

6. What type of training did you receive and for what length of time? What skills are most important for this career?

7. What do you like and dislike about your present job, work environment, company and industry?

8. In the position you now hold, what do you do on a typical day?

9. What specific advice would you give to students entering this field? What about internships or volunteer experience?

10. Note alumns using alumnae office. They may be in the same situation as you.

11. Alumni and alumnae using professional associations.

Questions to Ask Corporate Recruiters

1. What are some of the major issues facing your company and industry in the next few years?
2. How have you positioned your company in today's market? What makes your company different from the competition? How have you protected yourself against potential acquisitions?
3. What are your corporate growth projections for the next five years? What were they for the past five? Latest developments?
4. What are your plans for expansion? What companies are hiring people? (If not in your field today, maybe tomorrow.)
5. Can you describe your company "culture" (e.g., work environment, corporate atmosphere or "personality")?
6. What skills and characteristics do you regard as essential for a successful career in this industry and company?
7. What article and publication should I read? What professional associations should I consider joining?

If You're Due to Graduate Soon

Think about working with a state job-matching center like the Interstate Conference of Employment Security Agencies (ICESA), an independent Washington, DC-based firm that has information about state employment agencies. Write ICESA, Suite 142, 444 N. Capital Street N.W., Washington, DC 20001 or telephone (202) 628-5588.

Following Up Your Advice Meetings

Right Away (Write-ups and thank you letters)
After your meeting, write up your notes while everything is still fresh in your mind. How did people react to your presentation? How did you feel you did? Note feelings about this field, industry, and organization. Also list any new information, strategies, or referrals that you may have found out about. Take note of all correct names, titles, and addresses as well as new questions that may have surfaced. Note followup dates.

Send out a thank-you letter no longer than two to three days later.

Weeks Later
Follow up with a telephone update presentation, no later than two to

three weeks after you have had your advice meetings. The format for this update is shown in Fig. 15.18.

✦ ✦ ✦

FIGURE 15.18
Telephone update

> Hello, Mr. _____, this is Dennis Snedden, do you have a minute to talk? Have you received the thank-you note I sent you? (Yes.)
>
> Good. I wanted to make sure that you did and again I really appreciated the time we spent together and your candid advice.
>
> I promised you an update on the people and companies that I have contacted and have this to report . . .
>
> Mr. _____, since we last talked, have you thought of any other people that I should contact or is there a company that we might have missed before?
>
> Thank you for your support and help. I'll be in contact with you soon with another update.
>
> Good-bye.

✦ ✦ ✦

Announcement/Thank-You Letters

Let all contacts, in a positive way, know how you are doing and share with them how their advice has helped you. You owe it to them. It's good etiquette. *Note:* Never share your frustrations and worries, which they have no control over. When you complete your search, recontact all key contacts who helped you by sending each an announcement/thank you letter, which lets the contact know what you are now doing and that you didn't forget him or her. To me this type of letter is also a "touch of class" and one that is well received by all who receive them. An example of positive feedback that can come from such a letter is given in Fig. 15.19.

✦ ✦ ✦

FIGURE 15.19
Announcement/thank-you letter

> It is with great pleasure that I announce my new position as Chief Executive Officer of _____ in _____. This is a free-standing state-of-the-art comprehensive medical rehabilitation facility offering clinical inpatient and outpatient programs. It is owned and operated by

_____ located in _____.

This is a challenging and exciting opportunity for me. As the CEO, I will be responsible for the start-up and ongoing operation of this 60-bed hospital, which is currently under construction and scheduled to open in late spring, 199__.

I would like to take this opportunity to thank you for your excellent assistance during my job campaign. Your friendship, professionalism and support have played an important and influential role in helping me to secure this position.

My family and I will be relocating to _____ in early January, 199__.

If I can be of assistance to you or others in the future, please feel free to contact me. Until we relocate in January, I can be reached at home: ___/___-___. As soon as I settle into my new position, I will forward my new address and telephone number. Once again, thank you very much for your help and cooperation.

Sincerely,

John Doe

—————————— ✦ ✦ ✦ ——————————

Note: Everyone gets a thank you letter. Figure 15.20 is an example of the positive things that can come from them.

—————————— ✦ ✦ ✦ ——————————

FIGURE 15.20

December 15, 199__

Name
Address
City, State, Zip

Dear (Name):

Thank you for your letter of December 9. That letter confirms my opinion of you that you are a man of exception rather than of rule. Most people I have worked with on job searches over the years never bothered to inform me when their search concluded.

I want to congratulate you on your appointment. I really think it is good you are returning to a _____ position. I know the firm you are joining and have great respect for it.

This is a great way for you to begin the holiday season and I know you and your family will have a good one.

Good luck.

Very truly yours,

Name

✦ ✦ ✦

Once you have taken the time to make these contacts, by all means keep in touch, nurturing their growth with notes, letters, holiday cards, articles, and/or quick telephone calls, periodically to keep them "alive." Keep your 3"x 5" card system active with a tickler system for follow-ups. "Dead or inactive contacts" should be so labeled. Rate your contacts on a scale from 1–5 (No. 1, high, to No. 5, low) with the following information on each card: name (nickname), title, address, dates contacted, summary of discussion, information obtained, and names of companies/people, etc. Add to your contact list when you are not under the gun to do so.

> *Make new friends*
> *And keep the old.*
> *One is silver*
> *The other is gold.*
>
> — Children's Song

16.

Use of Video and Audio Tape Recorders

Whatever you
vividly imagine,
ardently desire,
sincerely believe,
and enthusiastically act upon
. . . must inevitably come to pass!

— ANONYMOUS

To perfect your networking, interview, and listening skills, especially if you test out as an introvert, you will need to use both the video camera and the tape recorder.

Video Camera

First, let me talk briefly about the use of the video camera. If you have never been in front of the camera, you will need to get used to it. It takes some doing, seeing and hearing yourself on camera for the first time can be an unsettling experience. I tell my clients that it is natural to feel nervous in front of the camera because it's a "phony situation." It's certainly not a natural one, and it's okay to have butterflies in your stomach—but visualize them as flying in a V formation for you. Most clients begin to relax when they start to picture this.

I have a client bring a blank video tape that can be shared with friends or spouse. We either do an advice (focus/indirect) interview or a mock job interview. This can last from 30 to 45 minutes. I naturally play the part of a tough interviewer and fire delicate, unexpected questions at them, like "how much money are you looking for?" I have even been known to take their resume, fold it and put it in my jacket to see what their response will be. Most clients are well prepared and don't take me on until they have practiced their presentation with friends, other clients, or a spouse.

The confidence and feelings of increased self-esteem that come from this exercise, I feel, are terrific to see. Most clients feel more in control of themselves. Their interpersonal skills definitely improve.

Mock Interview Critique and Assessment

After the session, I critique the client's presentation style on camera as well as answering any questions about the presentation. I always try to talk first, saying what I liked about what the client did (try to find at least three positives). This way I'm assured of getting his or her attention. I then mention things that I feel need to be strengthened to make the presentation more solid from my perspective. I particularly focus on body language (positive—how the client sits, movement), whether the client maintains good eye contact without overstaring, how positively and confidently he or she came across, how relaxed and at ease he or she was, whether their message was communicated concisely and clearly, whether the client is well prepared (asked good questions) and displayed both enthusiasm and a high energy level (Fig. 16.1). As we used to say in Dale Carnegie, "if you act enthusiastic, you will be enthusiastic." All in all, I want this experience to be positive and to boost that client's positive feelings.

✦ ✦ ✦

FIGURE 16.1
Presentation critique ideas

Characteristics for evaluation:

A. *Appearance & Mannerisms*

Grooming	Neatness
Dress	Nervousness
Manners	Poise and Bearing
Voice	Facial expression

B. *Home & Family Background*
Parents' occupations
Activities/interests
Friends

C. *Work*
Type liked best/least

Thing, idea or people-oriented
Reasons for changing job(s)
Salary, etc. progress achieved
Responsibilities required
Attendance record
Supervision experiences
Work attitudes/values

D. *Education*
Educational background
Major/minor
Grades
Courses liked/disliked

Tuition financing

Extracurricular activities/
leadership roles

E. Personality

Perseverance	Drive
Sincerity	Maturity
Initiative	Stability
Self-image	Alertness
Judgement	Motivation
Discipline	Aggressiveness
Confidence	Attitude
Friendliness	Ambition

F. Preparation for Interview

Company knowledge

Industry knowledge

Industry competition

Knowledge of open positions

Relevance of questions
(prepared list)

Interest shown in organization

Career path knowledge

Career opportunities/alternatives

G. Communications

Grammar	Presentation of ideas
Vocabulary	Ability to sell ideas
Expression	Voice delivery
Creativeness	Enthusiasm (the way
Organization	you come across)
and ideas	

H. Direction

Short range goals

Long range goals

Confidence in abilities

Goal/realism

Depth of information on goals

I. Management Potential (if applicable)

People skills

Civic activities

Leadership experiences

Team (project) experiments

J. Health

Physical limitations

Health problems (if any)

Overall physical condition

✦ ✦ ✦

I then leave, inviting the client to rewind the video tape to view himself or herself in action. I tell the client also to write down his or her observations for us to discuss next time and to complete a videotape self-assessment form (Fig. 16.2) to help facilitate that. It turns out to be a positive learning experience!

One need for caution that I remind clients of is not to come across as "the mechanical man or woman" even if you correctly anticipate or know what your response to a question is. I suggest the "pregnant" pause for five or six seconds (that can seem like a long time) and then slowly give the response. If you find yourself in this situation, try it. You'll come across a lot better.

✦ ✦ ✦

FIGURE 16.2
Videotape self-assessment form

1. Did I give the interviewer a friendly greeting?   Yes___ No___

2. Was I relaxed?   Yes___ No___

   Did I appear relaxed?   Yes___ No___

3. Did I make my interest in the organization and the career
   area clear?   Yes___ No___

4. Did I appear positive and confident?   Yes___ No___

5. Were my answers clear, complete and yet concise?   Yes___ No___

6. Was I enthusiastic and energetic?   Yes___ No___

7. Was my voice natural, emphasizing impact statements
   when appropriate?   Yes___ No___

8. Were my gestures natural, posture good, and "body
   language" positive?   Yes___ No___

9. Did I emphasize my skills and abilities?   Yes___ No___

10. Did I emphasize my related education?   Yes___ No___

11. Did I emphasize my related experience?   Yes___ No___

12. Did I display nervous mannerisms?   Yes___ No___

13. Did I maintain good eye contact?   Yes___ No___

14. Did I ask good questions?   Yes___ No___

15. Did I have a written list?   Yes___ No___

16. Would I have hired myself?   Yes___ No___

Which questions did I answer poorly? _____

_____

What did I do well? _____

_____

Ways to improve: _____

_____

✦ ✦ ✦

*Changing people's habits and way of thinking is
like writing your instructions in the snow during a
snowstorm. Every 20 minutes you must rewrite
your instructions. Only with constant repetition
will you create change.*

— DONALD DEWAR

Tape Recorder

The audio tape recorder also can be a valuable aid to improving your presentations. You can successfully record your telephone presentation setting up your advice interviews, the advice interview presentation, your responses to difficult interview questions (i.e., money questions), and even positive affirmations to help your self-esteem. Just playing these over and over again whether at home, in the office during breaks if the walls don't have ears, or in your car can help you tremendously. I suggest that you write out scripts before you do the recording. Make sure it's yours or that at least you are comfortable with the script. After you have practiced enough times, you can try some low-key presentations with family or friends—low-key in the sense that if you make a "boo boo," so what, no big deal. While you make these low-key rehearsals for advice meetings you can also have the tape recorder running for your playback and critique later. I even had a former client that would tape his telephone presentations and bring them in for me to listen to and comment on. He got high marks for ingenuity and creativity.

Helpful Presentation Hints:

1. *Do your "homework" or research on the company (companies) of interest.*
2. *Dress and act like a winner!* Be enthusiastic and keep responses concise and positive. If an interviewer wants you to elaborate on one of your answers, he or she will tell you so.

Enthusiasm

*Enthusiasm is one of the most powerful engines of success. When
you do a thing, do it with all your might. Put your whole soul
into it. Stamp it with your own personality. Be active, be
energetic, be enthusiastic and faithful, and you will accomplish
your object. Nothing great was ever achieved without enthusiasm.*

— RALPH WALDO EMERSON

Enthusiasm

*That certain something that makes us great—that pulls us out of
the mediocre and commonplace—that builds into us Power. It
glows and shines—it lights up our faces—Enthusiasm, the
keynote that makes us sing and makes men sing with us.*

*ENTHUSIASM — The maker of friends—the maker of
smiles—the producer of confidence. It cries to the world, "I've
got what it takes." It tells all men that our job is a swell
job—that the house we work for just suits us—the goods we have
are the best.*

*ENTHUSIASM — The inspiration that makes us "Wake Up
and Live." It puts spring in our step—spring in our hearts—a
twinkle in our eyes and gives us confidence in ourselves and our
fellow men.*

*ENTHUSIASM — It changes a deadpan salesman to a
producer—a pessimist to an optimist—a loafer to a go-getter.*

*ENTHUSIASM — If we have it, we should thank God for it. If
we don't have it, then we should get down on our knees and pray
for it.*

*Upon the plains of hesitation, bleached the bones of countless
millions who, on the threshold of victory, sat down to wait, and
waiting they died.*

— Anonymous

3. *If you don't understand some of the questions, don't be afraid to ask for
   clarification.*
4. *In a job interview, get the interviewer first talking about the company's
   needs and wants.* You will then be able to relate your experiences
   to what the organization wants.
5. *Size up your interviewer.* Be prepared to go with the flow in a natural way. Be yourself.
6. *See a model videotape of an ideal interview.* Discuss it with others or
   your counselor.

Winners vs. Losers

The Winner is always a part of the answer: The Loser is always a part of the problem.

The Winner always has a program: The Loser always has an excuse.

The Winner says, "Let me do it for you": The Loser says, "That's not my job."

The Winner sees an answer for every problem: The Loser sees a problem in every answer.

The Winner says, "It may be difficult, but it's possible": The Loser says, "It may be possible but it's too difficult."

A Winner listens: A Loser just waits until it's his turn to talk.

When a Winner makes a mistake, he says, "I was wrong." When a Loser makes a mistake, he says, "It wasn't my fault."

A Winner says, "I'm good, but not as good as I could be." A Loser says, "I'm not as bad as a lot of other people."

A Winner feels responsible for more than his job: A Loser says, "I only work here."

— ANONYMOUS

17.

Interviews and How to Handle Them

I've met men who have saved lives, built nations,
or unlocked the mysteries of the universe . . . and
the most easily observable thread which connected
these people was their ability to present well on a
job interview.
— WINSTON CHURCHILL TO FDR, 1944

Interviewing is a two-way communication process where you (interviewee) and the company (interviewer) gather information from one another to determine if there is a potential match. Many variables come into play during this process, such as what you "bring to the party" (skills, especially presentation and interviewing skills; abilities; and talents), whether you have positive self-esteem (attitude), and the way you dress.

Interview Types

There are many types of interviews. As a brief overview, I will describe them: *Directive interviews*—the interviewer works from an outline and asks a specific set of questions. This format can be used during a screening interview by personnel departments to screen out candidates (can also be one-on-one); *nondirective interview*—loosely structured format ("go with the flow"), questions are broad and general; *stress (interrogation) interviews*—long periods of silence, challenging of opinions and variety of situations to make you feel uncomfortable, i.e., unbalanced chair (not many organizations use this approach today); *group (board) interviews*—several individuals "ganging up" on one interviewee. Handle yourself the same as you would in a one-to-one interview, but make sure you direct your eye contact to the person who has asked you a question as well as using eye contact with each person. If other candidates are being interviewed with you, demonstrate to the interviewers that you are a compatible team player. Give each person there your best sales presentation. Also, there is the *telephone interview* — usually very specific questions about your work history and experience will be asked, done from long distance to see if it is worth the cost to fly the candidate in for a formal job interview. Can be exploratory on their part. Go with the flow. Keep responses short, crisp, and positive. Let your voice be upbeat and enthusiastic. Ask at the end what the next step is. And, of course, there is the *job interview* — this is the main event that you have been preparing so hard for (act accordingly). This is a performance on your part. These interviews can vary with the different types of personalities involved in the process. If you can talk about your accomplishments using carefully selected impact statements at strategic times with confidence in a very succinct way, the interviewing style of an individual will have little impact on how you do during the interview. Another point to remember is to speak clearly and answer questions concisely.

When I worked for Mobil Oil in Chicago during the mid-sixties as an Employee Relations Representative, I frequently went to many of the local college campuses to interview both undergraduate and graduate students. These screening interviews were planned so that I would interview a student for approximately 30 minutes. (Typical Format: 5 minutes to establish rapport, 10 minutes asking questions, 10 receiving and answering questions. I then took the remaining 5 minutes to close the interview and to write-up the candidate.

As recruiters, we were interested in areas such as intellectual ability (GPA), knowledge and experience, three-dimensional qualities, hobbies, sports, and other non-work-related activities, personal characteristics, and how candidates projected themselves (hopefully, enthusiastically). We were also interested in whether candidates participated in extracurricular activities, whether they held positions of leadership, and whether, on the basis of their "total image," they would fit into our company. If we had a positive gut feeling on the candidate and seemed to have excellent rapport (positive chemistry), that was a really big plus in that person's favor. As recruiters, we wanted candidates who were conservatively dressed and neatly groomed and had given some evidence that they had done their homework (note homework section) regarding our firm. The sharper candidates would ask me for one of my business cards at the close of the interview and soon follow up our meeting with a thank-you letter. I felt that this was a nice touch on their part.

The day's recruiting could be hectic at times, as we were usually kept busy interviewing for an entire day. At day's end, each recruiter completed a campus visit report, which was forwarded to our local regional office. The most promising "survivors" were then invited by letter to have a second interview at a plant or regional office site where they would most likely be interviewed by several people. The better candidates were then offered positions. I believe that most companies today still recruit in a similar fashion. I still reflect on a lot of positive days gone by in recruiting and knowing "pros" the likes of Bob Brocksbank, Bob Traill, Bob Killeen, and Paul Harbaugh—all gentlemen and outstanding Mobil recruiters!

Interview Strategies

As an interviewer, an interviewee and a career management counselor for close to 15 years, I offer the following strategies for getting ready for, taking, and following-up on an interview:

20 Pre-Interview Pointers

1. Plan to be on time (punctual) but not too early (10 minutes before is ideal). Size up the surroundings! Check in with the appointment secretary. Be courteous and friendly; take note of his or her name. You can freshen up. Plan to carry deodorant, breath spray or mints, comb or brush, six extra resumes (but never volunteer them), a trade journal, the *Wall Street Journal*, and a legal pad in your black leather attache case. Note: If you are going to be late, call ahead with a valid excuse.

2. Do homework (research) on the company and industry (competition)—find out as much about them as you can, i.e., products, number of employees, friends who work there, acquisitions or expansion (growth), sales, profits, locations, names and correct pronunciation of names of top executives (very important), customers, R&D; call their public relations department for a media kit or information from the marketing department, ask a stock broker for a prospectus or ask about a 10K report, annual report or *Value Line* review.

3. Prepare written questions related to the company and job (see suggested list). Bring some ideas with you.

4. Make sure you have correct directions as to the time, date, and place of the interview and the name(s) and titles of the people you will be interviewing. Take a practice run to learn the amount of time it takes to get there and where you can park. Maybe you'll want to take the rapid transit system (if so, take enough money). Know the company style of dress.

5. Plan to dress conservatively and neatly with blues and grays, dry-cleaned solid wool and wool blends preferred. Don't wear sun-

glasses or tinted lenses. Note how people dress in pictures in their annual report. Wear a red tie as a symbol of power and for good luck!

6. Carry a gold Cross pen, pocket pad, and list of references. Prepare a written statement about why you left your previous company and be prepared to discuss this topic freely, openly and comfortably.

7. Review possible difficult questions—think out responses. Don't memorize responses. Try to understand the concept. There can be several types of questions: *open-ended* (want you to talk)—e.g., "tell me about _____." Talk with a feeling of self-assurance. Interviewers usually ask who, what, where, when, why, and how type questions; no yes or no answers. *Closed-ended* (answer by yes or no; they don't want you to talk)—e.g., "Did you _____?"; *probe (penetration) questions* (want you to further explain)— e.g., "Please tell me more about _____"; and *compare/contrast questions.*

8. Practice role playing the interview with a friend, by using a tape recorder, or in front of a mirror. Practice helps to make perfect and helps you to relax. Remember—interviewing is a survival skill that requires planning and *much practice*! Soften your tone of voice.

> *Practice doesn't make perfect. Perfect practice makes perfect.*
>
> — VINCE LOMBARDI

9. Analyze the market by finding out what experience, technical expertise, and education is being stressed by talking to people who are working in areas of interest. Note current "buzz words." Check out newspapers, trade journals, and government publications to see what organizations are looking for. Placement offices at local schools might also have some ideas for you.

10. Remember—demand is always excellent for people who exhibit a positive outlook ("can do" attitude) toward life. Say and repeat positive statements at least twice a day. Visualize yourself having a positive interview experience. Tell yourself that you will enjoy the interview.

You never get a second chance to make a good, first impression.

— JOHN MALLOY

11. If you are a nervous type, take some mild tranquilizers before your interview or switch to a decaffeinated beverage.

12. Get plenty of rest before your interview (7 to 8 hours) and have a nutritious breakfast. Be determined to be alert. Where appropriate, be yourself and not too stiff and formal!

13. Be prepared to fill out an application. Don't write "see resume." Bring a written work history with you so you can copy the information and a pocket dictionary in case you need to check your spelling. Know the names of your previous bosses (and the correct spelling), and your job titles, places worked, size, sales, employees, etc. See application section in this book.

14. Best times to schedule interviews generally are Tuesday to Thursday mornings; if the company has mentioned something about travel expenses, you could ask how the firm would like to handle them.

15. Consider bringing examples of your work to demonstrate your best qualities, i.e., a portfolio. Focus on your successes and how you fit the organization. Focus on the organization's needs and problems and on how you relate to the firm and can increase its profits.

16. Don't go to an interview if you have no interest in the company, even though you say it is just for the practice. Forget it. Practice on your own. Create a positive image of you having a terrific interview.

17. As Socrates said, "Know thyself"—review your impact statements. Be ready to articulate your skills, abilities, talents, and experience! Especially mention cases in which you saved money, turned a profit or created new operating procedures that were successful.

18. Know what you want to do—be focused with regard to your job objective. Know your strengths as they relate to the needs and wants of the company.

19. Know what the company has that you want. Note size, locations, sales and profits, and future expansion plans. Determine how your work experience might fit in.

Use the preinterview checklist which follows:

- Appearance okay? Coordinated outfit? No fancy jewelry (few pieces and tasteful) or religious or social pins. Check out your shoes and socks, suit or dress, shirt, handkerchief, fingernails, hair, teeth, and other accessories, as well as your breath, before you go to the interview and when you arrive.

- Personal records in good shape?

- Dates of past employment clearly in mind?

- Past achievements recorded? Records of achievements, honors, etc.

- Know why you want the job?

- Can you say why you want it, CLEARLY?

- Do you know exactly what you have to offer?

- Is your approach organized? Tell yourself that you will have an outstanding interview because you are so well prepared!

- All important personal dates clearly in mind?

- Can you intelligently account for gaps in employment record (if any)?

- Completely briefed on company? Have you used the business reference library section, talked to switchboard operators and receptionists at places you are interested in, talked to suppliers, vendors, and distributors?

- Are you completely briefed on the job requirements? Plan to ask, when convenient, for a job description and a copy of the organization chart!

- List of intelligent questions ready?

- Opening remarks worked out?

- Reasons why the company should consider you. Problems you can solve.

- All factors concerning past employment in order?

- Do you know what points about yourself you want to emphasize? The name of the game is *value*.

- Five-year job goal worked out?

- Have you worked out methods to prove your worth?

- Ready to state how you could help the company?

- Ready to state how the company could help you?

- Occupational goal(s) worked out?

- Is your frame of mind good? Be an optimist that things *will* go well. Also remind yourself that this is not the end all and the be all. "If it's to be, it will be." Program yourself with positive thoughts.

> *A pessimist is one who when he has the choice of two evils chooses both.*
>
> — OSCAR WILDE

- Be ready with a warm and friendly smile.

The Beauty Of A Smile

A smile costs nothing but its value is priceless.
It enriches the one who gives it, yet it impoverishes him not.
It happens in a flash but the memory may last for days.
No one is so rich that he can get along without it.
No one is so poor that he cannot afford to give it.
A smile generates happiness in the home and good will in
business because it says, "I like you. You pleasure me."
If you meet an acquaintance or a friend who is too busy to give
you a smile — leave him one of yours.
No one needs a smile so much as the person who has none to give.

> — ANONYMOUS

- Have you rehearsed answers to possible questions? Be prepared also for nonbusinesslike questions, i.e., on your extracurricular activities?
- Rehearse answers to questions that employers are most likely to ask, i.e., my performance appraisal, have been excellent but the position as it now exists doesn't fit my long range career goals.
- Get together supporting documents; i.e., resumes (at least six extra), work samples, portfolios, transcripts, letters of reference, performance appraisals, etc. Don't volunteer extra information, unless asked.
- Know and make note of the names of interviewer(s). Plan to call them Ms. or Mr. unless you are told otherwise.
- Develop listening skills and oral communication skills.

Perhaps of all the creations of man, language is the most astonishing.

— LYTTON STRACHEY

- If you're sick the day before the interview, call to reschedule it if you don't think you can make it.

Interview Pointers:

Except ye utter by the tongue words easy to be understood, how shall it be known what is spoken? for ye shall speak into the air.

— I CORINTHIANS 14:9

1. Check interviewer's office for clues to hobbies, collectibles (i.e., books) and topics of mutual interest (i.e., decor). Use this as part of your opening discussion to draw the two of you closer. Don't talk about an interviewer's family or clothing.
2. While waiting, check house organs (company newspapers) and product displays. Collect samples if available. Have one of your mouth mints.
3. Be prepared and well-organized; project an image of self-confidence. Smile! Good posture is a must! Carry yourself erect. Walk and talk the success that you are!

Stand tall. The difference between towering and cowering is totally a matter of inner posture. It's got nothing to do with height, it costs nothing and it's more fun.

— MALCOLM FORBES

4. Keep responses short (specific), concise, upbeat, and positive. If a question just elicits a simple yes or no, try following that up with a related impact statement. Generate no more than two to three minutes of one-way discussion. If a question has negative overtones, turn it around and make it positive! Be enthusiastic! Show your *value*!
5. Note all interviewer names, titles, and correct pronunciation.

Treat them all as the most important people you've met. Greet them in an upbeat manner. Ask for their business cards if appropriate or make mental notes of the correct spelling.

6. Have a firm, dry handshake (no "Boston Fishes"—limp shakes) and direct eyeball-to-eyeball) contact. Note: Wash and dry hands in restroom before interview to ensure dry handshakes.

> *An eye can threaten like a loaded and leveled gun;*
> *or can insult like hissing and kicking; or in its*
> *altered mood by beams of kindness, make the heart*
> *dance with joy.*
>
> — RALPH WALDO EMERSON

7. Plan not to smoke or chew gum. Don't fidget, and keep your hands in your lap, out of the way.

8. Read the interview signals, especially nonverbals. Note body language, facial expressions, voice tone, and eye movement. Know the interviewer's "hot buttons." Follow up on favorable remarks. *Note:* The person who talks and interacts usually gets the job, all other factors being equal.

> *When we encounter a natural style we are always*
> *surprised and delighted, for we thought to see an*
> *author, and found a man.*
>
> — PASCAL

9. Act enthusiastic (upbeat), with a positive attitude! Think of times when you were relaxed, i.e., on the beach or near a babbling brook or a waterfall.

> *We don't know our presidents. We imagine them.*
> *We watch them intermittently and from afar,*
> *inferring from only a relatively few gestures and*
> *reactions what kind of people they are and whether*
> *they should be in charge. Much depends on our*
> *intuition and their ability at a handful of*
> *opportune moments to project qualities we admire*
> *and respect.*
>
> — MEG GREENFIELD

10. Use good active, intelligent, and interpersonal skills. "Like" the interviewer, and show it with your body language and genuine interest. Interviewers don't endorse people they don't have a positive chemistry with.

11. Find out about the position as early in the interview as you can, even if you have to assert yourself, i.e., "Before I tell you about myself, would it be okay if you told me what you are specifically looking for?" Note the duties, responsibilities, and authority.

12. In periods of silence, either ask questions or wait for the interviewer to end the silence.

13. Don't sit until invited. Also, don't stare at your watch during the interview.

14. Sell yourself using accomplishments in the form of impact statements. Don't be bashful. Lean forward as you talk about yourself. *Sell your value* to the organization as it relates to the firm's needs and wants (the ability to solve its problems and make contributions).

15. Find out when you can expect further word. Ask what the next step is. Get feedback.

16. A self-critique after every interview can be helpful. Write one up after each interview and learn from them. Note what can be improved. Did you feel you sold yourself successfully?

17. Don't apologize for things you can't change, e.g., your education, work history, or age.

It is not so much the being exempt from faults as having overcome them that is an advantage to us.
— ALEXANDER POPE

18. Stress your ability to work successfully as a team member and to get along well with others. Give them reasons to hire you. Remember: there is no "I" in team, as my son-in-law, Chip, has always said. Use the word "we" when speaking about an employer.

19. Remember that the interviewer generally controls the flow. Don't interrupt him. You control substance. Watch for signs that you've done your homework, as well as signs of interest, e.g., if the interviewer suggests a tour, introduces you to his or her boss, or spends a great deal of time with you.

Your listeners won't care what you say until they know that you care.

— ANONYMOUS

20. Keep the interview positive with self-confidence and positive statements. Don't name drop. Never criticize former boss(es) or company(ies). This is no time for sour grapes to surface or negative seeds to be planted. Always remember to turn negatives into positives.

21. Believe in yourself, and show it by the way you dress and present yourself. If you've had some adverse situations, what's important is how you have dealt with them.

22. Don't answer a question with a simple yes or no. Try to use impact statements. "Sell the sizzle, not the steak." If you are asked a difficult question, consider using a "pregnant pause" before you answer. That is a slight time delay of no more than five to six seconds while you collect your thoughts.

23. Ask for the interviewer's business card so you can send a follow-up thank-you letter. Send your letter immediately after the interview. Mention some nice things about the receptionist if applicable.

24. Remember: many times it's not what you say but how you say it. The tone of your voice is important.

The devil hath not, in all his quiver's choice, an arrow for the heart like a sweet voice.

— BYRON

25. If you are invited to lunch, order things that are easy to eat and middle priced. Do not order any liquor. In virtually all professional settings, the old advice about avoiding discussion of politics, sex, or religion still holds true.

26. Avoid discussions of money, benefits and vacations; know how to fill out an application blank. Note: For your information, if you're graduating from a school, ask the placement director or one of the visiting recruiters what starting ranges are in your field.

27. Lean toward the interviewer—send honest nonverbal messages.

28. Remember the three golden rules of interviewing—"Be yourself, know yourself, and sell yourself." Successful interviewing requires successful selling!

29. If it's a telephone interview, keep your resume, list of questions, and writing pad together, with a pen or pencil close by.

30. Thank the interviewer when you leave. Let him or her know you are impressed and would like to join the organization if you are truly interested. Ask what the next step is.

Seven Postinterview Pointers:

1. Send thank-you letter(s) no later than two or three days after the interview to all you visited with. Cite specifics of your meeting. Personalize each one.

2. Write down the questions you were asked and share with friends who may be also looking for a job.

3. Note what areas could have been handled better.

4. Were you adequately prepared? Did you give it your best shot?

5. How did you feel you did? Did you focus and refocus on your achievements?

6. Is this the kind of organization and the people that you would like to work for and with?

7. Complete the interview report form (Fig. 17.1).

✦ ✦ ✦

FIGURE 17.1
Interview report form

CALLED ON:

Company _____

Address _____

Person (Initial) _____

Title _____

Others _____

Date of Interview _____

INTERVIEW LEAD:

Recruiter _____   Referral _____   Ad _____

Recruiter Referral _____

Company/Recruiter _____

Title of Position _____

Salary Range _____

Company Job Needs/Wants (position description): _____

_____

Geographical Location of Position: _____

Established Rapport: _____

Presentation: _____

Interviewer Interest (supportive) _____

Self-Confident _____

Demonstrated knowledge about organization _____

Questions raised by myself/interviewer _____

_____

_____

Organization Chart Shown _____

Trial and/or final closing statement(s) made; How was the interview closed? _____

_____

_____

General reactions (pluses/minuses) _____

_____

_____

Interview length _____ Interview(self) evaluation _____

Follow-up _____

_____

Date _____

✦ ✦ ✦

Interview Aid (HORSE)

To help you during this important time, visualize yourself sitting on top of a horse charging into "the battle of the interview." This beautiful horse is your foundation for success, so think it. Fix it in your mind. This multimodal imagery and mnemonic device means:

- H. *Homework* (research) about the company or organization that you are going to be interviewing. Make a list of questions and bring them with you to the interview. These may be brought up when appropriate.

- O. *Obtain* information as early as you can in the interview as to what this company's position needs (nonnegotiable, usually) and wants (negotiable) are. Henry Ford was once quoted as saying, "Find a need and fill it." At least show you *can* fill it. Reviewing a job description that outlines duties, responsibilities, what you would be accountable for, and what authority you would have could be very helpful if they have one available. Ask yourself, what are the behaviors that will lead to success or failure in that position? Do they have an organizational chart that shows where that position fits in and what the possible career paths might be?

- R. *Restate* key needs and wants that you have heard to show your understanding. The interviewer will correct you if you're wrong or if he or she wants to clarify vague or incorrect points.

- S. *Stress* and match your accomplishments using impact statements as they relate to the company's perceived needs and wants when you have the opportunity; also stress the *FACTS* (Fit and Chemistry/Transferable Skills) as they relate to the interview. E.g., "I honestly feel that this is an excellent opportunity, that the 'chemistry/fit' is perfect and that my skills are indeed transferable. Would you not agree?" or "Wouldn't you agree that my skills fit with what you are looking for in this position?" If he or she says you make an excellent candidate, then move to *E.*

Note: The interviewer is interested in what you "bring to the party" (what you can do for their organization). You can assume the interviewer is interested when an interview lasts more than 40 minutes; when the interviewer talks about positions that are available in the company; when the interviewer reveals a lot about you; when the interviewer wants you to meet other organization personnel; when the interviewer "sells" the organization; when the interviewer asks if you would like a tour of the plant or office; when an invitation is made to go to lunch; when questions come up regarding money, availability, willingness to relocate or details about specific accomplishments or experiences; and when the need for someone with your experience is mentioned.

Signs of disinterest could be some of these: the interviewers haven't read your resume, frequent disturbances; i.e., phone calls while conducting interview, interviewer does little talking (no two-way conversation); and interviewer never speaks in terms of your solving their problems.

- E. *Examine* where you are going next by asking, "Considering all that we have discussed about this position, do you feel I make a viable candidate?" "Do I meet your qualifications? What do you think?" If so, "What is the next step?" or "Where do we go from here?" Try to determine if you are "in the running" for the position; try to learn what the timing is for making the selection and filling the position. Try to secure another appointment to continue the process by indicating that you continue to be very much interested in this position. Once again, express how excited you are about this opportunity and that it is your number one choice.

If you find out that you are "not in the running," ask for positive or negative feedback. "Could you tell me where I am weak?" and ask for referrals (turn the job interview into a possible advice interview). "Could you suggest other companies or people that I ought to be talking to?"

The next step may very well be a second interview after the first round of interviews has been completed, since the first interview should be and usually is an exploratory one for both parties. Leave with a positive attitude! If an offer is not made, note that it is highly unlikely for one to be made during the first interview. Remember not to try to do any negotiation during the interview. Get the offer in writing (if an offer is made) and then negotiate (see chapter 22).

Two or three days after your interview, take the time to send a personal thank-you letter to all the contacts you made during the interview. Key on your "continued enthusiasm" for this position, that you are very much interested in this opportunity, and how you once again feel that "the chemistry and fit" are right. You can also mention what your understanding of this job is and how aspects of your background relate to the position. Other points to mention would be questions you may have previously forgotten and additional qualifications not covered in the interview.

If you find out by letter that you are no longer a candidate, you can always write or call to find out why you didn't measure up to their expectations. Don't expect, though, to honestly get much feedback (the firm is ever concerned about its community image). Companies usually don't share that information with you. You might also inquire whether another branch, division, or subsidiary might be interested in you as a candidate.

Interview Questions

Introduction

- Practice questions out loud with a friend and a tape recorder.
- Answer questions carefully and concisely. Be brief and positive!
- Listen to questions; ask for clarification if need be. Take a moment to gather your thoughts before answering. It's all right to say, "I don't know."
- If you have skeletons in your closet, be ready with your answers. (Say that you learned from the experience.) Don't volunteer information regarding potential liabilities in your background. Interviewers don't want you to confess your weaknesses! Focus on the *positives* of your past experiences.
- Answer questions in terms of your background and the position to be filled.
- Never answer questions "off the top of your head." Pause and think about them if necessary. Remember the "pregnant pause" (five- to six-second delay).
- Know what questions are legal and illegal to ask. Know how to answer these (see 26 Difficult Questions on page 290).
- Slow down when you speak—talking at a faster rate can convey nervousness or a lack of self-confidence. Keep telling yourself you're doing OK, even when you don't believe it.
- Turn negatives into positives!

School

1. What did you major in?
2. Why didn't you do better in school?
3. Do you think your grades represent your effort in school? Could you have done better?
4. How would a teacher describe you?
5. What was the main thing you got out of going to high school/college?
6. What are your plans, if any, for further education?
7. What were your most significant accomplishments in school? What subjects did you like best/least?
8. How did you spend vacations while in school?
9. What extracurricular offices did you hold in school?

10. What specifically have you done in school that has enhanced your leadership qualities?

11. I see many students with good credentials like yours. Why should I hire *you*?

12. Tell me about what you did in school.

13. What kind of courses did you take? What were you best in; what did you have trouble with?

14. Where would you estimate you stood in your class in terms of overall academic excellence?

15. How did you feel about attending this school?

16. If you had to do it over again, would you have taken the same course of study and gone to the same school?

17. How did you decide on majoring in that field?

18. How did you pay for your education?

19. Did you feel your education was worthwhile? Why?

20. You don't have the technical knowledge this position requires. How could you handle it?

21. Do you think your education qualifies you for this position?

22. What are your aspirations for the future?

23. One of the things we want to talk about today is your educational background—tell me about it.

24. Do you enjoy doing independent research?

25. If you were hiring someone from this school, what qualities would you be looking for?

26. How has your education prepared you for a career?

27. What didn't you like about the school you attended?

28. Define success.

29. Who were your favorite teachers? What were your favorite courses?

30. What was your greatest accomplishment while in school?

31. How did you motivate yourself to get through school?

Self

1. Tell me about yourself.

2. What motivates you?

3. What are your short range and long range goals?

4. What are your three most important career accomplishments?

5. What are your greatest strengths? Weaknesses?

6. Are you creative? analytical? Give an example.

7. When you complain, what is it that you usually complain about?

8. How much money do you need to live on?

9. Why are you not earning more money at your age?

10. Did you ever get angry? Why?

11. What else should I know about you?

12. What kind of salary are you worth?

13. Where do you want to be five years from now?

14. How would you define the word "ambition"?

15. What are your feelings about controversial subjects, i.e., abortion?

16. Why should I hire you?

17. What was the last book you read? Movie you saw?

18. Describe your ideal job.

19. How do you think a friend would describe you?

20. Do you like working with people?

21. What are your hobbies and interests?

22. What do you think is the ideal job for you?

23. Have you developed a career plan for yourself? Tell me about it.

24. How would you describe yourself?

25. Sell yourself to me.

26. Tell me, how do you spend your free time?

27. What kinds of things do you like to do best?

28. How did you happen to get interested in that?

29. Tell me about your health.

30. Everybody has pet peeves; what are yours?

31. What else do you think I should know about you?

Business-related

1. Why do you want to work for us?

2. Why did you decide to enter this field?

3. Why did you leave your last job?

4. What have you been doing since your last job?

5. Will you travel? relocate?

6. What can you do for us that someone else can't?

7. With what other companies are you speaking?

8. What other positions are you considering?

9. How did you get along with your last boss?

10. What was the most difficult job you ever performed?

11. If you had a choice of a job right now, what would it be?

12. How do you think you can make the greatest contribution to this firm?

13. How would you describe your ideal boss? How was your last boss?

14. How many hours a week do you think a person should spend on his or her job? What are/were your major responsibilities and duties?

15. What job quality suggestions of yours have former employers adopted?

16. How well do you work under pressure? deadlines? Give examples.

17. What did you like best and least about your last job?

18. What tools, equipment, instruments, and machines have you operated in the past?

19. What is your philosophy of management?

20. Do you prefer line or staff work? Why?

21. Would you object to working for a woman? a man?

22. Would you describe a few situations in which your work was criticized?

23. How would you evaluate your present firm? Why are you planning to leave?

24. Tell me about times you weren't pleased with your performance.

25. Don't you feel you might be better off in a different-sized company? With different kinds of supervisory or managerial responsibility?

26. How long would you stay with us?

27. How long would it take you to make contributions to our firm?

28. In your present position, what problems have you identified that were previously overlooked?

29. Why did you apply for this job?

30. What do you think your former bosses would say about you if we called them?

31. What do you know about our organization?

32. Describe a typical day.

26 Difficult Questions

As a rule, don't answer open-ended questions. Ask for clarification; e.g., if asked, "What does your work history consist of?" You should say, "It would help me if you would explain which items on my resume are of most interest to you."

Make sure you *listen* to the questions and do your mental preparation for the interview by both writing out your answers to the questions and then reciting them until they become you.

Remember, keep your responses short, concise, and positive. The most important things you have to sell are yourself and your accomplishments.

1. *"Why should I hire you?"* "Because the chemistry and fit is right," "I have the transferable skills to do the job," or "I am a fast learner and can be up to speed in very little time."

2. *"Tell me about your time in school."* Treat it as a question.

3. *"What are some of the things about others that annoy you?"* "I try not to be upset by little things. It's a luxury I can't afford."

4. *"I'm not sure you are suitable for this position."* "Why do you say that?" You need information and time to think up a satisfactory reply. Counter with appropriate impact statements.

5. *"What is your greatest weakness?"* "I enjoy my work and always give each project my best. Therefore, when others don't do their best, it bothers me. I am aware of this weakness and I try to offset it with a positive example."

6. *"What upsets you?"* "People who are late to meetings, people who lie, people who don't follow through on commitments."

7. *"How long would you stay with our firm?"* "As long as we both continue to meet one another's needs."

8. *"Whom can we check as references?"* Be ready with a typed list of references.

9. *"What kinds of decisions are most difficult?"* "Difficult decisions for me are the ones I have to make when I don't have enough time to gather all the information I need to make the decision" or "deciding which of two excellent performers must be let go during a downsizing of operations."

10. *"What are your greatest strengths?"* Know what your skills are and describe them using your impact statements as they relate to the organization's needs and wants.

11. *"What do you see yourself doing five years from now?"* "Continuing to work my hardest to be the very best that I can be."

12. *"Tell me about yourself."* Ask where the interviewer would like you to begin. If he or she says, "you choose," indicate only experience, accomplishments and skills relevant to the position you are seeking. Keep it short, if possible.

13. *"What are your liabilities?"* Turn this around and make it positive by introducing a third party. "People that have reported to me have told me that I am a stickler for detail. That's true. When I have the bottom-line responsibility for making key decisions, I need detail in the reports of those reporting to me. If I don't have it, I have to go back and waste their time as well as mine. It's better if I have it up front."

14. *"What kind of money are you looking to make?"* If that question is on an application blank, write that you will discuss it in the interview. If it occurs in an interview, be *prepared to dodge it.* Remember the saying, "he or she who mentions money first loses." If the question is asked early in the interview, say "If it's okay with you, I would like to set that question aside for the time being and focus on the duties and responsibilities of the job. Is that all right?" Or, "By talking about money I might overprice or underprice myself. I feel we both need to exchange more information about each other and then get back to it. Okay?" If it is in the middle of the interview say, "It's not that money is not important to me; it is. But at this stage of my career, the chemistry and fit of the position are more important. I honestly believe if those two things are in place, money will take care of itself. Would you not agree?" "I would expect a salary commensurate with my experience, and which would be related to the duties and responsibilities of the position." If it's late in the interview, "I trust that you will respect me for what I am about to say, but I've always taken the professional stand never to discuss money unless there is a firm offer on the table. On the basis of my meeting today, I feel that this is an outstanding opportunity, 'the chemistry and fit' is right, my skills are transferable, and I am receptive to a job offer if you're inclined to make one." "I imagine that a salary range has been established for the position. I wonder what the company had in mind."

If you definitely need to give a figure because your back is to the wall, you can give them a total figure that is your base plus benefits which usually amounts to 40% of your base, i.e., $40,000 salary plus 40% would make a salary in the mid-fifties; "could be upper forties to sixties depending on company and the opportunity for growth and advancement."

If an offer does come and it's in the ballpark, don't say yes and don't say no, tell them you are assuming that they will put it in writing and that after you receive it you will get back to them within a few days (this is an acceptable business practice).

15. *"Why do you want to work here?"* "Because you have an excellent reputation within the community"—that is, assuming you've done your homework.

16. *"How long would it take you to make a contribution to our firm?"* "I would hope to make it shortly after joining your firm. Obviously it will take me some time to get my feet on the ground, but I see myself doing that rapidly."

17. *"Why are you leaving your current job?"* "I've gone about as far there as I can go." There was nowhere for you to go, you had the abilities, but there were too many people ahead of you. "I am looking for greater challenges and responsibilities." You weren't able to grow professionally as well as you thought you would. "I want to broaden my experience base." "I want to make more money." You're underpaid for your skills and contributions. "My boss and I had some philosophical differences and an amicable parting of the ways." "There has been a reorganizing of the business and a variety of the operations have been downsized." "We recently merged and there is a new management team."

18. *"I see that you've been unemployed since last year."* "That's not entirely true. I lost my job last year. It was one of the best things that ever happened to me, as I've had a chance to reevaluate my career goals and direction. Since that time I have been working for myself conducting an active campaign where I am getting out to meet good people like you in hopes that something of interest will surface along the way. I'm convinced that it will." "I haven't been out of work. I've never been so busy organizing my talents and trying to analyze where they would be of most service."

19. *"What do you think of your boss?"* "An outstanding person to have worked for. I really learned a lot."

20. *"What kind of people do you find it difficult to work with?"* "People who don't follow rules." "People who aren't hard workers."

21. *"Why have you changed jobs so frequently?"* Blame it on your youth. Indicate that you broadened your experience as a result of each job change and that has increased your worth. Note there are differences between being a *job hopper* and a *job changer*. A job hopper is someone who has moved several times in a short time with little salary increase or job improvement. (If you're one, group functional skills and don't mention specific companies/time frames on your resume.) A job changer shows a logical progression in position and pay. (Use either a functional or a chronological resume. Don't be apologetic.)

22. *"Why didn't you graduate or obtain a degree?"* Mention schools, courses, seminars, workshops, correspondence programs, company-sponsored sessions, etc., that you have attended as well as citing recent impact statements, your ability to learn quickly, and your transferable skills that match their needs and wants.

23. *"Why did you start your own consulting company?"* Be prepared to briefly explain and show a list of the companies and projects that you worked for and on. A well-prepared and thought-out portfolio that could be left discreetly with interested people could be a plus.

24. *"Are you interviewing with other companies?"* "Yes, I am, but on the basis of my interview today, your company is my number one choice."

25. *"Why did you select this school and major?"* Stress the research you conducted that went into making your decision. Companies look for analytical thinkers and problem solvers.

26. *Illegal Questions.* In many cases, personal questions unrelated to job qualifications are illegal for the employer to ask. Obtain a list of current legal and illegal inquiries from your state's Civil Rights Commission. A reference librarian may also be able to point you in the right direction if need be. Questions such as "are you married?" "have you ever been arrested?" "where were you born?" "are you pregnant?" or "do you have any handicap?" are examples of illegal questions.

Questions to Ask the Interviewer

Make your own list, but remember these points:

- Use the 5 Ws (who, what, when, where, why); with the addition of *how* you can obtain additional information.

- Find out about the officers of an organization by doing research. Standard and Poors has biographical sketches of the top industrial firms. Ask a reference librarian how to find this book. Most firms reflect the style of the top person. If backgrounds are similar, the fit could be there. Your research may provide some question ideas.

Here are 31 suggested questions for your list:

1. Time away from home?
2. Overtime needed?
3. Career path? Promotion?
4. When/where are employees transferred?
5. Any plans for company expansion and/or new product lines?
6. How long is the typical training program?
7. How many people are trained annually?
8. Does the company have a tuition reimbursement plan for education?
9. Can employees transfer from one part of the company to another?
10. Does the company have employee discounts?
11. Are there company cars or does the company reimburse for travel mileage?
12. Is there a dress code?
13. Future growth/expansion planned?
14. May I meet some of the employees that I will be working with?
15. Is this a newly created position? If not, what happened to the former incumbent?
16. Do you have a current job description that I might have?
17. How much of my first assignment will be on-the-job training?
18. Performance appraisal system? When are appraisals conducted?
19. May I see an organizational chart? Where does this position fit?
20. How does this position interact with the rest of the organization?
21. How would you describe the culture or climate of this organization?
22. What kind of support staff and budget does this position have at its disposal?
23. What are the positive and negative sides of working for this organization?

24. What makes your firm different from your competitors?

25. What is the company's record of employment stability?

26. How can you or will you utilize my skills?

27. Why do you think I should want to work for your organization?

28. Why do you enjoy working for your firm?

29. What are the challenging aspects of the job?

30. What latitude would I enjoy in determining my goals, work objectives, due dates, and measurement methods?

31. What are some of the more difficult challenges that a person would face if he took this job?

Turning Potential Interview Barriers Around

Self-image

You are what you think you are! If you think of yourself as a winner, you become a winner! Henry Ford was once quoted as saying, "Whether you think you're right or whether you think you're wrong, you're right!" It's the Pygmalion effect, or the self-fulfilling prophecy. Mohammed Ali used this very effectively in boxing when he proclaimed, "I am the greatest." Other athletes have used positive mind set to their advantage, and Norman Vincent Peale wrote about the power of positive thinking.

Too Much Education

Avoid mentioning all your degrees—only those applicable to the position you are applying for. Many companies will screen out candidates saying that they are "overqualified." I had a client who had several advanced degrees but took a part-time retail job to survive and pay his bills. You can bet when he had his interview and filled out his application that these additional degrees were not mentioned. That certainly contributed to why he was hired.

Not Enough Education

Stress transferable skills and accomplishments that relate to the company's needs and wants. Have Bachelor of Science or Arts Degree equivalent on resume. Indicate you are a fast learner.

Changing Career Directions

Don't mention major areas of degrees unless they are applicable to the area you are changing to. Note: you may be changing careers, but your skills are transferable. Stress, by being enthusiastic, your willingness to learn by working extra hours. Consider preparing a proposal of what you believe you can do for a firm now that you understand its needs. If you have found a problem that you can solve or really help an organization with, work up a proposal for them.

Too Old

People are living longer and are healthier. You are physically fit and mentally alert! What you are selling is your maturity and expertise! You are qualified! You will "sell" this to others with your enthusiasm and your boundless energy. If you think you are too old, you will be. So think positively, and concentrate on what you can do for an organization. Emphasize your reliability, tenaciousness, savvy, and proven problem-solving skills. Note the many people who became successes when they were over fifty. Focus on them. If they could do it, so will you! Check with AARP for leads of firms hiring older people.

I have worked with many clients over fifty, who once their attitude turned around and they were through their job-loss grieving state, they went on to terrific and fulfilling positions. Most older people have a strong work ethic. They don't mind working alone, at night, on weekends, or possible seasonal work. Anything to feel productive.

Too Young

Recruiters and interviewers can eliminate you if they think that you are too young (they say you don't have enough experience) or too old (they don't want to pay you what you're worth). They can slice it any way they want. You need to convince them that you are the person for the job by enthusiasm, positive attitude, how well you are prepared, and stressing how your educational experiences, internships, co-ops, and part-time and volunteer positions have contributed to your maturity and ability to analyze and solve problems. Companies in the nineties will be looking for promotable problem solvers (there is now and will continue to be a shortage of middle managers) and analytical thinkers with both computer and interpersonal skills.

Overly Specialized

I had a client who had not only a Bachelor's and Master's Degree in metallurgical engineering but a Ph.D. as well. He wanted to move further away from the technical to the management side of business. To help facilitate this, he completed another degree (MBA) which was his ticket to a management position. He, of course, will be stressing his ability to interact with people of all levels and his ability to manage which has come from his broad experiential base. He will also need to stress how he can use his technical expertise coupled with his management skills to solve plant problems.

Too Much of a General Education

This used to be the argument against liberal arts graduates. They weren't focused enough, or they were too broad-based. Sort of a jack of all trades, master of none. With change being as rapid as it is (I read that over one million pages of new material is published daily) and with us living in a computer age of "information overload," if you are now too specialized, you can become obsolete almost overnight. Generalists will need to point out the particular skills they have that match whatever position they are being considered for, that they are flexible, adapt easily to change, and have a willingness to learn the many facets of this business.

The Art of Listening During an Interview

Listening is an art and could very well be a science. Certainly you can't just say, I'll be an active listener, and expect to be one automatically. Listening is like any learned skill. It takes time and practice to perfect. They say a top executive spends 45 percent of his or her time listening. That is how important a skill it is, but tragically speaking, most executives, according to studies use only 25 percent of their listening skill. Why is this, you ask? Our minds have a definite tendency to wander, to daydream, thinking maybe of the next thing that we are going to say, anticipating in our mind where the speaker is taking us or simply just "tuning out" (shutting off) the speaker because we are not interested in what he is saying. To perfect your listening skills, research the courses on the market that will help you. Xerox, for years, had an outstanding course, "Effective Listening," that helped teach people to become effective listeners. Here are some guidelines to help you in the meantime to become a more effective listener during an interview:

1. *Work at it.* Think about the most important person whom you have ever met and how you listened to him. Do the same!

2. *Don't interrupt the interviewer*, even though you feel you know where he or she is taking you.

3. *Listen for key ideas.* Focus your remarks on these.

4. *Don't answer questions too quickly.* Pause, gather your thoughts and say what you want in a short, concise way. Brevity is the order of the day!

5. *Use the five types of listening responses to convey interest.* (Think of the word *CARPET*, like the red *carpet* treatment):

- *C*asual comments — "I understand," "that's unusual," "uh-huh."
- *A*sking for clarification — "Would you clarify that for me?"
- *R*eflect — reiterate or paraphrase (parrot) back to the interviewer what you believe you have just heard him say.
- *P*ause — look at the interviewer without saying or doing anything. Maintain good eye contact.
- *E*cho — repeat the last few words that the interviewer has just said.
- *T*ip — nod your head back and forth slightly to show understanding.

The Second Interview

This interview can vary from company to company, but usually you will be scheduled to meet with a number of people, all of whom will be asked to evaluate you, even those you may just have a meal with. The organization hopes to ascertain how well the candidate fits into the work location, in terms of both technical knowledge and personality. Make sure you confirm in writing that you will be coming in for the interview and have verified anything that they may have sent you.

The organization will pay the cost of your travel, usually, except in education. You are on your own there. Keep all your receipts, and be accurate about your costs. If the distance is a short one, most likely you would drive and receive a mileage allowance (now around 28-30¢ a mile). If your interview begins in the morning and you have to travel a distance, plan to arrive the night before so that you are well rested. In addition to travel, lodging, and meals, most organizations also will repay you for taxi fares, parking fees, tips, and emergency phone calls. Items not covered would be personal phone calls, valet expenses, tips over 20 percent, entertainment, magazines, tours, alcohol, cigarettes, and hotel stopovers in cities other than the one you are being interviewed in. Don't exaggerate your expenses; most organizations know the costs of travel.

15 Useful Pointers

1. Do your homework — research thoroughly.
2. Follow the same techniques and advice as for the first interview.
3. This interview is set-up to take a more technical in-depth look at you and can vary in length (half a day to two days). Express higher level of interest in the company and position.

4. Bring extra resumes (six), a portfolio (if applicable, or pick it up if you left it at the first interview), and a list of references. Copies of reference letters would also be all right.

5. Buy a local newspaper to aid in your research of the local cost of living.

6. Ask the Chamber of Commerce to send you materials.

7. Ask the interviewer about housing, community events, etc. Contact the leading real estate broker for a local relocation kit.

8. Plan to bring enough cash to cover expenses, as you may not be reimbursed for several weeks.

9. Be prepared for more penetrating questions about your technical expertise. Some questions may be designed to evaluate your analytical thinking and problem-solving skills. Many of your interviewers may not be skilled in interviewing.

10. Show confidence in yourself. Be enthusiastic with all you meet even if some are dull.

11. If the company has not explained how expenses are to be handled, ask them if they can give you an idea how they would like you to handle your interview expenses.

12. It's best not to bring anyone with you. A spouse or friend could be the exception if you pick up his or her expenses, but have the person stay behind at the hotel or motel.

13. Let your prospective boss bring up the subject of salary and benefits. If you haven't received an offer, an acceptable response is to state what the starting salaries were for last year's graduates or in an industry salary survey that you've seen and indicate that you would be expecting a salary in the same range or perhaps somewhat higher. Know at least your acceptable range.

14. Learn and use people's names. If many of the people you meet don't give you a business card, write down their names and titles in a notebook so that when you write someone a thank-you letter, you will be prepared.

15. Communicate your goals and technical training by practicing your interviewing skills.

37 Questions To Expect

1. What do you feel are the primary factors which determine an individual's or company's progress?

2. Would you rather work by yourself or with others?

3. How do you feel about doing _____, specifically?

4. What motivates you more—earning money or helping others?

5. In your past jobs, what was your relationship with your employers? Why did you leave? (Suggest that it was for a broader experiential base, higher salary, greater challenge, unique opportunity, etc.)

6. How do you respond to constructive criticism?

7. What have you learned from your past employment situations?

8. Do you feel comfortable asking for recommendations from past employers?

9. Why did you choose to go to college? to that school?

10. Which of your college years was most difficult?

11. What difficulties, if any, have you had in getting along with fellow students and faculty?

12. How do you handle your money?

13. What were the personal highlights of your school and college career?

14. At what age did you become self-supporting?

15. Do you prefer flexible working hours or the nine-to-five routine?

16. Do you see yourself as a competitive person?

17. Do you have an analytical mind? Give me an example.

18. How would you rate your general physical condition?

19. What do you do to stay in good physical shape?

20. What personality types are you attracted to?

21. What personality types rub you the wrong way?

22. Do you feel your grades should be considered by us as a statement of your abilities? Why or why not?

23. Do you enjoy athletics?

24. Would you prefer a research position as opposed to a public contact position?

25. What special abilities do you have that would be valuable to our company?

26. What productive and constructive things have you accomplished thus far in your life?

27. What were your specific achievements on each job you've held?

28. What achievements are you most proud of so far?

29. What motivates you to do your best work?

30. How have you prepared yourself for a career in _____?

31. What obstacles have you overcome successfully?

32. If you could design the perfect job for yourself, what characteristics would it have?

33. What other companies are interviewing you? Do you have any offers yet?

34. What are your job goals?

35. Do you plan to pursue further additional education? What type of degree? Why is this important to you?

36. Tell me about your long-term goals. (If answer is management, what makes you think you would be a good manager?)

37. Are you willing to relocate? to travel?

Note: Still keep your responses short and concise.

Questions That You Might Ask

1. Why is this position open?

2. What is the company's commitment to this department?

3. Do you have a five-year plan? May I see it?

4. Can you explain your budgeting process?

It has been my experience that job applicants who talk more in an interview working on the "chemistry" of the situation and who keep their responses concise have a better chance of getting called back to a second interview.

Preparation Ideas

Prepare for your second interview by

1. Selecting appropriate clothing.

2. Reviewing and practicing your interview and money questions with family, friends, or neighbors in front of a mirror or with a tape recorder. Go over questions that you feel can be sensitive and review your responses to many questions. This also helps to reduce interview stress. Remember that practice can make or help to make perfect. Write out your answers and practice reciting your answers, but don't memorize them!

3. Researching the company and the position you are interviewing for. Make a list of questions you'll ask.

4. Noting how your expertise and capabilities match the duties and responsibilities of the position. Notice where you are the strongest as well as vulnerable. Identify your key selling points.

5. Deciding how you will establish rapport, as well as the closing of the interview.

6. Not becoming discouraged as you persevere in your campaign. Be determined to succeed, no matter what. The key is to keep going! Tell yourself, "I will succeed!"

7. Not taking the very first job offer that comes your way unless you feel you desperately need it or are a new graduate.

8. Never treating an interview lightly; the same goes for questions over lunch. Be prepared and know yourself. Be familiar with what is on your resume and how you are going to communicate it effectively.

9. Remembering that companies are looking for thinkers and problem solvers.

10. Having an interview report form (see Fig. 17.1 on page 282) that you can fill out after the interview while everything is still fresh in your mind. Write a brief summary of what happened including what your next steps are, your follow-up plan, if there were any questions that you had trouble with and specific thoughts to improve your next interview. Staple business cards together with copies of all correspondence. The files can be kept in an interview file for documentation and future reference.

Consider using a postinterview checklist (Fig. 17.2):

◆ ◆ ◆

FIGURE 17.2
Postinterview checklist

	Yes	No
1. Were you relaxed, confident?	___	___
2. Did you "control" your part of the interview with good, solid questions?	___	___
3. Were your questions well thought out?	___	___
4. Did you listen?	___	___

5. Was your knowledge of the company adequate? _____ _____

6. Was your personal appearance flawless? _____ _____

7. Were your remarks well controlled? _____ _____
8. Did you jump to answer questions rather than listen carefully? _____ _____

9. Did you pause to consider possible answers? _____ _____

10. Were all facts about your record in good order? _____ _____

11. Did you prove your points? _____ _____

12. Were your background facts fluently presented? _____ _____

13. Did you sell, convince, persuade? _____ _____

14. Did you concentrate on the interviewer's remarks? _____ _____
15. During the interview, were your thoughts somewhere else? _____ _____
16. Were you able to justify your background in terms of the job requirements? _____ _____
17. Were you completely frank? _____ _____

18. Did you demonstrate that you really wanted the job? _____ _____
19. Were you able to furnish facts about why you could handle the job? _____ _____

20. Did you skip anything in preparing for the interview? _____ _____

21. Did you pre-examine all aspects of the job? _____ _____

22. Were you specific and definite in your statements? _____ _____

23. Were you specific and definite in your answers? _____ _____

24. Overall, did you do well? _____ _____

25. Have you written a thank-you note? _____ _____

------------------------------- ✦ ✦ ✦ -------------------------------

12. Preparing to gather interview information on the following to help you assess the organization:

   • Job description that outlines your duties and responsibilities.

   • Types and locations of available positions; whether there is much travel or relocation.

   • Company and departmental organization charts.

- Types of cosponsored training and development programs; do they have an tuition reimbursement plan? What percentage of your expenses does it cover?

- Career paths and promotion policies and procedures.

- Type of performance evaluation and appraisal program; e.g., HAY, factor comparison system, etc.

- Culture and work environment of the organization. Backgrounds of other employees?

- Mission statement of the organization. What is their market strategy? Can you see a copy of their five-year plan? What about the budgeting process?

- What type of management style prevails within the firm? e.g., autocratic, democratic, participatory, etc.

13. By knowing weak background areas and planning to offer some aspect of your experience (education or skills) that can offset them.

Interview Thank-You Letter

An interview thank-you letter (Fig. 17.3) that notes your interest and how enthusiastic you are about the position should be sent two or three days later to all that you interviewed with. This letter can have a friendly overtone to it, with many of the key areas tailored to the individual interviewer. The letter can be on standard or monarch size quality bond paper. Make sure there is a lot of white space and that the margins are correct.

────────────── ✦ ✦ ✦ ──────────────

FIGURE 17.3
Interview thank-you letter

Dear _____:

Thank you for the opportunity to meet with you last Monday and to discuss the position of _____. It is an exciting and challenging job, and I feel I have the breadth and depth of experience necessary to handle it successfully.

The background you require of managerial experience in both _____ and _____ is a unique one, and I know I possess solid skills in both of them. I also have prior experience managing and in marketing—all of which should assure success in the position of _____.

Regarding references, you may call Mr. _____, President of _____, at telephone number _____. He is very familiar with my work. Also, Mr. _____ will serve as a reference regarding my _____ experience. He is _____ and you can phone him at _____.

Again, thank you for your time and consideration. I look forward to our next meeting, as well as to meeting the President of the company.

Sincerely,

Name

✦ ✦ ✦

If you have received no response to your letter after a couple of weeks, you may wish to call the person who interviewed you with a "voice of enthusiasm" to check whether you are still a viable candidate. If so, ask whether the company needs any additional information from you and when it anticipates making a decision. If you have received a legitimate job offer, you can tell people so, but also say that the one you are talking to is still your "number one" choice.

If you are eliminated from the selection process, see if the interviewers will give you some feedback as to how they felt you did, how you can improve your skills, and whether they would be willing to refer you to some other people or companies that you should be visiting.

Realize that when organizations "select the right candidates," they usually are interested in:

1. *Interviewing them more than once* and getting team assessments of them.

2. *Determining whether the candidate has the necessary skills* to do the job and whether he or she has the right kind of personality to fit into the organization.

3. *Noting past records* as to whether they have or continue to make steady progress. Jobs with short durations can present problems.

4. *What their references have to say* about past performance.

5. *Whether they have social and emotional stability*; e.g., have they lived at an address a reasonable length of time?

6. *Whether they are upbeat, motivated persons.*

7. *Problems with dependents*, if they have them.

8. *Noting whether the candidate has failed to finish high school, college, or a program.*

9. *Kinds of social, community, or professional organizations this person belonged to.*

10. *How successful other family members have been.*

11. *Whether there is a military record and if so, evidence of leadership.*

12. *What ambitions, goals and objectives each candidate has for the future.*

13. *Whether the candidate has the "moxie" to do this job and will follow-up the interview on his/her own.*

The Optimist Creed

Promise Yourself—

To be so strong that nothing can disturb your peace of mind.

To talk health, happiness, and prosperity to every person you meet.

To make all your friends feel that there is something in them.

To look at the sunny side of everything and make your optimism come true.

To think only of the best, to work only for the best and expect only the best.

To be just as enthusiastic about the success of others as you are about your own.

To forget the mistakes of the past and press on to the greater achievements of the future.

To wear a cheerful countenance at all times and give every living creature you meet a smile.

To give so much time to the improvement of yourself that you have no time to criticize others.

To be too large for worry, too noble for anger, too strong for fear, and too happy to permit the presence of trouble.

— OPTIMIST INTERNATIONAL

Appendix: Questions from Interviewee

Note: Appendix courtesy of Dan Campbell.

Culture

• Are people encouraged to learn about the organization beyond their own department?

- Can you describe the person to whom I would report?
- Could you describe the overall philosophy of the firm's management?
- Do you anticipate a reorganization or change of command in the near future? If so, when will it happen and who will be involved?
- Has the company looked internally?
- Has your company ever had a strike? How are labor relations now?
- What is the history of the company?
- How do you feel about professional development courses, conventions, etc., as vehicles for enhancing professional growth?
- How do you deal with the grapevine? What is corporate policy towards the grapevine?
- How institutionalized is the company? Are new ideas encouraged? Can you describe a recent example?
- How many additional candidates are going to be interviewed?
- How many others are under serious consideration for this position?
- If you were me, would you want this job, and why?
- Is nepotism a factor in hiring?
- Is the incumbent still there? (if yes) Where will he or she be going?
- What characteristics are possessed by people who succeed in this position? In this company?
- What is the organization's mission? How does this department affect the accomplishment of that mission?
- What kind of a company is this in a qualitative sense? Is it a good place to work? Is the company fair to you?
- What kind of training is available to prepare me for higher level responsibilities and positions?
- What personality traits or qualities are critical to success in this position?
- Where do I stand?
- Where does this department fit in the organization's pecking order?
- What have previous occupants of this position gone on to? Why is the position vacant? (Where have previous occupants gone?)
- Who makes the final decision?

- What is the work environment?
- Would you describe the company's CEO? Is he or she typical of CEOs of the company's past?
- Would you speculate on possible career tracks within this organization starting from this position?

Goals, Objectives, Planning

- Do you feel that this company may be sold or merged some day?
- Have there been any recent organizational changes? If so, how have these changes affected this department?
- How do you like to run your company or department in terms of involvement in day-to-day operations?
- How does business look?
- Tell me about the most important projects the organization has recently begun. What projects are planned for the future?
- What are the company's five-year plans?
- What are the department's goals for the next five years?
- What are the periodic activities such as forecasting, planning, and reviewing progress, and how are they handled?
- What do you foresee as the future of your industry? How is your company addressing this future?
- What is the company's position in the marketplace? What is your market share? What are you doing to improve it?
- What part do you expect me to play in achieving organizational goals?
- Who are your major competitors, and what are their major strengths and weaknesses relative to yours? Are there strategies in place to take advantage of their weaknesses and overcome yours?
- What are the company's goals, both near and long term? What would (your/my supervisor's) goals be for his or her area of responsibility? What goals should be contemplated for the area I would have responsibility for?
- What do you or my prospective supervisor hope I would accomplish in three months, six months, twelve months, three years, five years, and ten years?
- What long and short term problems and opportunities do you

think my prospective area faces? What will I face in the first week, month, quarter, six months, one year, and two years?

- What short and long term problems and opportunities do you think exist for (a) the company, (b) the supervisor's area, and (c) the supervisor's superior's area?

- What do you foresee as the future of your industry? Export (per DUNS)/global?

- Who are your major competitors? Major product lines?

- What are your competitors strengths and weaknesses relative to you?

- Are performance reviews conducted? How frequently? How are they utilized? (promotion, salary increments, etc.)

- Could you describe the person to whom I might report?

- Do you have a written job description for the position?

- Does the company hire friends and relatives for key positions? How are budgets and purchase orders handled?

- What are some of the problems that a person you hire should address?

Management Style
- Are there any hidden goals in the hiring process that I don't fulfill? Is there a hidden agenda?

- How are promotions usually made? When do you decide to go outside the company to fill a supervisory job, and how is the decision made?

- How did you happen to join the company? What happened then?

- How did you move into your present job? How long?

- How do you evaluate various jobs and review performance? How are goals set? What criteria are used for measurement?

- How would you describe your management style?

- If you and I have differing viewpoints about a situation, how do you believe we should reconcile them?

- Is this a newly created job? (If not): What happened to the predecessor?

- Please describe your performance appraisal system. How do you identify and reward outstanding work?

- (To manager): Would you describe your management style?

- To whom does the information resources department report, separately to the president, to the administrative vice president, or to the finance department?
- What are the usual communication channels? How rigid or flexible are they?
- What is the chain of command here? Formal or informal?
- What sort of periodic "touch base" communications do you generally like to have?
- What sorts of things would you expect me to talk to you about? Which would I not bother you with?
- What things are you looking for in the person that fills this job?
- What problems are to be solved? What opportunities are there?
- Where do we go from here? (at the end of the interview)
- After six months, one year, two years, five years how will you know you made the right decision in hiring the person for this position?
- If the position were offered, why should I accept it?
- How do you, as a supervisor, like to operate in terms of assignments, delegation of responsibility, and authority, and general operating style?
- What are the characteristics you like in a subordinate; the characteristics you don't like?
- How frequently and in what manner will I and my supervisor meet on a regular basis, and how will we deal with particular problems?
- How frequently and on what matters do you, my prospective supervisor, interact with your superiors on a regular basis? How are particular problems or crises handled?
- (To supervisor) Why did you come here? Why do you stay? If you could change anything about your job, what would you change? What contact on what issues will I have with my supervisor's boss, his or her superior, and others at higher levels?
- What criteria will my supervisor use for my performance evaluation? How often are these conducted and how much time is involved?
- Why did my predecessor leave the position; what were his or her strengths, weaknesses, accomplishments, and failures? (If the position is newly created—what factors led to the decision that this position should be created?)

- What are the responsibilities of my peers and what are their strengths and weaknesses?

- What are the strengths and weaknesses of my prospective subordinates as you see them?

- With whom will I be interacting most frequently, outside the company, and what are their responsibilities and the nature of our interaction? What are their strengths and weaknesses?

- With whom will I be interacting most frequently, within the company, and what are their responsibilities and the nature of our interaction? What are their strengths and weaknesses?

- What freedom do I have to act; what budget is available to me for changes in staffing, promotion, salary increases? Use of consultants, requesting or purchasing software or hardware systems, venture capital for new ideas and approaches, implementing planned growth, implementing planned cutbacks? Changes within my area in regard to policies, procedures, practices, or performance expectations?

- What specific responsibilities of the position do you regard as most important? What are the other responsibilities?

Position Requirements

- What are the limits of my authority and responsibility? What do I have to get permission for? Inform others about after the fact? Discuss prior to action?

- What is the position for which this interview is being conducted?

- What qualities and qualifications are you looking for in a person to fill this position?

- What is it about my letter that interested you?

- Do my qualifications fit what you are looking for?

- How do you envision my background and skills complementing those of your staff?

- What are the characteristics and qualifications of the person you are seeking to fill this position?

- What are the five or six most important qualifications that you are looking for in an ideal candidate for the job?

- What authority will I have to handle my responsibilities?

- How do you think the company and its top leadership is perceived in the industry and in the local business community and why?

- What are its perceived strengths and weaknesses?

- What are the major challenges, rewards, and stimulations of the prospective position I might hold? Of your (supervisor's) job? Of your superior's job? Of my subordinate's job?

- What are the major frustrations as you see them of the position I might hold? Of your (supervisor's) job? Of your superior's job? Of my subordinate's job?

- What opportunities are there for growth in my prospective area of responsibility and for advancement in the company? On what kind of timetable?

- What professional, industrial, community, or public policy involvement do you feel it necessary for me to have, and in what depth?

- What social requirements does the job entail?

- What particular things about my background, experience or style interest you? Make you think I'll be successful? Give you some amount of concern? What experience, training, attributes, operating style, accomplishments, and personality factors should the ideal candidate for this job have?

- Could you describe the overall philosophy of the firm's management? The personality of _____, President? The personality of _____, VP?

- Could you describe the ("unique profit sharing plan" described in news release of such and such a date)?

- Is there a continuing education program for employees?

- What are the negative characteristics of the company?

- How long has the interviewer been there?

- What has been the interviewer's experience with the company?

Organization Resources

- What is the department size in terms of dollars, people, categories of people?

- How is the firm held? (corporation, partnership, proprietor?)

- How long does it take to fill an order? How does the system work?

- How many people will report to me in the job?

- How are sales generated? What is the size and organization of sales force?

- Is the computer pretty well integrated into your operations?
- Present size in dollars, employment, listed on stock exchange?
- What are the research and development facilities? The new products?
- What are the types of manufacturing facilities? Equipment? Warehousing?
- Where are union relations? Which unions?
- What are the firm's and department's weak points?
- What are the strengths of this firm? Department? What weaknesses, if any, would you expect me to shore up?
- What engineering support do we have?
- What is the percentage breakdown between raw material, in-process, and finished goods inventories? How controlled?
- What sort of operating information is available now? What sort of data processing support does your company have?
- When could we arrange a trip through the plant?
- Who are my peers, and what are their jobs?

Position Functions

- What are some of the first problems that the person you hire should address? What other problems will need immediate attention?
- What are the usual and typical daily activities of the job?
- What sorts of decisions would you expect me to make on my own?
- Would you please describe a typical day for the occupant of this position?

18.

Answering Ads:
Play Your Cards Right

*The most visible creators I know of are those artists
whose medium is life itself. The ones who express
the inexpressible—without brush, hammer, clay or
guitar. They neither paint nor sculpt—their
medium is being. Whatever their presence touches
has increased life. They see and don't have to draw.
They are the artists of being alive . . .*

— ANONYMOUS

Few People Get Jobs From Ads

People who don't know any better place their job campaign bets on answering ads (the top of the job campaign) as their primary activity, although it should be just a campaign filler. We know that fewer than 10 percent of people get their jobs through ads; answering ads is potentially time consuming, with small return for your effort as your letter competes with hundreds of other responses. Ads account for fewer than 3 percent of the jobs out there, and answering them pays little dividends. Companies use newspaper ads primarily for filling lower and middle management positions. Higher-paying positions are seldom advertised in newspapers or trade journals, although I have worked with a few clients who happened to "hit the lotto" with some high-paying small-size firms.

*As the saying goes, "Things may come to those who
wait, but only the things left by those who hustled."*

— ANONYMOUS

How Ads Are Used

We also know that over and above these companies, recruiters and agencies use ads to fatten their files for future organizational openings or to screen respondents for companies; venture capitalists use them for prospective clients; and some organizations use them to meet government equal opportunity requirements even though the position may already be filled. The ads are either direct (organization identified in the ad) or indirect (blind box ad, where the organization is not identified).

Still, some clients occasionally get their new jobs through ads, so I tell them to hedge their company bets by selectively answering ads and then go about their business. Answering an ad may not result in a job, but an important contact may possibly be made which could result in an advice meeting.

It's interesting to note what organizations are advertising, even if the positions are not quite what you're looking for. It at least lets you know that some things are possibly cooking within those firms. It also gives you a local economic indicator as to what companies are hiring. You can then phone your ABC contacts or others who work or used to work at the company placing the ad to find out which departments and decision makers are doing the hiring. Then you can plan to network into those companies or, as a last resort, send a broadcast letter to the decision maker. One never knows.

Ads are placed periodically in professional trade magazines, journals, alumni and alumnae placement newsletters, state employment bulletins, and newspapers. Most ads are for local positions, so it is important if you're answering ads to check all weekend local (metropolitan) and regional (city) newspapers in targeted geographical areas of interest. If you subscribe to one or more, the costs are tax deductible during your campaign. The *Standard Periodical Directory* and the *Standard Rate and Data Service Directory* can provide you with addresses of newspapers and journals of interest. The weekly *National Ad Search* collects a variety of ads and the cover page gives you addresses of leading newspapers. The *Wall Street Journal* publishes four regional editions: Eastern, Mid-West, Southern, and West Coast. Note: *The Mart* on Tuesday and a composite of regional ads appears weekly (available Monday on newsstands) in The *National Business Employment Weekly* (*NBEW*), a publication related to The *Wall Street Journal*, along with interesting articles about finding employment.

The Sunday edition of the *New York Times* has classified, business, education and health-professions sections. Note: Have a friend in New York send you the classifieds (the employment classifieds are not included in papers distributed outside of the Metro NY area). I suggest you check these out with your local reference librarian to see if they have any of the above. Might save you both time and money.

Ad Response Time

If a lot of people respond to an ad, it will take the organization many weeks to screen out and select the finalists. With that in mind, I suggest that it's all right to review back issues and answer ads up to one to two months old. I wouldn't go beyond $2\frac{1}{2}$ months. Most responses to fresh newspaper ads occur right away and are usually received two to four days after the ad has appeared (see Fig. 18.1).

✦ ✦ ✦

FIGURE 18.1
Ad response time

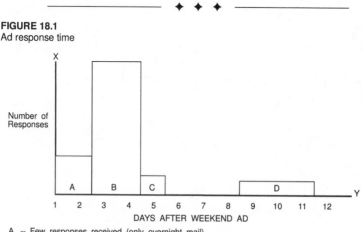

A. -- Few responses received (only overnight mail)
B. -- Most responses received; traditional response to ads
C. -- Trickle down (late response)
D. -- When you need to respond: 7 to 10 business days later; come in "After the Pack" (A & B)

✦ ✦ ✦

Later responses have a better chance of getting past initial cuts (seven to ten business days later, coming in after the crowd). People whose qualifications, capabilities, and experience don't quite match or fit are eliminated, and those whose responses are badly typed or written or appear messy no doubt are cut, too. Some are even eliminated because of their requested salary being either too high or too low or by providing too much information on their resumes that is used against them. Be prepared to receive "form letters" of rejection to a direct ad. Companies, for image sake, are usually obligated to send you a response. We used to code letters coming into Gulf Oil and then send out the appropriate form letter that matched the ideal response of that letter when we had a stack of them. It looked personal, but it really wasn't.

Note: Since monthly trade journal ads appear less frequently than weekly newspaper ads, those advertised positions may very well have already been filled through other sources. Also, the more often a publication publishes, you would like to think, the fresher the ads will be.

The Way to Answer Ads

There are essentially three ways to answer ads. The first and more traditional way entails following the specific directions (usually from the Personnel Department). By that I mean sending a cover letter (example of candidate's writing style) to the designated ad person, together with your resume and salary history. You'll see shortly why I don't recommend using this approach.

A second way to answer ads is to send a cover letter (Fig. 18.2) with your resume if you match the ad perfectly. I seldom see this happening. Most organizations are looking for "Superman" and seldom will they honestly find him or her (Fig. 18.3).

✦ ✦ ✦

FIGURE 18.2
Cover letter for answering ads

(Current Address w/phone number)

Date

30X XYZ
The Pittsburgh Press
34 Boulevard of the Allies
Pittsburgh, PA 15222

To whom it may concern:

I am responding to your ad for a _____ that was listed in Sunday's edition dated _____.

Some examples of my effectiveness that will interest you and match your ad well are:

- 4 to 5 important statements as they relate to the needs/wants of the ad
- or use the "matched" setup: Ad Requirements, Qualifications

I have a Bachelor of Science Degree from the University of Maine (top 5% of my class) and would be delighted to review my full salary history with you on a more personal basis when we get together.

I will be delighted to expand on my qualifications and background at a mutually convenient time. Please contact me at the above address or at either of the two listed telephone numbers, should you call my office I know you will be discreet.

Sincerely,

(Name)

Optional last paragraph

I am enclosing a copy of my resume as requested. I am prepared to answer any additional details or questions that you may have about it. Please contact me at the above address, etc.

✦ ✦ ✦

✦ ✦ ✦

FIGURE 18.3
Superman wanted

Exciting opportunity. Must be labor-relations expert, motivational psychologist, technical genius, production-control and time-management specialist, financial analyst, persuasive communicator, politician, safety and benefits consultant, teacher, disciplinarian. Ability to leap tall buildings a definite plus. Long hours. Low pay. Increasing responsibility without equivalent increases in authority, recognition, or reward. No tools, training, or support from superiors. No respect from subordinates. Negative feedback only. Candidates may send resumes to . . .

— ANONYMOUS

✦ ✦ ✦

Think of the company's requirements as one or more bars, and of your skills as a rectangle (Fig. 18.4). Even if there is not a perfect match, the position may be worth pursuing. Respond if you match 60 percent or better of the ad requirements. If A and B are what the company is looking for and your match is C (60 percent or better), go for it! Since there is employment activity within this firm, if you don't quite match this job, maybe you will with another position.

Even if you don't quite match, you may well be considered for other positions, now or in the near future, that might not even be advertised.

✦ ✦ ✦

FIGURE 18.4
"X" marks the job

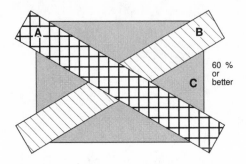

KEY

A -- Your experiences/qualifications
B -- Organization's needs and wants
C -- Arena and how you match it ("FIT")
    fluctuates in size depending on the
    movement of A and B

60 %
or
better

The third response, and the one I recommend for answering direct or blind (box) ads, is to send a one-page letter without attachments. This letter should emphasize successes in the form of your four to five best, most significant impact statements as they match the needs and wants of the ad (Fig. 18.5).

✦ ✦ ✦

FIGURE 18.5
Suggested direct ad response

(Date)
(7 to 10 business days after ad)

Dear Decision-Maker: Personal/Confidential

Since you are looking for a _____, you will be interested in my qualifications. (Notice I didn't say you might be or you could be. I was a little more deliberate and I wanted this first paragraph, obviously, to grab their attention in a positive way. You will also note that the name of the trade journal or newspaper that it appeared in is intentionally left out.)

I have _____ years of _____ experience with _____ organization and all of my positions have been related to _____. By way of introduction, some examples of my effectiveness are as follows:

- 4 to 5 key impact
- statements relating to
- needs and wants of
- the ad

I have a Bachelor of Science Degree (always spelled out) in _____ from _____ University and currently I am working on an advanced degree in _____.

    We should meet to discuss this opportunity and my qualifications. I will, therefore, call your office within the week to arrange a mutually convenient time. (Notice I have retained control rather than asking them to call me which they won't.)

Sincerely,

(Name)

✦ ✦ ✦

    We call this a "resume letter." Since the letter is something of a resume with some of your qualifications on it, you do not attach your resume. I believe first impressions are important, and when you enclose a resume, if you have any perceived negatives in it, it will be used to disqualify you. You want to see if you can catch the hiring persons (they are the decision-makers) with this letter and if you do, then you can follow it with your resume.

    If you are answering a direct ad (organization's name is on the ad), you will want to do some research on the firm to find who the hiring person is in your area of interest. Your research may even reveal certain qualifications that should be highlighted. You have to realize that you are coming in the back door, so to speak, so you don't mention the ad and any dates nor do you have to follow its rules (i.e., send resume and salary history).

    You might call the organization's switchboard to get the decision maker's name, indicating that you are a community organization and that you are updating your records, i.e., "Could you please give the correct spelling of the person who is Vice President of Sales (or the correct title) and while I have you on the phone, I would like to verify the mailing address." If the operator asks you why you need this information (he or she won't), you can say that you are preparing a personal letter for this person and you want to make sure that it's correct.

    Write to Personnel only if you are interested in that department. Remember that Personnel, as a staff department, is there mainly to disqualify candidates, not to qualify them. Having worked for several *FORTUNE* "Top Ten" companies' Personnel Departments, I can attest to this.

    If you feel uncomfortable doing this, as a "double barrel" alternative course of action, write separately to the identified decision maker and to the Personnel Manager for double exposure.

    Remember: never volunteer salary history information, as it can be used against you before you get your foot in the door and have a chance to present your case. Hopefully, your strong successes will carry you. Besides you are requesting an interview to present yourself and your qualifications.

Until you really know about the position and the organization, there really is no way for you to determine your salary requirements. You will want to retain as much control as possible in your letter by mentioning that you will call within the week to arrange a mutually convenient time. When you do call and the secretary asks you what your call is in regard to, you can say Mr. (her boss) and you have been in correspondence with one another and that he is expecting your call. It really is true!

If you feel you need to address salary, you can always state in your resume letter that the position's "chemistry and fit" is more important than the salary, which is negotiable or open.

Most ads are indirect (blind, box) and do not identify the organization (these are low-yield), and they allow these "secret organizations" to write a limited number of responses to interested candidates and to forget about replying to all the others. Although you're most likely not personalizing your blind ad responses, make an exception if you recognize the company, and write directly to it. *Note:* If it's your company, maybe your job is in jeopardy. Sometimes you find that the blind ad is a P.O. box and through your research, you locate the hiring firm; the format for this letter will be the same as for the direct letter with the exception of the final sentence, where you ask them to contact you.

If you haven't received a response from a blind ad in two to three weeks, I suggest a follow-up letter (shows initiative) referring to your earlier correspondence and how it must have gotten lost in the mail (Fig. 18.6). Give them a chance to save face!

✦ ✦ ✦

FIGURE 18.6
Blind (box) ad follow-up letter

To whom it may concern:

I am sending this letter as a follow-up to the one dated _____ that was sent three weeks ago. As "the fit" appeared to be an outstanding one when compared to my background, I thought I would send you a copy of it together with a copy of the original correspondence. Most likely the original got lost in the mail.

Please let me know what the status of this position is and what other information you might need from me. Thank you.

Sincerely,

(Name)

Enclosure

✦ ✦ ✦

If you need to maintain your secrecy while answering ads, use a relative's or friend's address with a different name to get information before committing yourself to responding to it.

If you notice an ad repeating itself, most likely it is a blind ad from an agency looking to stockpile potential candidates. If it is a company, there perhaps are more jobs over and above the position they are advertising for.

> *I will not die an unlived life.*
> *I will not live in fear*
> *of failing or catching fire.*
> *I choose to inhabit my days,*
> *to allow my living to open me,*
> *to make me less afraid,*
> *more accessible,*
> *to loosen my heart*
> *until it becomes a wing,*
> *a torch, a promise.*
> *I choose to risk my significance;*
> *to live so that which came to me as seed*
> *goes to the next as blossom,*
> *and that which came to me as blossom,*
> *goes on as fruit.*
>
> — ANONYMOUS

13 Suggestions

1. If you are worried about secrecy, avoid responding to blind (box) ads.

2. If you feel compelled to use salary figures, state a range 40 percent higher (compensation specialists say that your benefits today are worth at least 40 percent of your base).

3. When possible, use the phone to determine whether there is a feeling of mutual interest. Stress strengths as they relate to the organization's needs and wants. Call when there are no disturbances or interruptions. Have a resume nearby for ready reference. Always ask to schedule an interview for yourself.

4. Forget placing ads for yourself, i.e., "Chief Executive Officer-Chief Operating Officer, experienced in both Thrifts and Mortgage Banking, desires opportunity to transfer knowledge and skills to a small- to medium-sized financial institution for profitable results. Will relocate. Strengths: operations, lending, marketing and data processing." In my fifteen-plus years of career management counseling I have not yet known this to work.

5. Be selective in the ads to which you respond. Omit the ads that promise too much "pie in the sky."

6. Try other follow-up approaches if still interested. If you sent a resume letter the first time and didn't hear, try a cover letter with a resume. Send only to those where the "fit" is exceptional.

7. Rule: Write at least two levels higher than the position you are seeking. Your inquiry has more power if it "trickles down."

8. Publication ideas:

   • Note new business trends, openings, an organization's new hires, joint ventures, acquisition and expansions, mergers, and contract awards—especially government contracts, obituaries, and retirements. You might get some leads of where to write regarding new products, buildings, growth, and expansion.

   • Note people on the move (promotions, appointment, new hires, and transfers) that you can send a combined congratulatory and introductory letter to. Maybe they will consider you for employment on their "new" team if they are expanding or getting rid of deadwood.

   • Note companies moving in or out of your area from current or previous trade journals, newsletters, and newspaper articles. Research and find out what they are doing. Write to the decision makers of interested departments within these firms (Fig. 18.7). They might be sources for employment.

✦ ✦ ✦

FIGURE 18.7
Writing to decision makers

Dear Decision-Maker:
I recently read in the _____ that your organization is _____. Because of this news, I was wondering whether you would need an employee with my qualifications and experience.

By way of introduction, some examples of my effectiveness that fit with what you are doing are as follows:

• Choice impact statements
• as to what you mainly
• can "bring to the party."

We (or I and an appropriate member of your staff) should meet to discuss my background as it relates to your current situation. I will, therefore, call your office within the week to arrange a mutually convenient time.

Thank you.

Sincerely,

(Name)

✦ ✦ ✦

9. If you see a blind ad with a post office box (not a newspaper box, which is a private organization) and you wish to find out about the company (Fig. 18.8), call the postmaster at that zip code's post office and request that company's name. The Postmaster must inform you, by order of the United States Postal Administrative Support Manual Number 352.44. You may need to make your request by letter (Fig. 18.9), and then hopefully the postmaster will respond.

✦ ✦ ✦

FIGURE 18.8
Blind ad

INDUSTRIAL
ENGINEER

Manufacturing Engineer

Suburban Pittsburgh steel office furniture manufacturer is seeking two highly motivated and results-oriented individuals to fill immediate entry level openings in the Engineering Department.

A competitive salary and an excellent benefits package await the successful candidates.

A 4-year degree in industrial or mechanical engineering is required and experience in industry and plan operations a plus.

Send complete resume and salary history to:

Engineering Manager
P.O. Box XXX
Anytown, PA 01234

✦ ✦ ✦

✦ ✦ ✦

FIGURE 18.9
Letter to postmaster

Date

Postmaster
530 Allegheny River Boulevard
Oakmont, PA 15139

Dear Sir:
With reference to our telephone conversation today, I am requesting the company name and address of the holder of P.O. Box 330. This request is in accordance with your Administrative Support Manual #352.44e. I am enclosing a copy of their ad for your information. I look forward to hearing from you.

Thank you.

Sincerely,

(Name)

Enclosure—Copy of Ad

✦ ✦ ✦

10. When you use a person's name in the ad response, put "personal and confidential" both on the envelope and on the cover letter that you are using. Remember, most secretaries don't open this mail.

11. When you think you have found yourself in an ad, dissect the needs (the have-to-haves) and the wants (the negotiables) of the ad just by underlining them and then list them on a sheet of paper. You may even want to see how well you match them with your own experiences and successes (Fig. 18.10).

12. Enter all ads answered on your sheet (Fig. 18.11) so that you'll have a record of what ads have been answered by companies and those that need to be followed up by you.

13. Remember your potential employer is interested in what you bring to the party and whether he or she will get true value for the money invested. Stress those ideas in your ad response.

✦ ✦ ✦

FIGURE 18.10
Needs and wants

MANAGER OF AUDIT ADMINISTRATIVE SERVICES

Mellon Bank, a premier financial services institution, has an immediate opening for a manager of audit administrative services. This position is responsible for coordinating the Auditing Department Annual Operating Plan and assisting the division manager in developing and monitoring progress on the strategic plan, development and dissemination of corporate-wide auditing policies and procedures, and maintaining the Auditing Department Policies and Procedures Manuals.

CPA and five years experience preferred. MBA desirable.

We offer a competitive salary and benefit program. Qualified candidates should submit a resume and salary expectations for confidential consideration to M. Jane Doe, Mellon Bank, Room 1825, One Mellon Bank Center, 500 Grant Street, Pittsburgh, PA 15258

An Equal Employment Opportunity Affirmative Action Employer

NEEDS

1. Coordinating Auditing Department Annual Operating Plan.

2. Assist division manager in developing and monitoring progress on the strategic plan.

3. Development and dissemination of auditing policies and procedures.

4. Maintaining Auditing Department policies and procedures manuals.

WANTS
1. CPA and 5 years experience preferred.

2. MBA desirable.

✦ ✦ ✦

FIGURE 18.11
Ad status sheet

NO.	JOB TITLE	SOURCE	DATE	RESPONSE	RETURN	FUTURE ACTION

PART III

Getting To Where You Want To Be
Putting Your Gears Into Action

19.

Job Campaign Techniques:
Putting the Vision Into Practice as You Improve
Your Odds

Nothing in this world
Can take the place of persistence
Talent will not;
Nothing is more common
Than unsuccessful men with talent.
Genius will not;
Unrewarded genius is almost a proverb.
Education will not;
The world is full of educated derelicts.
Persistence
And
Determination
Alone
Are Omnipotent.

— CALVIN COOLIDGE

Campaign Attitude

All roads lead to the inevitable, the success of your job search, where persistence, patience, and faith in self pay off with a new job. If you have adequately prepared yourself with all the preliminaries, you should be ready for the main event where effort and courage meet. Make sure you have a job focus(es) before you begin and refine your goals as your campaign reveals more data. Psychologically you have to feel good because you are focused. You know your skills, abilities, and talents and what you have to offer. You're excited because you know what you're all about, you are looking ahead, and you know you are more prepared than the majority of your competition as you start your campaign. You have a "no-quit" attitude!

I will not have anything to do with a ship that does not go fast, for I intend to go into harm's way.
— JOHN PAUL JONES

Like most things in life, maintaining a positive attitude and a can-, will-do mindset throughout your campaign is a must! Radiate enthusiasm for what you are doing! This can be an interesting journey into self as well as an exciting time to hone existing skills and practice newly acquired ones. Be determined "to be the best that you can be," to say and visualize daily affirmatives to yourself, and to take and accept the responsibility for your campaign, remembering that only you can make things happen. "Results expected equals results achieved." Be determined to succeed! Direct and control your campaign momentum and keep it moving ahead. Take charge; speak and gesture with confidence. Consider this search as a marketing job where you are working for yourself, conducting an investigation, and that you are committing yourself to succeed no matter what. Stick to it! Set daily or weekly performance goals. Do not accept poor results or performance. There are no excuses for doing very little, even when the economy is sluggish. Remind yourself that if unemployment is at 7 percent, there is the other 93 percent who are working and that you will soon be part of those statistics. Success requires hard work! There is a job out there for you. Organizations always need good people. Constantly evaluate how you are doing. *Take responsibility for the management and effectiveness of your campaign!* Evaluate your progress weekly. Change options when needed. Be gutsy and create ways to meet key people, but don't give up.

I am a great believer in luck. The harder I work, the more I have of it.
— THOMAS JEFFERSON

You Are the Key

A well-executed job search takes patience, discreet perseverance, effort, a lot of time, a positive attitude, hard work, and follow-up. Put all vacations on hold. You will need to discipline yourself to plan and work long hours. "Plan your work and work your plan." There are no "cookbook solutions" to getting a job. No one is going to do the work for you, even a reputable search firm. You're going to have to do it yourself! It will require all the ingenuity and stamina you can muster. Seven to nine hours per day, six to seven days a week might not be out of the question. You will find that by conducting an aggressive campaign, you'll work harder and more creatively at your job search than at most jobs. Self-motivation and sheer determination are the orders of the day! I believe that the harder and smarter you work, the better the campaign results will be. One must realize that no matter how well one is organized, success is directly linked to whether one is willing to carry out a thorough, systematic, and well-organized campaign plan which includes a variety of strategies including networking to keep the momentum going. Networking can be a stumbling block to some who test as introverts or have not learned how to network effectively. These difficulties can easily be reversed, however, by effective instruction and counseling. People who have never been extroverts in the past become more so. Personalizing your campaign is important! Don't get desperate! Companies don't hire desperate job hunters.

As you actively go through this process, realize that most people have experienced job changes (moves, layoffs, etc.) during their careers, and they know what you are going through. I have seen articles that stated that young people today will each have as many as ten different jobs and possibly several different careers during their lifetime. The Bureau of Labor Statistics says that the average American now changes jobs about every four years. Change is inevitable. While new jobs are being created, old ones become obsolete. Effective campaigns require taking chances. Know that risk, by its very nature, produces fear. Confront and eliminate it from your mind. Be determined to overcome all obstacles. Discipline yourself to focus on your positives! List them: you are a survivor and you will survive; there is a job out there for a person with your talents; your family and support groups are 100 percent behind you; many people have gone, are going, and will go through what you are today; you are a good person; any others you may want to add to your list. Program yourself to be prepared to face the frustrating disappointments of unanswered letters, phone calls not being returned, form letters that are sent you, turndowns, rejections, etc. Realize you have no control over these very real things (rejection shock), so don't take them personally and tell yourself that their loss will be someone else's gain. Believe it! Learn from your mistakes! Realize that it may take many no's to reach some yesses.

What you do have control over, though, is your effort (time spent), attitude, commitment, persistence, belief you will succeed, dress (appearance), resume, how you research, and how you present yourself throughout your campaign. Keeping good campaign work habits and following through will help to minimize feelings of depression, which bring poor results and low self-esteem, which can in turn lead only to withdrawal. To find acceptance within yourself, you will have to positively assert yourself and risk any rejections that might come your way. You'll need to keep your mind active by immersing yourself totally in the hard work of the campaign. Effective campaigns of the nineties will require hard work, plenty of personal commitment, drive, desire, persistence, ingenuity, and self-knowledge. You will be as successful as you want to be, and your campaign will be as strong as your state of mind. (Sounds like my golf game.)

Failure is the first step toward success.
— CONFUCIUS

Campaign Time

If you are going to be laid off and you know it, start your campaign right away. The tendency will be not to do anything right away, as one is usually burdened down by depression, anxiety, and self-degradation. To survive, we need to begin. Also, before you leave your employer, see if you can negotiate for an excellent reference letter, extended medical coverage, and outplacement counseling and find out whether you are eligible for unemployment compensation. Most likely you are. You paid into it, and you deserve it.

I am always asked, "how long will my campaign take?" as if I have a crystal ball. It's like being asked, "how long will I live?" As with most things in life, the results of your campaign won't just happen right away. Begin with realistic expectations! Most productive campaigns last on the average of six to seven months if you are working and five to six if you are not. You should plan accordingly and even have a contingency plan if things don't work out ideally. Maybe you'll have to be retrained or you need more experience, which you can get from temporary work. A year might not be unusual in this day and age. Job searches take time, and a lot depends on your marketable skills and what needs are current in the job market. Allow extra time. There is an unwritten rule that states that it is easier to get a job when you have one. I believe that! If you are employed, take time each day to do some work on your campaign. Remember: "the walls have ears." Work *harder* and *smarter*. Don't be afraid to come to work early and leave late some evenings. It will help you on those days you need to take off early. Do so only for job interviews. Plan advice interviews for early morning, lunch (away from work site), evenings or weekends. Take personal or vacation days when needed, but only as a last resort. You will also want to consider writing articles for trade journals. Note: There is less pressure to get a job when you are employed, you are not perceived by others as being "damaged goods," and because of that, you will project a more positive attitude of being in control of your career.

If you're unemployed, make it your full-time job plan to spend at least 25 to 30 hours a week on your campaign. Set goals and a realistic timetable for yourself. There is also a rule of thumb, as I mentioned in an earlier chapter, that states for every $10,000 of straight salary you are looking for, it will take you one month. One has to be both patient and a hard worker! Invest in your daily time wisely. Be prepared to wait it out and budget your reserve funds accordingly, remembering that the following can impact on your campaign time: the current market (buyers' or sellers'), the time you are willing to spend, geographic areas of preference and how the hiring markets are in those places, your willingness to relocate to other parts of the country, salary and job titles and whether you are willing to take a cut in pay, working evening hours, your age (with some organizations), the quality and commitment of your effort, impressions created when taking interviews (advice and job), whether you have done the right research on organizations to position yourself in key places, and whether you can take trips to desired locations.

If a job is offered to you and it isn't quite what you were looking for, you may consider taking it if it could be used as a stepping stone to getting you to where you want to eventually be. Lesser-paying positions may have hidden benefits such as longer vacations, being part of a rapidly growing industry, profit sharing, free parking, annual bonuses, faster promotional opportunities. When my son took a job with Marriott, that was one of the many reasons he selected them.

According to my records, the following chart gives you some insight as to what the best months were for former clients to get a job (Fig. 19.1).

✦ ✦ ✦

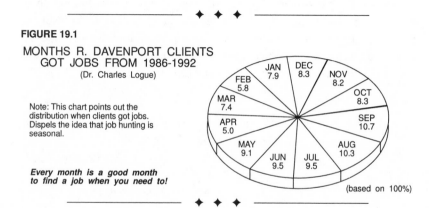

FIGURE 19.1

MONTHS R. DAVENPORT CLIENTS
GOT JOBS FROM 1986-1992
(Dr. Charles Logue)

Note: This chart points out the distribution when clients got jobs. Dispels the idea that job hunting is seasonal.

Every month is a good month to find a job when you need to!

JAN 7.9
DEC 8.3
NOV 8.2
FEB 5.8
OCT 8.3
MAR 7.4
SEP 10.7
APR 5.0
AUG 10.3
MAY 9.1
JUN 9.5
JUL 9.5

(based on 100%)

✦ ✦ ✦

Note: Learn to be patient, and don't expect overnight success. Diligence will pay off in the long run. Believe it! Also, there is no bad time to be looking for a job!

Campaign Finances

Figure out your campaign budget before beginning your campaign. Talk to all family members about your situation and involve them (especially younger children) in putting together the family budget. Tell them that you will need their help in making the budget work, as well as their continual support, and that everything will turn out fine! Many family members will fear change and what the future will bring. Your positive approach to all matters, including how to deal with the budget, will help all family members cope with the situation.

You will want to plan meetings with all of your creditors to explain your situation and to arrange minimum payments where possible, i.e., on your mortgage, pay only interest and put off principal payments to a later date.

If your campaign is taking you more time than you anticipated, you may want to consider a temporary or consulting job to help you pay the bills. Retail stores are always looking for help, and many cities have temporary agencies such as Robert Half that can assist you. Sometimes temporary or consulting jobs turn into full-time jobs.

Expect to pay for your campaign. Consider it as an investment in yourself and your career. While there are monetary and time expenses in working with a reputable career counselor, the cost is very small compared to the benefits you'll get from it. Most people, unfortunately, don't know how to market themselves (package their background and experience) to reach the "buying markets." You'll need to if you are going to survive in the nineties and the twenty-first century.

Keep records of campaign expenses in a daily diary, including travel, meals, postage, meeting attendance costs, parking, printing (e.g., resumes, photocopying charges), stationery (office supplies), telephone, and even career counseling costs. These expenses may be tax deductible. You will want to check with an accountant or tax specialist.

> *Whatever the mind can*
> *CONCEIVE and BELIEVE*
> *it can*
> *ACHIEVE*
> — THE MIRACLE MAN

Campaign Planning

You have to feel good that all is in place, and now all you have to do is to develop a well-thought-out, well-defined, and realistic campaign plan that will help get you to where you want to be. Consider it like planning a trip using a road map. You need to know where you are going and how to get there.

"Plan your work and work your plan." Remember: productive people are well organized and goal oriented. Campaign success will depend on how well you plan and your determination to make the plan work. Success comes to people who work hard at it. There are no shortcuts. A campaign is hard work. Individuals who are well prepared and well organized have the competitive edge. Plan to break your campaign down into bite-size pieces, or smaller strategies. Someone once asked, "how do you eat an elephant?" The answer is, "bite by bite." Or, "how do you climb a high mountain?" Answer: "step by step." Plan to set up a daily step-by-step campaign schedule for yourself. Set up a definite daily routine with starting and ending times. Don't be afraid to put in long hours if that is what it takes. Be determined to overcome all obstacles. Prepare a daily ABC (to-do) list for yourself: "A," what you must do; "C," what would be nice to do; and "B," what falls in between. This list will be revamped and revised at the end of each campaign day. Keep daily records and a weekly tally sheet! You should plan to check to see each day that you are not wasting time by doing nonproductive things. Evaluate your effectiveness! Keep your campaign momentum moving in a constant but positive way. Follow up all leads right away. Don't let them get cold!

Plan to have a written, clearly stated, and focused job objective and reasons why you want to move in that direction (you may have more than one focus). It is important that this be written, as we tend to honor things more within ourselves when we write them down. Around your focus, put together a market list of organizations from your research and homework, experience and contacts which are of interest to you and could possibly use your talents. Use SIC (standard industrial classification) codes. Plan to go after them "with a fever." Realize that your job is finding a new job! You may even consider industries other than your own but to which your skills are transferrable. Consider relocation and trying something new, especially in these turbulent times. You are working for yourself even though you may be unemployed. You are selling yourself and your skills.

Plan to identify all or most of your job wants: geographical area(s) of interest (local/relocation); size and type of organizations, large, medium, or small, schools; public or private sectors, profit versus nonprofit; travel, limited or not; position/title; partnership; independent contractor; office work;

reasonable work days; challenge; money; reasonable commuting time for work; limited pressure; time with family; ownership, etc.; from your research from directories, professional association journals, phone books, newsletters, newspapers, and other sources.

Set up alternative contingency plans by playing various scenarios through your mind and deciding what you would do if certain unexpected things happened.

Plan to also select campaign alternatives for yourself if your job objective doesn't work out for you, whatever the reason. Maybe you'll have to create a new direction with different strategies. Be flexible.

Plan weekly campaign strategies at least one week ahead of time. Set up all your meetings and utilize your campaign calendar. Plan what you want to accomplish, writing down "all the little things" that need to be done or followed through on so that "no stones are left unturned."

> *In life as in a football game, the principle to follow is: Hit the line hard.*
> — THEODORE ROOSEVELT

Plan to keep accurate and timely data so you can monitor your campaign results. Total up the results daily and weekly to note productivity. Plan to commit yourself to target numbers in all categories, e.g., research conducted, advice meetings held, periodicals scanned, phone calls, letters written, etc.

Personnel experts say job candidates become scarce around the holidays. If that is the case, why not plan to take advantage of this? According to *USA Today* (December 13, 1988), "people assume employers aren't hiring, so competition is less, hiring personnel are in better frames of mind and key people are usually at the office." Other reasons for expanding your job search during the holidays could be that there will be less competition from other sources (with people not submitting applications). Ads that do appear in newspapers could very well be high-priority positions. The fiscal year (new budgets) starts for many companies after December and June.

Plan to have at least three advice interviews per day if you are unemployed, meeting with people evenings and even on weekends if need be. Target yourself to do twenty to thirty things a week to keep your campaign moving ahead. If you're working, adjust accordingly.

Plan to work on Sundays, as they usually are nonproductive job campaigning days. Plan to handle your written correspondence (thank-you letters, introductory and broadcast letters), update your records, answer your ads, and plan your next week's schedule on this day.

Plan to keep your current job while you are looking for a new one. Psychologically speaking, it's easier to get a job when there is no pressure. Besides, you don't come across as damaged goods.

Plan not to take long weekends or vacations during your campaign. All energies should be focused on your campaign and getting to where you want. You can take a vacation just before you start your new job, if you feel you owe it to yourself and your family. Remember: the jobs go to those whose campaign is well planned, well marketed, and well executed. Most people, unfortunately, don't know how to plan and market themselves effectively. That, at least, is one of the reasons why some jobs don't necessarily go to the most qualified (aside from politics).

Plan to conduct an active, "people" campaign and to use a variety of your own innovative and creative strategies as you contact hundreds of people. Don't be afraid to experiment. I tell my clients that "anything within the letter of the law goes." What didn't work for someone else might in fact work for you. Cast your net wide! Expand it to the broadest base possible. There are no easy methods or cookbook solutions to finding a job! It requires a comprehensive plan and hard work. The more resources you tap or use, the more effective your campaign (the Law of Numbers). I really believe that! So "don't put all of your eggs in one basket." Develop and perfect the strategies that work best for you. People make their own luck, and they do it with well-thought out plans.

Plan to continue your campaign until you have a written job offer in hand. Be an optimist. Keep an open mind. Try to look at situations in different ways.

Prayer for Personal Achievement

Lord, I carry within me the basic wish
to fulfill myself as a person.
This is a noble ideal
that you want me to achieve
during my lifetime.
I feel I should bring to fruition
my being's potential.
Only in this way will I be able
to express the native traits
of my personality.
You encourage me, Lord, with your inspiration
and decisive influence.
Thus I can truly dedicate myself to this effort,

which integrates and fulfills me.
I want to begin by always accepting myself
as I am.
Keep far from me those ideas
that overstep my true capacity by far.
Direct me in this tangle of life
to what is truly beneficial
for my growth.
Give me always the ability to see,
without disguises and utopias,
the reality of myself and that of others.
Help me, Lord, to be myself,
and may I be so in the light
of your justice, truth, and love.
Amen.

— ANONYMOUS

Finally, after you get to where you want, start planning your next career step. Always have a plan or plans.

That Man Is A Success

Who has lived well, laughed often and loved much; who has
gained the respect of intelligent women and men and the love of
children; who never lacks appreciation of the earth's beauty or
fails to express it; who follows his dreams and pursues excellence
in each task; and who brings out the best of himself.

— ANONYMOUS

Don't Quit

When things go wrong as they sometimes will,
When the road you're trudging seems all up hill,
And you want to smile, but you have to sigh,
When care is pressing you down a bit,
Rest if you must, but don't you quit.
Life is queer with its twists and turns,
As every one of us sometimes learns,
And many a failure turns about
When he might have won had he stuck it out;
Don't give up though the pace seems slow—
You may succeed with another blow.

Success is failure turned inside out—
The silver tint of the clouds of doubt,
And you never can tell just how close you are,
It may be near when it seems so far;
So stick to the fight when you're hardest hit—
It's when things seem worst that you must not quit.
                                            — ANONYMOUS

93 Campaign Strategies

Your campaign success will be the result of you using several strategies and carefully weaving them in concert with one another as you successfully market yourself. Consider yourself a strategy manager. Take comfort in knowing that by reading this book and putting to use the majority of the ideas within, you will have more information about conducting an effective campaign than most of your competition. This thought alone should help in building your confidence and give you a "distinct competitive edge," especially during the nineties. You will need an edge.

The best approach to your developing a campaign plan is to answer the question, "where do you get the biggest bang for the buck?" Obviously, one that primarily utilizes networking and then encompasses all others in timely, imaginative, creative and organized ways. The more strategies you use, the more effective your campaign will be.

1. If you are looking for a job, for whatever the reason, don't start campaigning until your attitude is positive, you are through grieving, and you have effectively packaged yourself with most of the ideas from this book.

Career search can be a profound journey of
personal growth—not just a superficial choosing
and securing of a job.
                                  — BETTY NEVILLE MICHELOZZI

2. Seek and build the support of your family and friends right away. Don't delay. Job losses and career changes impact on everyone's feelings. Talk about how the trauma feels. Consider seeking emotional support from a qualified counselor, psychologist, or psychiatrist. The grieving process needs to be worked through so angry feelings can be reversed into positive ones. You need to tell yourself that it is normal to feel lost, alone, bitter and afraid when

confronting stressful issues. You need to tell yourself that all will be right and that you are a survivor—and tell your spouse, who will also be going through grieving, possibly more than you. Tell friends you will soon be looking for a job and will be able to use their help. You're not "using" them. They will want to help.

3. Assess your financial situation. Lay out at least a six-month survival plan; consider getting information about *The Banker's Secret Bulletin* by writing to the Good Advice Press, Box 78, Elizaville, NY 12523, and write to *The Tightwad Gazette*, RR 1, Box 3570, Leeds, ME 04263.

4. Write for information about a three-month bimonthly job bulletin service to Pro Net Job Bulletin, P.O. Box 51820, Palo Alto, CA 94303; also, consider subscribing to Exec-U-Net, 21 November Trail, Weston, CT 06883, (203) 226-5710 or (800) 637-3126 (9:00 a.m. to 5:00 p.m.), and The Search Bulletin, P.O. Box 641, Great Falls, VA 22006, (800) 486-9220 (24 hours) or (703) 759-4900.

5. Take a battery of valid and reliable career interest and aptitude tests to help you decide, confirm, and focus on your job objective(s). Develop a chart on yourself. A campaign will work as well as the information you have on yourself (self-assessment) and how that ties into what you are doing. Know that knowledge builds confidence. Note what makes you unique or unusual, what you do well. Assess your accomplishments, skills, values, and interests and your current job needs and musts, likes and dislikes, etc. What do friends praise you for?

6. Prepare a winning resume and quality portfolio which emphasizes what you can do for an organization. Stress your value (ideas, service, connections) and transferrable skills; tailor them for different situations if needed. Make sure you field test your resume with friends or, better yet, associates in your profession to see what suggestions they would make. If you need to maintain confidentiality, use a friend, keeping your name off the resume. Don't be embarrassed to call a friend for help. You may also consider using a box number rather than a street address.

7. Check your wardrobe and appearance. Be conscious of what good dress is and put your wardrobe and appearance in order. "When in Rome dress as the Romans do." If you are overweight, start a diet and exercise program for yourself. As the Nike ads state, "Just Do It."

8. Register with agencies and recruiters on a fee-paid basis only.

Contact the personnel offices of the better firms to find out what agencies and recruiters they use. Remember, though, that fewer than 10 percent of people get jobs through these firms and that they find people for jobs and not the other way around. They don't work for you but for organizations.

9. Send updated resumes to references with a note, thanking them for their support.

10. Correlate your test results and self-assessment with organizational research to insure the right slot for yourself. Match your personality with organizations. Which ones do you think you would fit best into? Do their working environment, culture, and way of doing business match yours? The heart of a well-done campaign can be the quality of your research. Use reference books, public filings, and annual reports in selecting desirable organizations. Start developing a target (one page) and market (more than one page) list of companies you feel you would be interested in, using the standard industrial classification codes (SIC).

11. Answer ads in professional trade journals in your area, as well as from radio, television, newspapers, business/professional publications, and ad sheets like the *National Ad Search* or *National Business Employment Weekly*. Consider answering ads with interesting firms where there is no match at all. They may reroute your letter. Realize, though, that fewer than 10 percent of people get jobs through ads. When you do, it's like hitting the lottery. Take note that newspaper ads, as my former boss Cap Beck commented, give you an indication of how active a market may be and what positions companies are hiring people for. You can write to the key decision maker in your field to see if there might be some interest.

12. Register with the placement office of the school(s) you graduated from. Find out what organizations recruit at your school and what they are looking for, also who hired last year and what jobs they went into. Make appointments and talk to the dean, placement director, and alumni or alumnae director. Obtain a copy of an alumni or alumnae directory to see if prominent former graduates may be working in some of your targeted organizations. Many offices contain directories and research materials. Consider the placement services of technical and professional societies and associations if applicable. Note *College Placement Annuals* and school job vacancy listings, and talk to academic departments,

faculty members, advisors, and staff. See if the placement office offers career development seminars, workshops, or career fairs. Note their bulletin boards for job leads. Contact school board members, directors, and trustees.

13. Consider placing position wanted ads in professional journals in your field.

14. Take a civil service exam at the nearest federal building to qualify for open positions with agencies such as the Postal Service; Department of Defense; Department of Labor; Department of Health and Human Services; Environmental Protection Agency; Internal Revenue Service; National Security Agency; and Federal Bureau of Investigation, as well as state and local positions, i.e., State Game and Park Commissions, State Employment Service, Probation and Parole Boards. Consult the *Federal Jobs Digest*, Breakthrough Publications, P.O. Box 594, Millwood, NY 10546, (800) 824-5000, and state government agencies for current labor conditions and who is hiring. Most post offices have application forms and information on job opportunities. You can also write to the U.S. Office of Personnel Management (formerly the Civil Service Commission), Washington, DC 20415; *Federal Career Opportunities*, Federal Research Service, Inc., P.O. Box 1059, Vienna, VA 22180-1059, (703) 281-0200; and *How to Locate Government Employment* (1987), Robert Hancock, Sylvia Carpenter and Jill Tucker, Broughton Hall Inc., 1919 State Street, Suite 112, Santa Barbara, CA 93101, (805) 687-7818.

County and municipal agencies could also be approached, i.e., YMCA/YWCA, agency dealing with aging, children's services, mental health/ retardation centers, civil defense, voter registration, sheriff, museums, American Heart Association, Diabetes Foundation, health services, hospitals, nursing homes, solicitor, tax office, water authority, police and fire departments.

15. Set-up weekly campaign support group meetings (others who are conducting active campaigns). Make a group formal commitment, i.e., "one for all and all for one." Others who are experiencing the same situation can be very supportive. Give your group a name, i.e., "The Highly Employables." Set agendas to discuss things such as weekly campaign progress, what techniques seem to work and not work, target and market lists. Discuss how to resolve common problems. Consensus decision making should set group action plans, agendas, and rotating leaders. Encourage or start a support group for spouses. Research projects for individu-

als can be assigned, e.g., checking out certain publications; critiquing all written and oral communications; reviewing films, audios and videos on job search subjects. Other ideas for consideration: comparing interview results and what was asked; comparing and critiquing resumes; giving role playing advice and advice on job interviews; sharing of journal and newspaper articles; inviting guest speakers to meetings (e.g., ministers, psychologists, financial planners, outplacement counselors, unemployment office representatives). Decide on the frequency of meetings and where you'll meet. Consider writing, with a self-addressed stamped business envelope, to Robert Bryant at 2303 West 11th Street, Wilmington DE 19805 for a free group meeting outline. For ideas in starting a network group, contact the following: Shirley Chambers, The Employment Network, Johnette Bldg., Suite 401, Monroeville, PA 15146, (412) 856-7979; Charles Beck Priority Two, Room 208, PNC Bank Building, Beaver and Blackburn Roads, Sewickley, PA 15143, (412) 741-8368; and the Interfaith Employment Group, 255 Washington Road, Pittsburgh, PA 15216, (412) 531-1007.

17. Befriend the reference librarian at your favorite library and seek help to locate research (homework sources). Some libraries have lending services which you can make available to yourself. Cities, counties, and states have directories of businesses and industries that you may target. Local Chambers of Commerce provide directories for nominal amounts. The U.S. Department of Labor publishes literature periodically on local and national job markets. Read financial magazines and business papers, i.e., *Barron's, Value Line.* Check the *Business Periodicals Index* for growth and rapidly developing firms. Note *FORTUNE* and *Forbes* magazine listings. Look up job titles that interest you. Isolate at least ten occupations or industries that interest you.

18. Become an expert at networking (making contacts). Once you are focused, ask job guidance from others already doing what you want to do. Remember: a successful job campaign is really all about jointly satisfying each other's needs (employer/employee). Networking is the best way to tap into the "hidden job market" (phrase that covers jobs that haven't been advertised or that the Human Resources Department doesn't know about). *Take note as to whether you are networking enough!* I have found that clients who conduct a paper campaign because it's comfortable (don't want to ask, too embarrassed to ask, don't feel they know anyone who

can help, or haven't perfected their skill) don't get the results that clients do with a mainly people campaign. Networking can be hard, but it is necessary! 65 to 85 percent of all jobs obtained come through this process, so it is worth your time to perfect your skills. Stop and think. How many of your jobs, either full or part-time, were obtained by networking? Most, I suspect.

Another interesting thought is that even though an organization might have a freeze on hiring, someone may be retiring, there might be an untimely death or a merger or acquisition might be taking place which could create some openings.

19. Follow-up *all* leads. Otherwise you lose control. Don't prejudge anything. Note interesting magazine and newspaper articles that describe start-up firms or places that are expanding their operations that you might follow up on. Keep your better contacts periodically advised as to what you are doing. If you are not getting the campaign results you want, change strategies, career direction or both.

20. Check out professional and technical associations of interest by using the *Encyclopedia of Associations*. If you are a member, many associations have placement or employment offices as a service. Consider joining local professional and social clubs to help you make contacts. Use membership directories, i.e., of the country club, as an information source. Find out what services or information is available to you as a member. Attend meetings to meet others from your profession. Contacts can and do give you job leads in your field.

21. When you land a job, keep campaign records and materials for possible later use. Maybe these can be shared with spouse, sons/daughters, friends, or neighbors. Records can also be used to plot progress and to note referrals.

22. Register with state employment offices (Bureau of Employment Security). Many have counselors trained to assist job-hunting people as well as a national computer base (called "Alex") of positions.

23. Check out all area (local) job information centers as well as community agencies, i.e., Urban League, Catholic Career Service, Information Hotline, Jewish Vocational Services, Job Advisory Service, etc. Some offer free or minimum-fee placement services.

24. Contact local Chambers of Commerce regarding their organizational directories, names of firms moving into the area, and those that are both profitable and expanding. Also note any directories

they might have of their membership and start contacting members.

25. Check to see what conventions and trade shows might be coming to town. Obtain listings of exhibitors. This is a great way to obtain information, make contacts, and exchange business cards.

26. Contact the League of Women Voters or courthouse for a listing of local publications and officials. Since many politicians are lawyers, the local or state bar association directory could also be of use for contacts.

27. Prepare a portfolio of yourself including copies of reference letters; self-assessment of your skills, abilities, and talents; more in-depth descriptions of experiences; copies of career test results; resume; transcript of grades; certificates; awards; and pictures of work sites and projects that you successfully completed (see chapter 14).

28. Create a position for yourself by preparing a company job proposal. Research the industry, target organizations and single out problem areas of need. Aim your solution(s) toward those needs after reviewing PR releases, annual reports, brochures, organization magazines, newsletters, newspaper and library articles as well as Chamber of Commerce materials. Also talk to people who work in that industry, people who have contact with people who work there, and individuals who are knowledgeable about that organization. Contact companies laying off people with your proposal. They may be hiring new people for newly developed operations. Remember: anything goes!

29. Many libraries and telephone business offices have White and Yellow Page directories for most metropolitan areas. Use them for potential organization leads and addresses.

30. Subscribe to trade journals, magazines, and newspapers for ads. Spend very little campaign time on ads due to questionable payback. It's comfortable, and that is why a lot of people "escape" into using just them.

31. Union personnel should check with hiring halls for possible job leads.

32. If you just lost your job (and were not fired for cause), register for unemployment compensation benefits right away! Remember: you paid into this fund and you are rightfully due your money.

33. Talk to friends. Let them know your situation and find out how

they got their jobs. Get feedback on opportunities and approach. Self-marketing is a must!

34. Consider approaching organizations (competition) in your industry and firms and vendors serving it both vertically and horizontally, i.e., consulting firms (e.g., Arthur D. Little, Andersen Consulting), banks and their business contacts.

35. Ensure that important letters or notes are read by sending them by registered letter, messenger service, telegram, or an overnight service like Federal Express.

36. Note news articles and "people on the move" items about persons with positions that look interesting to you. Consider writing to congratulate the newly hired or promoted person and letting them know you'd like to join their team. Follow up with advice interviews with them. Find out also how they got into the field, their background, whether they would recommend it to a person with your credentials, and how they could suggest getting into their field. Maybe they would serve as "conduits" into their companies.

37. Contact temporary help agencies that contract with organizations to provide services for specified periods of time (a way to get experience). My son Jon worked for a temporary agency for almost two years. One of his assignments led to a permanent position.

38. Ask relatives about jobs other than where they work. Let all know you are looking for a job. Get them working for you.

39. See if your area has computerized job banks. If it does, there will usually be an annual fee.

40. Contact people you know or possibly even people that you don't know in your profession located in other states.

41. Don't forget that secretaries can be helpful in suggesting alternate times to reach the boss. Have a friendly phone voice. If the secretary was of assistance in arranging a meeting, mention their name in your follow-up thank-you note. Don't send this personal and confidential, as you want them to read it when it comes in. You'll then have a friend for life.

42. If you are going in for a job interview, do your homework on the organization and the people you will be visiting with. Prepare a list of important topics you want to cover. Review your answer to the interview questions, especially the money ones, and then relax.

43. Write out short and long range and local and long distance campaign goals and strategies for yourself, even if you have to fantasize. Writing them down produces more commitment on your part to carrying them out.

44. During slow job markets, friends have proven to be the prime source of job leads. Organizations will run fewer ads, promote more from within, and try and fill all leftover openings from employees' friends.

45. Test your career direction by conducting advice interviews with people who are in positions you would like. This will help you to focus more on your career direction(s). Note: It is okay to have more than one career direction.

46. When contacting people (allow four hours per day as a rule if you're unemployed), write letters, make phone calls, and make "cold calls" in person. "Test the waters" to see what approach(es) work best for you. Keep generating leads until you get some job offers! Know organizational needs through research, why you are qualified, and "what you bring to the party" (transferrable skills).

47. All contacts get thank-you letters promptly (within 1–3 days). If someone suggests you see someone, do so in a timely manner. Keep contacts fresh by checking in with them periodically and sending them articles or personal notes when you come across them (even after you get your new job).

48. When you land your job, send out an announcement/thank-you letter to all key contacts.

49. Don't stop looking because someone says he or she will hire you. Unless you get the offer in writing with an actual starting date, keep your job campaign active! Think of as many different types of companies, job titles and positions which might use your experience and transferrable skills. Keep and meet realistic daily campaign goals. Remember: the more energy you put into your campaign, the quicker you'll get the results you want and can be proud of.

50. Note salary surveys that have been done by private organizations in your area of expertise. Periodic surveys are also done by the Department of Labor. You will then know what a fair and equitable salary is.

51. As embarrassing as it may seem to your ego, let everyone know you are looking for a job. Don't keep it a secret!

52. Check all your references. Ask them if they would send a "To whom it may concern" letter to you to hold for when it's needed.

53. Scan books on psychological testing, especially if you feel you will be tested. Go to a college Psychology Department and scan their books on psychological testing.

54. Attempt to identify blind ads and write to the hiring person in your area of expertise.

55. Look into job retraining programs that you might be qualified for offered at community and other colleges. A friend of mine, Max Money, was retrained in computer skills and now enjoys a new career.

56. Follow up on all unanswered phone calls and letters, especially while the leads are "hot."

57. Never show up late for or cancel an interview. Note: Realize that if you are late, you most likely will not get the job. Try your route beforehand to see how long it will take you under the most unfavorable conditions.

58. Follow up all interviews (both advice and job interviews) with a thank-you letter and telephone call, stressing your interest and excitement about this opportunity and yet not appearing too anxious.

59. Mail all material *Personal* or *Personal and Confidential*. Most secretaries don't have the authority to open the boss's personal mail.

60. Consider buying a business or starting your own (call business brokers in the Yellow Pages), or buying in as a partner if you are further along in your career and you have expertise to sell, e.g., as a manufacturer's representative.

61. If you are over fifty, consider #60, being a self-employed consultant, a consultant for a company, or a commissioned salesperson where time and effort will govern income. It's an excellent way to prove yourself in a low-key way, "get your foot in the door," and possibly create a full-time position for yourself.

62. Teachers or service personnel changing careers should assess the transferable skills they have (e.g., research, organization, instructional, leadership, people) that can be applied to another organization.

63. Visualize realistic campaign timetables for yourself and set your own demands.

Chance never helps those who do not help themselves.

— SOPHOCLES

64. You may want to do some community volunteer work part-time. It's an excellent way to meet people and could possibly work its way into a full-time job. Propose two to four week apprenticeships.

65. If you are conducting a long distance campaign, do the following: subscribe to local newspapers as well as local trade, civic, and other publications; note what organizations in the city you live in do business or have offices in the geographical area you're interested in; refer to copies of the interested cities' Yellow Pages; write the executive director of the chamber of commerce and ask for newcomers' printed materials as well as an industrial directory; plan a trip to your target area at least two to three months ahead of time. Set up your meetings before you leave; write introductory letters to senior executives, civic and union leaders, the Jaycees, religious leaders, educators, presidents of schools, government leaders, and people that you might know there even if they are old contacts. Tell them you wish to relocate, you need that person's help and would like information about the business climate, trends in the job market, and details about community living and working conditions—and that you don't expect them to know of a job. Another idea is to consider a mail drop in certain target cities. Send a resume with all letters as a matter of courtesy and respond to those that answer you by telling them of your continued interest and promise that when you make a trip there, you will call for an appointment.

66. Target three to four business lunches a week (if you can afford it) with your ABC contacts.

67. Respond even to negative responses, thanking them for their consideration. Maybe things will change and you'll be invited back.

68. Try to contact 5–10 companies each week from your market list whose size, location, product lines, or industry are to your liking. Write to the key decision maker and then follow up with a telephone call. Continually add new companies as your research uncovers them (companies that have problems for you to solve—that's where the jobs are) and eliminate those where

there is no longer any interest. Note recently promoted people and their former organizations.

69. For women, write to the Catalyst, 250 Park Avenue South, New York, NY 10003, (212) 777-8900, for a list of publications geared to the special needs of women in the market place.

70. Keep reminding yourself that face-to-face contact with potential employers is the most effective way to find a job. Jobs come through people contact, either by phone or in person. Sending out hundreds of resumes and letters thinking that doing so will give you results is but a dream and has an effectiveness rate of only about 2 percent.

71. Contact real estate companies in your target cities and ask for the relocation kits they give to newcomers. They will be extremely helpful during your campaign. If you have to move, request *The Moving Book* (an excellent booklet) from AT&T, P.O. Box 2000, 1235 N. Avenue, Nevada, Iowa 50201-9987, (800) 222-0400.

72. When trying cold calls, going door to door is not recommended. If you have developed a telephone presentation and worked out the bugs, you can try advice and information interviews over the phone. These calls should be preceded by an introductory letter, preferably using a mutual friend's name.

73. It is all right to make multiple contacts within a single organization. Sometimes a contact will "drop the ball." If you have made only one contact with that firm, you have lost out. Multiple contacts may be also used with answering ads.

74. Note comments regarding company products, advertisements, and new services mentioned in annual reports and the media. Write to public relation departments for information and press releases.

75. Ask influential people to make contacts on your behalf.

76. Follow up rejection letters. The person who read your original letter (perhaps a clerk) may have misunderstood.

77. See your former supervisor for a reference letter, referrals, and possible job leads. Before leaving, see if you qualify for unemployment benefits and extended medical coverage as well as job hunting (outplacement) counseling. Sometimes these can be negotiated.

78. Employers generally like to hire local people instead of people from out of town. Therefore, try to have a local address and phone number in the geographical areas of interest if possible.

79. Consider advertising yourself in an imaginative way (although this strategy doesn't usually pay off), e.g., renting a billboard on a busy street with your message or using a "walking billboard."

80. Prepare for job interviews as if your life depends on it. Don't criticize your former company or boss. Do your homework on the organization and review interview questions.

81. When you accept a new job, make sure you receive word that you have successfully passed your reference and security checks and physical and drug tests before you submit your resignation (if applicable). Don't send out any announcements or thank-you letters until all is confirmed. Therefore, never stop your campaign. I had a client, a few years ago, who had a verbal offer retracted two weeks after it was made. Needless to say, he not only lost out on two weeks of campaigning, but his self-esteem was shot for some time thereafter. I always tell clients to get offers in writing. Although nothing in life is ever guaranteed, at least it is a little more binding.

82. If you are unemployed and you are asked whom you are representing during your campaign, you should reply that you are representing yourself.

83. If you are over 40, write to 40 Plus of New York, 15 Park Row, Suite 810, New York, NY 10038, (212) 233-6086, for a brochure on their services and local chapters. Consider other industries, as your past ones may be too limiting.

84. Contact regarding their services: Exec-U-Net (job-leads newsletter), (800) 637-3126.

85. Consider putting your resume on line with a recruiting database firm, e.g., Peterson's Connexion Services, 202 Carnegie Center, P.O. Box 2123, Princeton, NJ 08543-2123, (800) 338-3282 or (609) 243-9111 (recent college grads).

86. If your campaign is slow and money is running out, consider turning a hobby or an avocation into a money-maker for yourself, e.g., an archer giving archery lessons to neighbors, being an antique dealer, etc.

87. Consider doing consulting, temporary, contract, part-time, or freelance work. Check out one of the consulting directories for firms to contact. It helps you to get your "foot in the door." Some recruiting firms place temporaries (call Executive Recruiter News at (800) 531-0007 for a list; the cost is ten dollars).

88. If you are conducting a long distance campaign, try these ideas:

- Write to the hiring person (in your discipline area) telling him or her that you will be relocating to that area and would like input regarding the business climate, the kinds of industries it has and whether they would recommend it as a place to live.

- To those replying, thank them for their response, give them dates when you will be going to the area and that you would like to set up an advice interview. Customizing your letter, attach a copy of your resume for their information, and retain control by telling them you will call them within the week to arrange a mutually convenient time, then follow through and do it! Note chapter 21, Marketing Yourself with Letters.

89. If you're a woman, especially with a family, consider job sharing, which allows career continuation while you are still raising children.

90. Give a party and invite key contacts.

91. Recontact organizations that previously sent you rejection letters. Do so after 60–90 days, restating your continued interest in the firm (things may have changed since your rejection).

92. Once you get where you want to be, reach out to others when they come in need! Share your experiences and feelings with them.

93. Consider making contacts for overseas work.

Your campaign can be very discouraging, frustrating and tiresome. Plan to attack it with dogged persistence. You'll meet some people who don't support it. Forget them and find those who do. Put together a plan with viable strategies that you believe will work for you. Make changes as you go. Remember: an error does not become a mistake until you refuse to correct it. Prepare to stretch yourself while you are conducting your campaign and to enjoy yourself. Don't let your campaign control you; you control it! Practice self-discipline! It can be a unique and enjoyable opportunity. When in doubt, use common sense! Make it so by being prepared, following through by executing your plan and keeping a "can do" attitude. Use all the parts in the selling of yourself; you'll be successful! (see Fig. 19.2)

✦ ✦ ✦

FIGURE 19.2
The whole equals the sum of the parts

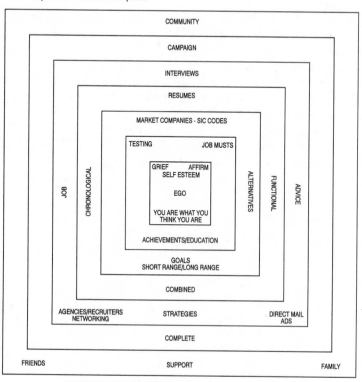

SELLING OF SELF: THE WHOLE EQUALS THE SUM OF THE PARTS

✦ ✦ ✦

One Day At A Time

There are two days in every week that we should not worry about.

Two days which should be kept far from fear and apprehension.

One of these days is yesterday, with its mistakes and cares, its faults and blunders, its aches and pains.

Yesterday has passed forever beyond our control.

All the money in the world cannot bring back yesterday.

We cannot erase a single word said,

Yesterday is gone.

The other day we should not worry about is tomorrow, with its possible adversities, its burdens, its large promise, or poor performance.

Tomorrow is beyond our immediate control.

Tomorrow's sun will rise, whether in splendor
or behind a mask of clouds.
But it will rise.
Until it does, we have no stake in tomorrow, for it is yet unborn.
This leaves one day . . . TODAY.
Any man can fight the battles of one day.
It is when you and I add the burdens of two awful eternities,
yesterday and tomorrow, that we break down.
It is not necessarily the experiences of today that disturbs
ones peace of mind.
It is of ten times the remorse of bitterness for something which
happened yesterday and the dread of what tomorrow will bring.
Let us, therefore, Live One Day At A Time.

— ANONYMOUS

20.

Registering with Employment Agencies and Executive Search Firms

Within our dreams and aspirations we find our opportunities.

— SUE ATCHLEY EBAUGH

Employment Agencies

Employment agencies (sometimes referred to as "flesh peddlers" or "job brokers") are organizations that obtain employer job vacancies primarily over the phone (entry level up to usually $40,000 per year) for the purpose of earning a one-time referral commission when the employer hires their referral. In short, they work for employers, not job candidates. Most states require that these agencies have state licenses and follow certain laws. Copies of these state laws can be obtained through the U.S. State Department of Labor (Bulletin 209) or the licensing bureau of the state in which you are interested. Despite the licensing requirements, though, many of these agencies are plagued by high staff turnover because employees are paid on commission based on a high volume of placements. If they don't get them, they leave. As a result, many agencies have people who are not too ethical—they may try to place you in any kind of job or maybe even try to hire you or sell you one of their available franchises. Many are franchise organizations.

You do not want to "shotgun" your resume to every agency in town. Overexposure makes you look as if you are desperate. Select a few (usually the best five) with excellent reputations that concentrate on or specialize in your field of interest. Don't expect much result. Fewer than 10 percent of people get jobs through agencies or recruiters. Give them, though, at least three months to uncover something. Don't expect too much because they are in business to fill jobs, not to get jobs for people. If one doesn't come up with anything, quietly register yourself with another agency. To uncover the better agencies, use friends (ask them if they have ever used one or know of anyone who has), directory guides, the Better Business Bureau, Chamber of Commerce, trade publications, personnel offices, classified newspaper ads and Yellow Pages ("Employment") for leads. I suggest that you do not use any that are not company "fee paid," unless you want to pay the fee.

Questions To Ask

Before you send your resume to either an agency or a recruiter, you may want to:

1. Find out if it specializes in your area of expertise. What is the size of the operation? How big is the staff and what are their backgrounds? How long have they been working there? How did they get your name?

2. Ask them how long the agency or recruiter has been in business. What organizations is it registered with (i.e., National Employment Association)?

3. How will you be marketed? Will confidentiality be maintained? Have they worked with others like you? How will your resume be handled? You can insist, if you want to, that they contact you before distributing your resume. If a position is open, ask why it is? If the person was fired, what was the problem? Ask to be sent written job specifications.

4. Ask if there is a contract. Who pays the fee? If you are asked to sign a contract, it usually demands 10 to 20 percent of starting annual salary if you take the job. (This can be deducted from income on your income tax.) Have an attorney look at the contract.

5. Ask to meet at the agency's office (if local).

Kinds of Agencies

There are three kinds of agencies you should be familiar with:

1. *General "all-around" agencies.* These agencies handle a wide variety of fields.

2. *Single-industry agencies.* These agencies specialize in a single field, e.g., advertising.

3. *Functional agencies.* These specialize within fields, e.g., in marketing.

After you have selected the agencies you want to register with, send a cover letter together with your resume. If the agency is located out of town, indicate that you are interested in relocating to that area, when you plan to be there, and when you will be available for interviews. You should state in your letter your salary requirements (usually your acceptable range) and at least four to five key accomplishments that make you marketable. The amount of time the agency gives you depends on that marketability and whether they have action projects which they feel you will match. If there is no current match, your resume will be placed in the file for possible future reference. If their client files need to be increased, "open blind ads" may be placed as a "come-on."

If you register with an agency, don't expect that it will help you very much, let alone write back to you. Fewer than 10 percent of people get their jobs through agencies or recruiters. Also, fewer than 8 percent of all professional, managerial, and executive jobs are listed with them (firms don't want to pay the fee). Consider it as "hedging" your campaign bet; if something materializes, it will be a blessing!

> *When a man has put a limit on what he will do, he*
> *has put a limit on what he can do.*
> — CHARLES M. SCHWAB

Executive Search Firms

Executive search firms (sometimes referred to as "recruiters," "headhunters," or "employment or management consultants"). These are non-licensed organizations who primarily handle senior executive management searches (average: three to four months) for jobs paying, usually, in excess of $50,000 per year, working for employers, not applicants. Top level firms only handle jobs with salaries in excess of $100,000. There are primarily two types of these firms:

1. *Retainer firms.* Such a firm has an exclusive contract and collects an upfront fee (30 to 50 percent of annual salary) or fee plus expenses (travel, lunches, and advertising) to locate a qualified candidate to be interviewed for a specific position. These firms are paid whether the candidate takes the job or not.

2. *Contingency firms.* These are paid only after the candidate has decided to take the position and has worked there successfully for a period of time. A one-time fee will usually be one percent for every thousand of the person's annual compensation (a $30,000 salary would mean a $300 fee). These firms are in competition with the others, with only the successful matchmaker getting paid by the company.

Note: If you are registering with the local office of a national firm, don't assume that your resume is being fed out to all the other offices. Each office usually is a franchise unto itself.

Questions To Ask

In addition to some of the questions you asked agencies, you may consider the following with recruiters:

- How do you operate? How are you perceived in the market-place? What is your turnover rate?
- What types of positions do you usually handle?
- What are some examples of companies you have as clients? Are the openings created by growth, turnover, or just an ongoing maintenance of staff?
- Do you work as an "exclusive contingency agency" for any firm?
- What is the education and business experience of your staff?

How They Work

Search firms are used by employers to screen candidates when high-level or sensitive positions are being filled, when the market may be tight, or when there are no viable in-house candidates. Some deal exclusively within one industry while others specialize in a certain industry function.

Usually recruiters are interested only in contacting employed, highly successful achievers, possibly in the news, who are career mobile. Almost all executive search firms work with people who are already employed by an organization. I guess there must be something about "damaged goods." They feel if you're working, you are all right!

Executive recruiters get names of potential candidates from a variety of reference sources: trade publications and directories, newspaper business articles, award articles, blind ads, conference and trade show speakers, school faculty members and deans, major competitors, business customers and clients, suppliers and vendors, consultants, business and support specialists, CPAs, bankers, attorneys, politicians and government officials, and the firm's own files.

These firms may approach you to ask if you know of any viable candidates for some "specs" that possibly mirror your background in hopes that you might even give your own name. If you are contacted as a potential candidate because your background looks like a match, ask if you can call back, as the caller has reached you at an inconvenient time. Then check the organization to see if it is listed in a recruiting directory or whether other friends or business associates have heard of them.

When you return the call, ask the recruiter the following: the correct spelling of the name, title and the firm's mailing address/telephone number. Ask them how they got your name, although they usually won't divulge their source; enough information may be given to you to make an educated guess as to the source. Ask about their experience and "track record" working with people of your background. Ask them about their size, other locations, customers, and the industries they handle. See if you can find out whether the position they are doing a search for is a division, subsidiary, or headquarters position. Ask what the job duties are. Who would be the subordinates and peers? Find out what the range for the position is. Prepare to give them salary information. Ask them how they maintain candidates' confidentiality. How are prospective employers contacted? And if they personally interview all candidates before referring them?

Selecting the Right Firm for You

If you are selecting executive search firms, select firms of repute, using the same selection criteria as you would an employment agency. Select firms in those areas of the country that you are interested in. Visit local recruiters if you can make an appointment for an interview to make an impression. If you do make a positive impression and they currently don't have an active search in your area, they no doubt will remember you for future opportunities. They may also be willing to contact some of your target firms that they have contracts with to help you secure an appointment. It also provides you with an opportunity to check out their working environment and whether you want them to be representing you (so to speak).

When you register with a recruiter, send a cover letter with your resume indicating your job objectives, salary range, and other information you think would be helpful (see Fig. 20.1 on page 362).

Sources of Agencies and Executive Search Firms

Names of employment agencies, executive search firms, executive recruiting consultants, and personnel placement services can be obtained from the following:

ACME (Association of Consulting Management Engineers)
521 Fifth Avenue, 35th Floor
New York, NY 10175

FIGURE 20.1
Sample agency/recruiter cover letter

February 10, 199__

Contact's Name
Title
Company
Street Address
City, State, Zip Code

Dear (Contact's Name):

Your organization has been recommended to me as a highly respected and very successful executive search firm, and one which may have a current search for a person with my experience and qualifications in operations or sales management.

I have twelve years of diverse management experience, having progressively more responsible positions with companies in the areas of Operations, Distribution and Sales Management, with profit and loss responsibilities. My experience includes preparation of departmental budgets, customer service, expense control, personnel management, inventory management, safety and quality control.

My personal attributes and abilities include:

- Operations and Sales Management experience in steel castings, aluminum forgings and fabricated metals.
- Ability to manage, lead and motivate people.
- Communicate and interact effectively at all levels.

Depending on location, size of the company and responsibilities of the position, my salary requirements are in the $50,000 to $60,000 range.

Should a client's interest seem compatible with my background objectives, I would welcome talking with you so we can arrange a meeting. I am enclosing my resume for your review.

Sincerely,

John Doe/eb

412/ _____ (Business)
412/ _____ (Residence)

Enclosed - Resume

American Management Association
Management Services Department
135 West 50th Street
New York, NY 10020
(212) 586-8100

Association of Executive Recruiting Consultants, Inc.
236 Park Avenue, Suite 1594
New York, NY 10169
(212) 949-9556

Association of Executive Search Consultants (AESC)
230 Park Avenue, Suite 1549
New York, NY 10169
(212) 949-9556

Directory of Executive Recruiters & Executive Recruiter News
Consultant News
Templeton Road
Fitzwilliam, NH 03447
(603) 585-2200
Note: This organization offers a set of mailing labels for the recruiting
offices listed in its directory.

National Association of Personnel Consultants (NAPC)
3133 Mt. Vernon Avenue
Alexandria, VA 22305
(703) 684-0180

The Recruiting and Search Report
P.O. Box 9433
Panama City Beach, Florida 32417
(904) 235-3733; (800) 634-4548

Contacts, as they are made, can be put on an agency/recruiter control
sheet similar to Fig. 20.2.

Additional Employment Sources

In addition to private employment agencies and executive search firms,
there are other places to look for job placement assistance. *The Encyclopedia
of Associations* has a list of organization addresses, information, and sched-

✦ ✦ ✦

FIGURE 20.2
Contacts with employment agencies/executive search firms

							FIRST NAME
							ADDRESS/ PHONE
							SECRETARY'S NAME
							SPECIALTY PERSON'S NAME
							DATE OF CONTACT
							MISCELLANEOUS

✦ ✦ ✦

ules of upcoming meetings. Many of these organizations (industrial, trade, technical, professional, social), publish job openings in their newsletters or professional trade journals.

School and college placement offices offer alumni and alumnae placement assistance for little or no money. I even suggest to some of my clients that they wander through some of the local offices even if they didn't graduate from that school. You never know what might be on a bulletin board, what free handouts might be available, or what ideas might surface. Schools publish alumni and alumnae magazines which contain a variety of class news releases. When I was teaching at the Oil Companies School in North Africa in the early sixties, a story about my experiences ran in my alumni magazine. This story provided the motivation for a graduating University of Maine student to apply for a position, and she was subsequently hired. You never know!

The key contact at these schools' offices is the Placement Director. Many of these directors will even administer tests or refer you to the school's counseling office for a battery of vocational tests, usually at no cost to students, alumni, or alumnae.

You will want to find out who your Alumni Director is. He or she may have some key business contacts within the community for you to contact or might even be able to refer you to some members of the school's board of trustees, who are usually successful business leaders. Obtain or order an alumni or alumnae directory while you are there. This may contain the names of some alumni or alumnae working for some of your target companies whom you can contact.

Campus fraternity, sorority, religious and other club organizations also have local and national directories that might be of use to you in your campaign as you network. These groups also may offer a variety of employment counseling, guidance or placement services for their members.

Other sources could be alumni or alumnae chapters throughout the country, professional organizations (e.g., Society for Advancement of Management), Retired Officers Associations, YMCA/YWCA, career counseling services, United States Employment Services (USES) in connection with state employment services—usually, though, they deal with few professional skills positions—civil service offices to take civil service exams, club directors, trade shows/conventions, church support groups, and personnel associations. Personnel association members usually have excellent connections with other local business leaders as well as some local employment agencies and recruiters that they might have used in the past.

Temporary employment agencies (e.g., Kelly Girls, Manpower, Robert Half) are also a viable option. They can be located in the Yellow Pages. My oldest son Jon had been out of school only a year and a half. He was trying to obtain a position in the financial/accounting field and to no avail. You might say he was between a rock and a hard place—a "Catch 22." Firms wanted to hire people with at least several years experience, which he didn't have. So where was he to go for that experience? He connected with a Robert Half Temporary Agency and they sent him out on temporary assignments, many for as long as eight months. These assignments, which lasted close to two years, were usually temporary work to replace an employee who was on leave or because that firm had a temporary overload of work. The agency billed the company for Jon's services and then paid him a certain percentage of the total (usually two-thirds). This experience served as an excellent apprenticeship period for him as he gained the experience he needed to add to his resume, eventually resulting in a full-time offer from one of the companies because they liked him and his work.

Working for a temporary agency also provides excellent insights and exposure to how industrial climates work and how politics (organization cultures) can vary from one company to another.

Touch of the Master's Hand

'Twas battered and scarred and the auctioneer
Thought it scarcely worth his while,
To waste much time on the old violin,
But he held it up with a smile.

"What am I bidden, good folks," he cried.
"Who'll start the bidding for me?"
"A dollar, a dollar," Then, "Two." "Only Two?"
"Two dollars, and who'll make it three?"
"Three dollars once; three dollars twice; And going
for three . . ."

But no.
From the room far back a gray-haired man
Came forward and picked up the bow.
Then, wiping dust from the old violin,
And tightening the loosened strings,
He played a melody pure and sweet
As a caroling angel sings.

The music ceased and the auctioneer
With a voice that was quiet and low,
Said, "What am I bid for the old violin?"

And he held it up with the bow.
"A thousand dollars, and who'll make it two?

Two thousand, and who'll make it three?
Three thousand once, three thousand twice,
And going, and gone," said he.
The people cheered, but some of them cried,
"We do not quite understand what changed its
worth."
Swift came the reply,
"The touch of a master's hand."

And many a man with life out of tune,
And battered and scarred with sin
Is auctioned cheap to the thoughtless crowd.
Much like the old violin.
A "mess of pottage," a glass of wine.
A game, and he travels on.
He is going "once" and going "twice."
He is going and almost "gone."

But the Master comes, and the foolish crowd
Never can quite understand
The worth of a soul and the change that's wrought
By the touch of the Master's hand.

— Anonymous

21.

Application Blanks:
Handle with Care

*I can stand what I know. It's what I don't know
that frightens me.*

— FRANCES NEWTON

Main Purposes

The application blank, as you know, is a personnel form for systematically collecting important information about each job applicant. You will usually have to fill one out for every position you apply for. If you are given an application blank to fill out, my suggestion is to ask if you can take two copies with you (a scratch copy and the one you will return), complete it at home, and send it in. Other than that, bring a "master" all filled out that you can refer to for correct dates, organizations, and titles, together with a typed list of your personal and business references.

An application blank has three main purposes:

1. *As a screening device* to eliminate candidates who are not qualified on the basis of such items as previous employment history (whether you're a job hopper), professional skills and education, references available, and memberships in professional organizations.

2. *As an aid to the interviewing process*, where facts from the form can be verified.

3. *As a possible tool* used by the institution to establish a successful employee profile. Application blanks of better employees can be reviewed to determine trends that can be used in the recruiting and selection process. As a former Director of Education for a fairly large hospital in the late seventies, I learned that turnover

of hospital staffs on the average was about 26 percent. Weighted application blanks were used by many hospitals and health care institutions to screen out applicants who did not "match the successful profile." This is not to say that it was the only way to select good employees, but together with the interviewing process it has proven to be fairly reliable in helping to reduce costly turnover rates.

Remember that application blanks can be used to eliminate you as a job candidate. You should never answer any question in a way which might be construed by the employer as being negative. It would be better to leave it blank. Leaving it blank is not the same as writing a false statement. Most applications ask you to sign at the bottom that all the information that you have given is true. Since omitting an answer is not the same as giving a false statement purposely and all the other information that has been given is correct, you should be willing to sign the document.

16 Ideas for Filling in the Blanks

1. Use a pocket dictionary.

2. Pay attention to directions. Use neat, uniform-size writing with blue or black ink unless you take the application blank home to type it at your convenience. (Consider no other colors than blue or black). A typed application would be my first choice, with no erasures or white outs.

3. For all salary questions (current salary, salary desired, etc.), print "will discuss during the interview, open, and/or negotiable."

4. If a question is not applicable, put "N/A." (Not applicable) Or draw a line through the blank to indicate that you didn't overlook that question.

5. If you are mailing an application blank back to an organization, make sure you have a well-written cover letter to accompany it.

6. Have all references typed on one sheet including names, titles, addresses, and telephone numbers.

7. Know which questions are lawful and unlawful to ask on an application blank. Information can be obtained from EEOC Compliance Manuals, the Bureau of National Affairs, Inc., Washington, DC.

8. Fill out the form; don't just attach a resume.

9. Be honest (employers more often than not *do check*).

10. Have no employment gaps. Fill in with school, parenthood, part-time job, or active job campaign (working for yourself).

11. Indicate your area code with your telephone numbers (residence/work) and zip code with your address.

12. If your school grades were just average and you have to list QPA, emphasize part-time work and school activities that you may have been involved in.

13. Keep all statements on your application blank positive. Avoid all negatives; e.g., Reason for leaving—long hours with low pay. Better—to broaden my experiential base and broaden/expand my skills.

14. When you print your first name, use your formal name, i.e., "Charles" rather than your informal one, i.e., "Chuck."

15. Print your full middle name, not an initial. If you don't have one, print N/A (not applicable).

16. If you have any physical limitations and the application calls for some of your medical history, print that you will discuss this section during the interview. Otherwise it may be used against you.

Never let your head hang down,
Never give up and sit down and grieve,
Find another way . . .
And don't pray when it rains,
If you don't pray when the sun shines.
— SATCHEL PAIGE

22.

Negotiating With Power:
Take the Cuffs Off

*When schemes are laid in advance, it is surprising
how often circumstances fit in with them.*
— Sir William Osler

Have the courage to act instead of react.
— Darlene Larson Jenks

It Starts With A Written Offer

Negotiation *does not begin* until you have a written job offer in hand. *I re-peat*—negotiation does not begin until you have a written job offer in hand. If an offer is not made, you don't negotiate and you definitely keep your job search active. You also, as I have mentioned before, "don't put all your eggs in one basket," even though there is that tendency when you think everything fits together. Your attitude has to be one that if you've done everything possible to enhance your candidacy, "whatever's to be, will be." If you don't get it, "their loss is going to be someone else's gain." That's what you have to think and believe.

If an offer is made that is "in your ball park," don't say yes or no to the offer, but ask them the following: "I'm assuming that you are going to put that offer in writing to me and once I have received it, I will have a few days to review it and get back to you. Is that all right?" If they say it isn't, mention to them that it is an acceptable business practice to put an offer in writing and that you would appreciate them doing so for you (Figs. 22.1 to 22.4).

As an aside, if the initial offer is way off the mark, you might assert yourself by saying something like, "I really feel that this is an excellent opportunity. I know that the 'chemistry' between us is terrific and that 'the fit' is perfect. I want you to know that I want to come to work for you for these reasons, as well as the fact that my skills are indeed readily transferable. But in all honesty, I am really disappointed in your offer!" Hopefully, as you remain quiet, they will make an offer to your satisfaction.

✦ ✦ ✦

FIGURE 22.1
Get the offer in writing

Date

Name
Address
City, State, Zip

Dear _____:
   Confirming our conversation of (date) , and further discussions with (third party), you are hereby formally offered the position of (job title) for our _____ operation at a salary level of $60,000 per year. Also, included are the Salaried Employee Benefits forwarded to your attention previously. In your case, we are extending the temporary living expenses on Page 12 of the benefit's package to cover all fair and reasonable expenses.
   I would like to take this opportunity to welcome you aboard our team and assure that you will find the group productive and exciting to work with. We sincerely welcome the addition of a professional such as yourself to this very key position in (company) . We have forwarded, for your acceptance, this offer for starting your new duties in (company) at the earliest possible date. Please acknowledge your acceptance of this offer by signing a copy of this letter and returning it to me.
   Very truly yours,

_____ COMPANY, INC.

Name
Title

ACCEPTED:

This _____ date of _____

✦ ✦ ✦

✦ ✦ ✦

FIGURE 22.2
Get the offer in writing

Date

Name
Address
City, State, Zip

Dear _____:

As per the agreement reached at our meeting on _____ in _____, we would like to offer you the following position and conditions of employment.

1. Your position will be _____, reporting directly to the President. Your areas of responsibility will be the sales of _____ and the traditional _____ Capital Equipment Lines on the national and international markets as assigned to our _____ Operations.
    You will also be responsible for the sale of the corresponding spare parts as well as the sale of _____ other auxiliary equipment related to our product line.
2. Your base compensation salary in _____ will be $_____ a year. The bonus in _____ and the following years will be established per the Company's standard bonus plan for executives and will be based on personal and company performance during each particular year.
3. The Company will provide a company car for you. Your car will be a _____. Eventual extras, such as a cassette player, sun roof, etc., will be at your charge.
4. In order for you to take advantage of the existing tax laws for house sales, you will be allowed up to ten weekend trips to _____ between _____ and _____. It is understood that you will try to combine these trips with customer visitations.
5. In addition to the above trips, your wife/husband will be allowed one trip to _____ for the duration of one week, including travel and living expenses, to explore the purchase or rental of your future living quarters in _____.
6. You will be reimbursed for the actual invoiced amounts for packing, transportation, insurance, and final unpacking at your new residence in the _____ area, of all your personal belongings from your present home in _____. The household items to include a maximum of one automobile.

7. You will be given a fixed amount of $_____ as an allowance for moving to compensate you for all travel and living expenses that you and your family will incur in making the total move.

8. You will be entitled to one week vacation in _____ and three weeks per year afterwards. (Fifteen working days.)

9. You will receive the standard Company retirement benefits.

10. You will be entitled to the medical, hospitalization, dental, vision and life insurance benefits now being offered to the Company executives.

11. In the unlikely event that the Company should elect to terminate your employment, you will be given six months of salary as a severance, should your termination occur during the first three calendar years. After the first three calendar years of service the severance will be in accordance with general Company policy for executives.

12. Your effective date of employment will be the earliest possible, but not later than _____.

Please return one copy of this letter countersigned by you for acceptance.

Very truly yours,

President

I accept the above conditions.

Mr./Ms. _____

◆ ◆ ◆

✦ ✦ ✦

FIGURE 22.3
Get the offer in writing

Date

Name
Address
City, State, Zip

Dear _____:

Pursuant to our conversation we are pleased to offer you the position of _____ for _____ effective as soon as your current employment terminates. The provisions for your employment are as follows:

1. Your salary will be $_____ per year.
2. In addition to your salary, _____ will provide a bonus for the first twelve months of employment at $_____ per month.
3. Along with your salary and bonus, _____ will provide a commission plan as follows:

   On $1.00 through $10,000,000 = .25%
   From $10,000,001 to $15,000,000 = .35%
   From $15,000,001 to $20,000,000 = .50%
   From $20,000,001 + = .75%

   Your commission program is based on a calendar year and booked business.

4. You will be provided a car allowance of $500 per month and a car phone allowance of $100.00 per month.
5. Your employment package will include the standard _____ Corporation benefits.

If you have any questions, please do not hesitate to call me.

Sincerely,

Name
Title

✦ ✦ ✦

FIGURE 22.4
Get the offer in writing

Date

Name
Address
City, State, Zip

Dear _____:

The purpose of this letter is to confirm the offer by _____ to you for employment on the following terms:

- Title: _____
- Salary: $_____ annually with a performance review after six months and annually thereafter.
- Bonus: Consistent with _____ policy at job level.
- Option Share: 500 shares of _____ Common Stock at date of issue price
- Benefits: Consistent with _____ policy.

(Name), we are very pleased that you have chosen _____ to continue your career and I look forward to working with you.

As we discussed, I will telephone your references this afternoon and I hope to hear from you concerning moving expenses as soon as possible.

Sincerely,

Name

What To Do After Your Offer Arrives

Once your written offer arrives, first discuss it with your spouse, family, or friends. Then enthusiastically telephone them with an upbeat attitude and positive tone to your voice. Many times as you well know, it's not what you say, it's how you say it. Do you say it with conviction and purpose?

The following is a sample scenario: "I received your offer and can honestly say that I'm very excited about coming to work for your company. There are, however, some minor items with respect to the letter that we need to talk about and resolve. I'm convinced that we will be able to do that. Because of the importance to me and to you since I will be working for you, I would like to meet with you in person as soon as possible rather than discuss them over the phone. Is that okay? When is a good time for you? Thanks again. I look forward to our get-together."

After pleasantries are exchanged at your next meeting and the question is asked, "with respect to the offer, what's on your mind?" You first say, is the salary negotiable? Americans aren't used to negotiating over prices. When working in North Africa, I found that it was expected that you make counteroffers in the marketplace. Companies today and in the nineties, I believe, will regard people with solid negotiating skills as being more valuable to the organization.

Remember: the company or the organization will always be negotiating with you for the lowest possible salary. By not speaking up in your own interest, you risk having the company decide that you are not much of a bargain at any price. If you don't think you're worth more money, the company won't, either. Also, any good organization will never withdraw an offer because you think you are worth more. The worst that could happen is that it will not budge off of the original offer. As an aside, some companies will try and get you for a lower salary by telling you that you'll have tremendous future opportunities there. Remember that nothing in this day and age is definite, especially if it is not stated in a written contract.

If you determine that the salary is negotiable, then ask, "would it be possible to be considered for $_____?" (I usually advise clients no more than $10,000 above the mentioned price. You want to keep it in a win-win mode; most likely around $5,000.)

If he or she responds by saying, "no, we can't go for $_____, but we can approve $_____," you say "fine" and then go on to your next item on your negotiations list.

If he or she says "no", you will need to ask if your job duties and responsibilities can be expanded so that the job can pay more. If the answer is again "no", you say "okay" and then ask if it would be possible for your job performance to be reviewed in three to six months and again six months after that, subsequently thereafter going on an annual review? If the answer is still "no," you will have to hope for some concessions as you review your list, i.e., you currently have four weeks vacation and you ask them "is it be possible to have four weeks vacation in lieu of the lack of salary increase?" If they say no, maybe they might come in at three which is certainly better than two. Maybe your job title can be changed within a few months and an employment contract specifying several months severance be granted if the salary can't be changed. Try and obtain at least those arrangements given to your equals.

Planning for Your Negotiating Session

You will want to be prepared for your negotiation session and plan for it. Accordingly, by reviewing Fig. 22.5 and selecting items applicable to your situation or at least those that you feel are, you will also want to single out those issues which you can compromise on and those that need to be resolved. You may even want to practice (role play), tape record, or videotape your practice sessions to see how your strategy flows.

———————— ✦ ✦ ✦ ————————

FIGURE 22.5
Negotiation checklist

Corporate perks (prerequisites) cover a variety of benefits which may or may not offer meaningful value to the employee. Remember when you negotiate, you do so for a compensation package—not just a salary. Also note that your prospective employer may not be able to negotiate some of these items as there may be a fixed company policy. However, others might be flexible, even if you are a part-time employee.

Answer questions Y–yes or N–no.

	Desired	Offered	Not Offered
Direct/Regular Income (Generally Taxable):			
Base Salary	___	___	___
Sign-on/Other (Year End)	___	___	___
Commissions	___	___	___
Bonuses, Corporate/Xmas, Annual, etc.	___	___	___
Profit Sharing	___	___	___
Stock Options (Date of Issue Price); Phantom Stock	___	___	___
Matching Funds	___	___	___
Investment Programs, Grants, Financial Counseling	___	___	___
Salary Review 3, 6, 9, 12 months	___	___	___
Deferred Salary Compensation	___	___	___
Cost of Living Increases (COLA)	___	___	___

Indirect/Other Perks (Generally Non-taxable):

A. Position:

Title ___ ___ ___

Line/Staff Relationships ___ ___ ___

Reporting Relationships (Organization Chart) ___ ___ ___

Functions, Overseas Travel ___ ___ ___

Responsibility/Authority/Accountability ___ ___ ___

Support (Personnel, Budgets), Secretary ___ ___ ___

Facilities, Equipment, Supplies, etc. ___ ___ ___

Pension Plans; Matching Investment Programs ___ ___ ___

Vacations (number of weeks), Holidays (extra time if need be) ___ ___ ___

Expense Account (Reimbursements; unrestricted), First Class ___ ___ ___

Gas, Mileage, Travel Allowances (Spouse) ___ ___ ___

Corporate Car, Phone Allowance ___ ___ ___

Free Parking (reserved) ___ ___ ___

Cafeteria/Executive Dining Room Privileges, Luncheon Clubs (private) ___ ___ ___

Use of Corporate Property (Vacation, Phone, Boat), Tickets, Lodge ___ ___ ___

Low Interest Loans, Short Term Loans ___ ___ ___

Country Club/Athletic or other Memberships, e.g., Civic, Health ___ ___ ___

Corporate Product Discounts ___ ___ ___

Office (size, location, window, drapes, furniture) ___ ___ ___

Entertainment Allowance (at-home) ___ ___ ___

Airline VIP Clubs, Frequent Flyer ___ ___ ___

Flexible Hours ___ ___ ___

Comp Time for Late Hours/Weekends ___ ___ ___

Work at Home Days ___ ___ ___

B. Health

Health Care Insurance (paid-up) ___ ___ ___

Medical, Dental, Vision ___ ___ ___

Life Insurance (Self and Family)   _____ _____ _____

Flight Insurance; Business Travel
Insurance   _____ _____ _____

Disability Pay Insurance, Accidental
Death   _____ _____ _____

Annual Company Physical and Dental
Exams (Self/Spouse)   _____ _____ _____

Personal Time (paid)   _____ _____ _____

Maternity Leave (Female/Male);
Funeral Leave   _____ _____ _____

C. Moving/Housing:

Packing, Moving, Storage, Unpacking,
Cleaning Reimbursement (direct)   _____ _____ _____

Payment for Family House Hunting   _____ _____ _____

Lodging between Homes (temporary)   _____ _____ _____

Additional Shipping Costs (Cars, R.V.'s,
Boats, Pets, etc.)   _____ _____ _____

Purchase of Home   _____ _____ _____

Mortgage Funds (Bridging Loans, etc.)/Rate
Differential, Low-Interest Rates   _____ _____ _____

Real Estate Brokerage Fee   _____ _____ _____

Prepayment Penalty   _____ _____ _____

Closing Costs   _____ _____ _____

Special Allowance for Installation of Home
Fixtures, Appliances, Carpets, Drapes,
etc. (incidentals)   _____ _____ _____

Company Purchase of Home   _____ _____ _____

Home Security Systems   _____ _____ _____

D. Termination:

Employment Contract (Senior Management
usually)—"Golden Parachute"   _____ _____ _____

Pension/Retirement Plan   _____ _____ _____

Deferred Compensation, Salary,
Continuance   _____ _____ _____

Severance (termination) Pay (1-3 year,
6 month - 1 year salary)   _____ _____ _____

Outplacement Marketing Services   _____ _____ _____

Health Care Insurance Benefits
Continuance _____ _____ _____

Insurance Conversion Privileges _____ _____ _____

Use of Office, Secretary, Phone,
Charge Cards _____ _____ _____

Noncompetition Terms _____ _____ _____

Release with Compensation in Case of
Merger/Acquisition _____ _____ _____

Consulting Fees After Termination _____ _____ _____

E. Other:

Estate or Financial Planning Assistance _____ _____ _____

CPA or Tax Assistance _____ _____ _____

Legal Assistance _____ _____ _____

Educational Tuition Refunds, Seminars _____ _____ _____

Career Counseling/Planning/
Pre-Retirement _____ _____ _____

Child Care _____ _____ _____

Right to Do Freelance Work On
Own Time _____ _____ _____

Personal Security _____ _____ _____

Sabbatical Leaves _____ _____ _____

Office Location/Size _____ _____ _____

Limousine Service, Company Jet _____ _____ _____

Company Suite When Traveling _____ _____ _____

Keogh Plan (401K); ESOP _____ _____ _____

Cafeteria Style Flex Plans _____ _____ _____

Prescription Drug Plan _____ _____ _____

Retiree Health Benefits _____ _____ _____

Subsidized Meals _____ _____ _____

Payroll Deduction - IRA (Other
Tax-Free Benefits) _____ _____ _____

Chauffeur Service _____ _____ _____

✦ ✦ ✦

You can ask if a medical exam and/or reference checking still needs to be done. Unresolved issues (major ones) can be approached by asking for assistance in resolving them. If these issues aren't resolved to your satisfaction, then the job can be turned down.

After your negotiating sessions, put your account of what has been agreed to in a confirmation letter (Figs. 22.6 and 22.7). Don't ask them to once again confirm things to you as you can just as easily do it. You might weaken your position or relationship.

◆ ◆ ◆

FIGURE 22.6
Confirmation letter

Date

Name and Title
Division
Company
Address
City, State, Zip

Dear _____,

It is with great pleasure that I accept your offer of employment with _____ in the position of _____. I believe the only item we discussed which was not covered in your letter was that of vacation time. After reviewing the _____ benefits material, I suggest that the best way to handle it is to recognize some amount of my prior service with _____ as equivalent _____ service for the purposes of vacation allotment only. Since I have 18 years experience, I recommend we establish an equivalent figure of 12 years service with _____.

We also agreed that both _____ and I have a strong interest in my assuming responsibility for a line position in the company with profit and loss responsibility in about two years.

I look forward to working with you and the other excellent people at _____. I can't tell you how many people have commented on the quality of your company and I look forward to a long and exciting career with the corporation.

Sincerely

Your Name

◆ ◆ ◆

✦ ✦ ✦

FIGURE 22.7
Confirmation letter

Date

Name and Title
Division
Company
Address
City, State, Zip

Dear _____:

As per our conversation of _____, I am pleased to accept the offer of _____ for the position of _____.

I am excited about this opportunity and am anxious to become a part of _____ management team. As you know, I feel that _____ is moving in the right direction and I want to be a part of that movement. I know that I have found the right "chemistry and fit" with you and the organization. Most importantly, I know that I will enjoy working with you in building a strong future for the company.

As we had discussed, the following is my understanding of the changes we made to the compensation package outlined in your letter dated _____.

1. item A.	$2,000 was added to the salary.
2. item B.	The six month review was eliminated.

The following items were not changed:

1. item C.	The review in June.
2. item D.	The Sickness and Accident benefits.
3. item E.	Health insurance.
4. item F.	The moving expenses.

As I mentioned, I would like to begin to familiarize myself with the company and, if possible, would like to receive some material to start that process. The material that I believe would be helpful includes the following:

1. The policy and procedure manuals.

2. Any employee information booklets or handouts (I have the employee guidebook and the benefit booklets).

3. The Department's annual reports for the last two years and the goals and objectives for those years.

4. Any employee newsletters or publications for the past few months.

Please feel free to add any material that you believe will be beneficial to me. If there is any problem sending the material to me, let me know and I will make arrangements to pick it up.

Once again, I am excited about this opportunity and am looking forward to starting on _____.

Sincerely,

Your Name

✦ ✦ ✦

Thoughts For A Confirmation Letter

Other thoughts for a confirmation letter (letter of agreement) might be as follows: "I am looking forward to my new position with (name of company) on (agreed date). It is my understanding that the following have been agreed upon and are in place: (items negotiated listed).

If you have conducted an active campaign, it's not unusual to have more than one offer to consider, you will need to compare and contrast them (pros and cons) by using evaluation sheets and information similar to the ones listed in Figs. 22.6 and 22.7.

What to Do When You Have an Offer(s) In Hand

If you have one offer "in hand" with one or more possibly pending, you might want to play "one-in-the-pocket" against the others by calling the company or companies you have not yet heard from. Call them and ask if you are still a "viable candidate" and if so, is there anything else that you can do to speed up the process?

If they say "no," tell them that "you are between a rock and a hard place," that you have received an offer from the XYZ Company and they are requesting a reply from you within the week. You'll need to tell the company that they are "your number one choice" and if there is anything that can be done to expedite the process, it would be appreciated! Maybe the "domino principle" will prevail (one falling domino brings the others nearby down). It has for many of my clients as they played one situation against another.

If you need time when reviewing several offers, you could say to a company that several firms have made you offers. Would it be possible to take an extra week or so to review these situations and then get back to them?" Maybe you will be lucky to gain some additional time for yourself. Use the criteria to evaluate job offers where applicable (Fig. 22.8).

———————————— ✦ ✦ ✦ ————————————

FIGURE 22.8
Critera to evaluate job offers

A. What values are important to you, your spouse, and/or your family?

Position (Long-Term Potential)
Predecessor's status
Use of degree skills
Degree of responsibility (ties)
Chance to develop new skills/ideas
On-the-job training
Variety of assignments/Work/Tasks
Title (status)/Independence
Chemistry (supervisors, peers, staff)
Travel requirements (%)
Decision-making opportunities (visibility)
Company Car

Career/Life Goals
Personal growth potential/Title
Relevance of knowledge
Relevance of experience
Fulfillment of long-range objectives
Promotional potential (fast track)
System for performance appraisal
Opportunity to obtain a mentor and learn new skills

The Company (Image)
Reputation/growth/vulnerability
Size (No. of employees, earnings)
Industry/Annual Sales
Product line/service(s) offered
Location (close to home) - you and spouse
Soundness/potential of company -

company literature
national/multi-national
Working conditions - information from current employees/hours
Corporate culture/political climate/ diversified/specialized/profit/ non-profit/public/private

Personal Goals
Career for spouse
Degree of sociability
Rural or urban setting (cost of living)
Career interests
Time flexibility
Personality needs
Values and ethics
Recreational habits
Commuting time
Work place variation

Financial Goals*
Salary potential
Bonus/incentives/commission
Profit-sharing
Stock options
Insurance programs
Moving expenses
Educational assistance
Vacation time
Sick leave
Health Club facilities

*To find out what you are worth, keep abreast of Trade Journals, Occupational Outlook Handbook, The College Placement Council, professional publications, regional hiring salaries, salary surveys, talk with recruiters and with organizations that hire people with your talents; also with your peers.

Future Boss (as best you know) Wants written reports; will serve as mentor/teacher/coach; gives feedback; holds regular meetings with staff; will let you "do your thing"; is available for discussions; leads by example.

B. What are your answers to the following questions?

1. JOB DESCRIPTION (Duties, accountability, responsibilities, authority) — Is there a job description for this position? Are the duties and responsibilities described clearly? Is there a clear statement of authority? Can the job description be upgraded?

2. JOB HISTORY (Growth and previous incumbent) — How old is the position? How long has the position been open? Who previously held the position? Why was he/she replaced? How long was he/she in it? Did he/she succeed or fail? How many predecessors were there? What happened to them? Why? Where will this job lead? Possibility of a layoff?

3. EMPLOYEES (their backgrounds and direction) — Who are the employees that I will work with; immediate superior; subordinates; peers in other departments; what are their job titles, background, age, personality, education, reputation, etc.? Turnover rate?

4. DEPARTMENT (long-standing or new) — Does the department have any short/long-range plans? Growth or consolidation? Downsizing? Does the department have its own budget? Who controls it? Has the department been successful? What is its reputation? How is the staff morale? Is there anyone on the staff who expected to be promoted to this position but was bypassed?

<table>
<tr><td>5.
ORGANIZATION/
FIRM</td><td>Where does this position fit into the organizational chart? Is there a chain of command? Are there multiple bosses? Overtime demands? Culture (conservative, participative, regimented)? How old is the firm? Is it private or public? How long has its senior management been in power? What have been its sales and losses over the past several years? Now? Does the firm have an expansion plan? What does the firm's annual report and the D&B report show about its credit rating and financial history? If the company is "Public", what do recent broker reports say about the firm? How does the firm and its products/services rate in its industry? What is the economic trend of the industry? Customers? Competition? Market?</td></tr>
<tr><td>6. ORIENTATION/
TRAINING</td><td>Are there new employee orientation programs? How do I become familiar with policies and procedures? Are there training programs? Are there other training programs? Is there an educational reimbursement policy?</td></tr>
<tr><td>7. COMMUNITY/
LIVING
CONDITIONS</td><td>Is there information on housing, religious/social organizations, schools, shopping, transportation, libraries, educational and recreational facilities, etc.? Does the organization involve itself in the community? Climate? Cost of living index (what is it)? Is there a Chamber of Commerce?</td></tr>
</table>

C. Workplace Comparisons
Check each of the questions against your offers.

	Offer #1	Offer #2	Offer #3
Is there chemistry with fellow workers/associates?	_____	_____	_____
Will you be able to be creative in your work?	_____	_____	_____
Will this position be a "stepping stone" to a better job?	_____	_____	_____
Will you be using your abilities to the fullest?	_____	_____	_____
Will your work be challenging?	_____	_____	_____
Will you be able to "stretch" yourself?	_____	_____	_____

Are there opportunities to expand
your talents?   _____ _____ _____

Is your commuting distance to
work all right?   _____ _____ _____

Are you truly excited about this
opportunity?   _____ _____ _____

Is the workplace formal or informal?   _____ _____ _____

List any additional ideas for consideration

_____

_____

_____

D. A Benefits Checklist

Pensions, profit sharing, life insurance and medical benefits - standards in many employee benefits packages - help determine the overall value of an employee's annual compensation. This checklist gives you a chance to figure out which benefit advantages and disadvantages may affect your situation.

PENSION

☐ What are the vesting requirements?

☐ When can I participate (often after one year)?

☐ How are payments computed (often years of services times percent of salary)?

☐ Worth today and at retirement?

☐ Cost-of-living provision (COLA)?

☐ Are there survivor benefits?

☐ How is the fund managed?

☐ What is the fund's current rate of return?

☐ Do I have an investment choice?

☐ What is the normal retirement age?

☐ Are payments made in a lump sum or on an installment basis?

☐ Disability provisions?

☐ How does the plan integrate with Social Security?

☐ Where are the funds invested?

PROFIT SHARING

Ask all the questions under the pension checklist plus the following:

☐ How much does the company pay into the plan?

☐ Are my monies matched by the company?

☐ Early withdrawals made without penalties?

☐ Under what conditions?

☐ Are there withdrawal penalties?

LIFE INSURANCE

☐ Do I qualify right away?

☐ Do I have to pay anything? How much?

☐ Is the coverage twice my annual salary?

☐ Can this change?

☐ What are excluded?

- [ ] What happens when I terminate employment? Make a temporary break in service?
- [ ] Double indemnity clause?
- [ ] When I terminate, may the plan be converted?
- [ ] Who provides the coverage?
- [ ] Is the payment made in a lump sum or in installments?
- [ ] Can I purchase extra coverage?
- [ ] What are the disability benefits?

MEDICAL

- [ ] When do I qualify for coverage?
- [ ] How are the payments broken down?
- [ ] What is included in my coverage?
- [ ] Does the policy cover basic/major medical expenses?
- [ ] What are the deductibles?

- [ ] What is the maximum amount (limit) the insurer will pay for an illness or accident?
- [ ] Are there accidents that are not covered?
- [ ] Are there limits to a hospital stays?
- [ ] Is there a maximum payment for a hospital room?
- [ ] Dependent coverage?
- [ ] What are the exclusions in the policy?
- [ ] Where are tests conducted?
- [ ] Are there provisions for psychiatric treatment, rehabilitation, dental, vision, etc.?
- [ ] What are the disability benefits? How much and for how long?
- [ ] Who provides the coverage?
- [ ] How long have they been a provider?
- [ ] Are there other plans such as HMOs?

✦ ✦ ✦

Note: You may want to seek counsel from several key network contacts regarding your offer(s). Use a model like Fig. 22.9 to help in the decision-making process in addition to checking salary survey information in your field, if applicable (Fig. 22.10).

✦ ✦ ✦

FIGURE 22.9
Decision chart

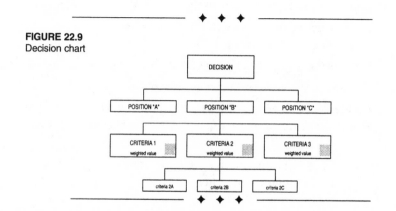

✦ ✦ ✦

✦ ✦ ✦

FIGURE 22.10
Salary surveys in special journal issues

Journal Name	Issue Date
Administrative Management	December
Business Week	May
Chemical Week	May
Datamation	April
Dun's Business Month	November
Engineering News Record	July
Industrial Chemical News	October
Industrial Engineering	June
Industrial Research & Development	March
Institutional Distribution	January
Purchasing	December
Sales & Marketing Management	October
Special Libraries	October

✦ ✦ ✦

In conclusion, remember that this process does not begin in earnest until you have that piece of paper (your written offer) in hand. Once you have it, be prepared to negotiate and enjoy the process. Find out, though, what are or can be the typical perks at your level.

How to Tell if a Company Is Interested in You

Clues to a company definitely being interested in you are as follows:

1. Request for references and then the contacting of those references.

2. Both parties feeling that there is a strong "chemistry." The interviewer knows all about you.

3. Volunteering to give you a plant or office tour. Discusses problems.

4. Wanting to schedule additional interviews.

5. Conducting a longer than usual interview (over 30 minutes). Expresses an interest in you. Questions you at length and takes notes.

6. The company representative wanting you to meet his boss or other workers. Praises his or her company.

7. Sharing benefit package material and other materials, e.g., instructions on medical exams.

8. Desire to talk about money.

Negotiation Ideas

1. He or she who mentions money first loses, so never reveal your current salary or what you're interested in. Be skillful and dodge the money questions when they come your way. Remember that you never discuss or negotiate salary or other benefits until you have an offer in hand. Note: Your organization, budget structure, value in the marketplace, and cost-of-living expenses can vary from place to place. The company extending an offer is paying you for your current worth, not what you were being paid by someone else.

2. Know what you are worth before negotiating your salary. Talk with friends who have similar jobs: agencies or recruiters, the placement director at your school, or personnel directors, or check salary surveys in special journal issues.

3. Never accept an offer when it is made. Don't say yes or no. Say you are assuming that the firm is putting it in writing and that once you receive it, you will review it and get back in a few days with your answer. Ask if that is all right. It is an acceptable business practice today to put an offer in writing.

4. If you need an extension for a decision, don't be afraid to ask a company for one. Maybe you are considering several options and you simply need a little more time for this decision.

5. If your company counters with a counteroffer after you said you were leaving, remember that those "blackmail situations" usually don't work out. Forget it and move on!

6. Side step the money questions as long as you can!

One of the most important things for all of you to remember is that no one has final authority over your destiny but yourself.

You may honor or respect a parent or a close friend, but the closest friend you will ever have is yourself. You must be a friend to yourself first, you must respect yourself first, you must be a success with yourself before you can be a success with others. The greatest treasure you will ever have is your self-image, a good opinion of yourself, and you must never let anyone take this away from you, no matter who it may be. If anyone does, he is opinionated and wants you to live his life, not your own.

Of course, you might listen to words of advice from a parent or friend; but in the final analysis, you must make the decision of what you want to be, if what you want to be is within your capabilities and your training, if what you want to be doesn't mean stepping on other people's toes. Go toward your goals aggressively, refusing to let anyone steer you from your course, because you must believe in your goals and you must drive to reach them.

Your goals, your parents' goals, your friends' goals are different. You must do the thing you feel you have to do; and you must apply the power. It is another way of saying that you must let your belief in yourself work for you, not against you. You must choose your career because you believe in it. Never choose a career to suit someone else. It is the beginning of failure and unhappiness. Respect the integrity of others, but respect your own integrity as well. You are the master of your destiny.

— ANONYMOUS

23.

Contracts:
Put Them In Writing

The greatest mistake you can make in life is to be
continually fearing you will make one.
— ELBERT HUBBARD

Employment Conditions

Institutions often offer contracts to define employment conditions for executives who are making over $70,000, although there have been situations where either an organization or an individual making less has insisted on one, perhaps because the company is rather new or at risk, including one that had filed for bankruptcy, had just been acquired or merged, or could be taken over; newly-formed companies that have a high risk of failing; and privately or family-owned companies, especially where one power group or personality controls the situation. An older person who is strongly interested in financial security for his family and being apart from organizational politics, especially with an uncertain economy and high cost of relocation, may also ask for a contract.

Precedents

You may check to see if the organization that you are dealing with has had a practice of offering employment contracts. Ask if the firm prepares employment contracts for a person at your level. That information will give you not only some insight but guidance as to what you should do. *Note:* A contract can be a simple letter stating the offer and your written reply, the easiest form if the company has no experience with formal contracts.

Company officials may say that they feel that your relationship should begin on a foundation of mutual respect and trust and that requesting a contract is a sign you don't trust them or that you don't have confidence in the future of the organization. This can be countered by talking about this age of uncertainty and saying that, with all due respect, you owe it to yourself and your family to protect your financial future. A contract would do that. Written contracts are usually for periods of three years or longer.

Parts of A Contract

A contract can be drafted by you with the help of an attorney; if you are offered one, have an attorney, a good CPA and/or a company officer check it. Note that all contracts, before agreed to, are negotiable. Points reviewed or discussed can be as follows:

- Specific job duties and how you will be paid.
- Severance (termination) terms, including outplacement marketing services together with extended insurance and health coverage (up to one year).
- A takeover (merger/acquisition) protection clause that provides for a reference letter if you leave and will be paid in full if this happens.
- Early retirement. Pension
- A stipulation that if either you or the firm have to sue, the loser pays the attorneys' fee and costs.
- Post-retirement counseling.
- Paying for relocation expenses.
- Paying extra compensation for undesirable (hardship) relocation.
- Noncompetition agreements—if you leave, for whatever the reason, such an agreement may set up a geographical restraint (you can't go after customers in certain territory if you're working for the competition) or an activity restraint (you can't take your customers with you if you leave).
- A "good faith clause"—insists on you not going to work for a competitor (whatever the definition) for at least six months to one year after you leave. (As an aside, this always seemed unconstitutional to me, especially when you're out of work and you need work.)
- Preservation of trade secrets (sometimes included with non-competition arrangements); these specify what is considered confidential, i.e., notes, records, computer disks.

- Deferred compensation, insurance, salary benefits to your family in case of accidental death and performance bonuses.
- Special benefits, such as retirement, disability, or vacations.
- Sign-on bonuses or other special perquisites.
- Stock options or other equity participation—purchase conditions and when stock is vested.
- Capital accumulation.
- Company car (with phone).

Live Each Day To The Fullest

*Live each day to the fullest. Get the most
from each hour, each day, each age of your life.
Then you can look forward with confidence,
and back without regrets.*

*Be yourself—but be your best self. Dare
to be different and to follow your own star.*

*And don't be afraid to be happy. Enjoy what is
beautiful. Love with all your heart and soul.
Believe that those you love, love you.*

*Forget what you have done for your friends, and
remember what they have done for you. Disregard
what the world owes you, and concentrate on
what you owe the world.*

*When you are faced with a decision, make that
decision as wisely as possible—then forget it.
The moment of absolute certainty never arrives.*

*And above all, remember that God helps those
who help themselves. Act as if everything
depended on you,
and pray,
as if everything
depended on God.*

— ANONYMOUS

PART IV

Building for Tomorrow
Be Strong and Sturdy as an Oak

24.

Owning Your Own Business: Taking The Right Steps

As Dale Dauten, author of *Taking Chances*, suggests, "Dare to be different. If mediocrity is your goal, imitate. If achievement is your goal, innovate."

Many of my clients, blue and white collar, who are either contemplating or are presently undergoing career changes, think about going into business for themselves. Some who may be otherwise unemployed, work initially as self-employed consultants to at least fill the time void that would occur on their resume if they weren't doing anything.

If you are at that point and managing your own business has crossed your mind, you may want to initially ask yourself the following questions:

1. Why do you feel the way you do? Have you learned the necessary skills to succeed on your own? Do you know what they are? If you don't have all the necessary skills, how do you plan to learn them?

2. Do you know what kind of product, service, or business you want? Do you enjoy working with people more than with things, or do you equally enjoy working with both? What research have you done on areas of interest? What books have you read on owning your own business? You'll need to both know and visualize what you want your business to be. You'll need to have a written mission statement or statement of purpose.

3. Whom have you talked with who has been successful in your area of interest? What was his or her career path? Have you sought advice from the Small Business Administration (SBA), 409 3rd Street SW, Washington, DC 20416, (202) 205-6780? Have you attended an SBA workshop? There may be an SBA office located near you. The SBA has instructional pamphlets available for reasonable prices; one free pamphlet is, "Are You Ready for Franchising?"

4. Have you sought advice from any professional organizations related to your area(s) of interest? Have you used any advice from retired executives or businessmen? See if there is a local SCORE (Service Corps of Retired Executives) organization in your community or reasonably nearby.

5. Do you see yourself as a hard worker, a self-starter, a person with a lot of energy and one who is not afraid to make the necessary moves and take the necessary risks to get ahead? If not, owning your own business may not be for you. This is definitely not a knee-jerk situation. Not everyone is an entrepreneur!

6. Have you talked to any manufacturer's representatives, sales representatives or customers who might give you some insights into your area(s) of interest? Have you asked for their reasons for success as well as a look at their financial statements? Do you know who your competition is? Are you thinking about a partner? What's his or her track record? Does his or her business plan and goals match or complement yours?

7. Is franchising for you? Have you read David Silver's book *Entrepreneurial Megabucks: The 100 Greatest Entrepreneurs of the Last 25 Years*, published by John Wiley & Sons, 605 Third Avenue, New York, NY 10158, (212) 850-6000. Do you fit the pattern or profile of successful entrepreneurs? Have you obtained the free SBA booklet, "Are You Ready for Franchising" or the free Federal Trade Commission pamphlet, "Franchise Business Risks"? As an aside, the U.S. Department of Commerce publishes a booklet entitled, "Franchise Opportunity Handbook," U.S. Government Printing Office, Superintendent of Publications, P.O. Box 371954, Pittsburgh, PA 15250. Have you looked at *A Business of Your Own: Franchise Opportunities*, Sterling Publishers, New York? Do you have your copy of *What You Need to Know When you Buy a Franchise*? Write for prices or publications list by contacting the International Franchise Association, 1350 New York Avenue, N.W., Suite 900, Washington, DC 20005, (202) 628-8000. Have you seen the *Franchise Annual* published by Info Press, Inc., 728 Center Street, Lewiston, NY 14092-0550, (716) 754-4669?

8. How much of a capital investment will you need? Will you need to take out a loan? What do you have for collateral? Assuming no money coming in for a year, do you have enough money saved to live? Will you be starting with an active or silent partner whose style complements your own? What about venture capital firms? Assuming you didn't have any money coming in for a year, how

much would you need to survive? Can you get started part-time, or would it be strictly a full-time operation? Have you put together a financial plan? Is a foreign company interested in you as a partner?

9. Have you written or called the Center for Entrepreneurial Studies, Graduate School of Business Administration, New York University, 44 West 4th Street, Suite 8-165B, New York, NY 100012, (212) 998-0070, for a complimentary subscription to *The Entrepreneurship Forum* (biannual). This publication includes information about the Center as well as commentary and research reports.

10. Have you read Charlotte Taylor's, *Entrepreneurial Workbook*, published by Plume Book, 375 Hudson Street, New York, NY (a step-by-step guide to starting and running your own business); *Straight Talk About Small Business*, by Kenneth Albert, McGraw-Hill, 1221 Avenue of the Americas, New York, NY 10022; *Setting Up Shop*, by Randy B. Smith, Warner Books, 1271 Avenue of the Americas, New York, NY 10020; and *In Business For Yourself: A Guide to Starting a Small Business and Running It Your Way*, Jerome Goldstein, Scribner's, 866 Third Avenue, New York, NY 10022. Other good books are *Test Your Entrepreneurial I.Q.* by Kathleen Hawkins and Peter Turla, published by Berkley Books, New York; *Successful Small Business Management*, Seigel and Goldman, Fairchild, NY; *Starting on a Shoestring: Building a Business without a Bankroll*, Arnold Goldstein, Wiley, New York; and *How to Start and Operate a Mail-Order Business*, Julian Simon, McGraw-Hill, 1221 Avenue of the Americas, New York, NY 10022.

11. Have you put together a solid business plan? Have a reputable attorney, a good CPA, or the president of a business check all contracts before they are signed?

12. Do you have a list of people to consult with if you need help?

13. Are you determined to set the highest of standards to be the best in your field that you can be?

14. Have you researched consulting firms (e.g., McKinsey & Company, New York) to see if you could sign on as an independent contractor?

Having answered those questions honestly, you should then be in a position to decide whether owning a business is for you. If so, good luck, and always look toward being successful!

Here are a few additional hints:

1. Some enterprising independent businessmen have used multiple box rentals with suite numbers in a variety of cities for image purposes even though they don't formally have offices in each. For information on mailbox rental firms, contact Mail Boxes, Etc., San Diego, California; Pak Mail, Inc., Denver, Colorado; Princeton Mail Services, Princeton, New Jersey; or the Association of Commercial Mail Receiving Agencies. There are even some that will give you an international postmark if you desire.

2. Find a need and fill it; build on your expertise; try and think of ways to improve small things; look at improving things that really bug you. Be creative in your thinking!

> *Man's reach should exceed his grasp.*
> — ROBERT BROWNING

3. Former clients who have gone into business for themselves successfully indicate the following ideas for success: setting and working toward goals; committing themselves to working long days, or whatever it takes; keeping a positive, upbeat attitude coupled with a strong desire for success; continuing to learn all they can about the business; surrounding themselves with good people; and never settling for second best!

25.

Internal Campaigning:
Making The Right Connections

*Good work counts to your advantage only if it is
seen, heard, and somehow recognized.*
— ADELE SCHEELE

"First impressions are lasting ones." How many times have you heard that
expression? It is very true, especially with a new job or a new assignment
or if you are trying to bounce back when you were or are on the ropes with
your present company. To assist you if you are in these kinds of situations,
the following internal campaign ideas may be of value:

1. Obtain or generate a *current job description* that outlines all your
   duties, responsibilities, what you're accountable for and what
   "real authority" and support that you have in carrying them to
   completion. Not only will this help you to set realistic, measurable and observable goals and objectives for yourself to monitor
   your performance, but it is a tool that could possibly be used at
   some later date if you have to update your resume.

2. Keep a *daily log or diary* of all transactions and interactions. This
   log is your documentation that can be used for weekly, biweekly,
   or monthly summations of your work activities. These summary
   reports can either be submitted to your boss as regular updates
   or, more importantly, can be saved by you and brought to performance reviews when you have them.

3. Use a *daytimer* (Day-Timers, Inc., Allentown, PA 18195-1551, call
   for information at (215) 395-5884) to keep track of your daily appointments and the addresses and telephone numbers of people
   you meet. *A folder for the business cards* you accumulate is another

must. One of my clients had plastic pages with as many as twenty slots (3 x 5) for his cards. It makes for an ideal networking starter list at a later date if needed.

4. Keep a business *photo album* with appropriate labels and documentation for possible later research, report, or portfolio or proposal use; e.g., photos from seminars, workshops, tours, and visits.

5. Always *clean off your desk* or work area at day's end. Make sure you at least keep your desk locked. I never thought this way until I had a desk broken into; several confidential files were taken. It was my fault for not being sharp enough to keep my desk locked.

6. Have a good *gold pen/pencil* set, e.g., Cross pen, A. T. Cross Co., 120 Albion Road, Lincoln, RI 02865, with you at all times, together with a pad for taking notes. For image sake, never have plastic pens in your pocket.

7. Know what is expected of you (*benchmarks*). Verify them with the boss. Review all duties and responsibilities in your job description. Update at least annually with new accomplishments. Don't be afraid also to ask questions. Check with your boss when he or she wants something accomplished as to what his or her priorities are, what kind of feedback he or she wants, and when he or she wants it. Communicate with your boss on a daily basis for four to six weeks and then start your own internal campaign by noting those around you (for instance, team player versus non-team player). Write up a brief description of key people as you interact with them, noting their positive attributes, their strengths, and those people that can help you. Try to improve your position within the company. Set your sight on the position you ultimately want to hold and the salary you want to earn. Develop logical stepping stones and a time frame. "Give in order to get!" Show loyalty and give others credit.

8. Draw up an *organizational diagram* indicating real lines of power. Note where your department fits. Offer daily hellos and goodbyes to all. Be an extrovert!

9. Start being an *avid reader*. Conduct additional research on all the organization goals and how it reaches those goals. Read annual reports, balance sheets, 10K reports, news releases, stock market studies, the *Wall Street Journal*, daily local newspapers (note local issues and editorials), and other items of interest. Send articles to key contacts with handwritten notes.

10. Check with *people who report to you* to determine what they think their responsibilities are; offer to be a mentor for newer, younger employees; know what their business goals are. Maybe you can help them reach their goals!

11. Develop a *personal action plan* for your own betterment with short- and long-range goals for your first year and obtain approval from your boss. Plan to attend outside seminars and conferences. Jot down all contributions on a daily basis. Use these jottings to prepare a weekly or monthly update (progress report) for your boss. Keep them also for your performance reviews. Prepare presentations and make contacts with those who can help you implement your objectives—individuals who have the knowhow, the power, and top management support. Take the initiative to see them. Update your plan at least annually.

Every noble work is at first impossible.
— THOMAS CARLYLE

12. Use *coffee breaks* and lunch times to build relationships as well as to establish contacts with others. Offer your commitment to the achievement of their goals.

13. Try to volunteer when you can for *team projects* and opportunities to work on task forces or committees. It's a great way to demonstrate your skills, knowledge, and abilities. Be visible! Always be on the lookout for ways that you can help your institution. If people praise your work, ask them to write "to whom it may concern" for your file. Cultivate peer relationships.

First you start acting the part. Pretty soon people think of you in terms of the part. Before long, you become the part.
— DEBRA A. BENTON

14. Determine *where your strengths are*, what areas you need to improve, and what your goals, steps, and timetable are to accomplish them. Plan always to be punctual! Start work early each day. If you are going to be late, take the time to call and let others know. You are always as close as the nearest telephone.

15. Be active *within your community*. Join a professional organization and seek a prominent position. Develop and cultivate your network! Seek opportunities to write for trade journals. This can help to give you an audience with prospective employers.

16. Meet with your boss from time to time (at least every three months) to review your job description and how well you are doing. Don't wait until your once-a-year performance evaluation meeting. Take responsibility for your career direction. Measure your performance constantly. Select issues to be worked on, and run them by your boss.

17. If you had a network before this new job, still keep everyone informed. Keep them "alive." Hopefully, you sent all campaign contacts a thank-you and announcement letter informing them of your progress regarding your new job. Clip and save articles for them.

18. Note the following 33 internal campaigning thoughts:

Assignments

- Ask for additional assignments.
- Complete assignments as soon as possible.
- Provide solutions and alternatives instead of problems.
- See problems as challenges/opportunities, and from the organization's point of view.
- Obtain assignments that offer exposure to other managers and executives.
- Keep records of everything (e.g., work correspondence). You never know when you'll need the documentation.
- Bring weekly/monthly work summations to performance appraisal meetings.
- Rate your boss's promotional chances.
- Always be prepared to move if the organization wants you.
- Use your current assignment as a "career stepping stone" every two to three years. Plan your next move from your current position.
- Try and find the reason behind each assignment. Maybe there is a "hidden agenda."
- Be enthusiastic in your work.
- Keep personal integrity and organizational work ethics.

- A lack of negative criticism does not equal positive praise. In other words, no news is not necessarily good news.
- Always obtain constructive criticism of your work. Don't take things personally.
- "Take the heat" (blame) if your subordinates mess up and correct it right away.
- Note dead-end positions and salary freezes.
- Learn to delegate authority. Use "buck slips" or brief notes.

Skills

- Advertise your skills by outstanding performance. Like the Ford Motor Company says, "Quality is Job One."
- Note the career paths in your vocational discipline. Start planning!
- Develop new skills and competencies through training and educational courses.
- Obtain line, not staff positions. Get where the rubber meets the road.
- Practice your public speaking skills. Sign-up for Toastmasters.

Personal Relations

- Avoid discussing controversial subjects (if possible).
- Never underestimate your social responsibilities. Your social graces will be tested.
- Try to avoid internal politics and cliques. Be positive!
- Be loyal to the organization and demonstrate it!
- Recognize employees for their work. A short, positive note does wonders.
- Enrich your personal life by getting involved in your community and making many personal contacts.
- Ask others for their advice about your career. Always cultivate a mentor.
- Talk to all employees as friends. They can help you succeed!
- Talk about ideas and never about people.
- Build bridges with your associates. Never burn them!

19. Contrary to belief, *a new broom doesn't always sweep clean.* If man-

agement changes, try to "lie low in the weeds," as one of my former bosses said, for at least six months. Observe and take notes. Keep your mouth shut.

> *Simple strategies well executed produce dramatic results.*
>
> — ANONYMOUS

20. Set aside *emergency money.* You never know in this day and age of mergers and acquisitions when you might need it.

> *It was the best of times, it was the worst of times. . . .*
> — CHARLES DICKENS, *A Tale of Two Cities*

21. Treat your family to a *mini-vacation* before you start your new job. They deserve it!

22. As one former senior project manager of ours, Mac Matter, would say all the time, "*Let the boss be boss.*" Build a positive relationship. You don't do this by taking on the boss. You may win the battle but lose the war. Make him or her a hero! If, for whatever reason, you can't get along, try to transfer to another department.

23. Remember to constantly *weigh your words* and your actions. They affect others around you. Prove your ability to work as a team member.

24. Study and *observe the successful people* in your institution and seek their advice and counsel.

> *You can see a lot by observing.*
> — YOGI BERRA

25. *Plan the next step* in your job and career—never be without achievable goals (only successful if they benefit both your employer and you).

26. Continue your *formal or informal education.* Acquire knowledge to reinforce your strengths. Learn how your job fits into related

functions and how your predecessor dealt with the job if it's not a new one.

27. Never present a problem without *suggesting a constructive solution* or plan. Maybe even several alternatives, too.

> *If you're not part of the solution, you are part of the problem.*
> — ELDRIDGE CLEAVER

28. Be determined to start each day with a *smile*, while keeping good physical health and a positive attitude!

29. Establish a reputation for doing your assignments well and *on time*. How well determines your job success.

> *Yet all experience is an arch wherethrough | Gleams that untraveled world.*
> — ALFRED, LORD TENNYSON

30. When you are in control of your job, *add new responsibilities* with your boss's approval.

> *Love doesn't just sit there, like a stone; it has to be made, like bread; remade all the time, made new.*
> — URSULA K. LEGUIN

31. Take *time to consider* problems (challenges) before taking action. Avoid instant emotional reactions.

> *Lost time is never found again.*
> — BEN FRANKLIN

32. Respond to *phone or memo inquiries* as soon as possible.

33. Learn to *reach a consensus* in meetings and don't verbally attack co-workers even if you are right.

34. Learn to know *what work can wait* and what can't. Set up a daily "to do" list. Be happy in your work.

> *We are as happy as we make up our minds to be.*
> — ABE LINCOLN

35. Learn to *delegate work* when possible.

36. Shirley Sloan Fader, in *Business Week*'s "Guide to Careers", says there are 20 things that your boss will expect you to know:

   - Get work done on time—don't make excuses.
   - Get job done—don't aim for perfection.
   - Take the initiative and do more than is expected.
   - Ask yourself what could go wrong—anticipate problems.
   - Handle problems yourself.
   - Be punctual.
   - Take being at work seriously.
   - Don't be a squeaky wheel.
   - Choose your battles carefully.
   - Expect to lose sometimes—don't hold a grudge.
   - Deal with the decision makers—this is the best way to get action.
   - Understand the boss's language—that is what he/ she really wants.
   - Get an overall picture. Learn what others are doing.
   - Get along with co-workers.
   - Never discuss business in public places. Be discreet.
   - Develop a sense of timing.
   - Don't lie or lose credibility.
   - Read industry publications, i.e., trade publications.
   - Get to know your peers.
   - Make no assumptions.

37. *Never look back.* Change is with us. It is inevitable. Remember that most key events in your career will be those that cause you to change.

38. If you have a *fear of the unknown* because of your new job, realize that it is natural and everyone experiences it until settling in. Immerse yourself in your work for your first several months, and you will find yourself growing in self-confidence.

39. Work with and *befriend all secretaries*. They control a lot of the office situations. They understand company policies and can assist and advise you in many matters.

40. Don't be afraid to *ask others questions*. Maintain confidentiality by not gossiping.

41. *Don't socialize in the office* or cultivate an office romance.

42. According to the *Executive Compensation Service* (ECS), most companies (50.4 percent) give new employees a raise at the end of the first year, with 41.8 percent of the companies giving them their first raise within the first six months. Most of the companies (29.4 percent) gave a 5 to 6.9 percent raise, whereas 29.1 percent of the companies gave a 7 to 8.9 percent raise. Average raises by all companies surveyed was 7.9 percent.

43. *Plan your future.* Think of your next step(s). What are your options? Use best and worst case scenarios (what if?). Realize that nothing is definite during these times. Assess your future with your current employer—how healthy is it? How have profits been? Have there been any tell-tale signs of things to come, e.g., projects held up or put on an indefinite hold, hiring freezes, not replacing people who have retired or left the organization, delaying merit increases or just not giving any increases, responsibilities (duties) being reduced, etc.? If so, maybe you need to be working on your next campaign.

> *The man who starts out with the idea of getting rich won't succeed: you must have a larger ambition. There is no mystery in business success. If you do each day's task successfully, stay faithfully within the natural operations of commercial time, and keep your head clear, you will come out all right.*
> — JOHN D. ROCKEFELLER

Success is not rare—it is common. It is a matter of adjusting one's efforts to obstacles and one's abilities to a service needed by others. There is no other possible success. But most people think of it in terms of getting; success, however, begins in terms of giving.

— HENRY FORD, SR.

26.

The Year 2000:
Moving Toward The Future

*Enter to grow in wisdom, depart better to serve
country and mankind.*

— HARVARD UNIVERSITY

*Education isn't a preparation for life, education is
life itself.*

— JOHN DEWEY

As we move through the nineties toward the year 2000, we are immersed in a period of transition and much change brought on by mergers, acquisitions, leveraged buyouts, and foreign competition and investment. The only way to survive will be to consider viable options. These options could include job retraining, starting one's own entrepreneurial venture, and learning to effectively market oneself and then to creatively respond and adapt to whatever changes one faces.

We read almost every day about organizations laying off, cutting-back, downsizing, streamlining, and restructuring their operations. Who would have thought just a short time ago that stateside manufacturing jobs would be decreasing the way they are, whereas service jobs would be on the rise? This trend is projected to continue.

The mighty steel union, which at its height numbered 1,110,000 members, is down now to slightly over 637,000, and blue chip organizations like IBM, GM, and AT&T are trimming their employee rolls.

Peter, Paul, and Mary have sung "the times they are a changing" many times. The lyrics seem more and more applicable today. Many organizations continue to cut their middle managers; long-time loyalty is being paid back by early retirements, and lifetime job security, if there ever was such a thing, is a practice of the past. Individuals in the years to come will have as many as ten to fifteen jobs during their five to six careers, so it will pay to be flexible.

In the years to come, we will have to "know ourselves" and then, after examining market data, decide career directions and geographical locations for our career moves.

> *The future belongs to those who believe in the beauty of their dreams.*
> — ELEANOR ROOSEVELT

The United States Department of Labor has reported that the work force trends by the year 2000 will be as follows:

- The population and the labor force will grow very slowly over the next decade. By the year 2000, the workforce will increase by only one percent annually.

- The pool of young workers entering the labor market will shrink; 16–24-year-olds accounted for 20 percent of the work force in 1985, but will decline to 16 percent by 2000.

- The proportion of the labor force that is minority will increase substantially. By 2000, one of five new labor force entrants will be a minority youth.

- With the decline in young workers, the average age of the workforce will increase from 35 today to 39 in 2000.

- More women will enter the work force, although the rate will decrease. By the year 2000, about 47 percent of the workforce will be women. Sixty percent of working-age women will be at work.

- International competition and technological change means that many new and existing jobs will require higher levels of analytic skills. The level of workplace literacy required will continue to rise beyond the mere ability to read and write.

- Rapid turnover and change of industries and firms will require workers to adjust more quickly and more often. Some American workers will change jobs five or six times during their work lives.

- Between now and 2000, labor markets may be tighter than at any time in recent history. Employers may face skill shortages. This could lead to the export of jobs overseas, bidding up of wages for qualified workers, automation investments, or spending more to train and educate new employees.

The Social Security Administration projected (in *2000—A Strategic Plan*) the following:

- There will be 10 million more Americans over age 65 than in 1980 (35 million versus 25.7 million).
- Birth rates will continue to decline.
- Baby boomers will continue to affect the disability rolls and will begin entering their retirement years by 2010.
- Labor force growth will fall to an annual rate of 1.1 percent in the late 1990s.
- Labor force participation will increase in most segments of the population.
- Many of the new technologies emerging now in the marketplace, such as artificial intelligence, expert systems, optical disks, speech recognition and synthesis, and smart cards will become fully mature.
- Increased use of fiber optics and satellites will facilitate communications networks to meet the needs of the ever-increasing number of customers.

The Hudson Institute (*EMA Journal*) speculates that the work force profile of the year 2000 will mirror the following: "90% of the new jobs will be in the service sector, whereas only 8% will be in manufacturing; as there will be an older work force, median age will rise to 39 in 2000; there will be higher communicative skills required with increases in professional and managerial jobs and an increased need for flexibility, retraining, job mobility, more competition and quality conscience."

What we do today will determine where we will be tomorrow. We need to know ourselves today—what our career skills and strengths are, what the market data is telling us (take note what purchasing agents are saying about the economy and its direction)—and then put together a market plan to effectively sell ourselves. That is how we will survive the changes that are being imposed upon us. We need to be the captains of our own ship and thus the creators of our own destiny.

Nothing in the world can take the place of persistence. Talent will not; nothing is more common than unsuccessful men with talent. Genius

will not; unrewarded genius is almost a proverb.
Education alone will not; the world is full of
educated derelicts. Persistence and determination
alone are omnipotent.

— ANONYMOUS

The quality of a man's life is measured by how
deeply he has touched the lives of others.

— CHARLES WALCOTT

PART V

Additional Resources
"The Proof of Pudding Is in the Eating"

27.

Homework: You Need To Do It!

The future is purchased by the present.
— SAMUEL JOHNSON

To keep a lamp burning we have to keep putting oil in it.
— MOTHER TERESA

Two-Way Street of Information Gathering

I can easily recall my mother and father asking me, when I was in high school, whether I had completed my homework. So, too, when one gets older, is it important to do your homework on those markets and target institutions that mirror your interests. The impression that you will make with companies when you interview with them is in direct proportion to the quality of your homework. Therefore, know as much as you can about these organizations of interest because they, in turn, will try and know as much as they can about you. It will be a two-way street of information gathering. By you doing your homework, you will send a positive signal to that organization that you really do care about it, are interested in what it is about, and have possibly found some problems or trends which you know you could help them solve them.

Sources

Primary

Homework sources can be separated into two parts. First there are the *primary sources* of people who know the organization and who have answers to many of the questions listed under homework information. These contacts can include customers, vendors, competitors, current and former employees, and trade associations that the organization may belong to and their membership. Visit places that sell the firm's products and talk to the people who sell them. What are the pros and cons? Local business leaders may know of the organization, e.g., the Junior Chamber and the Chamber of Commerce, local bankers and other financial experts such as investment analysts, stock brokers, economists, and accountants, as well as members of the Better Business Bureau and representatives of the economic development agency. Local economic and business forums are often supported by business schools or other agencies and should be attended for interesting insights into the local economy.

Secondary

The second homework source for doing in-depth research on target employers (employers who would have a need for your background) is the *secondary area*. This area includes a multitude of sources that a person can use to do research including mailing lists, organizational directories, prospectuses from brokers and agencies, computer database services (i.e., Dialog, Palo Alto, CA 94304, 415/858-2700), and personal contacts (Fig. 27.1). A lot of this research comes from published information about the organization and its key officers, e.g., 10K, proxy statements, annual reports, and organizational newsletters. The following career homework sources are not meant to be all-inclusive but to give you at least a starting point for your homework. Most of the listed directories are available at your local business, college or university, and public libraries. Befriend your reference librarian!

◆ ◆ ◆

FIGURE 27.1
Homework information checklist

Find Out These Things About the Company
Name, address, telephone number
Major product(s), service(s), process(es), market(s), global
Major competitors/share of market
How old company is (history)—stable
Philosophy/mission statement/policies/objectives
Total sales, financial condition (assets/liabilities); new
developments
Company credit rating
Culture/quality of life/personality (FIT)
Locations—Plants/offices/outlets/headquarters
Ethics
Employment Practices
Size (current/former)/number of employees

Expansions (acquisition and mergers)/growth potential/ market share/moves

Labor turnover (voluntary or otherwise layoffs and causes; promotions

Industry trends/trouble spots—contracts canceled

Annual report—who are outside directors, key officers and board members (is it a representative or a captive board?)—Note Standard & Poor's *Biographical Directory*

Age of top management/ backgrounds

Recent items in the news (releases); magazine articles

People you know in the firm—how do they feel about working there?

Present price of stock

Type of facilities/equipment/ machinery used

Related industries, trends, problems

Community

(Primarily for individuals relocating) Does company play an active part in the community?

Schools/libraries/taxes/recreational facilities

Religious/commuting time/shopping

Transient/stable

Cost of living/real estate (resale values)

Trade Association Memberships

Board of Trustee (schools/hospitals) members

Note Local Trade Shows/Conventions

Position

Scope/responsibilities/duties/ authority

Job description/organization chart

Training (formal/OTJ); seminars; associations

Advancement/mobility

Travel/relocation (east, west, urban, rural)

Salary structure

Department performance

Persons working with (age/personality)

Budget/staff/morale

Why hire externally?

People bypassed?

Time position open

Name of recruiter/key hiring person/potential boss (correct spelling and pronunciation)

Typical career path for position being interviewed for

Professional jargon/"buzz" words

Predecessors

Number of bosses

Long range plans for this department

Orientation program for new employees

Compensation

(See salary negotiation section)

Employee Benefits

Moving/selling homes

Stock options/perks

✦ ✦ ✦

The Key to Serenity

*When you know and believe without questions or
doubt that in all you do, God is there to help, you
hold in your hand the golden key to peace and joy
and serenity.*

— HELEN STEINER RICE

Career Homework Sources

An active job campaign means using a variety of career homework sources. You will want to refer to many of these sources as you put together a market list of organizations that you are interested in, as you more specifically prepare your institutional target lists for the companies you want to work for and as you gather information of these organizations. (*Note:* Many of these sources are outdated before they hit the street. Always verify with switchboard operators names (correct spelling), titles, addresses, and telephone numbers.)

Associations

American Academy of Nursing
2420 Pershing Road
Kansas City, MO 64108

American Association for Counseling and Development
5999 Stevenson Avenue
Alexandria, VA 22304
(703) 823-9800

American Association for the Advancement of Science
1333 H Street NW
Washington, DC 20005
(202) 326-6400

American Association of Advertising Agencies (AAAA)
666 Third Avenue, 13th Floor
New York, NY 10017
(212) 682-2500

American Bankers Association
1120 Connecticut Avenue NW
Washington, DC 20036
(202) 663-5000

American Chemical Society
Education Division
1155 16th Street NW
Washington, DC 20036
(202) 872-4600

American Iron & Steel Institute
1101 17th Street NW, 13th Floor
Washington, DC 20005
(202) 452-7100

American Management Association (AMACOM)
135 West 50th Street
New York, NY 10020
(212) 586-8100

American Marketing Association
250 South Wacker Drive, Suite 200
Chicago, IL 60606
(312) 648-0536

Association for Computer Machinery
1515 Broadway, 17th Floor
New York, NY 10036
(212) 869-7440 or (212) 575-1520

Association for School, College and University Staffing (ASCUS)
1600 Dodge Avenue, Suite 330
Evanston, IL 60201-3451
(708) 864-1999

Association of Executive Recruiting Consultants, Inc.
230 Park Avenue, Suite 1549
New York, NY 10169
(212) 949-9556

Association of Management Consulting Engineers (ACME)
521 5th Avenue, 35th Floor
New York, NY 10175
(212) 697-9693

Chemical Specialties Manufacturers Association
1913 Eye Street NW
Washington, DC 20006
(202) 872-8110

Federation of Organizations for Professional Women
2001 S Street, NW, Suite 500
Washington, DC 20009
(202) 328-1415

Financial Executives Institute (FEI)
P.O. Box 1938
Ten Madison Avenue
Morristown, NJ 07962-1938
(201) 898-4600

The Institute of Electrical and Electronics Engineers
345 E. 47th Street
New York, NY 10017-2394
(212) 705-7900

National Association for Female Executives (NAFE)
127 West 24th Street, 4th Floor
New York, NY 10011
(212) 645-0770

National Association of Accountants
Ten Paragon Drive
Montvale, NJ 07645
(201) 573-9000

National Association of Manufacturers
1331 Pennsylvania Avenue NW, Suite 1500 N
Washington, DC 20004
(202) 637-3000

National Association of Purchasing Management
2055 E. Centennial Circle
P.O. Box 22160
Tempe, AZ 85285
(602) 752-6276

National Association of Temporary Services (NATS)
119 St. Asaph Street
Alexandria, VA 22314
(703) 549-6287

National Management Association (NMA)
2210 Arbor Boulevard
Dayton, OH 45439
(513) 294-0421

National Retail Federation
100 West 31st Street
New York, NY 10001
(212) 244-8780

National Society of Black Engineers (NSBE)
1454 Duke Street
P.O. Box 25588
Alexandria, VA 22313-5588
(703) 549-2207

National Society of Professional Engineers
1420 King Street
Alexandria, VA 22314
(703) 684-2800

National Technical Association (NTA)
P.O. Box 7045
Washington, DC 20032
(202) 829-6100

National Tooling and Machining Association
9300 Livingston Road
Ft. Washington, MD 20744
(301) 248-6200

Plastics Institute of America
Steven's Institute of Technology
277 Fairfield Road, Suite 100
Fairfield, NJ 07004
(201) 808-5950

Public Relations Society of America (PRSA)
33 Irving Place, 3rd Floor
New York, NY 10003-2376
(212) 995-2230

Rubber Manufacturers Association
1400 K Street NW, 10th Floor
Washington, DC 20005
(202) 682-4800

Homework Sources

Accountants' Index. American Institute of Accountants. A comprehensive index by author, subject and title to books and articles on finance and accounting.

Almanac of Business and Industrial Financial Ratios. Englewood Cliff, NJ: Prentice-Hall (annual).

Alumni and Alumnae Directories: Contact your alumni or alumnae office. Maybe some graduates of your school are working at some of your target companies.

Alumni and Alumnae Newsletters.

American Men and Women of Science. R.R. Bowker Database Publishing Group, 121 Chanlon Road, New Providence, NJ 07974, (908) 464-6800.

American Journal of Public Health: Lists openings in Public Health.

Annual Reports. Offer a summary of all the operations for the year, products involved, highlight events, and names of key personnel, plus budgetary data you may want to see. In addition to the balance sheet and the auditor's report, The Annual Report also contains a letter from the chairman reflecting the culture, goals, and directions of the organization. Your library should have annual reports of nearby companies plus leading national ones. Turn first to back of report to note the CPA firm that did the auditing. If you come across a "subject to," it could mean a problem. Note also the footnotes and what they say. Check out the chairman's report, which reflects the overall economic condition of the company and where it is going. Note the presented balance sheet and find out what the earnings per share are and what the debt-to-equity ratio is. Compare this report with previous ones to note trends. Annual reports also give you a clue to the colors of acceptable business dress and what generally is worn in a formal setting.

Analysts Handbook. Composite corporate per share data, by industries. New York: Standard & Poor's Corp. (annual, with monthly supplements).

AT&T Toll Free Directory. Many companies have toll-free numbers. Call 1-800-555-1212 to see if one does. This obviously will save you money.

Best's Insurance Reports, Property and Casualty. A.M. Best Company, Ambest Road, Oldwick, NJ 08858, (908) 439-2200. Gives in-depth analyses, operating statistics, financial data, and officers of over 1,300 major stock and mutual property-casualty insurance companies. In addition, provides summary data on over 2,000 small mutual companies and on several hundred casualty companies operating in Canada.

Best's Insurance Reports, Life and Health. Supplies individual company reports in addition to summary of smaller companies similar to the property and casualty reports.

Books. Note bibliography section for some suggested readings.

Books in Print. R.R. Bowker/Xerox. Lists publishers and other titles.

Bureau of Labor Statistics Reports. Bureau of Labor Statistics, Inquiries and Correspondence, 2 Mass Avenue, NE, Washington, DC 20212, (202) 606-6020. Write for catalogue and list of publications.

Business Conditions Digest (BCD). Washington, DC: U.S. Dept. of Commerce, Bureau of Economic Analysis. Statistics and charts, emphasizing leading cyclical indicators of use to business analysts.

Business Index. Information Access Co. Up-to-date information to be used with microfiche reader.

Business Periodicals Index. New York: The H.W. Wilson Company. Monthly, with periodic cumulations. A subject index to several hundred periodicals in accounting, banking, economics, finance, insurance, labor, management, marketing, and specific business and industries. A good source to find out information about private companies.

Business Organizations, Agencies and Publications Directory. Gale Research, Inc., 835 Penobscot Building, Detroit, MI 48226-4094, (313) 961-2242.

Business Publication Rates & Data. Standard Rate and Data Service, Inc., 3002 Glenview Road, Wilmette, IL 60091, (708) 256-6067. Names and addresses of the trade publications in thousands of fields listed by topics.

Case Placement Letter. Suite 400, 11 Dupont Circle, Washington, DC 20036, (202) 328-5942.

Chamber of Commerce Directories. Many are available for free or a nominal charge. Contact targeted Chambers.

Chronicle of Higher Education. 1255 23rd Street NW, Suite 700, Washington, DC 20037, (202) 466-1000. Lists all types of college and university positions.

Civil Service Commission. Federal, state, county, city. Take civil service exam.

College Placement Annual. 62 Highland Avenue, Bethlehem, PA 18017, (215) 868-1421. College Placement, Inc., Published annually; offers one-page descriptions of hundreds of companies.

Consultants and Consulting Organizations Directory. Detroit: Gale Research, Inc., 835 Penobscot Building, Detroit, MI 48226-4094, (313) 961-2242; 3 vols. 7,000+ firms, individuals, and organizations engaged in consultation for business and industry. Includes executive search firms and is broken out by specialty and geography.

Contacts. See Networking section. Work on perfecting these skills.

Corporate Technology Directory. Corporate Technology Information Services, Inc., 12 Alfred Street, Suite 200, Woburn, MA 01801, (617) 932-3939..

Crain's Business Publication. Circulation Department, 740 N. Rush Street, Chicago, IL 60611, (312) 649-5200. Has publications for some targeted cities.

Directory of American Firms Operating in Foreign Countries. World Trade Academy Press, 50 E. 42nd Street, New York, NY 10017, (212) 697-4999.

Directory of College Recruiting Personnel. College Placement Council, Inc., 62 Highland Avenue, Bethlehem, PA 18017, (215) 868-1421.

Directory of Consultants. National Association of Regulatory Commissioners, Box 684, Washington, DC 20044, (202) 898-2200.

Directory of Corporate Affiliations. National Register Publishing Co., Inc., 3004 Glenview Road, Wilmette, IL 60091, (708) 256-6067. Provides detailed information on "who owns whom" as a result of mergers and acquisitions. Contained are companies listed on the New York Stock Exchange or the American Stock Exchange, the *"Fortune* 500" and others. This directory is useful when one is seeking out the detailed corporate structure of a parent company, or when a company is not listed in other directories because it is a subsidiary, division, or affiliate.

Directory of Directories. Detroit: Gale Research Company, 835 Penobscot Building, Detroit, MI 48226-4094. This is what its title says. Strong in sources of information about particular industries.

Directory of Executive Recruiters. Consultant's News. Kennedy and Kennedy, Inc., Templeton Road, Fitzwilliam, NH 03447, (603) 585-2200.

Directory of Foreign Firms Operating in the United States. World Trade Academy Press, Inc., 50 E. 42nd Street, New York, NY 10017, (212) 697-4999.

Directory of Management Consultants. Consultant's News, Kennedy and Kennedy, Inc., Templeton Road, Fitzwilliam, NH 03447, (603) 585-2200.

Directory of New England Manufacturers. Companies classified by state and industry with executive names. George D. Hall Company, 50 Congress Street, Boston, MA 02109, (617) 523-3745.

Directory of U.S. Labor Organizations. BNA Books, Bureau of National Affairs, Inc., 9435 Key West Avenue, Rockville, MD 20850, (202) 452-4200.

Dun and Bradstreet's Million Dollar Directory (Annual). 3 Sylvan Way, Parsippany, NJ 07054-3896, (201)455-0900. Volume I contains an alphabetical listing for U.S. businesses with a net worth of $1 million or more. Included for each company are the address, phone number, officers, products or services, standard industrial classification (SIC), sales, and number of employees. In Volume II, the yellow pages list companies geographically, the blue pages list the companies by SIC, and the white pages are an alphabetical listing of officers and directors. A companion volume is the *Middle Market Directory*, which lists about 31,000 companies with net worth of $500,000 to $999,999 (similar to Standard & Poor's Register). Also publishes *America's Corporation Families: Billion Dollar Directory, International Affiliates, Principal International Businesses,* and *Corporate Managements.*

Dun's Employment Opportunities Directory. Dun and Bradstreet. Reference Book. Bimonthly. 4 volumes. A geographic listing for all types of U.S. and Canadian firms. Prior to using this directory, however, you must establish the desired location, i.e., state or province and city. Includes an SIC number for each firm, and in most instances contains a code for estimated financial strength and composite credit appraisal.

Economic Indicators. Washington, DC: United States Government Printing Office, Prepared for the Joint Economic Committee by the Council of Economic Advisors, U.S. basic economic indicators.

Education Week. 4301 Connecticut Avenue, NW, Suite 250, Washington, DC 20008, (202) 364-4114.

Employment Agencies/Recruiters. See chapter 20.

Encyclopedia of Associations: National Organizations of the United States. Gale Research, Inc., 835 Penobscot Building, Detroit, Michigan 48226-40946. A guide to thousands of national organizations of all types, purposes, and interests. Gives names and headquarters addresses, telephone numbers, chief officials, number of members, staffs, and chapters and descriptions of membership, programs and activities. Includes lists of special committees and departments, publications and a three-year convention schedule. Cross-indexed. Useful in locating placement committees which can help you learn of specific job openings in your field of interest; getting membership lists of individuals in order to develop personal contacts; learning where and when conferences are being held so that you can attend them to develop personal contacts and position leads.

Encyclopedia of Business Information Sources. Gale Research, Inc., 835 Penobscot Building, Detroit, MI 48226-4094. A general resource book that will lead to all other sources, including directories listing companies. Look up the word *marketing* and you will find information about handbooks and manuals, bibliographies, trade associations, and statistical sources.

F&S Index of Corporations and Industries. Predicasts, Inc., 11001 Cedar Avenue, Cleveland, OH 44106, (216) 795-3000. Cumulates monthly, quarterly, and annually. Indexes articles on companies and industries that have appeared in over 750 selected financial publications and in brokerage house reports. Excellent source to use to find information on private companies.

F&S Index International. Predicasts, Inc., 11001 Cedar Avenue, Cleveland, OH 44106, (216) 795-3000. Monthly, cumulates annually. Indexes articles on foreign companies and industries that have appeared in over 750 foreign and U.S. trade journals.

Fairchild's Financial Manual of Retail Stores. Fairchild Publications, 7 West 34th Street, New York, NY 10001, (212) 630-4000. Provides statistical information on major retail stores and chains in the United States; lists companies alphabetically.

The Foundation Directory. M. Lewis, ed., Columbia University Press, Foundation Center, 79 Fifth Avenue, New York, NY 10003-3076, (212) 620-4230.

Guide to American Directories. B. Klein Publications, P.O. Box 8503, Coral Springs, Florida 33065, (305) 752-1708. A listing and description of thousands of directories with several hundred major industrial, professional, and mercantile classifications. Useful in locating membership names and titles. Calling the publisher or library and asking for specific information or a copy will expedite your research.

Jane's Major Companies of Europe. McGraw-Hill, 1221 Avenue of the Americas, New York, NY 10020, (212) 391-4570. More than 1,000 companies in 16 major countries are represented. Arrangement is in alphabetical order by company name. Front indexes include a listing by country and a classification of companies by industry groups.

Using State Industrial Directories

Almost every company that does business within each state is listed in the state's industrial directory. These directories give information about their products, sales, officers, etc. Using your state directory, you can select companies in different industries which might use your skills, abilities, and talents. Companies are listed alphabetically, by town and county, and by products and services. Each company has a Standard Industrial Classification (SIC) code which defines what that company manufactures.

The SIC number consists of four digits (e.g., 8711):

- The first two digits are the Major Group (e.g., 87 Engineering and Management Services).
- The third digit is the Sub-Group Number (e.g., 871 Engineering and Architectural Services).
- The fourth digit is the Specific Industry Number (e.g., 8711 Engineering Services).

Steps:

1. Visit your state employment security office or nearby library and use the directory.
2. Go through the index of the SIC numbers at the front of the book and write down the ones that interest you.
3. Then find the geographical area that interests you and pick out the names and addresses of the companies from the state directories that have the SIC number you want.
4. Then find out the hiring person in your area of expertise. Send that person a broadcast letter. Also, you can contact the Public Relations officer or Treasurer's office of that company for information to help in your homework.
5. Keep flexible and have several alternative plans of action.

Here are the directories, by state:

Alabama Directory of Mining & Manufacturing: Alabama Development Office, c/o State Capital, 401 Adams Avenue, Montgomery, AL 36130, (205) 242-0400.

Alaska Business License Directory: Business Licensing Section, P.O. Box D, Juneau AK 99811-0800, (907)465-2550.

Directory of Arizona Exporters: Phoenix Chamber of Commerce, 34 West Monroe, Suite 900, Phoenix, AZ 85004, (602) 254-5521.

Directory of Arkansas Manufacturers: Arkansas Industrial Development Foundation, P.O. Box 1784, Little Rock, AR 72203, (501) 682-1121.

California Manufacturers Register: Database Publishing Co., 523 Superior Avenue, Newport Beach, CA 92663, 800-888-8434.

Directory of Colorado Manufacturers: University of Colorado, Business Research Division, Campus Box 420, Boulder, CO 80309, (303) 492-8227.

MacRae's State Industrial Directory (Connecticut): Business Research Publishing, 817 Broadway, 3rd Floor, New York, NY 10003, (800) 622-7237.

Delaware Directory of Commerce & Industry, 1633 Central Street, Evanston, IL 60201, (708) 864-7000.

Manufacturers Directory, Metropolitan Washington, DC: Metropolitan Washington Board of Trade, 1129 20th St., NW, Washington, DC 20036, (202) 857-5900.

Directory of Florida Industries: Florida Chamber of Commerce Management Corp., Box 11309, Tallahassee, FL 32302-3309, (904) 425-1200.

Georgia Manufacturing Directory: Georgia Department of Industry and Trade and Tourism, Box 56706, Atlanta, GA 30343, (404) 656-3607.

Hawaii Business Directory: Hawaii Business Directory, 1164 Bishop Street, Suite 1007, Honolulu, HI 96813, (808) 526-2287.

Idaho Manufacturing Directory: Center for Business Development & Research, College of Business and Economics, Moscow, ID 83843, (208) 885-6611.

Illinois Manufacturers Directory: Manufacturers News, Inc., 1633 Central Street, Evanston, IL 60201, (708) 864-7000.

Indiana Industrial Directory: Harris Publishing Co., 2057 Aurora Road, Twinsburg, OH 44087, (216) 425-9000.

Directory of Iowa Manufacturers: Manufacturers News, Inc., 1633 Central Street, Evanston, IL 60201, (708) 864-7000.

Directory of Kansas Manufacturers & Products: The Kansas Department of Commerce & Housing Economic Analysis Section, 700 SW Harrison, Suite 1300, Topeka, KS 66603-3712, (913) 296-3481.

Kentucky Directory of Manufacturers: Kentucky Dept. of Commerce, Business and Industry, Capital Plaza Tower, Frankfort, KY 40601, (502) 564-4886.

Directory of Louisiana Manufacturers: Department of Economic Development, Box 94185 Capitol Station, Baton Rouge, LA 70804-9185, (504) 389-0227.

Maine Manufacturing Directory: Tower Publishing Company, 34 Diamond Street, Box 7220, Portland, ME 04112, (207) 777-9813.

Directory of Maryland Manufacturers: Harris Publishing Co., 2057 Aurora Road, Twinbury, OH 44087, (216) 425-9000.

Directory of Massachusetts Manufacturers: George D. Hall Co., 50 Congress Street, Boston, MA 02109, (617) 523-3745.

Michigan Manufacturers Directory: Pick Publications, 24151 Telegraph, Suite 280, Southfield, MI 48034, (313) 443-1799.

Minnesota Directory of Manufacturers: K&G Publishing, 250 Prairie Center Drive, Eden Prairie, MN 55344, (800) 800-MINN.

Mississippi Manufacturers Directory: Harris Publishing Co., 2057 Aurora Road, Twinsburg, OH 44087, (216) 425-9000, (800) 888-5900.

Missouri Industrial Directory: (Year) Harris Publishing Company, 2057 Aurora Road, Twinsburg, OH 44087, (216) 425-9000.

Montana Manufacturers and Products Directory: Department of Commerce, Business Development Division, 1424 9th Avenue, Helena, MT 59620, (406) 444-4780.

Directory of Nebraska Manufacturers: Dept. of Economic Development, P.O. Box 94666, Lincoln, NE 68509, (402) 471-3111.

Nevada Industrial Directory, Gold Hill Publishing Co., Inc., P.O. Drawer F, Virginia City, NV 89440, (702) 847-0222.

MacRae's State Industrial Directory—Maine/New Hampshire/Vermont (New Hampshire): Business Research Publishing, 817 Broadway, 3rd Floor, New York, NY 10003, (800) 622-7237.

Directory of New Jersey Manufacturers: George D. Hall Company, 50 Congress Street, Boston MA 02109, (617) 523-3745.

New Mexico Manufacturing Directory: Harris Publishing Co., 2057 Aurora Road, Twinsburg, OH 44087, (216) 425-9000, (800) 888-5900.

The New York State Directory: Cambridge Information Group, 7200 Wisconsin Avenue, Bethesda, MD 20814, (800) 227-3052.

Directory of Manufacturing Firms in North Carolina: North Carolina Department of Commerce, Industrial Development Division, P.O. Box 25249, 430 North Salisbury Street, Raleigh, NC 27611, (919) 733-4151.

Directory of North Dakota Manufacturers: Economic Development Commission, 1833 E. Bismarck Expressway, Bismarck, ND 58504, (701) 224-2810.

Ohio Manufacturers Directory: Manufacturers News, Inc., 1633 Central Street, Evanston, IL 60201, (708) 864-7000.

Directory of Oklahoma Manufacturers: Oklahoma Commerce Dept., Attn: Deborah Lee, P.O. Box 26980, Oklahoma City, OK 73126-0980, (405) 843-9770.

Directory of Oregon Manufacturers: State of Oregon, Dept. of Economic Development, 775 Summer Street, NE, Salem, OR 97310, (503) 373-1200.

MacRae's State Industrial Directory (Pennsylvania): Business Research Publishing, 817 Broadway, 3rd Floor, New York, NY 10003, (800) 622-7237.

Rhode Island Directory of Manufacturers: Rhode Island Dept. of Economic Development, 7 Jackson Walkway, Providence, RI 02903, (401) 277-2601.

South Carolina Chamber of Commerce Directory: South Carolina Chamber of Commerce, 1301 Gervais Street, Columbia, SC 29211, (803) 799-4601.

South Dakota Manufacturers & Processors Directory: Manufacturers News, 1633 Central Street, Evanston, IL 60201, (708) 864-7000.

Tennessee Manufacturers Directory: Manufacturers News, 1633 Central Street, Evanston, IL 60201, (708) 864-7000.

Directory of Texas Manufacturers: Bureau of Business Research, University of Texas, Austin, TX 78712, (512) 471-1616.

Utah Directory of Business and Industry: Utah Dept. of Employment Security, 324 S. State Street, Suite 500, Salt Lake City, UT 84111, (801) 538-8700.

Vermont Buyers & Sellers Directory: Tower Publishing, 34 Diamond Street, Box 7720, Portland, ME 04112, (207) 774-9813.

Virginia Industrial Directory: Virginia State Chamber of Commerce, 9 S. Fifth Street, Richmond, VA 23219, (804) 644-1607.

Washington Manufacturers Register: Database Publishing, 523 Superior Avenue, Newport Beach, CA 92663, (800) 888-8434.

West Virginia Manufacturers Register: Manufacturers News, 1633 Central Street, Evanston, IL 60201, (708) 864-7000.

Classified Directory of Wisconsin Manufacturers: Wisconsin Manufacturers and Commerce, Box 352, Madison, WI 53701-0352, (608) 258-3400.

Wyoming Directory of Manufacturing and Mining: Wyoming Economic and Stabilization Board, Herschler Building, Cheyenne, WY 82002, (307) 777-7284.

Other

International Alliance of Professional and Executive Women's Networks. 8600 LaSalle Road, Baltimore, MD 21286, (410) 472-4221.

International Directory of Corporate Affiliations. Reed Reference Publications, P.O. Box 31, New Providence, NJ 07974, (908) 464-6800.

Libraries. Locate your local business public and university libraries. Many of these sources are there. Work with the reference librarian on any homework questions and/or specific research you have.

Mailing Lists. For example: Hugo Dunhill Mailing Lists, Inc., 630 Third Avenue, New York, NY 10017, (212) 682-8030, outside NYS (800) 223-6454; R. L. Polk & Company, P.O. Box 305100, Nashville, TN 37230-5100, (615) 899-3350; Alvin B. Zeller, Inc., 224 5th Avenue, New York, NY 10001, (212) 689-4900 or (800) 223-0184.

Magazines. *Barron's, Business Horizons, Business Week* (especially hot growth companies and industry outlook issues), *Dun's Review, Ebony, Financial World, Forbes* (note their annual feature in November on "The Largest Private Companies in the U.S.," *Fortune, Inc* (note their annual top 500 listing of industrial companies in the April and May issues and service companies in June), *Glamour, Harvard Business Review, Entrepreneurs, Money, Newsweek, Saturday Review, Success, Time,* and *The Economist.* Read to learn about industries of interest, the current "buzz words," and where things are happening. Companies of possible interest can be looked up in the industrial directories.

Mergers and Acquisitions. The Journal of Corporate Venture. LR Publishing Company, 229 S. 18th Street, 3rd Floor, Philadelphia, PA 19103, (215) 790-7000.

Million Dollar Directory Series. Dun's Marketing Services, 3 Sylan Way, Parsippany, NJ 07054-3896, (201) 455-0900.

Monthly Labor Review (U.S. Bureau of Labor Statistics). Washington, DC: U.S. Dept. of Labor, Bureau of Labor Statistic, 441 G Street NW, Washington, DC 20212, (202) 606-7828. Current statistics on employment, unemployment, hours and earnings, wholesale and retail prices.

Moody's International Manual. 99 Church Street, New York, NY 10007-0300, (212) 553-0300. Annual. Financial and business information on more than 3000 major corporations in 100 countries. Corporations are listed alphabetically under country names. Each country section is preceded by summary statistics relating to a demographic and economic profile. Front blue pages contain an alphabetical listing of all corporate entries. Center blue pages include financial and economic statistical tables, exchange rates, consumer price index.

Moody's Industrials. This reference covers only those companies whose securities are traded. Firms are listed alphabetically by firm name. *Moody's* contains a good synopsis of firm size, location, products, plants, and officers. Other Moody's Publications: Prospective employers not falling into the "industrial" classification are generally covered by some other Moody publication, such as *Moody's Public Utilities, Moody's Rail-*

roads, and *Moody's Banks, Insurance, Real Estate, and Investment Trusts*. Information included is similar to *Moody's Industrials*.

National Trade and Professional Associations of the United States and Labor Unions. Columbia Books, Inc. Publishers, 1212 New York Avenue NW, Suite 330, Washington, DC 20005, (202) 898-0662. Lists national trade and professional associations with national memberships, chief officers, date of annual meeting. Also ranks associations by financial size.

Newspapers. Use back issues, look up several employment sections and want ad listings for trends in your job target areas. Note articles on plant openings, new products, new companies, people on the move, local stock reports, which companies "advertise" and which ones do not, etc. (See list of periodicals). Note: cities such as Baltimore, Dallas, Philadelphia, and Pittsburgh have a *Business Times* that will provide interesting local information. Obituaries provide leads to an organization possibly because of an untimely death. Usually positions are not filled right away; or, if the company promotes from within, there still may be a job vacancy that you may qualify for.

I have used these two national ad summation services: *National Ad Search*. P.O. Box 2083, Milwaukee, Wisconsin 53201, (414) 351-1398 (*note:* NAS indexes the ad, saving you time) and *National Business Employment Weekly*, Box 300, Princeton, NJ 08543-0300, (609) 520-4305.

O'Dwyer's Directory of Corporation Communications. J.R. O'Dwyer Co., Inc., 271 Madison Avenue, New York, NY 10016, (212) 679-2471. Lists companies and the largest trade associations; indicates Formal Public Relations/"corporate communications"; surveys how companies define, organize, and staff their public relations operations.

The Occupational Outlook Handbook. U.S. Government Printing Office. Describes over 800 jobs and gives the training, job description, working conditions and employment outlook.

Personnel Department. Ask for company literature from this department. Other company sources can be public relations, treasurer's office, and interviewer's secretary. Ask for annual report, product literature, brochures and in-house newsletter.

Placement Office. Register at your school and get information on organizations/job listings.

Polk's World Bank Directory. North American Edition (U.S., Canada, Mexico, Central America, and Caribbean). R.L. Polk Company, P.O. Box 305100, Nashville, TN 37230-5100. A major detailed directory listing banks and other financial institutions and government agencies by address; also includes geographic indexing with maps, names, and titles of officers. Useful for corporations and government agencies. Also, *Polk City Directory*.

Predicasts. Cleveland: Predicasts, Inc. Quarterly. A service that abstracts both short- and long-range forecast statistics for basic economic indicators and for specific products (by SIC number). Citations of journal articles from which forecasts are derived are a basic feature.

Principal International Businesses. New York: Dun & Bradstreet, Inc. (annual), 299 Park Avenue, New York, NY 10171, (212) 593-6800.

Prospectus. In addition to financial and historical data, this supplies information on the directors, officers, and insiders including backgrounds, holdings, and compensation. Ask local stock broker for companies of interest.

Readers' Guide to Periodic Literature. H.W. Wilson Company, 950 University Avenue, Bronx, NY 10452-9978, (800) 367-6770.

Reference Book of Corporate Managements. Dun & Bradstreet, Inc., 99 Church Street, New York, NY 10007, (212) 553-0300.

Salary Surveys. Write to the following for information: Northwestern University, Endicott—Lindquist Report, Placement Center, Evanston, IL 60201; Michigan State University Placement Services, East Lansing, MI 48824; or Assembly of Collegiate Schools of Business, 605 Old Ballas Road, Suite 220, St. Louis, MO 63141-7077, (314) 872-8481.

Securities and Exchange Commission Bulletin. Extensive information on companies' finances or operations (i.e., officer salaries, bonuses, perks). Available to the public upon request, these reports will give you more detailed information than the annual report. Ask for the company's 10K, 10Q, and 8K reports. Contact the treasurer's office of public information or public relations officer of the corporation; a local business library, college or university library, or bank library; the office library of a public accounting business; or National Investment Inc., P.O. Box 104, Greenhills, Mandaluyong, Metro, Manilla, Philippines.

SEC Filing Companies. Bethesda, MD: Disclosure, Inc. (Annual). To determine whether a company is public or private. Lists parent companies currently required to file reports with the Securities & Exchange Commission. Available at no charge from Disclosure, 5161 River Road, Bethesda, MD 20816, (301) 951-1300.

Security Industry Yearbook. Published by the Securities Industry Association, Inc., 120 Broadway, New York, NY 10271, (212) 608-1500. This book profiles numerous large and small investment companies, ranks them, and includes names of corporate officers.

Small Manufacturers Directories. Find out if your community has any.

Standard Corporation Records. Standard & Poor's Corp., 1221 Avenue of the Americas, New York, NY 10020, (212) 512-4900. Loose-leaf; bimonthly with daily supplements. Comparable to Moody's but in addition, it has a daily news section which is a good source for up-to-date information on public companies.

Standard Directory of Advertisers. Reed Ref. Publishing, P.O. Box 31, New Providence, NJ 07974, (708) 464-6800. Lists companies doing national and regional advertising with their names, telephone numbers, products, or services; executives and their titles are included, as well as the advertising agency handling the account, account executives, time and amount of appropriation, media services used, and distribution. Companies are listed by product classification and in alphabetical and trade name indexes. A useful source in locating marketing officers, names of parent companies, subsidiaries, and affiliates. A known trade name can be used to locate the manufacturer. Also publishes *Standard Directory of Advertising Agencies.*

Standard Industrial Classification Manual. Washington, DC: U.S. Government Printing Office, 1987. Order from National Technical Information Service, 5285 Port Royal Road, Springfield, VA 22161, (703) 487-4650. This classification scheme of specific industries was developed by the federal government to facilitate the collection and presentation of statistical data on all industrial establishments. The four-digit SIC code is a major tool for the defining of businesses and industries as well as for classifying their suppliers and customers.

The Standard Periodical Directory. Oxbridge Communications, 150 Fifth Avenue, Suite 302, New York, NY 10011, (212) 741-0231. Describes periodicals and directories in hundreds of subject categories.

Standard and Poor' Register of Corporations, Directors and Executives. 25 Broadway, New York, NY 10004 (3 volumes), (212) 208-8000. A guide to the business community providing information on public companies of the United States. *Volume I, Corporate Listings*: Alphabetical listing by business name of corporations including addresses, telephone numbers, names, titles of officers and directors, public firms' (SIC) Standard Industrial Classification codes (for company/industry cross referencing), annual sales, number of employees, some division names, principal and secondary businesses. *Volume II, Directors and Executives*: Alphabetical list of officers, directors, trustees, partners, etc., and their principal business affiliations with official titles and business and residence addresses. Where obtainable, year and place of birth, college, year of graduation, and fraternal memberships are listed. *Volume III, In-*

dexes: Lists companies by SIC and geographically. It also contains an obituary section and a listing of officers and companies.

Standard and Poor's Register Supplement (Quarterly). Standard and Poor's Register of Corporations, Directors and Executives, 25 Broadway, New York, NY 10004, (212) 208-8000. Gives corporation director revisions and directors and executives revisions (an updating of data for the above volumes).

State Employment Agencies. Provide aptitude testing, career advising and job placement. The service is free.

Stock Reports. A relatively unbiased source of information available at any stockbroker's office for organizations that are sold by shares to the public. Several research services provide the brokers with data that can help you analyze the company's potential for growth, stability, and other relevant factors. Prospectuses on companies can also be obtained free.

Survey of Current Business. Washington, DC: U.S. Bureau of Economic Analysis (U.S. Department of Commerce) Washington, DC 20230, (202) 523-0777. One of the most useful sources for current business statistics.

Thomas Register of American Manufacturers and Thomas Register Catalog File. Thomas Publishing Company, 5 Penn Plaza, 250 W. 34th Street, New York, NY 10001, (212) 695-0500. Useful in locating many specific product manufacturers both large and small not listed in any of the other preceding directories. Also contains a listing of all U.S. Chambers of Commerce. *Volumes 1-7*: Products and services listed alphabetically. (Brand names and index in Volume 7). *Volume 8*: Company names, addresses, and telephone numbers listed alphabetically with branch offices, capital ratings, and company officials. *Volumes 9-12*: Catalogues of companies listed alphabetically and cross-indexed.

Trade Directories of the World. Croner Publications, 34 Jericho Turnpike, Jericho, NY 11753, (516) 333-9085 (also London, U.K.). Trade directories listed by continent, country and trade or profession. Also lists import/export directories.

Trade Publications. Some trade publications may provide articles about a specific company or industry, e.g., *Computer Age, Computerworld, Datamation, IBM Systems Journal, Popular Computing.*

Trade Show Exhibitor Directories.

The Value Line Investment Survey. Value Line, Inc., 711 Third Avenue, New York, NY 10017, (212) 687-3965. Section 1: Summary and Index issued weekly; inserted at front of Ratings and Reports (replacing the previous week's index). Section 2: Selection and Opinion filed in separate binder holding about 25 weekly editions; gives Value Line's opinion on the stock's outlook and advisable investments. Section 3: Ratings and Reports issued weekly; 13 most recent weekly editions on file; 1700 stocks classified into 92 industry groups. Value Line catalogues stocks at their most recent prices with current rankings for timeliness and safety.

Venture Capital Directory. Information about 450 organizations supplying venture capital to new businesses. Names individuals who might have knowledge of job openings in new growth businesses. Technimetrics, Inc., 80 South Street, New York, NY 10038, (212) 509-5100.

Ulrich's International Periodicals Directory. Reed Reference, 121 Chanlon Road, New Providence, NJ 07974, (800) 521-8110. Describes 60,000 periodicals and directories published throughout the world.

U.S. Bureau of Labor Statistics. Handbook of Labor Statistics. Washington: Government Printing Office (Annual), Bureau of Labor Statistics, 2 Mass Avenue, NW, Washington, DC 20212, (202) 606-5886. A one-volume source for major labor statistics. For current statistics, see the Bureau's *Monthly Labor Review.*

Ward's Directory of 51,000 Largest U.S. Corporations (also *Ward's Directory of 49,000 Private U.S. Companies*). Ward's Business Directory of U.S. (private and public companies) Vol. 1 and Vol. 2, Gale Research, Inc., 835 Penobscot Building, Detroit, MI 48226-4094, (800) 877-4253. Ranks public, private companies and subsidiaries by sales and industry, (800) 521-0707.

Who's Who in America. Reed Reference Publishing, 121 Chanlon Road, New Providence, NJ 07974, (800) 521-8110. Contemporary biographies including life and career data of noteworthy individuals, including, most likely, the president of the company you may want to work for.

Who's Who in Finance & Industry. Reed Reference Publishing, 121 Chanlon Road, New Providence, NJ 07974, (800) 521-8110. Also *Who's Who in: Government, East, West, South Southeast and America.*

Yellow Pages. Throughout the U.S., lists literally millions of companies and businesses. Go to your nearest telephone business office. It usually has directories from all over the U.S. or at least will be able to direct you where you might find them. Some local libraries carry them.

Specialized Directories

Accounting
American Institute of Certified Public Accounts (AICPA). Annual survey, 1211

Avenue of the Americas, New York, NY 10036-8775, (212) 596-6200. Directories list both private practitioners and accounting firms.

Takce the CPA Challenge. AICPA, P.O. Box 2209, Jersey City, NJ 07303-2209, (800) 862-4272.

Advertising

Standard Directory of Advertisers. (4,400 leading advertising agencies in U.S. with key executives (4,000 U.S., 400 foreign), major accounts, geographic index). Reed Reference Publishing, P.O. Box 31, New Providence, NJ 07974, (908) 464-6800.

Apparel

American Apparel Manufacturers' Association Directory. Lists member firms and executives. American Apparel Manufacturers Association (AAMA), 2500 Wilson Boulevard, Suite 301, Arlington, VA 22201, (703) 524-1864.

Automobiles

Ward's Automotive Yearbook. Auto industry executives. Ward's Communications Inc., 28 West Adams Street, Detroit, MI 48226, (313) 962-4433.

World Motor Vehicle Data. Motor Vehicle Manufacturers Association of the United States, 7430 Second Avenue, Suite 300, Detroit, MI 48202, (313) 872-4311.

Banking

Corporate Finance Blue Book. Reed Reference Publishing/Professional Books, P.O. Box 31, New Providence, NJ 07974, (908) 464-6800.

Broadcasting

Broadcasting Yearbook. Broadcasting Publications, Inc., 1705 Desales Street, NW, Washington, DC 20036, (202) 659-2340.

Television and Cable Factbook. Warren Publishing, Inc., 2115 Ward Court, N.W., Washington, DC 20037, (202) 872-9200.

Canada

Canadian Trade Index. 13,350 companies classified by product and location. Contains executive names. Canadian Manufacturers' Association, 75 International Boulevard, Entobicoke, Ontario, Canada M9W6L9, (416) 798-8000.

Construction/Real Estate

National Roster of Realtors. Stamats Communications, Inc., 427 Sixth Avenue, SE, Cedar Rapids, IA 52406, (319) 364-6032.

Drugs

American Druggist Blue Book. All drug manufacturers. American Druggist, 60 E. 42nd Street, No. 449, New York, NY 10165-0449, (212) 297-9680.

EDP

Computers and Computing Information Resources Directory. Gale Research Company, 835 Penobscot Building, Detroit, MI 48226, (313) 961-2242.

Electronics

American Electronics Association Directory. American Electronics Association, 5201 Great American Parkway, Santa Clara, CA 95054, (408) 988-1777.

Electronic Manufacturers Directory. 7,500 manufacturers classified by location. Harris Publishing Co., 2057 Aurora Road, Twinsburgh, OH 44087, (216) 425-9000.

Engineering—Teaching/Research

Engineering College Research & Graduate Study. Lists 200 engineering colleges with names of department chairmen and research directors. American Society for Engineering Education, 11 Dupont Circle, N.W., Suite 200, Washington, DC 20036, (202) 986-8000.

Engineering Times. National Society of Professional Engineers, 1420 King Street, Alexandria, VA 22314, (703) 684-2875.

Food

Chilton's Food Engineering's Directory of U.S. Food Plants. Chilton Co., Chilton Way, Box 2035, Radnor, PA 19089, (215) 964-4440.

Progressive Grocer's Marketing Guidebook. Lists supermarket chain stores and major food wholesalers in 79 major U.S. markets. Contains names of key executives. Progressive Grocer, 4 Stamford Forum, 6th Floor, Stamford, CT 06901-3202, (203) 325-3500.

Thomas Food Industry Register. Manufacturers and wholesalers of food by product type and state. Thomas Publishing Company, One Penn Plaza, 250 W. 34th Street, New York, NY 10119, (212) 290-7341.

Franchising

Directory of Franchising Organizations. Pilot Books, 103 Cooper Street, Babylon, NY 11702, (516) 422-2225.

Gas Utility

Browns Directory of North American and International Gas Companies. Executive of American and Canadian Gas utilities. Advanstar Communications, 7500 Old Oak Boulevard, Cleveland, OH 44130, (216) 826-2839.

Directory of Gas Utility Companies. U.S. utility companies with key executives. Midwest Oil Register, Inc., 1345 E. 15th Street, Tulsa, OK 74120, (918) 582-2000.

Glass

Glass Factory Directory. National Glass Budget, Box 2267, Hempstead, NY 11550, (516) 481-2188.

Health Care

American Hospital Association Guide to the Health Care Field. American Hospital Association Services, Inc., 840 North Lake Shore Drive, Chicago, IL 60611, (312) 280-6225.

Hospital Blue Book (Annual). Billian Publishing, 2100 Powers Ferry Road, Atlanta, GA 30339, (404) 955-5656.

High Tech (See EDP)

Computers and Computing Information Resources Directory. Martin Connors, ed. Gale Research Co., 1986, 835 Penobscot Building, Detroit, MI 48226, (313) 961-2242.

Hotels

Directory of Hotel and Motel Systems. American Hotel Association Directory Corporation, 1201 New York Avenue, N.W., Washington, DC 20005-3931, (202) 289-3100.

Hotel and Motel Red Book. Donald E. Lundberg, Van Nostrand Reinhold Co., Inc., 115 5th Avenue, New York, NY 10003, (800) 842-3636.

Imports

Directory of United States Importers. 30,000 companies classified by location and type of product imported. Contains names of owners and key executives. The Journal of Commerce, 2 World Trade Center, 27th Floor, New York, NY 10048, (212) 837-7000.

Import/Export

American Export Register. 25,000 importers and exporters classified by product. Contains names of executives. American Register of Importers & Exporters Inc., 5 Penn Plaza, 250 W. 34th Street, New York, NY 10001, (212) 695-0500.

Insurance

Who's Who in Insurance. Underwriter Printing & Publishing Co., 50 East Palisades Avenue, Englewood, NJ 07631, (201) 569-8808.

International Companies

Directory of American Firms Operating in Foreign Countries. 4,200 American companies with overseas subsidiaries. Classified by product and country. Contains names of U.S. executives in charge. World Trade Academy Press Inc., 50 East 42nd Street, Suite 509, New York, NY 10017-5480, (212) 697-4999.

Encyclopedia of Associations: International Organizations. Gale Research, Inc., 1989, 835 Penobscot Building, Detroit, MI 48226, (313) 961-2242.

Labor Unions

Directory of U.S. Labor Organizations (Biennial). The Bureau of National Affairs, Inc., BNA Books, P.O. Box 6036, Rockville, MA 20850-9914, (800) 372-1033.

Directory of National Unions & Employee Associations. Lists unions with officers names. Superintendent of Documents, U.S. Printing Office, Division of Public Documents, Washington, DC 20402, (202) 783-3238.

Law

Law and Legal Information Directory (Biennial). Gale Research, Inc. 1988, 835 Penobscot Building, Detroit, MI 48226, (313) 961-2242.

Who's Who in American Law. Reed Reference Publishing, P.O. Box 31, New Providence, NJ 07974.

Mining

E/MJ International Directory of Mining. Maclean Hunter Publishing Company, 29 N. Wacker Drive, Chicago, IL 60606, (312) 726-2802.

Newspapers

Bacon's Publicity Checker: Newspaper Volume. Includes listings of 1,700 daily and 8,000 weekly newspapers. Bacon's Publishing Company, 332 South Michigan Avenue, Suite 900, Chicago, IL 60604, (312) 922-2400.

Oil

Worldwide Refining & Gas Processing Directory. Penn Well Publishing Company, Box 1260 Tulsa, OK 74101, (918) 835-3161.

Overseas

Foreign Service Journal. American Service Association, 2101 E. Street, N.W, Washington, DC 20037, (202) 338-4045.

Paper

Paper Industry Management Association Magazine. Pulp and paper mill executives. Paper Industry Management Association, 2400 East Oakton Street, Arlington Heights, IL 60005, (708) 956-0250.

Pharmaceutical

Pharmaceutical Marketers Directory. Communications Inc., 7200 W. Camino Real, Suite 215, Boca Raton, FL 33433, (407) 368-9301.

Public Relations

Public Relations Register. Public Relations News, 7811 Montross Road, Potomac, MD 20854, (301) 340-2100.

O'Dwyers Directories. O'Dwyer Publications, 271 Madison Avenue, New York, NY 10016, (212) 679-2471.

Who's Who in Public Relations. PR Publishing Co., Dudley House, Box 600, Exeter, NH 03833, (603) 778-0514.

Publishing

For directories in the publishing field (e.g., *Literary Marketplace*) write to Reed Reference Publishing, P.O. Box 31, New Providence, NJ 07974, (908) 464-6800.

Purchasing

Standard Directory of Advertisers and *Thomas Register.*

Research

Research Centers Directory. 5500 research centers in all fields. Includes names of research directors. Gale Research, 835 Penobscot Building, Detroit, MI 48226, (313) 961-2242.

Retailing

Fairchild's Financial Manual of Retail Stores. Fairchild Publications, 7 East 12th Street, New York, NY 10003, (212) 630-4000.

Textiles

Davison's Textile Buyer's Guide. Textile Mills & Dyers with executives' names. Davison's Publishing Company, P.O. Box 477, Ridgewood, NJ 07451, (201) 445-3135.

Training

Training and Development Organizations Directory. Gale Research Company, 835 Penobscot Building, Detroit, MI 48226, (313) 961-2242.

Transportation

American Motor Carrier Directory. K-III Press Inc., 424 W. 33rd Street, New York, NY 10001, (800) 221-5488.

If you have important information at hand about the organization you are interested in, your interview questions can certainly be more substantive. This clearly gives evidence to those you are interviewing with that you are dedicated to this field, have spent time on research, and have made the decision that this is definitely the occupation for you.

If you want to read articles and newspaper stories about private companies, refer to the *Business Index, Business Periodicals Index,* or *Predicasts' F&S Index.*

As you do your homework and collect information, it is suggested that you keep all information in large manila envelopes, slit lengthwise and properly labeled with organization name, address, zip code, telephone number, and key hiring people and names of any secretaries you have talked to. (*Note:* Record the decision-maker/hiring person in your area of expertise. Start with that person rather than the Human Resources Director unless you are in that discipline.)

Index cards (3"x 5") may also be used to put homework information on and then placed in the appropriate envelopes. Information on a card can include executives and titles; consumer products/services; image; kind of business; organization name; names of individuals to contact; address, zip code, and telephone number; principal major competitors; similar companies; finance data (net sales, return on investment, profit, stock ratings); questions about the company; how you feel you "fit" with the company; and any extra comments or notes that you feel you wanted to make as a result of your homework. Fit is a "biggie." You need to decide if you are comfortable with how the firm does things and how motivated you can be by how it does business. If the answer is a definite yes, then you certainly can move ahead with your campaign.

> *Lord, make me an instrument of your peace*
> *Where there is hatred . . . let me sow love*
> *Where there is injury . . . pardon.*
> *Where there is doubt . . . faith.*
> *Where there is despair . . . hope.*

Where there is darkness . . . light.
Where there is sadness . . . joy.
O Divine Master, grant that I may not so much seek
To be consoled . . . as to console,
To be understood . . . as to understand,
To be loved . . . as to love,
        for
It is in giving . . . that we receive,
It is in pardoning, that we are pardoned,
It is in dying . . . that we are born to eternal life.

— St. Francis

28.

Job Hunters and Counselors Bibliography:
Books, Publications,
and Organizations with Job Listings

*Luck is a crossword where preparation and
opportunity meet.*

— Anonymous

This job hunter's bibliography contains a listing of some useful career and
life-planning books and other publications that could be of use to you. It is
not meant to be complete or all-encompassing, but it is to be used as an additional resource as you conduct or work on your job campaign. It should
be noted that many of these resources, in themselves, contain listings that
you may want to consider using.

Books

Adams, Bob, Inc. *The JobBank Series* (a separate edition for 20 U.S. cities
and one national edition for all 50 states), Bob Adams, Inc., 260 Center
Street, Holbrook, MA 02343. Offers complete contact information on
employers in specific geographic areas of the U.S. (617) 767-8100.

Alexander, Sue. *Finding Your First Job*, Dutton, New York 1980.

Allen, Jeffrey G., *How to Turn an Interview into a Job*, Simon & Schuster,
New York, 1983.

Allen, Jeffrey, and Jess G. Gorkin. *Finding the Right Job in Midlife*, Simon &
Schuster, New York, 1985.

Alman, Brian M., *Self-Hypnosis: A Complete Manual for Health & Self-Change*,
2nd ed., International Health Publications, San Diego, 1991.

Angel, Juvenal L. *The Complete Resume Book & Job Getter's Guide*, Pocket Books division of Simon & Schuster, New York, 1990.

Applegath, John. *Working Free: Practical Alternatives to the 9-to-5 Job*, AMA-COM, New York, 1982.

Ashley, Sally. *Connecting: A Handbook for Housewives Returning to Paid Work*, Avon, New York, 1982.

Avrutis, Raymond. *How to Collect Unemployment Benefits: Complete Information for All 50 States*, Prentice-Hall, Englewood Cliffs, NJ, 1983.

Azrin, Nathan, and Victoria B. Besalel. *Job Club Counselor's Manual: A Behavior Approach to Vocational Counseling*. PRO-ED, Austin, TX, 1980.

Baldridge, Letitia. *Complete Guide to Executive Manners*, Rawson Associates, New York, 1985.

Barker, Raymond C. *You Are Invisible*, 2nd ed., DeVorss, Marina Del Rey, CA, 1986.

Barrett, James, and Geoffrey Williams. *Test Your Own Job Aptitude: Exploring Your Career Potential*, Viking Penguin Books, Bergenfield, NJ, 1981.

Bayless, Hugh. *The Best Towns in America: A Where-To-Go Guide for a Better Life*, Houghton Mifflin, Boston, 1983.

Beatty, Richard H. *The Five Minute Interview*, John Wiley & Sons, New York, 1986.

Berkey, Rachel L. *New Career Opportunities in the Paralegal Profession*, Arco, New York, 1983.

Bermont, Hubert. *How to Become a Successful Consultant in Your Own Field*, 3rd ed., Prima Pub., 1991.

Bernard, S., and G. Thompson. *Job Search Strategy for College Grads*, Bob Adams, Inc., Holbrook, MA, 1984.

Biegeleisen, Jacob. *Job Resumes: How to Write Them, How to Present Them, Preparing for Interviews*, Putnam, New York, 1991.

Biegeleisen, Jacob. *Make Your Job Interview A Success*, 3rd ed., Arco Books, New York, 1991.

Birsner, E. Patricia. *The Forty Plus Job Hunting Guide*, Facts on File, New York, 1990.

Bixler, Susan. *Professional Presence: The Total Program for Gaining that Extra Edge in Business*, Putnam, New York, 1992.

Bixler, Susan. *The Professional Image*, Putnam, New York, 1985.

Blanchard, Kenneth, and Spencer Johnson, *The One Minute Manager*, Berkley Publications, 1987.

Boe, Anne. *Is Your "Net" Working?* John Wiley & Sons, Inc., New York, 1989.

Bolles, Richard, *What Color is Your Parachute?: A Practical Manual for Job-Hunters and Career Changers*, (Annual) Ten Speed Press, Berkeley, CA.

Bolles, Richard. *The New Quick Job-Hunting Map*, Ten Speed Press, Berkeley, CA, 1990.

Bostwick, Burdette E. *Resume Writing*, 4th ed., New York: John Wiley & Sons, Inc., New York, 1990.

Bostwick, Burdette E. *111 Proven Techniques and Strategies for Getting the Job Interview*, Wiley, New York, 1981.

Briggs, James and Robert B. Nelson, *The Berkeley Guide to Employment for New College Graduates*, Ten Speed Press, Berkeley, CA, 1984.

Brown, V., M. Thompson, and H. Harmison. *Selecting and Studying Prospective Employers*, Iowa State University Research Foundation, Inc., 1983. (Discusses using placement services and provides a comprehensive categorized list of references.)

Brown, Duane. *Career Choice and Development*, Jossey Bass, San Francisco, CA, 1990.

Butler, Pam. *Self-Assertion for Women*, Harper & Row, San Francisco, 1992.

Calano, James and Jeff Salzman. *CareerTracking: Twenty-six Shortcuts to the Top*, Simon & Schuster, New York, 1988.

Calhoun, Mary E. *How to Get the Hot Jobs in Business and Finance*, Harper & Row, New York, 1986.

Campbell, David P. *If You Don't Know Where You're Going, You'll Probably End Up Somewhere Else*, Argus Publications, Allen, Texas, 1990.

Casewit, Curtis W. *How to Get a Job Overseas*, Arco, New York, 1984.

Catalyst Staff. *Marketing Yourself*, Putnam & Sons, New York, 1980. Catalyst is a nonprofit organization that encourages the participation of businesswomen and publishes career development materials and resume writing guides. Write or call them: 250 Park Avenue South, New York, NY 10003, (212) 777-9000.

Catalyst Staff. *When Can You Start?*, the complete job-search guide for women of all ages, Macmillan Publishing Co., Riverside, NJ, 1981.

Catalyst Staff. *What to do With the Rest of Your Life*, Simon & Schuster, New York, 1980.

Chapman, Jack. *How to Make $1000 A Minute: Negotiating Salaries and Raises*, Ten Speed Press, Berkeley, CA, 1987.

Chastain, Sherry. *Winning the Salary Game: Salary Negotiation for Women*, John Wiley and Sons, Inc., New York, 1980.

Cho, Emily. *Looking, Working, Living Terrific 24 Hours A Day*, Putnam, New York, 1982.

Cohen, Herb. *You Can Negotiate Anything*, Bantam Books, New York, 1983.

Cohen, Lilly, and Dennis R. Young. *Careers for Dreamers & Doers: A Guide to Management Careers in the Nonprofit Sector*, The Foundation Center, Westbury, NY, 1989.

Cornish, Edward. *Careers Tomorrow*, World Future Society, Maryland, 1988.

Covey, Stephen R., *The Seven Habits of Highly Effective People*, Fireside, New York, 1989.

Cox, Allan J. *Achiever's Profile*, AMACOM, New York, 1991.

Coxford, Lola. *Resume Writing Made Easy*, 4th ed., Gorsuch Scarlsbrick, Arizona, 1991.

Cramer, Kathryn D., *Staying on Top When Your World Turns Upside Down*, Viking (Penguin), New York, 1991.

Croft, Barbara L. *The Checklist Kit for Resume Writing & Job Application Letters*, Different Drummer Press, Des Moines, IA, 1982.

Davidson, Jeffrey P. *Avoiding the Pitfalls of Starting Your Own Business*, Walker & Company, New York, 1988.

Davis, George, and Gregg Watson. *Black Life in Corporate America*, Doubleday-Dell, New York, 1985.

Dawson, Roger. *You Can Get Anything You Want, But You Have To Do More Than Ask*, Simon and Schuster, New York, 1987.

Deal, Terrence, and Allen Kennedy. *Corporate Cultures: The Rites & Rituals of Corporate Life*, Addison-Wesley, Reading, MA, 1982.

De Prez, Caroline S., and Richard J. De Prez. *Resume Manual for the Military: A Complete Job Hunting Guide for Present and Future Veterans*, Arco, San Diego, 1984.

Dickhut, Harold W. *The Professional Resume and Job Search Guide*, Prentice-Hall, Englewood Cliffs, NJ, 1981.

Diggs, R. N. *The Great Job Hunt*, Progressive Publications, Homosassa Springs, FL, 1986.

Dowling, Collette. *The Cinderella Complex—Women's Hidden Fear of Independence*, Pocket Books, New York, 1990.

Elsea, Janet G. *First Impression, Best Impression*, Simon & Schuster, New York, 1986.

Faux, Marian. *The Complete Resume Guide*, 3rd ed., Arco, New York, 1991.

Fear, Richard A and R.J. Chiron. *The Evaluation Interview*, 4th ed., McGraw-Hill, New York, 1990.

Feingold, S. Norman, and Hansard-Winkler, Glenda Ann. *900,000 Plus Jobs Annually*, Garrett Park Press, Garrett Park, MD 20846, 1982.

Fields, Daisy B. A Woman's Guide to Moving Up in Business and Government, Prentice-Hall, Englewood Cliffs, NJ, 1983.

Figler, Howard, *Complete Job-Search Handbook*, Henry Holt & Co., New York, 1988.

Fisher, Roger, and William Ury. *Getting to Yes*, Penguin Books, Bergenfield, NJ, 1991.

Fox, Marcia R. *Put Your Degree to Work*, W. W. Norton & Company, New York, 1988.

Foxman, Loretta D. *The Executive Resume*, 2nd ed., Wiley & Sons, New York, 1989.

Foxman, Loretta D. *Resumes That Work: How to Sell Yourself on Paper*, Wiley & Sons, New York, 1993.

Frankl, Viktor E. *Man's Search for Meaning*, Simon & Schuster, New York, 1988.

Friedenberg Joan and C. Bradley. *Finding a Job in the U.S.A.*, Passport Books, Illinois, 1986.

Fraser, Jill A. *The Best U.S. Cities for Working Women*, Plume Books, New York, 1986.

Frailey, L. E. *Handbook of Business Letters*, 3rd ed., Prentice-Hall, Englewood Cliffs, NJ, 1991.

Gale, Barry and Linda. *Discover What You're Best At: The National Career Aptitude System and Career Directory*, Simon & Schuster, New York, 1990.

Gawain, Shakti. *Creative Visualization*, Bantam, New York, 1983.

Gerberg, Robert Jameson. *Robert Gerberg's Job Changing System*, Performance Dynamics, Andrews & McMeel, Parsippany, New Jersey, 1986.

German, Donald R. and Joan W. *How to Find a Job When Jobs are Hard to Find*, Amacom, New York, 1981.

Germann, Richard, and Peter Arnold. *The Job and Career Building*, Ten Speed Press, Berkeley, CA 1982.

Gilligan, Carol. *In a Different Voice*, Harvard University Press, Cambridge, 1982.

Glossbrenner, Alfred. *How To Look It Up Online*, St. Martin's Press, New York, 1987.

Goffman, Erving. *Gender Advertisements*, Harper and Row, New York, 1988.

Goldstein, Harold, and Bryna Shore Fraser. *Getting a Job in the Computer Age*, Peterson's Guides, Princeton, NJ, 1986.

Good, C. Edward, *Does Your Resume Wear Blue Jeans?* Blue Jeans Press, Word Store, Charlottesville, VA, 1985.

Gottfredson, G. D., J. L. Holland, and D. K. Ogawa. *Dictionary of Holland Occupational Codes*, Consulting Psychologists Press, Palo Alto, CA, 1982. (Also available from Psychological Assessment Resources, Inc.)

Grayson, Stuart, *The Ten Demandments of Prosperity: Dynamics for Successful Living*, Putnam, New York, 1989.

Grones, Freda. *Fifteen Tips on Writing Resumes*, Career Publishers, Orange, CA, 1987.

Greiner, Larry E., and Robert O. Metzger. *Consulting to Management*, Prentice-Hall, Englewood Cliffs, NJ, 1983.

Grice, Charles Richmond, Jr. *Fifteen Tips on Handling Job Interviews*, Career Publishing Inc., Orange, CA, 1987.

Gunderson, John G. *Get That Interview, Write a Winning Resume*, Focus (Practice Management) Publications, Honolulu, HI, 1980.

Half, Robert. *On Hiring*, Dutton, 1986.

Half, Robert. *The Robert Half Way to Get Hired in Today's Market*, Bantam, New York, 1983.

Harragan, Betty Lehan. *Games Mother Never Taught You: Corporate Gamesmanship for Women*, Warner Books, New York, 1989.

Hart, Lois Borland. *Moving Up! Women and Leadership*, AMACOM, New York, 1980.

Helmstetter, Shad, *What To Say When You Talk To Yourself*, Grindle Press, New York, 1986.

Henning, Margaret, and Ann Jardim. *The Managerial Woman*, Simon & Schuster, New York, 1988.

Higginson, Margaret, and Thomas Quick. *The Ambitious Woman's Guide to a Successful Career*, AMACOM, New York, 1982.

Hill, Napoleon. *Think and Grow Rich*, Random-Fawcett, New York, 1987.

Hillstrom, J. K. *Steps to Professional Employment*, Barrons, New York, 1982.

Hochheiser, Robert M. *How to Work for a Jerk: Your Success is the Best Revenge*, Vintage Books, New York, 1987.

Holland, J. L. *Making Vocational Choices: A Theory of Vocational Personalities and Work Environments*, 3rd ed., Pysch. Assess., 1992.

Holtz, Herman. *Beyond the Resume: How to Land the Jobs You Want*, McGraw-Hill, New York, NY, 1984.

Hyatt, Carole. *Shifting Gears: Mastering Career Change*, Simon & Schuster, New York, 1992.

Irish, Richard K. *Go Hire Yourself an Employer*, Dell, New York, 1987.

Jackson, Tom. *Guerrilla Tactics in the Job Market*, Bantam Books, New York, 1991.

Jackson, Tom. *The Perfect Resume*, Anchor Books, New York, 1990.

Jacobson, Kenneth C. *Retiring from Military Service*, Naval Institute Press, Annapolis, MD, 1990.

Jameson, Robert. *The Professional Job Hunting System*, Performance Dynamics, New Jersey, 1981.

Kanchier, Carole. *Dare to Change Your Job and Your Life*, Master Media,Ltd., New York, 1991.

Kaplan, Glenn. *The Big Time: How Success Really Works in 14 Top Business Careers*, Congdon & Weed, 1990.

Keyes, Ken. *How to Enjoy Your Life in Spite of It All*, Love Line Books, 1990.

Kennedy, Marilyn. *Career Knockouts*, Follett Publishing Co., Chicago, 1980.

Kishel, Gregory and Patricia. *Cashing in on the Consulting Boom*, Wiley, New York, 1985.

Kline, Linda, and Lloyd L. Feinstein. *Career Changing: The Worry-Free Guide*, Little, Brown, and Co., Boston, 1982.

Kleiman, Carol. *Women's Network*, Ballantine/Fawcett, New York, 1980.

Kocher, Eric. *International Jobs, Where They Are—How To Get Them*, Addison-Wesley, Reading, MA, 1989.

Krannich, Ronald L. *Re-Careering in Turbulent Times*, Impact, Manassas, VA, 1983.

Krannich, Ronald L., and William J. Banis. *High Impact Resumes and Letters*, Impact, Manassas, VA, 1992.

Kravette, Steve. *Get a Job in 60 Seconds*, Bantam, 1983.

Kroeger, Otto, and Janet M. Thuesen. *Type Talk*, Delacarte, New York, 1988.

Kushner, Harold. *When Bad Things Happen To Good People*, Schochen Books, New York, 1989.

LaBella, Arleen, and Delores Leach. *Personal Power*, CareerTrack, Boulder, CO, 1983.

LaBier, Douglas. *Modern Madness: The Emotional Fallout of Success*, Addison-Wesley, Reading, MA, 1986.

Lathrop, Richard. *Who's Hiring Who*, Ten Speed Press, Berkeley, CA, 1989.

LaRouche, Janet, Janice and Regina Ryan. *Strategies for Women at Work*, Avon, New York, 1984.

Levering, Robert, Milton Moskowitz, and Michael Katz. *The 100 Best Companies to Work for in America*, Doubleday, 1993.

Levine, Steven. *Who Dies?* Doubleday Engerbook, New York, 1989.

Lewis, Adele. *How to Write Better Resumes*, Barrons, Woodbury, NY, 1989.

Lewis, A., and B. Lewis. *How to Choose, Change, Advance Your Career*, Barron's Educational Series, New York, 1983.

Lewis, William. *Resumes for College Graduates*, Prentice-Hall, Englewood Cliffs, NJ, 1984.

Ley, D. Forbes. *The Best Seller*, Sales Success Press, Newport Beach, CA 1986.

Lucht, John. *Rites of Passage at $100,000+ . . . , The Insiders Guide to Absolutely Everything About Executive Job Changing*, Viceroy Press, New York, 1988.

MacKay, Harvey. *Sharkproof*, Harper Business, New York, 1993.

Martin, Phyllis. *Martin's Magic Formula for Getting the Right Job*, St. Martin's Press, 1987.

Malloy, John T. *Dress for Success*, Warner Books, New York, 1988.

Marks, E., and A. Lewis. *Job Hunting for the Disabled*, Barron's Educational Series, Inc., New York, 1983.

Matteson, Michael T. and J. M. Ivancevich. *Controlling Job Stress: Effective Human Resources and Management Strategies*, Jossey-Bass, The Free Press, New York, 1982.

McDaniels, Carl. *Developing a Professional Vitae or Resume*, Garrett Park, Garrett Park, MD, 1990.

McHugh, John. *Interviewing for Jobs*, EMC Publishing, St. Paul, MN, 1981.

McLaughlin, John E., and Stephen K. Merman. *Writing a Job-Winning Resume*, Prentice-Hall, Englewood Cliffs, NJ, 1980.

Medley, H. A. *Sweaty Palms: The Neglected Art of Being Interviewed*, Ten Speed Press, Berkeley, CA, 1992.

Molloy, John T. *Dress For Success*, Warner Books, New York, 1988.

Moore, Charles Guy, *The Career Game*, National Institute of Career Planning, New York, NY 1978.

Munschauer, John L. *Jobs for English Majors and Other Smart People*, Petersen Guides, Princeton, NJ, 1991.

Nadler, Burton J. *Liberal Arts Power! What It is and How to Sell It on Your Resume*, Peterson's Guides, Princeton, NJ, 1989.

Nivens, Beatryce. *The Black Women's Career Guide*, Doubleday, New York, 1987.

O'Brien, Mark. *High Tech Jobs for Non-Tech Grads*, Prentice-Hall, Inc., Englewood Cliffs, NJ, 1986.

Olmstead, Barney, and Suzanne Smith. *The Job Sharing Handbook*, Ten Speed Press, Berkeley, CA, 1985.

Osher, Bill, and Sioux Henley Campbell. *The Blue Chip Graduate*, Peachtree Publishers, Ltd., Atlanta, GA, 1987.

Ostrander, Sheila, and Lynn Schroeder. *Superlearning*, Dell, New York, 1984.

Parker, Yana. *The Damn Good Resume Guide*, Ten Speed Press, Berkeley, CA, 1989.

Parker, Yana. *The Resume Catalog: 200 Damn Good Examples*, Ten Speed Press, Berkeley, CA, 1988.

Payne, Richard A. *How to Get A Better Job Quicker*, The Taplinger Publishing Company, Jersey City, NJ, 1988.

Pearson, H. G. *Your Hidden Skills: Clues to Careers and Future Pursuits*, Mowry Press, Wayland, MA, 1981.

Pell, Arthur R., and George Sadek. *Resumes for Computer Professionals*, Monarch Press, New York, 1984.

Peters, Thomas, and Robert Waterman. *In Search of Excellence*, Warner Books, New York, 1988.

Petras, Ross and Kathryn. *The Only Job Hunting Guide You'll Ever Need*, Poseidon Press, New York, 1989.

Petras, Ross and Kathryn. *Jobs*, Prentice-Hall, Englewood Cliffs, NJ, 1993.

Pogrebin, Letty Cottin. *Growing Up Free: Raising Your Child in the 80's*, McGraw-Hill, New York, 1980.

Pollack, Sandy. *Alternative Careers for Teachers*, Harvard Common Press, Cambridge, MA, 1984.

Richardson, Jerry. *The Magic of Rapport*, Meta Pubns., New York, 1988.

Roesch, Roberta. *You Can Make It Without A College Degree*, Simon & Schuster, New York, 1986.

Rogers, E. J. *Getting Hired: Everything You Need to Know About Resumes, Interviews, and Job-Hunting Strategies*, Prentice-Hall, Englewood Cliffs, NJ, 1981.

Sanford, Linda T. *Women and Self-Esteem*, Penguin, New York, 1985.

Schmidt, Peggy J. *Making It on Your First Job When You're Young, Ambitious, and Inexperienced*, Petersens Guides, Princeton, NJ, 1991.

Scholz, Nelle and Judith Prince. *How to Decide: A Workbook for Women*, College Bd, New York, 1985.

Schuller, Robert H. *Tough-Minded Faith for Tender Hearted People*, Bantam, 1985.

Sher, Barbara, and Annie Gottlieb. *Wishcraft: How to Get What You Really Want*, Ballantine, New York, 1986.

Sitzmann Marion, and Reloy Garcia. *Successful Interviewing*, National Textbook, Washington, DC, 1983.

Smith, Manuel. *When I Say No, I Feel Guilty*, Bantam Books, New York, 1985.

Smith, Michael H. *The Resume Writer's Handbook*, Barnes & Noble, Savage, MD, 1987.

Stumpf, Stephen and Celeste K. Rodgers. *Choosing a Career in Business*, Simon & Schuster, New York, 1984.

Tarrant, John. *Perks and Parachutes: How to Get the Ideal Employment Package*, Fireside, New York, 1986.

Tavris, Carol. *Anger: The Misunderstood Emotion*, Simon & Schuster, New York, 1989.

Thain, Richard. *The Mid-Career Manual*, Prentice-Hall, Englewood Cliffs, NJ, 1982.

Toffler, Alvin. *The Third Wave*, Bantam Books, New York, 1984.

Usher, Harland. *How to Get a Job with "No Experience" or "Not Enough"*, Ell Ell Diversified, 1981.

Washington, Tom. *Resume Power: Selling Yourself on Paper*, Mt. Vernon Press, Bellevue, WA, 1990.

Weeks, Francis William and D.A. Jameson. *Principles of Business Communication*, Stipes Publishers, Champaign, IL, 1984.

Weinstein, Robert V. *Jobs for the 21st Century*, Collier Books, New York, 1983.

Weinstein, Bob. *Resumes for Hard Times, How to Make Yourself a Hot Property in a Cold Market*, Fireside, Hamden, CT, 1986.

Wilson, Robert F. *Better Resumes for Executives and Professionals*, 2nd ed., Barrons, Happauge, NY, 1991.

Wood, Orrin G., Jr. *Your Hidden Assets: The Key to Getting Executive Jobs*, Dow Jones Irwin, Homewood, IL, 1986.

Wool, John D. *How to Write Yourself Up*, Richards Publishing, Phoenix, NY, 1983.

Wright, John. *American Almanac of Jobs and Salaries*, Avon, New York, 1987.

Yate, Martin John. *Knock 'em Dead: The Ultimate Job Seeker's Handbook*, Bob Adams, Inc., Holbrook, MA, 1993.

Note: Check with your local bookstore for a current *Dictionary of Publishers* if you can't locate a particular book, you can at least contact the publisher. The cost of books can be tax deductible if they are used to locate a job or promotion within the buyer's "continuing trade or business" (IRS Code Section 162, Revenue Ruling 75-120).

> *Above all else, be the very best you can be.*
> — ANONYMOUS

Publications and Organizations with Job Listings or Assistance

The Air Jobs Digest. World Air Data, P.O. Box 70127, Washington, DC 20088, (301) 984-0002.

American Association for Counseling and Development, 5999 Stevenson Avenue, Alexandria, VA 22304, (703) 823-9800; (800) 347-6647.

American Society of Public Administration, 1120 G Street, Suite 700, Washington, DC 20005, (202) 393-7878.

APA Newspaper Directory. Alabama Press Association Rate and Data Guide, Commerce Center, Suite 1100, 2027 1st Avenue N., Birmingham, AL 35203, (205) 322-0380.

Career Opportunities News. Employment Opportunities Made by Employers at the Time of Publication—A Six Month Projection of Anticipated Openings, Box 190F, Garret Park, MD 20896, (301) 946-2553.

The Chronicle of Higher Education. 1255 23rd Street NW, Suite 700, Washington, DC 20037, (202) 466-1000.

College and School Placement Offices.

Company (in-house) job postings.

The Connection (published twice a year), for Business Opportunities in Engineering and Surveying, Microprecision, Inc., P.O. Box 10, Wilsonville, Oregon 97070, (503) 682-3181.

Contract Weekly. C.E. Publications, Inc., P.O. Box 97000, Kirkland, WA 98083-9700, (206) 823-2222.

Crystal-Barkley Corporation. Attn: John C. Crystal Center - Life/Work Design, 152 Madison Avenue, New York, NY 10016, (212) 889-8500.

Engineering News-Record (ENR). 1221 Avenue of the Americas, New York, NY 10020, (212) 512-3549.

Federal Bar News and Journal. 1815 H Street, N.W., Suite 408, Washington, DC 20006-3697, (202) 638-0252.

Federal Career Opportunities. Federal Research Service, Inc., 243 Church Street NW, Vienna, VA 22180, (703) 281-0200.

ICMA Newsletter. The International City Management Association, Suite 500, 777 North Capitol Street NE, Washington, DC 20002-4201, (202) 289-4262.

Intercristo. Christian Placement Network, P.O. Box 33487, Seattle, Washington, 98133, 1-800-251-7740, ext. 10 (4 printouts during each 3 month's time).

The Northwestern Lindquist-Endicott Report. (Annual) Northwestern University Placement Center, Scott Hall, 601 University Place, Evanston, IL 60201, (708) 491-3700.

International Employment Hotline. Cantrell Corp., P.O. Box 3030, Oakton, VA 22124, (703) 620-1972.

The Job World, Inc. Directory. 499 Highway 434, Suite 2113, Altamorite Springs, FL 32714, (407) 788-6232.

Jobs Available. P.O. Box 1040, Modesto, CA 95353, (809) 571-2120.

Legal Services Corporation. (Twice a month). 7 51st Street NW, 11th Floor, Washington, DC 20002-4205, (202) 336-8800.

National Ad Search. The National Want-Ad Newspaper, P.O. Box 2083, Milwaukee, WI 53201, (414) 351-1398.

The National Weekly Job Report, Overseas Jobs. (Monthly) Career Link, Inc., P.O. Box 11720, Phoenix, Arizona 85061, (602) 841-2134, 1-800-453-3350.

Peterson's Guides. Box 2123, Princeton, New Jersey 08543-2123 (MBA/College Grad Guides), (609) 243-9111.

Public Administration Times. American Study for Public Administration, 1120 G Street, Suite 700, Washington, DC 20005, (202) 393-7878.

Public Personnel Exchange. Drake University, Des Moines, IA 50311.

Security. 1350 E. Touhy Avenue, Box 5080, Des Plaines, IL 60017-5080, (708) 635-8800.

The Search Bulletin. (Executive job leads twice a month) P.O. Box 641, Great Falls, VA 22066, 1-800-486-9220 (24 hours) or (703) 759-4900.

The Wall Street Journal National Business Employment Weekly. A weekly compilation of career-advancement positions from the four regional editions of *The Wall Street Journal*—published each Sunday. Wall Street Journal, 420 Lexington Avenue, New York, NY 10170, (800) Job Hunt.

Where quality starts with the fundamentals.
— RAYTHEON COMPANY

Other Worthwhile Publications

Careers and the MBA, Bob Adams, Inc., 260 Center Street, Holbrook, MA 02343, (617) 767-8100, 1993.

Careers Tomorrow: The Outlook for Work in a Changing World. World Future Society, 7910 Woodmont Avenue, Suite 450, Bethesda, Maryland 20814, (301) 656-8274, 1983.

College Placement Council Annual. The College Placement Council, 62 Highland Avenue, Bethlehem, PA 18017, (215) 868-1421.

Directory of Franchising Organizations, Pilot Industries, Inc. 103 Cooper Street, Babylon, NY 11702, (516) 422-2225.

Doss, Martha M. *The Directory of Special Opportunities for Women*, Garrett Press, P.O. Box 190F, Garrett Park, MD 20896, (301) 946-2553. Another publication obtained from Garrett Press is *The Women's Organizations: A National Directory* (lists women's professional and trade associations, network groups and research centers specializing in women's issues).

Education Directory. U.S. Department of Education, Superintendent of Documents, U.S. Government Printing Office, Washington, DC 20402.

Employment Marketplace. Employment Marketplace, P.O. Box 31112, St. Louis, MO 63131, (314) 569-3095.

Careers for the 90s. Research and Education Association, 61 Ethel Road West, Piscataway, New Jersey 08854, (908) 819-8880.

Jenkins, Michael D. *Starting and Operating a Business in Pennsylvania*, The Oasis Press/PSI Research, 300 North Valley Drive, Grants Pass, OR 97526, (800) 228-2275 or (503) 479-9464.

Kennedy's Career Strategist. Career Strategies, 1150 Wilmette Avenue, Wilmette, IL 60091, (708) 251-1661.

Lindquist, Carolyn Lloyd, and Pamela L. Feodoroff, eds., *Where to Start Career Planning*, Cornell University Career Center, Peterson's Guides, Inc., P.O. Box 2123, Princeton, New Jersey 08543-2123, 1989-1991, (800) 338-3282.

MBA Employment Guide. Association of MBA Executives, Inc., Publishers, 227 Commerce Street, E. Haven, CT 06512, 1984.

Occupational Outlook Quarterly. U.S. Department of Labor, Bureau of Labor Statistics. Quarterly published by the Superintendent of Documents, 2 Massachusetts Avenue, Washington, DC 20212, (202) 783-3238. Another publication available from the printing office is called *Merchandising Your Job Talents.*

Seminars Directory, (Annual). Gale Research, Inc., 835 Penobscot Building, Detroit, MI 48226, (313) 961-2242.

Teacher Magazine, Suite 250, 4301 Connecticut Avenue, NW, Washington, DC 20008, (202) 364-4114.

International School Experience: Teaching and Administrative Opportunities Abroad. (Pamphlet). International School Services, P.O. Box 5910, Princeton, New Jersey 08543, (609) 452-0990.

The Industrial Marketing Communications Planning Guide. Ken O'Neill Publisher, 132 East 45 Street, New York, NY 10017, (212) 599-3188.

The JobBank Series. Bob Adams, Inc., 260 Center Street, Holbrook, MA 02343, (617) 767-8100. Books for 20 major U.S. cities.

The Kiplinger Washington Letter. The Kiplinger Washington Editors, 1729 H Street, N.W., Washington, DC 20006, (202) 887-6400.

Unity Magazine. Christian Publication, Unity Village, MO 64065, (816) 599-3188. Yearly subscriptions published monthly.

Working Woman's Guide to Her Job Rights. Women's Bureau/U.S. Department of Labor, 200 Constitution Avenue, NW, Washington, DC 20210, (202) 219-6652, 1984.

Food For Thought
The Man Who Lived by the Side of the Road

He sold hot dogs. He had no radio. He had trouble with his eyes, so he had no newspaper. But he sold good hot dogs. He put up a sign on the highway telling how good they were. He stood by the side of the road and cried, "Buy a hot dog, mister." And people bought. He increased his meat and bun orders, and he built a bigger stand to take care of his trade.

*His son came home from college to help him. His son said,
"Father, haven't you been listening to the radio? Business is
terrible. The international situation is terrible, and the domestic
situation is even worse."*

*The man thought, "Well, my son has been to college. He listens to
the radio and reads the papers, he ought to know."*

*So the man cut down his bun order, took down his advertising
signs and no longer bothered to stand on the highway to sell hot
dogs. His hot dog sales fell almost overnight.*

"You were right, son," said the father. "Business is really terrible.

*The moral of the story—turn off the radio, ignore the
newspapers and maybe this will be your best year ever!*

— ANONYMOUS

A Hug

*It's wondrous what a hug can do.
A hug can cheer you when you're blue.
A hug can say, "I love you so,"
or "Gee, I hate to see you go."*

*A hug is "welcome back again" and
great to see you! where've you been?
A hug can soothe a small child's pain
and bring a rainbow after rain.*

*The hug! There's just no doubt about it—
we scarcely could survive without it.
A hug delights and warms and charms.
It must be why God gave us arms.*

*Hugs are great for fathers and mothers,
sweet for sisters, swell for brothers,
and chances are your favorite aunts
love them more than potted plants.*

Kittens crave them, puppies love them.
Heads of state are not above them.
A hug can break the language barrier
and make your travels so much merrier.
No need to fret about your store of 'em—
the more you give, the more there's more of 'em.

— ANONYMOUS

29.

Supplemental Aids:
Audio and Video Tapes

*Do not follow where the path may lead. Go instead
where there is no path and leave a trail.*

— ANONYMOUS

Tapes, be they audio or video, can reinforce a variety of the ideas that
you've been exposed to while reading this book.

Excellent sources of audio tapes are the following:

Nightingale-Conant Corporation
7300 North Lehigh Avenue
Niles, IL 60714
(800) 525-9000

Contact them for their catalogue and order tapes that meet your
needs. Sample tape programs:

- Dyer, Dr. Wayne. *How to Be a No Limit Person*
- Nightingale, Earl. *Lead the Field*
- Schuller, Dr. Robert. *Possibility Thinking*

The Napoleon Hill Foundation
1440 Paddock Drive
Northbrook, Illinois 60062
(708) 998-0408

Excellent sources of video tapes include these:

The Video Catalogue Co., Inc.
561 Broadway
New York, NY 10012
(212) 334-0340
Executive Dressing for Men and *Career Dressing for Women*

Motivational tapes and records are also available for loan purposes at many public libraries.

> *The difference between a successful person and others is not a lack of strength, not a lack of knowledge, but rather a lack of will.*
> — VINCENT T. LOMBARDI

> *The most important thing about fame is what it means to those who will never have it.*
> — JAMES SALTER

> *The quality of a person's life is in direct proportion to their commitment to excellence, regardless of their chosen field of endeavor.*
> — ANONYMOUS

30.

Sharing Your Ideas and Resources

The earth has music for those who listen.
— WILLIAM SHAKESPEARE

I would like to invite all readers to submit any updates, corrections, changes, new ideas, personal career stories about what worked for them, and testimonials regarding the effectiveness of some of the ideas in this book. Many of these may be incorporated into future revisions. Also, if you have some favorite inspirational poems, graphs, or stories that you want to forward, they too would be greatly appreciated. Please direct correspondence to:

Charles Logue
R. Davenport Associates
1910 Cochran Road, #844
Pittsburgh, PA 15220-1107

Thank you/in hoc.

P.S. You may also use the above address for arranging presentations, workshops and seminars.

The greatest compliment you can pay to this book is your referral to friends and loved ones. For other copies, send check or money order to Bob Adams, Inc., 260 Center Street, Holbrook, MA 02343.

In the deepest part of our soul,
In truest parts of our humanity,
We have the need to create,
To transform the viciousness and mediocrity
of the world into sunlight and peace.
Welcome to this place where you can
dare to be in your dreams,
dare to be strong,
dare to be vulnerable.
All power to the imagination,
Love and good courage.
— THE LIVING STAGE THEATER COMPANY

It is attitude, not aptitude, that governs altitude.
— ANONYMOUS

Index

About The Author

Charles H. Logue, Ph.D., CCDC (certified career development consultant), an authority on career management, has consulted and guided the destinies of hundreds of clients. He has over fifteen years of career management experience, most recently as vice president of R. Davenport Associates. He has moderated and conducted workshops and seminars on the subject. He has also been a consultant and after-dinner speaker for many organizations and firms.

Dr. Logue's background uniquely combines the theoretical (education) with the practical (organizational experience). He received his undergraduate degree in economics from the University of Maine, his guidance and counseling degree from Tufts University, and attended the evening school MBA program at Duquesne University before receiving a graduate fellowship at the University of Pittsburgh, where he received his Ph.D. He has been on the evening school faculty of the University of Pittsburgh Katz Graduate School of business since 1980, taught courses for the Community College of Allegheny County, and taught for two years in North Africa. He served as a First Lieutenant infantry/airborne in the U.S. Army.

Beyond his educational achievements, Charles Logue has worked for Mobil Oil Corporation both in New York and Chicago as an employee relations representative and at the corporate headquarters of the Gulf Oil Corporation in Pittsburgh as their U.S. program coordinator, working with Kuwaiti students. He also served five years as director of education for a women's hospital and as flight attendant/customer training manager for a major U.S. airline.